"In Darwin's day, a living cell was thought to be quite simply—for all practical purposes—little more than a microscopic blob of gelatin. Today we know that the cell is among the most organized, complex structures in the universe. Through clear and engaging writing, Fuz Rana lays out what contemporary science has learned about the cell's design, and he poignantly and provocatively shows that it is the handiwork of not only an Intelligent Designer but specifically the God revealed in Scripture."

—**Hank Hanegraaff**, president, Christian Research Institute;
host, *Bible Answer Man* broadcast

"As I sat in a class on cell biology at MIT, a thought kept going through my head: *This cannot have just happened; someone must have made it this way!* I am not the only one who ever thought this. In this book Dr. Rana takes us on a far more detailed tour of the inner chemistry of the cell and shows why that intuition is indeed well-founded; in fact, many new discoveries in biochemistry only make the conclusion stronger. Like William Paley's *Natural Theology*, which aimed to overwhelm the skeptics with example after example of 'contrivance,' or design, Dr. Rana's book builds a strong cumulative case for design, and thus a Designer, from the way the cell works. Those of us who know the Designer can rejoice with awe at the magnificence of these designs, and we can pray that this book will help those who do not know the Designer to seek after him."

—**C. John Collins**, professor and chairman, department of Old Testament, Covenant Theological Seminary

"Zoologist Richard Dawkins defines *biology* as 'the study of complicated things that give the appearance of having been designed for a purpose.' Fazale Rana's book plausibly argues that we are dealing with more than the appearance of design. In his well-researched, carefully argued book, he further advances the case for the complex cell's actual design. The remarkable phenomenon of the cell is one that naturalism is profoundly hard-pressed to explain."

—**Paul Copan**, Pledger Family Chair of Philosophy and Ethics, Palm Beach Atlantic University

"Fazale Rana's welcome sequel to *Origins of Life* makes a significant contribution to the growing scientific literature pointing to intelligent design. This comprehensive and clearly written book develops a panoply of converging biochemical arguments that demonstrate that the best explanation points to a mind of unimaginable proportions. *The Cell's Design* aptly uses the metaphor of an artistic masterpiece in its development of an analogy between human and biological designs."

—**Kenneth Boa**, president, Reflections Ministries, Atlanta;
president, Trinity House Publishers, Atlanta

The CELL'S DESIGN

How Chemistry Reveals the Creator's Artistry

Fazale Rana, PhD

BakerBooks

a division of Baker Publishing Group
Grand Rapids, Michigan

© 2008 by Reasons To Believe

Published by Baker Books
a division of Baker Publishing Group
P.O. Box 6287, Grand Rapids, MI 49516-6287
www.bakerbooks.com

Second printing, July 2008

Printed in the United States of America

Library of Congress Cataloging-in-Publication Data
Rana, Fazale, 1963–
    The cell's design : how chemistry reveals the Creator's artistry / Fazale Rana.
        p.   cm.
    Includes bibliographical references and index.
    ISBN 978-0-8010-6827-0 (pbk.)
        1. Cytochemistry—Religious aspects—Christianity. 2. Intelligent design (Teleology). I. Title.
BL255.R36 2008
215′.7—dc22   2007052069

Scripture is taken from the HOLY BIBLE, NEW INTERNATIONAL VERSION®. NIV®. Copyright © 1973, 1978, 1984 by International Bible Society. Used by permission of Zondervan. All rights reserved.

In Memory of
Abdul Rahman "Ray" Rana

For
Arlene and Freddie

CONTENTS

List of Illustrations   9
Acknowledgments   13
Introduction: A Rare Find   15

1. Masterpiece or Forgery?   23
2. Mapping the Territory   35
3. The Bare Essentials   53
4. Such a Clean Machine   69
5. Which Came First?   97
6. Inordinate Attention to Detail   109
7. The Proper Arrangement of Elements   125
8. The Artist's Handwriting   141
9. Cellular Symbolism   169
10. Total Quality   183
11. A Style All His Own   203
12. An Elaborate Mosaic   225
13. Coloring Outside the Lines   245
14. The Masterpiece Authenticated   269

Epilogue   285
Notes   287
Glossary   314
Index   327

ILLUSTRATIONS

Figures

1.1 The Explanatory Filter   25

2.1 The Cell (*with inset*)   37

2.2 Protein Structure   44

2.3 Phospholipid Structure   46

2.4 Phospholipid Bilayer Structure   47

2.5 Membrane Proteins   47

2.6 Fluid Mosaic Model   48

2.7 DNA Structure   49

2.8 Chromosome Structure   51

2.9 Central Dogma of Molecular Biology   52

4.1 The Bacterial Flagellum   71

4.2 F_1–F_0 ATPase   72

4.3 Assembly of the Bacterial Flagellum   75

4.4 The AcrA/AcrB/TolC Complex   76

4.5 Virus Structure and Life Cycle   79

4.6 Viral DNA Packaging Motor   80

4.7 The Myosin Linear Motor   82

4.8 Dynein   83

4.9 Brownian Motion and Brownian Ratchets   92

4.10 The BiP Brownian Ratchet   94

5.1   DNA Replication and Cell Division   100
5.2   mRNA Splicing   103
5.3   Ribosome Structure   104
5.4   Chaperone Activity   106
6.1   Aquaporin Structure   113
6.2   Amino Acid Side Groups   114
6.3   Proton Wire   116
6.4   Collagen   117
7.1   Nucleotide Structure   131
7.2   DNA Backbone and Side Chains   132
7.3   The Phosphodiester Bonds of RNA   133
7.4   Differences between Deoxyribose and Ribose   133
7.5   Gene Structure   135
7.6   High-Energy Bonds of ATP   138
8.1   Carbohydrate Structures   147
8.2   The *Lac* Operon   149
8.3   Base-Pairing Rules and the Even Parity Code of DNA   161
9.1   Error Minimization Capacity of the Genetic Code   176
9.2   The Histone Octamer   179
10.1   tRNA Structure   188
10.2   Protein Synthesis at the Ribosome   190
10.3   RNA Polymerase Production of mRNA   194
11.1   LUCA and the Tree of Life   217
11.2   Semiconservative DNA Replication   219
11.3   DNA Replication Bubble   220
11.4   The Proteins of DNA Replication   222
12.1   Bilayer Assemblies   230
12.2   Fatty Acids and Micelles   239
13.1   The Futile Cycle of Glycolysis   252
13.2   Pseudogenes   257
13.3   Two Metabolic Fates of Proteins   263

Tables

3.1   Genome Sizes of Life's Simplest Organisms   56
3.2   Minimum Genome Sizes for Photoautotrophs   57
3.3   Estimates of the Essential Genome Size   59
8.1   Cellular Sentences   143
8.2   Parity Bit Assignment   159
9.1   The Genetic Code   172
11.1   Examples of Molecular Convergence   207

ACKNOWLEDGMENTS

This book represents the sacrifice and hard work of many people, not just the author's. I want to thank my wife, Amy Rana, and my children—Amanda, Whitney, and Mackenzie—for their love, encouragement, and understanding when this book project took "priority" over family matters.

Each member of the Reasons To Believe team has supported me with their friendship and encouragement in this endeavor and I am grateful. Kathy and Hugh Ross deserve a special mention for their inspiration and the opportunities they have given me.

I especially want to acknowledge the editorial department (staff and volunteers) who dedicated themselves to this book as if it was their own labor of love. Thank you Patti Townley-Covert, Sandra Dimas, Marj Harman, Linda Kloth, Kristi Sandberg, and Colleen Wingenbach for your expert editorial guidance and help with all the little chores that must be done during a book project. Thank you Jonathan Price and Phillip Chien for designing the many figures found in this book.

The critical peer-review of scholars Dr. Matt Carlson, Dr. Russell Carlson, Richard Deem, Dr. Lyle McCurdy, Amy Rana, Kenneth Samples, and Dr. Jeff Zweerink was invaluable, and this book is better for it. Still, I assume all responsibility for any errors found herein. I'm indebted to Joe Aguirre, Ken Hultgren, Dr. Dave Rogstad, Dr. Hugh Ross, Kenneth Samples, and Dr. Jeff Zweerink for our many stimulating conversations in the hallway and during lunch. These discussions helped to directly and indirectly shape the contents of this book.

I also want to thank my friends at Baker Books, especially Bob Hosack and Paul Brinkerhoff, for their efforts on this project and for their belief in our work at Reasons To Believe.

Charles Marion Russell, *Riders of the Open Range* (Reproduced by permission from Private Collection/
Peter Newark Western Americana/The Bridgeman Art Library)

INTRODUCTION

A Rare Find

"What would you like to be when you grow up?" As a child, I usually answered, "I don't know."

Yet deep down inside I knew exactly what I wanted to be—an explorer. I never told anyone my desire though, because I was convinced there weren't any new territories left to discover and explore.

By the time I entered college and was ready to choose a career path, I decided (at my father's urging) to enroll in a premed program. Not long afterwards, I began taking courses in chemistry and biology. That's when I realized I'd been wrong as a youngster. An abundance of scientific "lands" remained to investigate! For me, the most exciting of all was the molecular world inside the cell.

My fascination with life's chemical systems prompted me to change my course of study and launched my career as a biochemist. I joined a band of scientific explorers who—with the aid of electron microscopes, spectrometers, chromatographs, ultracentrifuges (and an assortment of other laboratory techniques)—made available new vistas on the inner workings of the cell.

The Most Fascinating Discovery of All

The forays made by biochemical adventurers into the cell's molecular environs have opened up windows on life at its most fundamental level.

Scientists have fairly complete knowledge about the chemical composition of the cell's structures and contents. We know, for the most part, how living systems extract energy from the environment and convert it into a form that the cell can use for its operations. We are beginning to grasp the relationship between the structure of biomolecules and their function. And, we understand how the cell stores and manages the information needed to carry out life's activities. The molecular basis for inheritance and the chemical processes responsible for cell division stand in full view.

As amazing as these insights are, for me, the most fascinating discovery made by scientific pioneers has little to do with the cell's structures or activities. Rather, it is the sheer beauty and artistry of the biochemical realm.

Biochemistry as Art

So far, only a small portion of the splendor of life's chemistry has been captured in scientists' attempts to represent the structures, chemical interactions, and operational mechanisms of biochemical systems. Still, the magnificence of the cell's inner workings is evident even in the "crude" images produced by biomolecular explorers.

In some ways, biochemists who attempt to depict what they've "seen" on the molecular frontiers inside the cell are like the cowboy artists of the past. Artists like Charles M. Russell (1864–1926) sought to convey the adventure and majesty of the Old West on canvas for those who would never get a chance to experience it firsthand. Still, the best artist could never fully capture the actual splendor of a sunset over the western horizon or the panoramic sweep of the snow-covered Rocky Mountains.

Though the remarkable depictions "painted" by biochemists are available for people to ponder, those who have never worked directly on biochemical problems can't fully appreciate the grandeur of the cell's molecular domain. Too much of the beauty is lost in the scientific translations.

Biochemistry's Impact

Unlike art, which some argue should be done strictly for its own sake,[1] the last half-century of biochemical advance has been more than "science for science's sake." The ever increasing understanding of the cell's chemistry has revolutionized our day-to-day lives. Biochemistry drives many of the technological advances in biomedicine, agriculture, and even industry.

But as important as these biochemical applications are, perhaps the most significant outcome of the so-called molecular biology revolution is universal recognition that biochemical systems appear to be designed.

This elegance, evident in virtually all aspects of the cell's chemistry, carries profound philosophical and theological significance that prompts questions about the origin, purpose, and meaning of life. Though I once embraced the evolutionary paradigm, its inadequate explanations for the origin of life coupled with the sophistication and complexity of the cell's chemical systems convinced me as a biochemistry graduate student that a Creator must exist.[2]

A Controversial Beginning

Theists and atheists alike can see design in biological and biochemical systems. Even the well-known evolutionary biologist Richard Dawkins, an outspoken atheist, acknowledges that "biology is the study of complicated things that give the appearance of having been designed for a purpose."[3]

While the indicators of design in biological and biochemical systems are not controversial, their source is. For me, and many others, biochemical design is best explained as the handiwork of a Creator.[4] Yet, the majority in the scientific community maintains that the design found in the biological and biochemical realms is the product of a naturalistic evolutionary process. According to this view, natural selection operates on random variation again and again to yield structures and systems that *appear* intentional but, in fact, are not.

The late Francis Crick, who shared the Nobel Prize for discovering the structure of DNA, cautioned, "Biologists must constantly keep in mind that what they see was not designed, but rather evolved."[5] So even though life's chemistry looks as if it's the product of a Creator, many in the scientific community suppress this obvious intuition.

Recent advances in biochemistry, however, make this resistance harder and harder to accept. Life scientists now have research tools they only dreamed about a few years ago. Researchers routinely isolate the fragile, complex molecular assemblies that constitute the cell's chemical systems. New techniques allow biochemists to manipulate the cell's structures and processes at a molecular level and visualize its chemical constituents at an atomic level. All this progress has led to remarkable insight into the cell's chemistry. This detail reveals biochemical systems that seem far more purposeful, intricate, and sophisticated than ever imagined.

As biochemists learn more about the details of the cell's chemical systems, the appearance of design becomes increasingly pervasive and profound. Currently, hundreds of scientists who represent a range of scientific disciplines express skepticism about "the ability of random mutation and natural selection to account for the complexity of life."[6] This skepticism largely fuels the recent resurgence of the creation (intelligent design)/evolution controversy in America.

Darwin's Black Box

In spite of the mind-boggling evidence for biochemical design, most works that explore the creation/evolution controversy give life's chemical systems cursory attention, typically confined to a chapter or two. As far as I know, few, if any, provide a book-length treatment. The chief exception is Michael Behe's *Darwin's Black Box*, a seminal work (originally published in 1996) that presents a potent case for intelligent design from a biochemical perspective. In this book, Behe argues that biochemical systems, by their very nature, are irreducibly complex.

According to Behe, irreducible complexity describes "a single system composed of several well-matched interacting parts that contribute to basic function, wherein removal of any one of the parts causes the system to effectively cease functioning."[7]

Behe makes the case that irreducibly complex systems cannot be produced from protosystems by the Darwinian process of slight incremental changes that inch towards the finished product. Any protosystem that lacks even one of the parts that contributes to "basic function" is nonfunctional. Even if all the essential components are present, they too must interact with one another in a "just-so" fashion, or that system will not function. If the protosystem doesn't have function, then natural selection can't operate on it to produce an improved form. Without function, natural selection has nothing to select.

Irreducibly complex systems, and hence biochemical systems, must be produced all at once. Therefore, it's completely within the bounds of rational thought to conclude that irreducibly complex biochemical systems came into existence through intelligent agency.

The case for intelligent design made in *Darwin's Black Box* is compelling. Still, Behe's explanation rises and falls on the perceived validity of the concept of irreducible complexity. Several scientists have leveled significant challenges against this argument.[8] And, even though Behe has responded to these critics, many skeptics remain unconvinced.[9]

Darwin's Black Box primarily argues for intelligent design by emphasizing the inability of natural selection to generate irreducibly complex systems in a gradual stepwise evolutionary process. And because natural processes can't explain irreducibly complex biochemical systems, they must be designed. Critics generally view this approach as a god-of-the-gaps argument—illegitimately evoking God as the explanation whenever science cannot account for some feature or process in nature. Critics maintain that the case for intelligent design rests on a lack of understanding and reject Behe's argument on this basis alone.

These objections motivated me to write this book.

An Increasing Weight of Evidence

Irreducible complexity is but one of a vivid ensemble of biochemical features that individually and collectively point to intelligent design. *The Cell's Design* goes beyond irreducible complexity and communicates a vast range of amazing properties that characterize life's chemistry.

The never before compiled evidence shows that the cell displays far more than a single feature that reflects intelligent design at the biochemical level. Rather, a magnificent gallery of awe-inspiring characteristics signify a Master's brilliance at work. While skeptics may not be impressed by the irreducible complexity of biochemical systems, perhaps they will respond differently to a growing collection of evidence that leads to one conclusion—a supernatural basis for life.

The hallmark indicators of design displayed in the cell's chemistry make a case for a Creator based on what scientists know, not on what we don't understand. Instead of arguing for creation by relying on the perceived inability of natural processes to generate life's chemical systems, this approach frames the support for intelligent design in positive terms by highlighting biochemical features that reflect the Creator's signature.

The Lay of the Land

In many respects, Behe pioneered the biochemical case for intelligent design in *Darwin's Black Box*. *The Cell's Design* continues this exploration and strives to make the biochemical case for a Creator much more compelling.

Chapter 1 describes and justifies the approach used to argue for intelligent design in biochemical systems—one that relies upon the weight of interrelated evidence. Chapter 2 consists of a brief overview of cell biology and biochemistry. This section provides the necessary background to appreciate the elegant and powerful design that can only be seen in the details of the cell's chemical systems.

The next ten chapters describe separate biochemical arguments for design. Each one indicates the work of an intelligent and creative mind. Collectively, these arguments constitute a compelling weight of evidence for a supernatural basis for life.

Chapter 13 responds to one of the most common challenges leveled against arguments for intelligent design: imperfections found in nature. Chapter 14 unveils the biomolecular masterpiece found in the cell and, in doing so, authenticates the biochemical intelligent design argument.

In most works of this nature, the authors are quick—perhaps too quick—to declare the inability of evolutionary processes to produce certain features of the biological realm. Their argument goes something like this: "If evolution can't produce it, then a Creator must have." *The Cell's Design* avoids this negative approach. Instead of focusing on what evolution can or cannot do, this book emphasizes the aspects of biochemical systems that make a positive case for intelligent design.

Biochemical systems are complex and in nearly every case incompletely understood. Scientists are still working out what they believe to be the possible mechanisms for evolutionary change. Often there simply isn't enough understanding to say for certain if evolutionary processes can or cannot generate specific biochemical characteristics. Of course, the burden of proof should be on evolutionary biologists to explain in detail how biochemical systems originated all on their own.

In a few cases though, enough understanding already exists to critically evaluate the likelihood of evolutionary mechanisms generating specific properties of life's chemistry. This is true for the origin of the genetic code (chapter 9), the convergent beginnings of many biochemical systems (chapter 11), and the emergence of cell membranes (chapter 12). In these cases, a detailed critique of the evolutionary paradigm accompanies the positive case for intelligent design.

I invite you to come and explore the molecular world of the cell and perhaps you'll be as captivated by the beauty and artistry of the molecular landscape as I am. As we look at the systems that constitute life at its most fundamental level, it is my hope that the weight of the evidence will convince you that biochemical design results from a Creator's hand, a Divine Artist.

The technical terminology that is so much a part of cell biology and biochemistry can feel overwhelming for many people. So, the details have been limited to those necessary to show the Creator's fingerprints. However, the Creator's signature style is ultimately most evident in the finer points of the cell's chemistry. Please keep in mind, that for an Artist's work to be fully appreciated, one must take the time to study its subtleties and nuances.

Unfamiliar terrain never guarantees a simple path. But struggling over, around, and through the obstacles can lead to vistas of unimagined beauty and splendor as nature's art comes into view. It's definitely worth every effort to get there.

But, before unfolding the map that supplies the necessary directions, it's important to come up with a strategy to determine whether the cell is actually a masterpiece of a Divine Artist or only appears that way.

The Unknown Masterpiece (Reproduced by permission from © Mark Harris)

1

MASTERPIECE OR FORGERY?

Sometime in the early 1970s, a junk dealer came across five ink drawings while clearing out a deceased woman's apartment in London. He hung onto them for several years, after which time one of them wound up in the hands of a Brighton art dealer. Eventually, that dealer showed the mysterious drawing to Mark Harris, an art aficionado, who concluded that the piece might well be an unknown work by Picasso.[1]

This drawing, referred to as Picasso's *The Unknown Masterpiece*, has provoked a heated controversy between his estate and Harris. The estate and its beneficiaries deny the drawing's authenticity.

In the face of this rejection, Harris and his collaborators began amassing a large body of evidence to support their claim that Picasso, indeed, painted the masterpiece.

To make the case, Harris points to hallmark features of Picasso's work. For example, a fingerprint rolled into the wet ink at the time the drawing was made, appears near the bottom of the piece. Many artists in the early 1900s, including Picasso, began fingerprinting artwork to stave off fraud. This mark could conclusively identify the work as a Picasso if compared with his known fingerprint. However, the estate refuses to comply, officially insisting that Picasso did not fingerprint his work during the 1930s.

While photographing the painting, Harris also discovered what seems to be Picasso's dated signature. A Scotland Yard handwriting expert identified features in the signature consistent with those from other Picasso works.

The drawing also contains a number of features characteristic of other Picasso works and appears to have connections to several specific pieces. Both Mark Harris and Melvin Becraft (author of *Picasso's Guernica: Images within Images*) place Picasso's *The Unknown Masterpiece* between his 1925 work, *The Three Dancers*, and his 1937 work, *Guernica*. Picasso was known to carry ideas and themes from work to work. *The Unknown Masterpiece* links themes, symbolisms, and hidden imagery in *The Three Dancers* with those found in *Guernica*—connections not previously apparent.

Harris also recognized themes that reflect the events of Picasso's life at the time *The Unknown Masterpiece* was created. The year 1934 was a time of intense crisis for Picasso. The tragedies he experienced appear in the imagery of the mysterious drawing. Related symbolism depicting these circumstances also occurs in other Picasso pieces of the same period.

It remains to be seen if Harris's case for authenticity convinces the Picasso estate and the art world. Still, he has assembled what appears to be a compelling argument on the painting's behalf.

The approach used by Harris to argue for the authenticity of *The Unknown Masterpiece* can also be used to make the case that life's chemistry has been created by a Divine Artist. Before articulating and defending this approach, a discussion on methods to detect intelligent design reveals how difficult this undertaking can be.

Detecting a Master at Work

Most people are pretty good at distinguishing between the work of an intelligent agent and the outworking of natural processes. It's usually not that difficult, for example, to discriminate between an unusually shaped rock and an arrowhead intentionally made out of stone. Philosopher Jay Richards and astronomer Guillermo Gonzalez point out in their book *The Privileged Planet* that most individuals have no idea how they make the distinction between an intelligently designed object and one generated by natural processes. They just intuitively do.[2]

Usually people can trust their intuition. Still, as Richards and Gonzalez discuss, subjective bias and the capacity of natural processes to yield objects that mimic design make the possibility of false positives (i.e., mistaking the product of blind processes for intelligent design) a troubling reality.

To avoid false positives, a rigorous and formalized scheme to reliably detect the activity of an intelligent agent is necessary. In *The Design Inference*, William Dembski pioneers and proposes such a methodology—something he calls an "explanatory filter."[3] This filter consists of a sequence of three yes/no questions that guide the decision process of determining whether an intelligent mind has been at work (see figure 1.1). Based on this filter—if an event, system, or object is intentionally produced by a designer, then it will (1) be contingent, (2) be complex, and (3) display an independently specified pattern. According to the filter, to be confident that an event, system, or object has been produced by an intelligent designer it can't be a regularity that necessarily stems from the laws of nature, and it can't be the result of chance.[4] According to Dembski, the explanatory filter highlights the most important quality of intelligently designed systems, namely, specified complexity. In other words, complexity alone is not enough to indicate the work of an intelligent agent; it must conform to a pattern. And, that pattern must be independently specified.

If an event, system, or object successfully passes through the filter, then, Dembski argues, it must emanate from the activity of an intelligent agent. The filter ensures that the product of natural processes is not mistaken for deliberate design. And yet, while this approach avoids false positives, it is plagued

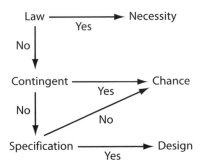

Figure 1.1. The Explanatory Filter
Three questions are used to determine if an event, system, or object stems from the activity of an intelligent agent. Can it be explained as a consequence of the laws of nature (necessity)? If yes, then it is not designed. If no, then can it be explained as a consequence of chance (contingent)? If yes, then it is not designed. If no, then does it display a specified pattern (specification)? If no, then it is not designed. If yes, then it must be the product of an intelligent designer.

by false negatives. For example, the filter will fail to register intelligent design if the agent operates in a way that mimics natural processes or in a manner that simulates chance.[5] In other words, if God created life using evolutionary processes, the filter may not be able to detect his involvement.

Filtering Out Forgeries

Can the explanatory filter be used to detect intelligent design in biochemical systems? Dembski says "yes." In *Intelligent Design*, he describes the relationship between specified and irreducible complexity. Biochemist Michael Behe argues that irreducible complexity is an indicator of biochemical intelligent design; but according to Dembski, irreducible complexity is a type of specified complexity.[6] The specified pattern is the simultaneous co-occurrence of components required for the system to have minimal function.

Behe argues, and Dembski agrees, that Darwinian evolutionary mechanisms cannot generate irreducibly complex biochemical systems.[7] In terms of formally applying the explanatory filter, this limitation means that biochemical systems are not a regularity produced by the outworking of nature's laws. Biochemical systems are contingent, complex, and conform to an independently specified pattern (irreducibility).

The explanatory filter seems to effortlessly identify irreducibly complex biochemical systems as the product of an intelligent agent. Careful consideration of the questions posed at the first and second decision points, however, exposes potential problems that could clog the filter.[8] The first decision node seeks to determine if an event, system, or object is contingent or a necessary consequence of the laws of nature. While it certainly seems as if irreducibly complex biochemical systems are contingent, there are biochemists who disagree. Some scientists maintain that life's origin (and hence the origin of biochemical systems) is a cosmic imperative built into the laws of nature.[9]

The notion that biochemical systems are a necessity can be questioned on numerous grounds.[10] Still, given the current state of scientific knowledge, it can't be ruled out with absolute certainty. Nobody really knows if life is a cosmic imperative or not. The question posed at the first decision point in the explanatory filter can't be answered with a simple "yes" or "no."

Further complicating the first decision is the view held by many origin-of-life researchers that the origin of biochemical systems stems from both necessity and chance. In other words, the answer to the question posed at the filter's first stage is not either "yes or no" but both "yes and no." Again, scientific challenges to this view can be raised, but the current state of scientific knowledge makes it impossible to decisively rule out an evolutionary explanation for life's origin that appeals to both necessity and chance.

Potential problems confront the second decision point in the filter as well. Simple visual inspection of most biochemical systems reveals their complexity. Yet, are biochemical systems so complex they can't be explained by chance alone or more appropriately by chance operated on by some selection process? Intuitively, it does indeed seem as if this is the case. But biochemists lack the knowledge to substantiate this conclusion.

In many respects, biochemical knowledge is still in its infancy. For example, biochemists still don't understand the relationship between amino acid sequence and protein structure, let alone function (see page 42). To rigorously demonstrate that biochemical systems are so complex that they defy a naturalistic explanation, biochemists need this basic understanding. Establishing the relationship between amino acid sequence and protein function is no trivial exercise and will take decades of concerted effort by the biochemical research community. So, there is no way to answer the second question posed by the explanatory filter with any level of certainty.

The point is not to debate the validity of the explanatory filter as a design detection methodology. Rather, it is to describe a suitable, practical approach that can demonstrate whether or not the cell's chemical systems are the work of a Creator. In principle, the filter seems capable of detecting intelligent design. But in practice, at least with respect to biochemical design, it can't be used to establish intelligent causation—until much more is learned about biochemical systems and the potential of naturalistic processes to generate them.

So what would constitute a workable approach for detecting intelligent design in biochemical systems?

Predictable Patterns

In spite of the potential problems associated with the explanatory filter, Dembski appears to be onto something really important with his concept of specified complexity as a marker for intelligent design. Systems intentionally produced by human designers typically display certain hallmark characteristics. That is, these types of systems conform to a pattern or specification that exists independent of the system. These patterns are strong indicators that an intelligent human agent has been involved.

Pattern (or specification in Dembski's words), and not necessarily complexity, appears to be the most important property when it comes to recognizing the work of human intelligence. In defining what he means by design, Dembski notes that

> when intelligent agents act, they leave behind a characteristic trademark or signature. . . . It is *design* in this sense—as a trademark, signature, vestige or fingerprint—that this criterion for discriminating intelligently from unintelligently caused objects is meant to identify.[11]

In the quest to detect deliberate mindful design, the only thing needed is to identify a pattern that reflects the work of an intelligent agent. Once established, this pattern can be used as the standard and compared with events, systems, or objects suspected to be the work of an intelligent agent.

When people distinguish between the work of an intelligent agent and the outworking of natural processes, it's not intuition they use. Rather, whether they realize it or not, they are using pattern recognition.

Though simple, this approach is profoundly powerful. For example, art aficionado Mark Harris is using pattern recognition in his quest to demonstrate that *The Unknown Masterpiece* is authentic. Harris has identified a set of features that characterize Picasso's work. This set of features constitutes the pattern Harris uses as a reference or standard against which *The Unknown Masterpiece* is compared.

Pattern matching is quite common in science as well. For example, analytical chemists routinely use pattern recognition as a way to determine the identity of an unknown chemical compound by comparing the physical, chemical, and spectral properties for a series of known standards with those possessed by the unknown substance. The identity of the unknown compound is revealed when its characteristics closely match those possessed by a known chemical entity.

Identifying an Original

While it's relatively straightforward to establish a pattern that reflects Picasso's work or one that helps determine the identity of an unknown material, how could it be possible to specify a pattern that reflects the activity of a Creator? How could a Creator's fingerprint possibly be recognized in nature?

In the quest to identify the Divine Artist's signature in nature, two things would be useful: (1) a set of criteria that universally describes the behavior of an intelligent designer and (2) some understanding of the Creator's properties and capabilities.

Unfortunately, no universal criteria for the behavior of an intelligent agent exists. The only example available to base the pattern on is the behavior of human designers. Is it legitimate to generalize human behavior to form a set of criteria that universally describes the activity of any intelligent agent? Could it be that, in general, other intelligent creators behave in ways distinct from human designers? Do human creators function in a way that deviates from the norm? This problem threatens to frustrate the use of pattern recognition to detect a Creator at work in the natural realm, unless the behavior of human designers can somehow be connected to this Divine Artist's work.

To maintain that the Creator is an unidentified Genius is not sufficient. In order to gain insight into his or her or its characteristics and ability, an identity must be specified. Assuming the intelligent designer is the God described in the Old and New Testaments, the Bible reveals information that offers a limited but useful perspective on how he operates.

The biblical account of humanity's origin establishes the link between human designers and the Creator. The Genesis 1 creation account and Genesis 5:1–2 teach that God created human beings (male and female) *in his image*.[12] This declaration implies that humans bear a similarity to their Maker, at least in some ways.

Scripture doesn't explicitly define what is meant by the image of God. Over the centuries, theologians have discussed and debated this topic. Some believe the image describes humanity's resemblance to God, while others think the image of God allows humans to function as his representatives or viceroys on Earth.[13] A consensus of ideas identifies four characteristics:[14]

- Human beings possess a moral component. They inherently understand right and wrong and have a strong innate sense of justice.
- Humans, though physical, are also spiritual beings who recognize a reality beyond this universe and physical life. Mankind intuitively acknowledges the existence of God and has a propensity towards worship and prayer.

- Human beings relate to God, to themselves, to other people, and to other creatures. There is a relational aspect to God's image.
- Humanity's mental capacity reflects God's image. Human beings possess the ability to reason and think logically. They can engage in symbolic thought. People express themselves with complex abstract language. They are aware of the past, present, and future. Human beings display intense creativity through art, music, literature, science, and technical inventions.

The intellectual component of God's image holds the greatest relevance for pattern recognition as evidenced in human beings. This mental likeness reveals itself in human creativity (art, music, literature, and technical inventiveness). As God is a Creator, so too are human beings—they are minicreators. Being a reflection of their Maker implies that the hallmark characteristics of humanly designed systems will mirror those that were divinely designed.

The expectation, however, is that humanly produced systems would, at best, be an imperfect reflection. If biochemical systems are indeed the product of a Master Creator who made man in his image, then the defining characteristics of those systems should be analogous to the hallmark characteristics of humanly crafted systems. At the same time, the cell's chemical systems should be clearly superior to anything produced by the best human minds.

Much like Dembski's explanatory filter, any design detection protocol that relies on pattern recognition is bedeviled by false negatives. Consequently, this approach *under*determines intelligent design. Pattern recognition will not detect the Creator's activity if he works in a way that mimics natural processes or simulates chance. Additionally, there are many technologies that humans have yet to discover. If the Creator employed any of these as-yet-unknown technologies in the design of biochemical systems, they will remain unrecognized as part of the pattern that reflects his artistry.

Investigating the Claim

Pattern recognition represents a form of analogical reasoning. One of the most common forms of reasoning, analogical thinking is not only an integral part of day-to-day decision making, but also factors significantly into legal and scientific reasoning. The proper way to reason using analogies must be kept in mind to effectively employ pattern recognition while searching for the Creator's signature within biochemical systems.[15]

Analogical thinking employs inductive reasoning. As such, it is not neat and tidy. Conclusions are not certain but probabilistic.

This type of reasoning involves comparing events, systems, or objects. If they are highly similar, then it can be concluded they are the same in some way. If, however, they are significantly dissimilar, such a conclusion would be unwarranted.

For example, when two systems labeled A and B are compared, if A possesses properties a, b, c, d, e . . . and z—and B possesses properties a, b, c, d, e . . .—it is reasonable to conclude that B possesses property z as well. This conclusion becomes even more likely if the property z somehow relates to properties a, b, c, d, e. . . .

To properly reason from analogy, several factors must be considered:

- The relevance of similarities is critical. The properties being compared must be relevant to the conclusion.
- The number of similarities that are part of the analogy impacts the likeliness of the conclusion. The greater the number of similarities the greater the validity of the conclusion.
- The number of events, objects, or systems that enter into the comparison influences the conclusion. The greater the number of separate comparisons, the more probable the conclusion.
- The diversity of the events, objects, or systems compared has bearing on the conclusion. Greater diversity translates into greater confidence about the conclusion reached through comparison.
- Disanalogy is important. In addition to shared similarities—the ways in which the events, objects, or systems differ must be considered.

Mark Harris's case for the authenticity of Picasso's *The Unknown Masterpiece* illustrates the principles that constitute effective analogical reasoning. Harris hasn't relied on a single piece of evidence but rather on a weight of evidence—a number of similarities. These similarities are relevant to Picasso's authorship. They are also quite diverse in nature.

Any one of the individual pieces of evidence cited by Harris points to Picasso as the painting's creator. Still, in isolation, each piece of evidence can be dismissed by plausible counterexplanations. Someone might have forged Picasso's signature or perhaps a kindred spirit memorialized his tragic circumstances. Yet, all the evidence combined points to the same conclusion—Picasso drew *The Unknown Masterpiece*. With each piece of data that supports this conclusion, it becomes more difficult to defend alternative explanations and the less likely it becomes that the painting is fraudulent.

In addition, the case for authenticity doesn't rest simply on the weight of evidence amassed by Harris but on how some pieces of evidence interrelate. For example, the themes in *The Unknown Masterpiece* not only explain those in *The Three Dancers* and *Guernica* but also depict the timely events that bridge gaps between the appropriate dates. The way these pieces of evidence nicely "dovetail" with one another makes for a compelling claim.

Finding God's Fingerprints

Various lines of evidence can also make a powerful case that life's molecular artistry stems from the Creator described in the Bible. To be convincing, this position must be built upon a weight of evidence. For an idea to gain credibility in the scientific arena, it must find support from a collective body of data that works in concert to support one conclusion. Skeptics are within their rights to regard a single piece of evidence or a single line of reasoning as marginal in support of intelligent design. However, if a litany of diverse evidence exists, it becomes less tenable to reject a supernatural basis for life, even if naturalistic explanations for the emergence of biochemical systems have been advanced.

Instead of making the argument that evolutionary processes cannot generate irreducibly complex biochemical systems, the approach used here maintains that irreducible complexity—a property that frequently characterizes humanly designed systems—is one of the indicators of intelligent design because such specified complexity results from forethought and planning. Now, Behe's concept of irreducible complexity (delineated in *Darwin's Black Box*) contributes to an overall pattern that points to the Creator's work in biochemical systems. Some of the details of this template—like molecular motors, chicken-and-egg relationships, fine-tuning and optimization, molecular convergence, pre-planning, quality control, biochemical information, the genetic code, and the fine-tuning of the genetic code—are discussed in chapters 3–12.

God of the Gaps

Unfortunately, too often Christian apologists or intelligent design advocates who argue for the work of a Creator focus on the perceived inability of natural processes to explain life's chemistry. By default, they conclude that the cell's biochemical systems must be designed. And, as skeptics rightly point out, this conclusion doesn't necessarily follow. For these critics, the case for biochemical intelligent design, and hence biblical creation, rests on faulty "god-of-the-gaps" reasoning.

Scientists admit they still have an incomplete understanding of many aspects of life's chemistry, and many Christians and design theorists exploit this lack of knowledge. Skeptics rightly maintain that the evidence for intelligent design often rests merely on what science doesn't know, not on what has been discovered. Because science operates with partial knowledge, new discoveries and new insights always hold the potential to fill in the gaps and explain what the laws of chemistry and physics can accomplish. According to this critique, once science fills in the gaps, the evidence for a Creator will vanish.

Compiling the Evidence

Rather than use a negative approach that relies on gaps in understanding, the subsequent chapters make use of pattern recognition to identify the God of the Bible's involvement in bringing life into being. Such a method makes it possible to build a *positive* case for biochemical intelligent design. This approach inherently depends on what science currently knows about life's chemistry and how the organization of biochemical systems relates to the characteristics of humanly designed systems—not on what science doesn't know.

To demonstrate purposeful design, the cell's biochemical systems will be probed for the hallmark features of intelligent creativity in the same way that Mark Harris uncovered Picasso's telltale signatures in *The Unknown Masterpiece*.

This strategy anticipates scientific advance and looks for future studies to uncover additional characteristics that reflect intelligent design as knowledge gaps become filled. From a theological standpoint, it is reasonable to expect that the cell's chemical systems should reflect the Creator's "signature," if life's origin has a supernatural basis (Rom. 1:20).[16] This "signature" manifests itself as evidence for deliberate design.

Is the artistry found in biochemical systems the authentic work of a Divine Artist, or is it a forgery produced by natural processes? The following chapters seek to answer this question. But first, to guide this exploration the next chapter provides a description—a map of sorts—of the cell and its molecular constituents.

Jan Vermeer, *The Artist's Studio* (Reproduced by permission from Kunsthistorisches Museum, Vienna, Austria/The Bridgeman Art Library)

2

MAPPING THE TERRITORY

One of the best known works by Dutch painter Jan Vermeer (1632–1675) is *The Artist's Studio*. This baroque piece depicts an artist in a brightly lit studio painting a carefully posed subject. On the wall behind the young woman hangs a large map.[1]

Speculation abounds as to the meaning of the map. Some think it makes political commentary; others maintain the map is an allegory for the spread of the artist's reputation.[2]

Maps frequently find their way into works of art. Artists often use them as a device to critique a specific culture. A map can also signify power and sovereignty over a particular territory.[3]

Biologists also use maps. Over the last half-century, researchers have used light and electron microscopes to systematically map the cell's interior. Application of biochemical techniques has increased knowledge about the structural and compositional makeup of the subcellular world. These biological and biochemical depictions of the cell's interior become the maps that represent science's growing control over life at its most fundamental level.

Studying the biological map that hangs in the Divine Artist's studio supplies the background necessary to appreciate the elegant sophistication of the cell's chemical systems. This exploration also sets the stage for understanding biochemical design as the Creator's craftsmanship.

Sighting the New World

The same year that Jan Vermeer painted *The Artist's Studio* (1665), Robert Hooke discovered cells.[4] Following his initial work, a number of biologists reported the existence of cells in plants and animals. These discoveries culminated in the cell theory developed independently by Matthias Schleiden in 1838 and Theodor Schwann in 1839.

This theory states that cells are the fundamental units of life and the smallest entities that can be considered "life." As a corollary, all organisms consist of one or more cells. Most life-forms on Earth are single-celled (bacteria, archaea, and protozoans). Multicellular organisms (plants, animals, and fungi) are made up of specialized cells that carry out the many activities necessary for life.

Most cells are between 5 and 40 microns in size. (A micron is one-millionth of a meter.) The average width of a human hair ranges between 20 and 180 microns. An idealized cell is defined by a cell boundary or *membrane*. This structure separates the cell's interior from the exterior surroundings. The *cytoplasm* (made up of water, salts, and organic molecules) forms the cell's internal matrix. *Organelles* are large structures embedded within the cytoplasm. These compartments carry out specific functions for the cell. A membrane, similar to the cell membrane, surrounds most organelles. The *nucleus* houses the cell's genetic material (DNA). Like other organelles, a membrane also surrounds the nucleus (see figure 2.1).

Two Different Worlds

By the mid-1950s, biologists recognized two fundamentally distinct cell types: eukaryotic and prokaryotic. Eukaryotic cells contain a nucleus, organelles, and internal membrane systems. Unicellular protists and multicellular fungi, plants, and animals are examples of eukaryotic organisms.

Prokaryotic cells are typically about one micron in diameter. These cells appear to be much simpler than eukaryotic cells. Apart from a cell boundary, prokaryotes lack any visible defining features. They don't have a nucleus, organelles, or internal membranes. Their genetic material consists of "naked"

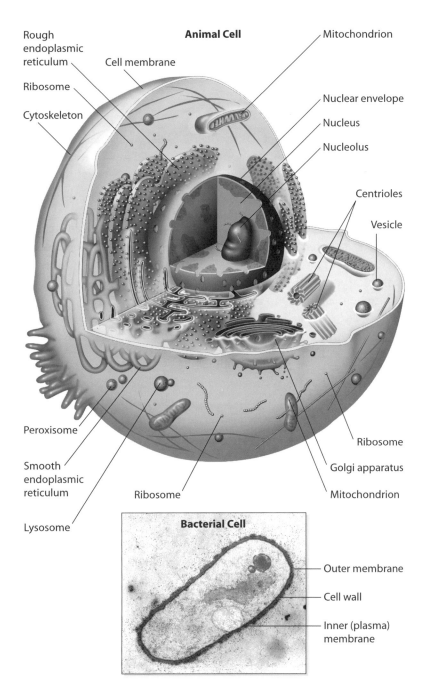

Figure 2.1. The Cell (*with inset*)
A schematic of a typical animal cell. A representation of a bacterial cell is found in the inset.

highly coiled DNA that resides in the cytoplasm. Bacteria and archaea are prokaryotic organisms. Archaea are similar to bacteria in appearance, but fundamentally differ in their biochemical makeup.

Zooming In

In many ways the Internet has made life much easier. It's now commonplace to go to a website, click a computer mouse a few times, and pull up a map of nearly any location in the world. Perhaps most useful of all is the capability to zoom in to get a more detailed view of a specific area or to zoom out for a better perspective on the surrounding region.

The previous section took a quick look at the downloaded map of the cell. The next two sections progressively zoom in to view the eukaryotic cell's territory in greater detail. First, the internal biological features within a typical eukaryotic cell are explored. Then, the focus moves in even tighter on the biochemical makeup of these subcellular structures.

Cell Membranes

Cell membranes are thin and cannot be seen with a light microscope. They are only 7.5 to 10 nanometers thick. (A nanometer is one-billionth of a meter.) Electron micrographs show cell membranes to resemble a sandwich cookie. The inner and outer surfaces appear dark (due to high electron density), whereas the membrane's interior looks like vanilla cream (due to low electron density).

The cell membrane (also called the plasma membrane) creates a protected environment within the cell. Isolation from the cell's surroundings makes it possible for life's activities to occur in an efficient manner. Cell membranes are like plastic sandwich bags that hold the cell's contents and regulate the flow of materials into and out of the cell. (The molecular makeup of cell membranes is described in the next section, p. 45.)

Cytoplasm

Generally, biologists refer to all the material inside the plasma membrane, excluding the nucleus, as the cytoplasm. Specifically, cytoplasm (or more precisely the cytosol) is the liquid suspension composed of water, salts, molecules, and molecular aggregates that surrounds the organelles and other structures inside the cell.

Cytoskeleton

A network of filaments extends throughout the cytoplasm and attaches to the plasma membrane and organelles. Biologists refer to this filamentous network as the cytoskeleton. It imparts structural integrity to the cell and forms the framework for the cell's shape and movement.

The cytoskeleton is not permanent. It assembles and disassembles in various locales within the cytoplasm as needed. This threadlike structure functions as a "railway system" that the cell's machinery uses to ferry organelles and other cellular cargo from place to place within the cell.

Three types of filaments make up the cytoskeleton: microtubules, intermediate filaments, and microfilaments. These filaments are made up of proteins. (Proteins are discussed in more detail in the next section, p. 42.) Microtubules are long slender tubes 20 to 25 nanometers in diameter and are composed of the protein tubulin. Intermediate filaments are about 8 to 10 nanometers in diameter. They consist of ropelike assemblies of protein fibers that intertwine. Microfilaments, which consist of the protein actin, are only 6 nanometers in diameter.

Nucleus

The most prominent feature and control center inside eukaryotic cells is the nucleus. This large organelle houses DNA (deoxyribonucleic acid), the cell's genetic material. (DNA's molecular structure is described in the next section, p. 48.) The DNA in the cell's nucleus interacts with proteins to form chromosomes. Within the nucleus is a dense area called the nucleolus.

A double membrane system surrounds the nucleus. The inner and outer membranes connect at various points to form nuclear pores. These pores control the passage of materials in and out of the nucleus. The outer membrane is continuous with a network of membranes in the cytoplasm called the endoplasmic reticulum.

Ribosomes

Within the nucleolus, ribosomes (see p. 102) are assembled. Once put together, ribosomes are exported from the nucleus to the cytoplasm and endoplasmic reticulum. These subcellular particles measure about 23 nanometers in diameter and consist of two subunits, one large and the other small. Ribosomes are made up of proteins and RNA (ribonucleic acid) molecules.

The cell may contain up to a half-million ribosomes. These indispensable particles play the central role in protein synthesis. Ribosomes are distributed throughout the cell in the cytoplasm. Some are attached to the cytoskeleton and some are embedded in the endoplasmic reticulum membranes.

Endoplasmic Reticulum

A complex system of membrane tunnels and sacs, the endoplasmic reticulum concentrates near the cell's nucleus and accounts for over 50 percent of the cell's membranes. It is a continuous tubelike structure with a single internal space, the lumen. This space acts as a compartment that keeps materials separated from the rest of the cell. The endoplasmic reticulum connects the outer membrane of the nucleus's envelope to the plasma membrane.

Two regions constitute the endoplasmic reticulum. One region, the *rough endoplasmic reticulum*, has ribosomes associated with the outer surface of the endoplasmic reticulum membrane. Proteins made by these ribosomes are deposited into the lumen for further biochemical processing. The endoplasmic reticulum functions like an assembly line with a conveyor belt that prepares and processes proteins for export. Proteins transported into the lumen eventually (1) make their way into lysosomes and peroxisomes, (2) become incorporated into the plasma membrane, or (3) are secreted out of the cell.

No ribosomes are associated with the *smooth endoplasmic reticulum*. This area produces small round membrane-bound sacs (vesicles) that contain the proteins processed in the lumen. These vesicles typically make their way to the Golgi apparatus.

Golgi Apparatus

Stacks of flattened membrane-bound sacs that look like a pile of pita bread make up the Golgi apparatus. Numerous small vesicles surround these membrane stacks. This organelle makes biochemical modifications to the contents of vesicles that originate from the endoplasmic reticulum and then distributes these vesicles to different locations throughout the cell. Materials due to be secreted into the cell's exterior also pass through the Golgi apparatus.

Lysosomes

Membrane-bound vesicles, lysosomes pinch off from the Golgi apparatus and vary in size. They contain about forty different types of digestive enzymes and break down food, unneeded molecules, and damaged cell components. This action allows the components that make up these structures to be reused by the cell. Lysosomes are like the cell's recycling bins.

Peroxisomes

Similar in appearance to lysosomes, peroxisomes also bud off from the Golgi apparatus. However, they contain oxidative enzymes instead of digestive enzymes. A peroxisome's enzymes detoxify materials harmful to the cell by oxidizing them, much in the same way that liquid bleach sanitizes.

Mitochondria

Roughly the size of bacteria, mitochondria possess their own genetic material in the form of a small circular piece of DNA. Two membranes surround these large organelles: an outer membrane and a highly folded inner membrane. Unlike other organelles in the cytoplasm, cells cannot make mitochondria from scratch. Mitochondria come from preexisting mitochondria through a replication and division process. The cell's nucleus controls this replication.

Acting as the cell's power plant, mitochondria carry out biochemical reactions that extract energy from organic materials. This energy is stored in the form of high-energy chemical compounds used by the cell to power its processes.

The number of mitochondria per cell varies depending on the cell's energy requirements. Cells that utilize a significant amount of energy, like those found in muscle and the liver, require several thousand copies of this organelle.

Chloroplasts

Double-membrane organelles, chloroplasts are found only in plant cells. Like mitochondria, they have their own DNA and replicate themselves. Additionally they contain stacks of internal membrane sacs. Pigments in the membranes of the sacs absorb light energy so the chloroplasts can carry out photosynthesis. Chloroplasts are like solar cells converting sunlight into useable energy.

The Cell Wall

Plant cells have a porous cell wall that lies on the outside surface of the plasma membrane. This porosity allows water and nutrients to pass through the cell wall to the plant cell surface. In contrast to cell membranes, the wall that surrounds plant cells is visible with a light microscope. Composed of primarily cellulose (a large sugar molecule that consists of glucose subunits), the cell wall gives the plant cell its shape. The wall also cements adjacent plant cells together.

Extracellular Matrix

In all multicellular organisms, the space surrounding the cells consists of a fluid and an irregular network of fibers. The cells often help create the extracellular environment by secreting materials produced inside the cell. This extracellular matrix holds cells together to form tissues. Cells migrate through this matrix and interact with one another in the extracellular environs.

Enlarging the Molecular Domain

Taking a close look at the internal biological features of the cell gives a broad overview of the layout of the land. Even with this level of detail, however, much of the cell's landscape remains hidden from view. The only way to get a thorough picture of the cell's inner works is to zoom in even further on the cell's membranes, cytoplasm, and organelles. These structures are ultimately composed of molecules. This section describes the biochemical makeup of the cell and discusses how its molecular constituents interact to form its subcellular features.

Proteins

These "workhorse" molecules of life take part in essentially every cellular and extracellular structure and activity. Some proteins help form structures inside the cell and in the cell's surrounding matrix. They are dissolved in the cytosol and the lumen of organelles or they aggregate to form larger structures like the cytoskeleton. Structural proteins also associate with the cell membrane in a variety of ways (see p. 46). Proteins called enzymes catalyze chemical reactions. Enzymes are perhaps the most important type of protein. These biomolecules speed up the rate of chemical transformations by bringing the molecules together so they can react more readily. Other proteins harvest chemical energy, serve in the cell's defense systems, and store and transport molecules—and that's only a few of their roles.

Proteins are made up of one or more polypeptides. These chainlike molecules fold into precise three-dimensional structures. This architecture determines the way the polypeptides interact with each other and consequently determines the protein's function (see figure 2.2).

Polypeptides form when the cellular machinery links smaller subunit molecules called amino acids together in a head-to-tail fashion like beads on a string. Each amino acid possesses a specific set of chemical and physical properties. Cells employ twenty different amino acids, which (in principle) can link up in any possible order to form a polypeptide.

Each amino acid sequence imparts a unique chemical and physical profile along the polypeptide's chain. This profile determines how the polypeptide chain folds and, therefore, how it interacts with other polypeptide chains to form a functional protein. The amino acid sequence ultimately determines a polypeptide's function because a specific sequence will fold into a specific structure, and structure dictates function (see figure 2.2).

Because proteins are such large complex molecules, biochemists categorize protein structure into four different levels: primary, secondary, tertiary, and quaternary structures (see figure 2.2).

A protein's primary structure is the linear sequence of amino acids that make up each of its polypeptide chains. The secondary structure refers to short-range, three-dimensional arrangements of the polypeptide chain's backbone arising from the interactions between chemical groups that make up its backbone. Three of the most common secondary structures are the random coil, alpha (α) helix, and beta (β) pleated sheet (see figure 2.2). Tertiary structure describes the overall shape of the entire polypeptide chain and the location of each of its atoms in three-dimensional space. The structure and spatial orientation of the chemical groups that extend from the polypeptide backbone are also part of the tertiary structure. Quaternary structure arises when several individual polypeptide chains interact to form a functional protein structure.

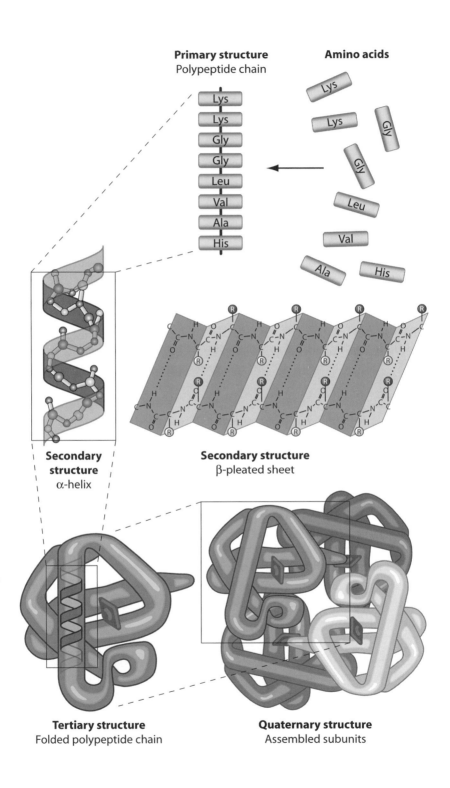

Primary structure
Polypeptide chain

Lys
Lys
Gly
Gly
Leu
Val
Ala
His

Amino acids

Lys
Lys
Gly
Gly
Leu
Val
Ala
His

Secondary structure
α-helix

Secondary structure
β-pleated sheet

Tertiary structure
Folded polypeptide chain

Quaternary structure
Assembled subunits

Enzymes have special regions on their surfaces called active sites. These locations can be either pockets or crevices. Chemical reactants bind to the active site. The binding of these molecules is highly specific. Once bound, the reactants are held in the just-right orientation in space so that the reaction between them readily takes place. By facilitating the interactions between chemical reactants, enzymes speed up the rate of chemical reactions. Other proteins, like receptors, have binding sites on their surfaces as well. These regions are similar to active sites.

Cell Membranes

Two classes of biomolecules interact to form cell membranes: lipids and proteins. Lipids, a structurally heterogeneous group of compounds, share water insolubility as a defining property. They also readily dissolve in organic solvents. Cholesterol, triglycerides, saturated and unsaturated fats, oils, and lecithin are familiar examples of lipids.

Phospholipids are the cell membrane's major lipid component. A phospholipid's molecular shape roughly resembles a distorted balloon with two ropes tied to it (see figure 2.3). Biochemists divide phospholipids into two regions that possess markedly different physical properties. The head region, corresponding to the "balloon," is soluble in water or hydrophilic (water-loving). The phospholipid tails, corresponding to the "ropes" tied to the balloon, are insoluble in water or hydrophobic (water-hating).

Chemists refer to molecules, like phospholipids, that possess molecular regions with distinct solubility characteristics, as amphiphilic (ambivalent in its likes). Soaps and detergents are amphiphilic compounds known to virtually everyone.

Amphiphilicity has great biological importance. Phospholipids' schizophrenic solubility properties play a key role in cell membrane structure. When added to water, phospholipids spontaneously organize into sheets that are two molecules thick called bilayers. When organized into a bilayer, phospholipid molecules align into two monolayers with the phospholipid head groups adjacent to one another and the phospholipid tails packed

---

Figure 2.2. Protein Structure
Biochemists categorize protein structure into four different levels. Primary structure is the linear sequence of amino acids that make up the polypeptide chains. Secondary structure refers to the three-dimensional arrangement of the polypeptide chain's backbone. The α helix and β pleated sheet are the two most common types of secondary structures. Tertiary structure describes the overall shape of a polypeptide chain. Quaternary structure arises when individual polypeptide chains interact to form a functional protein.

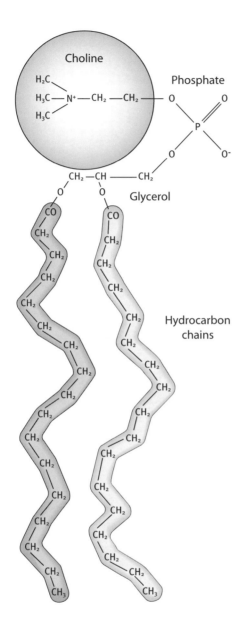

together closely. The mono-layers, in turn, come together so that the phospholipid tails of one monolayer contact the phospholipid tails of its companion monolayer. This tail-to-tail arrangement ensures that the water-soluble head groups contact water and the water-insoluble tails sequester from water (see figure 2.4).

This arrangement of phospholipids into a bilayer structure gives cell membranes their sandwich-cookie appearance in electron micrographs. The head groups that form the cell membrane's inner and outer surfaces are electron dense, rendering them dark. The phospholipid tails are less electron dense and, therefore, appear light.

Proteins associate with the cell membrane in a variety of ways. Peripheral proteins bind to the inner or outer membrane surfaces. Integral proteins embed into the cell membrane. Some integral proteins insert only slightly into the membrane interior, while others penetrate nearly half-

Figure 2.3. Phospholipid Structure
Schematic representation of a typical phospholipid superimposed on its molecular structure. The phosphate head group region (circle) is soluble in water while the hydrocarbon tails are insoluble.

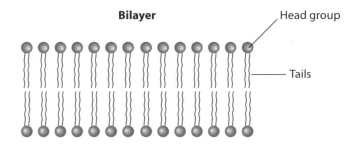

Figure 2.4. Phospholipid Bilayer Structure
A small segment of a bilayer. This structure spontaneously forms when phospholipids are added to water. Note the tail-to-tail arrangement.

way into the membrane's core, and still others span the entire membrane (see figure 2.5).

Membrane proteins serve the cell in numerous capacities. Some proteins function as receptors, binding compounds that allow the cell to communicate with its external environment. Some catalyze chemical reactions at the cell's interior and exterior surfaces. Some shuttle molecules across the cell

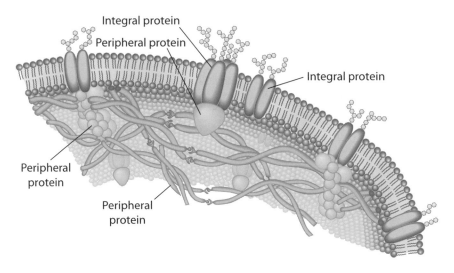

Figure 2.5. Membrane Proteins
A small segment of a typical cell membrane. Proteins associate with the cell membrane in a variety of ways. Peripheral proteins bind to the inner or outer membrane surfaces. Integral proteins embed into the cell membrane.

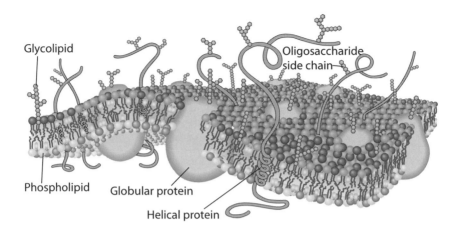

Glycolipid

Oligosaccharide
side chain

Phospholipid   Globular protein

Helical protein

Figure 2.6. Fluid Mosaic Model
A segment of the cell membrane illustrates the fluid mosaic model. The phospholipid bilayer
functions as a two-dimensional fluid that serves as both a cellular barrier and a solvent for
integral membrane proteins. The membrane proteins and lipids freely diffuse throughout the
cell membrane.

membrane; others form pores and channels through the membrane. Some
membrane proteins impart structural integrity to the cell membrane.

Since the early 1970s, the fluid mosaic model has provided the framework to understand membrane structure and function. This model views
the phospholipid bilayer as a two-dimensional fluid that serves as both a
cellular barrier and a solvent for integral membrane proteins. The fluid
mosaic model allows the membrane proteins and lipids to freely diffuse
laterally throughout the cell membrane. Beyond the bilayer structure and
asymmetry, the fluid mosaic model fails to attribute structural and functional organization to cell membranes (see figure 2.6).

DNA

DNA consists of chainlike molecules known as polynucleotides. Two
polynucleotide chains align in an antiparallel fashion to form a DNA molecule. The two strands are arranged parallel to one another with the starting
point of one strand, the 5′ end (reads "five prime"), in the polynucleotide
duplex located next to the ending point of the other strand, the 3′ end (reads
"three prime"), and vice versa. The paired polynucleotide chains resemble a

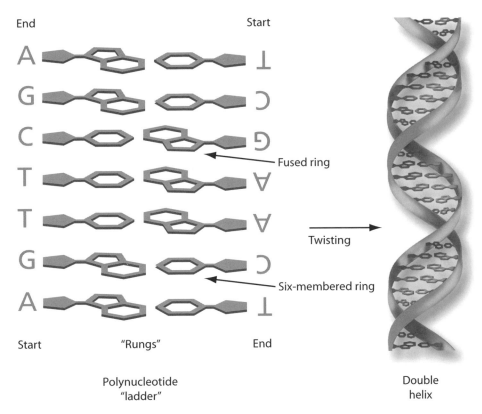

Figure 2.7. DNA Structure
DNA consists of chainlike molecules that twist around each other forming the well-known DNA double helix. The polynucleotide chains of DNA are formed from four different nucleotides—adenosine (A), guanosine (G), cytidine (C), and thymidine (T).

ladder with the side groups extending from the backbone interacting with each other to form rungs. The coupled polynucleotide chains twist around each other forming the well-known DNA double helix.

The cell's machinery forms polynucleotide chains by linking together four different subunit molecules called nucleotides. The four nucleotides used to build DNA chains are adenosine, guanosine, cytidine, and thymidine—famously abbreviated A, G, C, and T, respectively (see figure 2.7).

DNA stores the information necessary to make all the polypeptides used by the cell. The sequence of nucleotides in DNA strands specifies the sequence of amino acids in polypeptide chains. The nucleotide sequence that codes the amino acid sequence of a particular polypeptide (or other functional products) is known as a gene. Through the use of genes, DNA stores the information functionally expressed in the amino acid sequences of polypeptide chains.

Proteins interact with DNA to make chromosomes. These structures only become visible in the cell nucleus when the cell divides. Each chromosome consists of a single DNA molecule that wraps around a series of globular protein complexes. The globular proteins are called histones. These structures repeat to form a supramolecular structure that resembles a string of beads (see figure 2.8). Biochemists refer to the "beads" as nucleosomes.

The nucleosomes coil to form a structure called a solenoid. The solenoid further condenses to form higher order structures that comprise the chromosome proper. Between cell division events, the chromosome exists in an extended diffuse form that is not detectable. Prior to and during cell division, the chromosome condenses to form its readily recognizable compact structures.

Central Dogma of Molecular Biology

The central dogma of molecular biology describes how information stored in DNA becomes functionally expressed through the amino acid sequence and activity of polypeptide chains (see figure 2.9). DNA does not leave the nucleus to direct the synthesis of polypeptide chains. Rather the cellular machinery copies the gene's sequence by assembling another polynucleotide, messenger RNA (mRNA). Scientists refer to the process of copying mRNA from DNA as transcription.

A single-stranded molecule, mRNA is similar, but not identical, in composition to DNA. One of the most important differences between DNA and mRNA is the use of uridine (U) in place of thymidine (T) to form the mRNA chain.

Once transcribed from the DNA, mRNA migrates from the nucleus of the cell into the cytoplasm. At the ribosome, mRNA directs the synthesis of polypeptide chains. The information content of the polynucleotide sequence is then translated into the polypeptide amino acid sequence. The polypeptide chain then folds to form a fully functional protein.

Much more about the cell's biochemical and biological systems could be discussed. More details appear in subsequent chapters as the need arises. For now, this brief introduction offers a sufficient view of the cell's landscape to

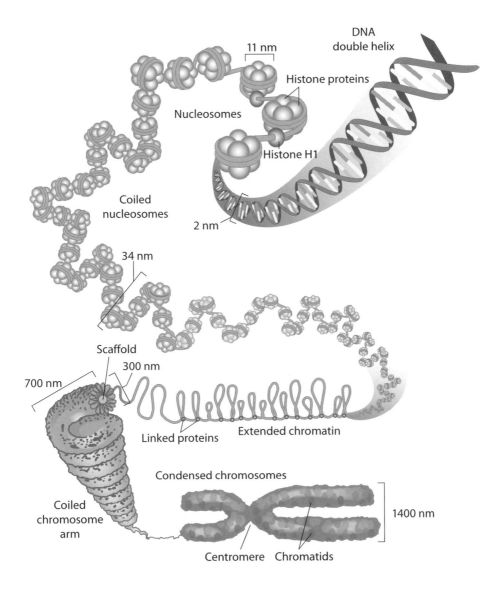

11 nm

DNA
double helix

Histone proteins

Nucleosomes

Histone H1

Coiled
nucleosomes

2 nm

34 nm

Scaffold

300 nm

700 nm

Linked proteins

Extended chromatin

Condensed chromosomes

Coiled
chromosome
arm

1400 nm

Centromere   Chromatids

Figure 2.8. Chromosome Structure
DNA and proteins interact to make chromosomes. Their fundamental structural elements are
nucleosomes. Each nucleosome consists of a single DNA molecule that wraps around a series of
globular protein conglomerates made up of histones. The nucleosomes further coil and condense to
form the chromosome proper.

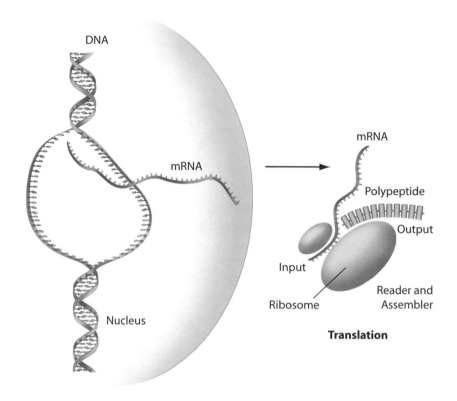

Transcription

Figure 2.9. Central Dogma of Molecular Biology
This concept describes how information stored in DNA becomes functionally expressed
through the amino acid sequence of polypeptide chains. The cellular machinery copies the
gene's sequence by assembling another polynucleotide, messenger RNA (mRNA). Once
assembled, mRNA migrates from the nucleus of the cell into the cytoplasm. At the ribosome,
mRNA directs the synthesis of polypeptide chains.

appreciate its organization, complexity, and elegant design. (For access to
a list of animations of biochemical activities in the cell, see reference.[5])

Is it possible to substantiate this molecular design as a masterpiece on
prominent display in the Divine Artist's studio? The next chapter begins
to develop the case for biochemical intelligent design by examining the
minimum complexity of the simplest life-forms.

3

THE BARE ESSENTIALS

Pablo Picasso and Georges Braque revolted against the artistic tradition of the early 1900s by refusing to imitate nature. They rejected the visual appeal of paint texture and color and abandoned the play of light on form and movement. Instead, Picasso and Braque established the Cubist school of art. This approach fragmented three-dimensional objects and redefined them as a series of interlocking planes.[1]

However, Cubism was short-lived. The movement dispersed shortly after World War I. Still, its reach extended throughout the twentieth century.

Influenced by Cubism, minimalism began in the late 1950s with the exhibition of Frank Stella's Black Paintings at the Museum of Modern Art in New York.[2] Like Cubists, minimalists reacted against what they saw as the pretentiousness of more expressive and traditional art movements. They sought to reduce art to the smallest number of colors, shapes, lines, and textures. These artists wanted their viewers to experience art without the distraction of composition, themes, and the elements of more traditional work.

Not confined exclusively to the art world, minimalism has also impacted music, architecture, and philosophy. Recently, a type of minimalism has even found its way into biochemistry.

It's becoming fashionable for biochemists to strip away all the excesses of the cell's chemical systems. The scientific community thinks that by eliminating the distraction of superfluous biochemical systems, they'll gain fundamental insight into life's indispensable chemical processes. Reducing life to its bare essentials will help scientists achieve a better definition of life and provide insight into its origin.

Complexity is often considered an indicator of design. But as Dembski's explanatory filter highlights, complexity, in and of itself, does not necessarily indicate the work of a Creator. Only complexity that conforms to a specified pattern does. The immense complexity of the cell's chemical systems obscures these hallmark characteristics of design. To see those intricate details, the cell's biochemical excesses must be eliminated.

So, scientists have focused attention on the simplest known life-forms, prokaryotes. These microbes come close to the minimal requirements for life. Biochemists find genome size a convenient measure of complexity. (The term "genome" refers to an organism's entire hereditary information stored in the nucleotide sequences of DNA.) The chief information housed in an organism's genome is the instructions the cell's machinery uses to make proteins.

Proteins take part in virtually every biochemical process and play critical roles in nearly every cell structure (see chapter 2, p. 42). Cataloging the number and types of proteins present in an organism gives biochemists important insight into its structures and operations, and hence, biological complexity.

The cell's machinery uses the information encoded in the nucleotide sequences of genes to manufacture proteins. The genome of eukaryotic organisms consists of both genes that encode proteins (and other useful products) and noncoding DNA sequences. The genome structure of prokaryotes, however, is far simpler. For the most part, only protein-coding DNA sequences make up their genomes. In prokaryotes, generally one gene corresponds to one protein. Therefore, knowledge about the number and types of genes present in a prokaryote's genome yields insight into the number and type of proteins present in the organism. And this relationship makes genome size a good initial measure of biological complexity.

Biochemical Minimalism

One of the most important advances in biochemistry over the last decade has been the emergence of techniques to sequence, analyze, and manipulate genomes. These methodologies, still in their infancy, fall within the scope of the new scientific discipline of genomics and pave the way for biochemists to define life's minimal complexity. Genomics cross-sects genetics, molecular biology, biochemistry, and computer science.

In 1995 The Institute for Genomic Research (TIGR) reported the first-ever genome sequence. TIGR scientists tried out their new "shotgun" sequencing strategy and determined the DNA sequence of the *Hemophilus influenzae* genome.[3] (This bacterium has been implicated in bronchitis, meningitis, and pneumonia.) Since this time, scientific reports of fully sequenced genomes have poured forth.

A fairly large database of microbial genomes now exists. Biochemists easily add several genomes to this database per month.

Less Is More

Biochemists have gained insight into life's minimum complexity by surveying the microbial database of sequenced genomes to identify the simplest. Table 3.1 samples the results.[4] To date, *Pelagibacter ubique* holds the record for having the most streamlined genome—at least for a free-living, self-sufficient prokaryote. This microbe, which accounts for 25 percent of microbial cells in the open ocean, possesses 1,354 gene products.[5] (A gene product refers to both proteins and functional RNAs like ribosomal and transfer RNA.)

Based on the *P. ubique* genome, it appears that the least complicated (for independently existing life) contains about 1,350 genes. Given the relatively small number of sequenced genomes currently available to assess life's complexity, it may well be that the minimum requirement for independent life extends below that number. To date, however, all genomes smaller than 1,350 gene products belong to parasitic microbes, organisms that aren't self-sufficient and must rely on the biochemistry of the host organism they invade.[6]

P. ubique gets by with a reduced genome because it feeds on the abundance of organic debris in the oceans. These organisms, which belong to a group called heterotrophs, don't require the proteins that produce the organic food stuff needed to support their activities. Heterotrophs get their nutrients from organic materials they eat.

Table 3.1
Genome Sizes of Life's Simplest Organisms

Organism	Domain	Approximate Genome Size
Pelagibacter ubique	Bacteria	1,354
Thermoplasma acidophilum	Archaea	1,509
Aquifex aeolicus	Bacteria	1,512
Picrophilus torridus	Archaea	1,535
Helicobacter pylori	Bacteria	1,591
Methanopyrus kandleri AV19	Archaea	1,692
Methanococcus jannaschii	Archaea	1,738
Streptococcus pyogenes	Bacteria	1,752
Methanobacterium thermoautotrophicum	Archaea	1,855
Thermotoga maritima	Bacteria	1,877
Thiomicrospira crunogena XCL-2	Archaea	1,922

In contrast, autotrophs survive by generating the organic materials they need using inorganic compounds and energy sources found in the environment. Two types of autotrophs exist: chemoautotrophs and photoautotrophs. Chemoautotrophs use chemical energy extracted from the environment as an energy source to produce organic materials. Photoautotrophs produce food stuff by using light energy. It's quite likely the minimum genome size for autotrophs is somewhat larger than the minimum heterotrophic genome because of the additional metabolic systems required to harvest energy from the environment and to produce organic materials from inorganic compounds.

Table 3.1 suggests that chemoautotrophs require a minimum genome size in the range of about 1,500 to 1,900 gene products to exist independently. Even in 1999, when the first microbial genome sequences were becoming available, evolutionary biologist Colin Patterson recognized that the 1,700 genes of *Methanococcus* are "perhaps close to the minimum necessary for independent life."[7]

Table 3.2 provides a list of minimum genome sizes for photoautotrophs.[8] Based on limited data, it appears as if that minimum falls roughly between 1,700 and 2,300 gene products—larger than required for chemoautotrophs.

Table 3.2
Minimum Genome Sizes for Photoautotrophs

Organism	Domain	Approximate Genome Size
Prochlorococcus marinus MED4	Bacteria	1,716
Prochlorococcus marinus SS120	Bacteria	1,884
Chlorobium tepidum TLS	Bacteria	2,288
Thermosynechococcus elongatus BP-1	Bacteria	2,475

This sampling of microbial genomes indicates that the simplest life-forms capable of independent living require roughly between 1,300 and 2,300 gene products depending on the organism's specific lifestyle (heterotrophic, chemoautotrophic, or photoautotrophic). Each gene product represents one of the cell's molecular parts. Even with unnecessary biochemical systems stripped away, the simplest life-forms appear remarkably complex.

Down to the Nitty Gritty

The discovery of parasitic microbes with reduced genome sizes (like *Mycoplasma pneumonia* and *Borrelia burgdorferi* with 677 and 863 gene products respectively) indicates that life exists, though not independently, with genome sizes less than 1,350 genes.[9] Because they are parasites, these microbes must exploit the host cell's metabolism to exist. (In general, parasitic microbes can get by with reduced genome sizes because of their reliance on host cell biochemistry.)

Two of the most extreme examples of parasitic genomes belong to *Mycoplasma genitalium* and *Nanoarchaeum equitans*.[10] *M. genitalium* parasitizes the human genital and respiratory tract. *N. equitans* lives as a parasite attached to the surface of an independently existing hyperthermophilic host (*Ignicoccus*). The *M. genitalium* genome possesses about 480 gene products, whereas the genome of *N. equitans* consists of about 550.

Because these genomes are so extensively pared down, they help determine the bare minimal requirements for life (assuming building block molecules such as amino acids, nucleotides, sugars, and fatty acids are readily available). Researchers find these parasites useful for identifying the "nonnegotiable" biochemical systems that must be present for an entity to be recognized as a form of life.

A significant percentage of parasitic genomes are dedicated to mediating interactions between the parasite and its host and, therefore, can be considered as nonessential to a strictly minimal life-form. So the bare essential genome is quite likely much smaller than 480 to 550 gene products. Researchers have employed both theoretical and experimental approaches to identify the essential gene set that defines "life."[11]

In Theory

To theoretically construct the minimum gene set, biochemists compare genomes looking for commonly shared genes. Researchers reason that these common genes constitute the minimum gene products necessary for life. The first study of this type was conducted in 1996 by scientists from the National Institutes of Health. This seminal work compared the genomes of the two parasites, *M. genitalium* and *H. influenzae*, and estimated the size of a minimum genome to be about 256 genes.[12]

In 1999, an international team of scientists estimated the minimum number of genes for life to be about 246.[13] These investigators developed a universal minimal gene set by comparing the genomes of representatives from life's three domains—Eubacteria, Archaea, and Eukarya.

Since then, biochemists have conducted more sophisticated theoretical studies using an expanded database and have determined that the number of shared genes found among representatives of all life-forms falls between 60 and 80. Still, due to horizontal gene transfer, these researchers conclude that the Last Universal Common Ancestor (LUCA)—evolution's hypothetical organism from which all life derives—must have possessed 500 to 600 genes.[14] These most recent studies, however, have uncovered inherent problems with theoretical genome comparisons. Researchers now question if these types of comparative analyses are the best way to identify the minimal gene set.

In the Lab

Experimental strategies to ascertain the minimum number of genes needed for life are also being pursued. These protocols ("knock-out experiments") involve either the random or systematic mutation of genes to determine those indispensable for life. If researchers can grow the microbe after a gene has been disabled, then the gene is deemed nonessential. While some of the first studies were done with parasitic microbes (because of their reduced genome sizes), biochemists are now applying these techniques to a wide range of prokaryotes. Table 3.3 summarizes the results of some of these studies.[15]

Table 3.3
Estimates of the Essential Genome Size

Organism	Technique	Essential Gene Products
Bacillus subtilis	Site-specific Mutagenesis	254–450
Bacillus subtilis	Systematic inactivation of genes	192
Mycoplasma genitalium	Global transposon mutagenesis I	265–350
Mycoplasma genitalium	Global transposon mutagenesis II	382
Hemophilus influenzae	High-density transposon mutagenesis	478
Staphylococcus aureus	Rapid shotgun antisense method	168
Escherichia coli	Genetic footprinting technique	620
Pseudomonas aeruginosa	Library of transposon insertion mutants I	300–400
Pseudomonas aeruginosa	Library of transposon insertion mutants II	335
Mycobacterium tuberculosis	Subsaturation mutagenesis postgenomic analysis	1,490

The methods used to determine the essential gene set for minimal life are in their infancy. Still, these initial experimental studies collectively indicate that life in its most stripped-down form requires somewhere between 200 and 500 genes. Even though some biochemists think that theoretical estimates of minimal genome size are flawed, those measurements come fairly close to those obtained experimentally.

In the Cell

The genome of bacterial intracellular symbionts (endosymbionts) provides another means to determine the size of the minimal gene set. These parasites permanently reside inside the cells of the host and possess dramatically reduced genomes. Scientists believe that the gene sets of intracellular symbionts are close to what is fundamentally essential for life. In contrast, the genomes of extracellular parasites (like *M. genitalium*) consist of both genes essential for life and those that mediate host-parasite interactions.

One of the smallest endosymbiont genomes is possessed by species of *Buchnera*. These microbes make their living inside the cells of aphids. While the genome size of the different *Buchnera* species varies, the smallest ones are estimated to contain between 350 and 400 gene products.[16]

In 2003, a research team compared the five completely sequenced genomes of insect endosymbionts and discovered they shared 313 genes.[17] The scientists concluded that this number is close to the minimum amount needed to sustain an intracellular symbiont. In 2006, a team of molecular biologists determined that the genome of the extreme endosymbiont, *Carsonella ruddii*, consisted of only 182 gene products.[18] This quantity is likely to be a good measure of the bare essential requirements for life. Again, this insight into the minimum gene set from endosymbionts coincides with values obtained from theoretical and experimental estimates.[19]

In the Future

Though the genomic tools to assess life's minimum complexity are powerful, they are still crude. In years to come, biochemists will undoubtedly develop more sophisticated ways to identify life's bare essentials.

One exciting plan involves synthetically reconstructing the presumed minimum genome (based on the *M. genitalium* knock-out experiments) and inserting it into a *M. genitalium* cell with its DNA removed.[20] By systematically exploring synthetic variants of the minimum genome, it should be possible to rigorously establish the essential gene set.

This approach faces a number of significant technical hurdles, however. The chief difficulty is synthesizing a DNA molecule hundreds of thousands of nucleotides long. (On average, a gene product is about 1,000 nucleotides in length.) Some progress towards this goal has been made. Independent research teams have synthesized from scratch the genomes of the poliovirus (7,000 nucleotides long), the bacteriophage $\varphi X174$ (5,400 nucleotides long), and the *E. coli* polyketide synthase gene cluster (32,000 nucleotides long).[21] As remarkable as these advances are, a DNA segment 32,000 nucleotides in length is a long way from one hundreds of thousands of nucleotides long.

While much of the focus has been on genomics with its top-down approach to life's minimum complexity, other researchers are using a different strategy, one that starts at the bottom and works its way up. This bottom-up approach generally entails producing artificial cell membranes and using them to encapsulate some of the basic components of the cell's molecular machinery.[22]

Though just getting started, this research effort is making some remarkable progress. Scientists from Rockefeller University in New York have successfully produced a membrane-encapsulated artificial cell about the size of a bacterium. And, it is capable of generating proteins.[23] The researchers extracted the biochemical machinery responsible for protein synthesis from *E. coli* and encapsulated it within a phospholipid bilayer system. They also introduced DNA molecules containing the genes that code for pore-forming proteins. These proteins associate with the cell membrane and form pores that serve as conduits for amino acids to enter the artificial cell. The influx of amino acids provides an ongoing supply of the raw materials needed to make proteins. Though far from a living entity (because it can't replicate itself), this artificial cell helps define life's essential systems.

In the Divine Artist's Studio

To create a masterpiece, an artist typically performs one process after another—sketching, refining, adding color, shading, intensifying, and perfecting. Much like art, biochemists have discovered that life also requires a series of steps.[24] These steps include:

- assembly of boundary membranes
- formation of energy capturing capabilities by the boundary membrane
- encapsulation of macromolecules (like proteins, RNA, and DNA) within the boundary membrane
- introduction of pores into the boundary membrane that can funnel raw materials into the interior space
- production of systems that allow the macromolecules to grow
- generation of catalysts that speed up the growth of the encapsulated macromolecules
- provision for the macromolecules to replicate
- introduction of information into one set of macromolecules that directs the production of other macromolecules
- development of mechanisms to cause the boundary membrane to subdivide into two smaller systems that can grow
- production of the means to pass information-containing macromolecules to the daughter products of the subdivision process

Origin-of-life researcher David Deamer stated, "Looking down this list, one is struck by the complexity of even the simplest form of life."[25]

The bottom-up method involved with identifying the process lends itself more readily to identifying life's essential biochemical operations than genomics' top-down strategy. Still, key insight into life's essential features has come from knock-out experiments and theoretical studies. These two complementary approaches both indicate that life in its bare minimal form requires genes that control DNA replication, cell division, protein synthesis, and assembly of the cell membrane. Minimal life also depends upon genes that specify at least one biochemical pathway that can extract energy from the environment.

Internal Composition

As biochemists labor to determine the minimum number of gene products needed for life, microbiologists are making discoveries that revolutionized the scientific community's understanding of prokaryotes. These advances indicate that life's bare essentials extend far beyond the number of proteins that must simultaneously occur for life to exist. Life's minimum complexity also requires organization of these gene products within the cell.

Prior to the mid-1990s, microbiologists had a simple view of prokaryotes as "vessels" that contained a jumbled assortment of life molecules randomly dispersed inside the cell. In short, microbiologists did not think these organisms possessed any type of internal organization.

This perception stood in sharp contrast to the remarkable internal organization displayed by the complex cells (eukaryotes) that make up the multicellular fungi, plant, and animal kingdoms as well as single-celled protozoans. Eukaryotic cells possess numerous internal compartments—membrane systems, a nucleus, organelles, a cytoskeleton, and other components that organize the cell contents at the subcellular and even molecular level (see chapter 2).

Now the traditional view of prokaryotes is changing. Microbiologists have begun recognizing that these microbes display a remarkable degree of internal organization. This ordering, however, does not involve subcellular structures. Rather the arrangement occurs at the molecular level—both spatially and temporally.[26] Microbiologists Lucy Shapiro (Stanford) and Richard Losick (Harvard) said:

The use of immunogold electron microscopy and fluorescence microscopy to study the subcellular organization of bacterial cells has revealed a surprising extent of protein compartmentalization and localization.[27]

Shapiro and Losick point out that in some cases, this internal ordering of proteins appears nonessential for cell survival. In other instances, however, the organization clearly involves essential cell activities. A few examples of extraordinary internal organization in prokaryotes include a bacterial chromosome(s), DNA polymerase, cell-division proteins, the bacterial cytoskeleton, and bacterial internal compartmentalization.

Bacterial Chromosomes

Unlike eukaryotic cells (which have DNA and proteins associated to form chromosomes inside the cell nucleus), bacteria and archaea possess one or more small naked pieces of DNA that loop to form a twisted circle. Microbiologists long thought that this bacterial DNA diffused freely and randomly throughout the cell and that when the cell divided, the segregation of the two duplicated DNA molecules between the daughter cells was a passive process.

It turns out, however, this view is incorrect. Microbiologists now know that the bacterial DNA has to have a specific orientation within the cell. Moreover, during cell division, a complex ensemble of proteins must not only segregate the two newly reproduced DNA circles, but also must maintain the chromosomes in the correct orientation—if not, cell death results.[28]

Bacteria also contain plasmids, extremely small extrachromosomal pieces of circular DNA. Once again it was long regarded that these plasmids were randomly dispersed and free to migrate throughout the cell. As with the bacterial chromosome, though, scientists have now determined that even plasmids cluster and localize inside the cell.[29]

DNA Polymerase

DNA polymerases duplicate DNA molecules during cell replication. Instead of moving along the DNA double strand, like a "train on a track," to produce two copies of DNA from the parent DNA molecule, microbiologists have determined that DNA polymerase must be localized near the middle of the cell.[30] In other words, instead of being randomly distributed throughout the cell, these enzymes must be situated in a specific region. Microbiologists now view bacterial DNA polymerases as "replication factories" anchored precisely in the cell. Their activity during cell replication seems to be intimately connected to the machinery that orients and segregates the bacterial chromosome.

Recent work also indicates that DNA topoisomerases also must be precisely situated in the bacterial cell. These enzymes control the topology of the DNA molecule by introducing and relaxing the supercoiling of DNA molecules. If DNA topoisomerases don't localize with the replication origin, the bacterial chromosome will not become properly oriented within the cell.[31]

Cell-Division Proteins

Bacterial cell division, in which the mother cell divides near its midplane to produce two daughter cells, requires dynamic spatial and temporal localization of several proteins. The FtsZ protein is key in this process. Several copies of FtsZ accumulate at the middle of the cell and aggregate to form a ring that extends around the inner surface of the cell wall.[32] During cell division, the FtsZ ring contracts to pinch the mother cell into two daughters. Disruption of this ring assembly results in cell death.[33]

An ensemble of proteins regulates the way FtsZ binds to the inner cell wall and ensures that the FtsZ ring forms at the proper location.[34] For example, the Min C and Min D proteins keep the FtsZ proteins from binding to the wrong place in the cell wall. The Min E protein interacts with Min C and Min D proteins to promote FtsZ binding at the cell's midplane. Any disruption of FtsZ, Min C, Min D, or Min E function and interactions compromises cell replication.

Recent work indicates that the Min C, Min D, and Min E proteins rapidly oscillate inside the bacterial cell from pole to pole in a spiral fashion. This back and forth movement plays a critical role in establishing the FtsZ ring at the cell's midplane.[35]

Bacterial Cytoskeleton

Microbiologists traditionally thought that bacteria lacked a cytoskeleton. In fact, the absence of a cytoskeleton was considered a defining feature of prokaryotic cells, one that distinguished them from eukaryotic cells. According to tradition, only complex eukaryotic cells possessed a cytoskeleton.

Recent advances completely overturn this long-standing view of bacteria. Research revealed that these microbes possess complex cytoskeletal structures with components that correspond to the cytoskeletal elements found in eukaryotic cells.[36] The FtsZ ring, which locates to the cell's midplane and plays a central role in cell division, is properly understood as a cytoskeletal component corresponding to tubulin in eukaryotic cells. The MreB protein, which corresponds to actin in eukaryotic cells, forms a helical structure that spans the length of nonspherical bacterial species. The MreB complex helps establish cell shape and serves as a "track" to ferry molecules around inside the bacterial cell.

Another bacterial cytoskeletal component that corresponds to intermediate filaments in eukaryotic cells is crescentin. This protein plays a role in determining cell shape. It even appears that the spiraling action of the Min proteins—C, D, and E—form an additional helical cytoskeletal structure independent of the one formed by the MreB protein.[37]

Bacterial Internal Compartmentalization

Traditionally, microbiologists considered the lack of internal compartmentalization and the absence of organelles to be *the* defining features of prokaryotic cells. According to tradition, only complex eukaryotic cells possessed organelles and displayed subcellular compartmentalization. But this conventional view of prokaryotes is incorrect. Recent advances have uncovered examples of compartmentalization within bacteria and have even identified the existence of bacterial organelles.

One example of a bacterial organelle is the carboxysome.[38] This organelle consists of a protein shell that houses the enzymes involved in carbon fixation reactions. The carboxysome sequesters these enzymes from the rest of the cell. Carbon fixation reactions are sensitive to the environment and could not proceed unprotected in the cytoplasm. Carboxysomes even have pores that allow influx of the raw materials needed to carry out the carbon fixation reactions and the outgo of reaction products.

When initially detected in bacterial cytoplasm, microbiologists thought carboxysomes were viral particles that had invaded the cell. The paradigm that prokaryotes lacked internal compartmentalization was so pervasive that no one could envision these inclusions actually being organelles. It was only after carbon fixation enzymes were found associated with carboxysomes that this deeply entrenched paradigm was abandoned. Organelles, like carboxysomes, are widespread among bacteria.

The last decade of research has overturned the traditional view of bacteria. These little "bags of molecules" actually display an incredible degree of internal organization. They also possess exquisite composition of biochemical activity in spatial and temporal terms. As microbiologists continue to probe, more examples of structural and functional organization are sure to be discovered.

Bacterial internal organization seems to be universal among microorganisms and seems to be a property necessary for life. It adds another dimension to life's minimal complexity. In other words, minimal life not only requires the simultaneous occurrence of a relatively large number of gene products, but also their spatial and temporal organization.

A Complex and Well-Organized Masterpiece

When minimalists created a piece of art, they wanted the viewer to experience it without the distractions that can come from the composition, theme, and other devices of more traditional works. Similarly, over the past several years, biochemical minimalists have attempted to strip life of its superfluous systems so scientific viewers can contemplate life in its bare essence.

Though still very much in formative stages, these efforts have been quite successful. Scientists are honing in on the minimum number of genes and essential biochemical systems necessary for life in its various forms (parasitic, heterotrophic, chemoautotrophic, and photoautotrophic). Most striking in these preliminary results is their remarkable complexity.

It appears as if a lower bound of several hundred genes exists, below which life cannot be pushed and still recognized as "life." In *Darwin's Black Box*, biochemist Michael Behe argues that individual biochemical systems are irreducibly complex.[39] The initial insight into life's minimal complexity indicates that it's not just individual biochemical systems that are irreducibly complex; so is life itself. Systems produced by human designers are often irreducibly complex. This feature is a hallmark characteristic of intelligent design.

Behe makes the powerful case that irreducibly complex systems cannot emerge through an undirected stepwise process. The incredible complex nature of minimal life, likewise, makes it difficult to envision how natural evolutionary processes could have produced even the simplest life-forms—whether parasitic, heterotrophic, or autotrophic.

In *Origins of Life*, Hugh Ross (an astronomer) and I reach the identical conclusion by considering the probability of the essential gene set coming into existence simultaneously. According to this analysis, it is superastronomically improbable for the essential gene set to emerge simultaneously through natural means alone.[40] If left up to an evolutionary process, not enough resources or time exist throughout the universe's history to generate life in its simplest form.

The overthrow of the traditional view of prokaryotes—as little bags of assorted molecules haphazardly arranged inside the cell—also substantiates the case for life being a divinely created masterpiece. Microbiologists now understand that these microbes display exquisite spatial and temporal organization at the molecular level. This organization adds an extra dimension of complexity that has yet to be explained away by naturalistic evolutionary processes.

Common experience teaches that it takes thought and intentional effort to carefully organize a space for functional use. By analogy, the surprising internal composition of prokaryotic cells bespeaks of intelligent design. Instead of resembling a preschooler's messy fingerpainting, the interior of the simplest cell is best described as a carefully planned and marvelously executed work of art—one that masterfully carries out life's most basic processes in living color. Disrupting this arrangement is often lethal.

This chapter focused on the general biochemical features of the simplest life-form—the essential gene set and internal molecular organization—which indicate that life's chemistry is the work of a Creator. Instead of being restricted to the minimal biochemical requirements for life, the next several chapters reveal the rich and full artistry of life's chemical systems. Chapter 4 shows the profound intricacy of molecular motors.

4

SUCH A CLEAN MACHINE

For some, automobiles are works of art. For a few, like Ken Eberts, automobiles are the subject of art. Perhaps it's no accident that Eberts became one of the world's most preeminent automotive fine artists.[1] He began his career as an automotive designer for the Ford Motor Company, creating the very concepts that eventually fueled his passion for painting. Now his artwork conveys the excitement that's very much a part of car history.

Automobiles make fascinating subjects because they cultivate a sense of exhilaration and nostalgia. Their form, color, and gloss, plus the way light plays on their surface, make them aesthetically enticing.

While it's generally the automobile's exterior that inspires art, that's not the only part of a vehicle considered a thing of beauty. Ask any racecar mechanic who marvels at a gleaming engine under the hood—the motor of a mean machine can be even more awe-inspiring than the exterior. Teams of engineers often labor long and hard to create the elegant engines that power automotive "works of art."

Such a motor makes for a quintessential example of a humanly designed system. Every feature stems from forethought and careful planning. These engineering masterpieces consist of numerous components that precisely and necessarily interact to achieve power. Machines operate according to the laws of physics and chemistry, but cannot be reduced to them.[2]

Nature's laws cannot explain an automobile engine's origin. A mechanical wonder like a motor is irreducibly complex, and this characteristic indicates that the engine was intelligently designed.

Motors and machines are found not only under the hoods of automobiles. They are also found inside of cells. One of the most remarkable advances in biochemistry during the last part of the twentieth century has been the recognition that many biochemical systems function as molecular-level machines. Remarkably, some of these biomolecular motors bear an eerie resemblance to humanly designed engines. Yet, these biomachines are far superior in construction and operation than their man-made counterparts.

Biomachines make a powerful case for biochemical intelligent design and reinvigorate one of history's most well-known arguments for a Creator's existence: the Watchmaker argument popularized in the eighteenth century by William Paley, a British theologian.

A Gallery of Molecular Motors

For an artist, there may be no greater form of recognition than to have his work featured and displayed for the general public to appreciate. Since 1968, Eberts has produced over one thousand original paintings that are part of collections all over the world. His works have been exhibited throughout the United States, and over twenty-five art galleries have honored him with one-artist shows.

The biomolecular art show that follows honors its Creator no less. Thanks to a decade or so of biochemical advance, just a few of the Divine Artist's many biomolecular machines are now on display for people to contemplate.

As in any exhibit, not every piece may be equally stimulating. Often observers stroll through the displays until something of interest catches their eye. Then it's easy to get caught up in every fascinating nuance.

A Magnificent Motor

The bacterial flagellum has become the "poster child" for Intelligent Design.[3] The flagellum looks like a whip and extends from the bacterial cell surface. Some bacteria have only a single flagellum, others possess several. Rotation of the flagellum(a) allows the bacterial cell to navigate its environment in response to various chemical signals (see figure 4.1).

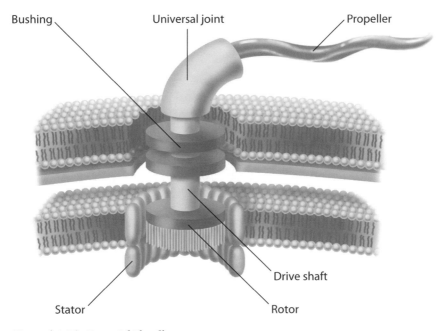

Bushing   Universal joint   Propeller

Drive shaft

Stator   Rotor

Figure 4.1. The Bacterial Flagellum
The proteins of the bacterial flagellum form a literal rotary motor.

An ensemble of over forty different kinds of proteins makes up the typical bacterial flagellum. These proteins function in concert as a literal rotary motor. The bacterial flagellum's components stand as direct analogs to the parts of a man-made motor, including a rotor, stator, drive shaft, bushing, universal joint, and propeller.[4]

The bacterial flagellum is essentially a molecular-sized electrical motor. The flow of positively charged hydrogen ions through the bacterial inner membrane powers the flagellum's rotation.[5] As research continues on the bacterial flagellum, its machinelike character becomes increasingly evident.[6]

Cruising throughout Nature

The rotary motor, F_1–F_0 ATPase, plays a central role in harvesting energy for cellular use.[7] F_1–F_0 ATPase associates with cell membranes. The mushroom-shaped F_1 portion of the complex extends above the membrane's surface. The "button of the mushroom" literally corresponds to an engine turbine (see figure 4.2).

Stator

Turbine

Rotor

Cam

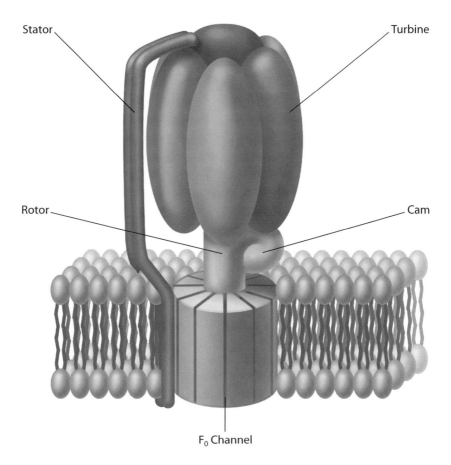

F_0 Channel

Figure 4.2. F_1–F_0 ATPase
The rotary motor F_1–F_0 ATPase consists of a rotor, cam, turbine, and stator.

The F_1–F_0 ATPase turbine interacts with the part of the complex that looks like a "mushroom stalk." This stalklike component functions as a rotor.[8] The flow of positively charged hydrogen ions (or in some instances sodium ions) through the F_0 component embedded in the cell membrane drives the rotation of the rotor.[9] A rod-shaped protein structure that also extends above the membrane surface performs as a stator. This protein rod interacts with the turbine holding it stationary as the rotor rotates.

The electrical current that flows through the channels of the F_0 complex is transformed into mechanical energy that drives the rotor's movement. A cam that extends at a right angle from the rotor's surface causes displacements of the turbine. These back-and-forth motions are used to produce ATP (adenosine triphosphate). The cell uses this compound as a source of chemical energy to drive the operation of cellular processes.

Back It Up

V-type ATPases bear a strong structural resemblance to F_1–F_0 ATPases. Like their counterparts, V-type ATPases are rotary motors replete with a turbine, rotor, cam, and stator.[10] They pump hydrogen, sodium, and potassium ions establishing electrical potentials across cell membranes. Roughly speaking, the V-type ATPases operate in a reverse mode compared to the F_1–F_0 ATPases. For V-type ATPases, the breakdown of ATP, mediated via the turbine, drives the rotation of its rotor. This rotation forces positively charged protons, sodium, or potassium ions across the cell membrane through the channel of the V-type ATPase.[11]

For the Long Haul

Bacterial conjugation refers to the transmission of DNA between bacterial cells. The protein complex responsible for transporting DNA across the cell envelope associates with the cell membrane. This DNA-transporting complex consists of multiple copies of the protein TrwB. Recent structural studies of the TrwB protein complex indicate that its architecture closely resembles the turbine of the F_1–F_0 and V-type ATPases.[12] The TrwB complex pumps DNA across the cell membrane through a channel that forms when the TrwB subunits interact.[13] The DNA molecule corresponds to the protein rotor in the F_1–F_0 and V-type ATPases.

Expelling the Exhaust

Recently, two independent teams of biochemists characterized the structure of the AcrA/AcrB/TolC complex isolated from the bacterium *Escherichia coli (E. coli)*. Their work uncovered another type of rotary motor that functions as an integral part of a literal molecular-level peristaltic pump (see figure 4.4).[14]

These devices push fluids through a tube using positive displacement.[15] A flexible tube carefully positioned within a circular pump casing contains

An Efficient Assembly Line

The production of the bacterial flagellum resembles a well-orchestrated manufacturing process. Its assembly pathway displays an exquisite molecular logic that results in the orderly production of this particular motor. Each step in the process seems to have been planned with subsequent steps in mind.

The information required to produce the more than forty proteins that make up the bacterial flagellum resides with the bacteria's DNA (see chapter 2, p. 48). In bacteria, genes specifying proteins involved in the same cellular process often lie next to one another along the DNA molecule. Biochemists use the term *operon* to describe a grouping of these juxtaposed genes. The flagellar genes, organized into over fourteen different operons, cluster into three operon classes: Class 1, Class 2, and Class 3 (see figure 4.3).

The flagellar operons are typically "turned off," making no proteins until the bacterial cell "senses" that the time has arrived to produce flagella. When this happens, the Class 1 operons "turn on" directing the production of two proteins. The two Class 1 proteins, in turn, activate Class 2 operon genes. The Class 2 operons turn on one at a time according to the spatial positioning of the proteins within the flagellum.

Proteins forming the innermost structures of the flagellum, such as the rotor and stator, are produced first followed by the proteins forming the drive shaft and bushings. Once the stator, rotor, drive shaft, and bushing (called the basal body) have been assembled, the Class 3 operons turn on and the Class 2 operons shut down. The genes of the Class 3 operons produce the proteins that form the universal joint and whiplike flagellum.

This well-orchestrated process of gene expression ensures that the proper proteins are present at the proper time during the assembly of the flagellum. The cell avoids wasting precious resources by making proteins only when needed. Additionally, improper assembly of the flagellum will result if proteins are made ahead of time. For example, if the cell makes the protein forming the whiplike flagellum before the basal body comes together, this protein will assemble into a whiplike structure inside the cell.

Watching almost any manufacturing process evokes appreciation for the efficient and orderly production that depends on careful planning, design, and engineering. Witnessing the assembly of bacterial flagella elicits the same type of response. The biochemical pathway to their structure and assembly evokes a sense of awe at the engineering brilliance involved.[16]

the fluid. A rotor fitted with rollers, shoes, or wipers compresses part of the fluid-filled tube as it rotates. This compression causes the part of the tube in contact with the rotor to collapse, forcing the fluid through the tube. In turn, the tube opens up as the rotor continues to turn allowing fluid to flow from a reservoir into the pump in a process known as restitution.

AcrA/AcrB/TolC is found in numerous types of bacteria (including several pathogenic microbes). It imparts resistance to noxious chemicals

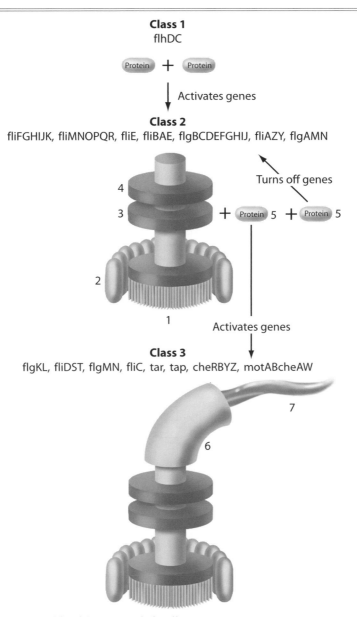

Class 1
flhDC

Protein + Protein

↓ Activates genes

Class 2
fliFGHIJK, fliMNOPQR, fliE, fliBAE, flgBCDEFGHIJ, fliAZY, flgAMN

4

3 + Protein 5 + Protein 5 Turns off genes

2

1 Activates genes ↓

Class 3
flgKL, fliDST, flgMN, fliC, tar, tap, cheRBYZ, motABcheAW

7

6

Figure 4.3. Assembly of the Bacterial Flagellum
Flagellum assembly proceeds through a well-orchestrated process that ensures the right proteins are produced at the proper time. Class 1 operons direct the production of two proteins. The two Class 1 proteins, in turn, activate Class 2 operon genes (fliFGHIJK, fliMNOPQR, fliE, etc.). The Class 2 operons turn on, one at a time according to the spatial positioning of the proteins within the flagellum. Once the Class 2 operons shut down, the Class 3 operons direct the production of proteins to complete the assembly of the flagellum.

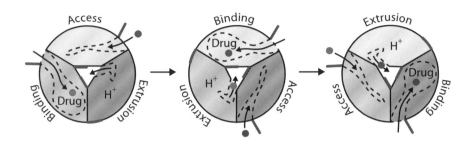

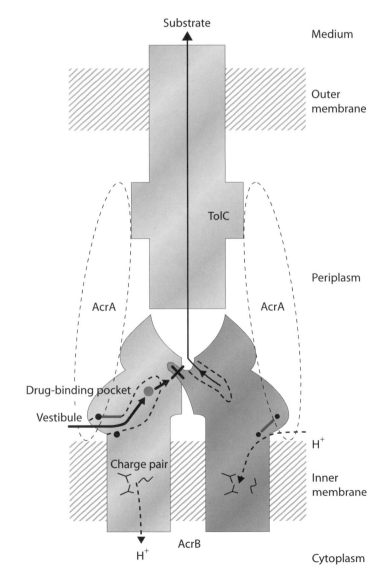

in the environment. This protein ensemble spans the bacterial inner and outer membranes and pumps structurally diverse compounds from the cell's interior to the external environment. Such a process minimizes the level of harmful materials in the cell, dramatically limiting their deleterious effects.

As part of its action, the AcrA/AcrB/TolC complex also recognizes and removes a wide range of antibiotics from the cell. This activity confers pathogenic bacteria with multidrug resistance. Biochemists refer to AcrA/AcrB/TolC as a multidrug transporter (MDT) and expend considerable effort to understand its structure and function to more effectively combat antibiotic resistance.

The primary component of AcrA/AcrB/TolC MDT is AcrB, which consists of three identical protein subunits that span the bacteria's inner membrane. The AcrB ensemble functions like a rotary motor. In response to the flow of positively charged hydrogen ions through the inner membrane (an electrical current), each subunit alternately binds antibiotics (or other offending materials) in the cell's interior and, through a three-step rotation, transports these materials by a peristaltic mechanism into a compartment formed by the AcrA.

The enclosure formed by this accessory protein bridges the space between the inner and outer membranes. Once in the AcrA porter, the noxious materials are collected by a funnellike structure that's part of TolC. This accessory protein spans the outer membrane. Once undesirable materials pass through the TolC channel, they are expelled into the cell's exterior.

A Spinning Spindle

Based on recent structural studies, biochemists have proposed that a protein complex isolated from a virus operates as a molecular rotary motor. If their proposal is correct, this viral motor will be the first of its type to be identified in biological systems.[17] This viral motor, a DNA translocator, generates the mechanical force needed to (1) transport viral DNA into newly formed viral capsules (capsids) during viral assembly and (2) inject viral DNA into the host cell during infection.

Viruses are subcellular particles composed of a protein capsid that houses viral genetic material (either DNA or RNA).[18] The capsid forms as a result

Figure 4.4. The AcrA/AcrB/TolC Complex
The AcrA/AcrB/TolC complex is a rotary motor that operates as a literal molecular-level peristaltic pump.

of the interaction of multiple copies of identical protein subunits. Some viruses also have a protein tail that extends from the base of the viral capsid. Like the capsid, this viral tail consists of several protein subunits (see figure 4.5).

When present, the viral tail plays an important role in the infection process. The tail binds the virus to the target cell's surface and injects the viral genetic material into the host cell.

Once inside the cell, the viral genetic material uses the host cell's enzymatic machinery to make copies of the virus's components. Viral proteins and genetic material then assemble forming multiple copies of the virus. Over time, the newly produced virus particles cause the host cell to rupture. When it bursts, the newly formed viral particles are released to repeat the infectious cycle.

The DNA translocator motor resides in the tail region near the base of the viral capsid. The "heart" of the motor is the head-to-tail connector. This cone-shaped structure forms through the interaction of twelve protein subunits (see figure 4.6).

The wide end of the connector fits into the opening found at the base of the viral capsid. The narrow end serves as the point of DNA entry during the viral assembly process. Six separate viral RNA molecules encircle the connector at the base of the viral capsid to form scaffolding. This structure acts as a binding site for five ATPase molecules. (ATPases are a class of proteins that break down ATP [adenosine triphosphate], an energy-storing molecule.)

ATP breakdown causes energy to be released, making it available to power cellular processes. According to one model, the activity of the viral ATPases drives the rotation of the connector. This rotation causes the viral DNA double helix, which interacts with the narrow end of the connector, to spiral into the viral capsid. In other words, due to the helical character of the DNA molecule, it becomes a spindle, the connector serves as a ball race, and collectively the capsid base, RNA scaffold, and viral ATPases form a stator.

Interestingly, the chemical groups that form the external surface of the connector in contact with the rotary motor's "stator" have "oily" properties. The "oily" surface functions as a lubricant allowing the connector to rotate with relative ease during DNA translocation.

Recent experimental work, however, raises questions about the rotary mechanism of the viral DNA packaging motor.[19] Researchers failed to

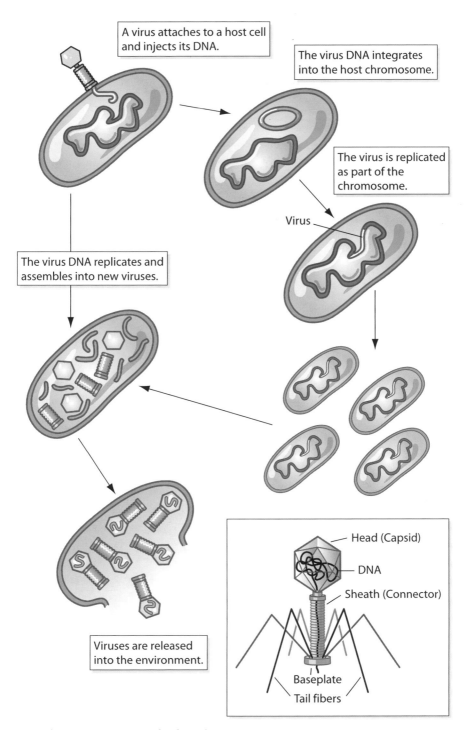

A virus attaches to a host cell and injects its DNA.

The virus DNA integrates into the host chromosome.

The virus is replicated as part of the chromosome.

Virus

The virus DNA replicates and assembles into new viruses.

Viruses are released into the environment.

Head (Capsid)

DNA

Sheath (Connector)

Baseplate

Tail fibers

Figure 4.5. Virus Structure and Life Cycle

Viral DNA Packaging Motor

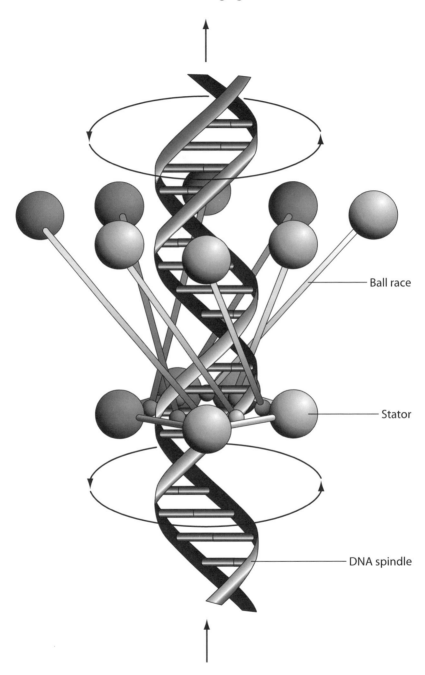

Figure 4.6. Viral DNA Packaging Motor
This motor consists of a spindle, ball race, and stator. The viral DNA double helix
corresponds to a spindle. The connector serves as a ball race. Collectively the capsid base,
RNA scaffold, and viral ATPases form a stator.

detect rotation of the connector during the DNA packaging operation. Instead, it appears that the connector may act as a valve to prevent DNA from "leaking out" of the capsid once driven into the head by the viral motor. They note that, "the spring-like shape of the connector suggests, indeed, that through compression and expansion, the connector may act as a 'Chinese finger trap' allowing the passage of the DNA in one direction during packaging but preventing its exit in the reverse."[20]

Even though it's not clear to biochemists how the DNA viral packaging motor operates, its machinelike character is not in doubt.

A Swiveling Motor

The molecular motor myosin generates the force that produces muscle contraction and transports organelles throughout the cell. In contrast to the biomotors just discussed, myosin is not a rotary motor. Rather, it's a linear motor with a rigid lever arm. Myosin also possesses a molecular hinge that functions as a pivot point for the swinging lever arm (see figure 4.7).[21]

Through genetic engineering and biophysical studies, researchers have directly (and indirectly) observed the swing of myosin's lever arm and the swiveling of the myosin hinge.[22] These measurements of the myosin motor in operation provide convincing proof of the swinging lever arm model for myosin motor function and myosin's machinelike character.

Riding the Rails

Dynein is a massive molecular motor that plays a role in generating a wavelike motion in eukaryotic flagella (which possess a fundamentally different structure than bacterial flagella). These motors also move cargo throughout the cell along microtubule tracks that are part of the cell's cytoskeleton (chapter 2, p. 39). In addition, dynein helps maintain the Golgi apparatus (chapter 2, p. 40) and plays a role in cell division (mitosis).[23] (See figure 4.8.)

Three domains make up dynein. The microtubule binding domain connects to the AAA-ring domain through a stalklike structure. The AAA ring consists of six identical protein subunits that form a hexameric ring with a central opening. Another stalklike structure extends from the AAA ring.

Two Positions of the Myosin Lever Arm

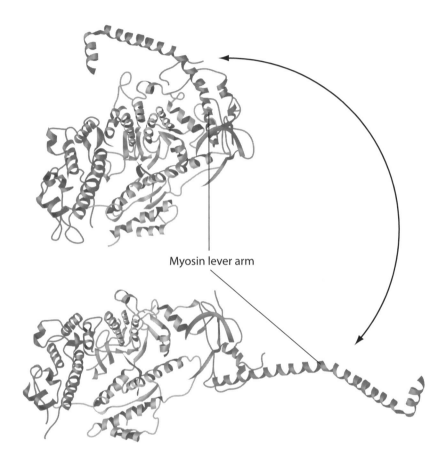

Myosin lever arm

Figure 4.7. The Myosin Linear Motor
A linear motor, myosin possesses a molecular hinge that functions as a pivot point for the
swiveling of a rigid lever arm.

This domain binds the cargo that dynein transports around the cell along
microtubules.[24]

The dynein motor changes chemical energy into mechanical motion.
At the release of chemical energy, the motor's power stroke alters the angle
between the cargo-binding stalk and the stalk that connects the AAA

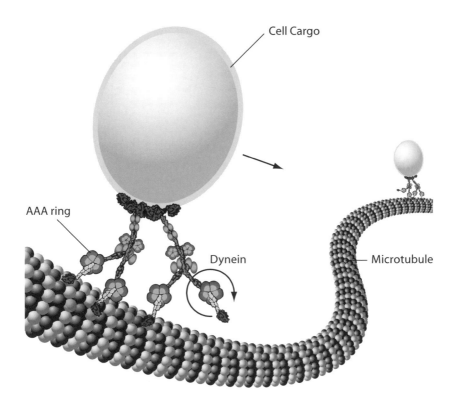

Figure 4.8. Dynein
Dynein is a massive molecular motor that moves cargo throughout the cell along microtubule tracks. Dynein's power stroke alters the angle between the cargo-binding stalk and the stalk that connects the AAA ring to the microtubule.

ring to the microtubule. It also increases the size of the AAA ring's central opening. The structural change in the AAA ring drives the angle change between the two stalks. This angle change leads to the movement of dynein along the microtubule.

Remarkably, the distance that dynein moves along the microtubule for each power stroke varies with the size of the cargo attached to this molecular motor. As the load increases, the distance that dynein moves per power stroke decreases. It appears that the dynein motor literally shifts gears in response to the load.[25]

Other Biomechanical Marvels

Recent structural studies also indicate that a number of protein complexes, though not molecular motors, possess components that resemble parts of man-made devices. One remarkable example is RNA polymerase II.

RNA polymerase II. In 2000, researchers from Stanford University reported the structure of the RNA polymerase II backbone at 3.5 Å resolution.[26] This complex consists of twelve protein subunits that work together to synthesize messenger RNA using DNA as a template. Produced this way, messenger RNA contains the information necessary to direct the synthesis of proteins at ribosomes.

Because of the large size, fragility, complexity, and low abundance of RNA polymerase II in the cell, its structural analysis took nearly twenty years to complete.[27] The results, however, were well worth waiting for—they led to a Nobel Prize.[28]

RNA polymerase II has a remarkable machinelike character. Its subunits form a channel that houses the chainlike DNA template. "Jaws" help grip the DNA template to hold it in place during RNA synthesis. The newly formed RNA chain locks a hinge clamp into place as the chain exits the channel. A funnellike pore then delivers the small subunit molecules to the channel where they are added to the growing end of the RNA chain.

DNA replication. A number of protein complexes that participate in DNA replication possess a clamp that holds onto DNA strands.[29] Because of DNA's helical structure and other torsional stresses on the molecule, the proteins that replicate DNA encounter considerable torque. The clamp helps these proteins grip the DNA molecule while maintaining their precise position along the DNA double helix. As replication takes place the proteins involved in DNA replication move along that spiral. The clamps allow these proteins to rapidly slide along the DNA during the replication process.

Thioredoxin reductase. Structural characterization at 3.0 Å resolution reveals that thioredoxin reductase function is built around a ball-and-socket joint.[30] This protein, isolated from the *E. coli* bacterium, assists in the transfer of electrons between molecules. During the catalytic cycle, the enzyme undergoes a conformational rearrangement that involves the 67° rotation of one of its domains around a clearly defined swivel surface.

RNA polymerase II, DNA sliding clamp proteins, and *E. coli* thioredoxin reductase represent just a few of the many protein complexes that possess components qualitatively identical to certain parts of man-made devices. The origin of these biomolecular motors and machines can be explained by a new version of an old argument.

The Watchmaker Argument Updated

Experience teaches that machines and motors don't just happen. Even the simplest require thoughtful design and manufacture. This common understanding undergirds one of history's best known arguments for God's existence.

The Watchmaker line of reasoning was best articulated by Anglican natural theologian William Paley (1743–1805). In the opening pages of his 1802 work *Natural Theology; or, Evidences of the Existence and Attributes of the Deity Collected from the Appearances of Nature*, Paley sets forth his famous analogy.

> In crossing a heath, suppose I pitched my foot against a *stone*, and were asked how the stone came to be there; I might possibly answer, that, for any thing I knew to the contrary, it had lain there for ever. . . . But suppose I had found a *watch* upon the ground, and it should be inquired how the watch happened to be in that place; I should hardly think of the answer which I had before given, that, for any thing I knew, the watch might have always been there. Yet why should not this answer serve for the watch as well as for the stone? Why is it not as admissible in the second case, as in the first? For this reason, and for no other, viz. that, when we come to inspect the watch, we perceive (what we could not discover in the stone) that its several parts are framed and put together for a purpose, *e.g.* that they are so formed and adjusted as to produce motion, and that motion so regulated as to point out the hour of the day; that, if the different parts had been differently shaped from what they are, of a different size from what they are, or placed after any other manner, or in any other order, than that in which they are placed, either no motion at all would have been carried on in the machine, or none which would have answered the use that is now served by it. . . . This mechanism being observed . . . , the inference, we think, is inevitable, that the watch must have had a maker: that there must have existed, at some time, and at some place or other, an artificer or artificers who formed it for the purpose which we find it actually to answer; who comprehended its construction, and designed its use.[31]

For Paley, the characteristics of a watch and the complex interaction of its precision parts for the purpose of telling time implied the work of an intelligent designer. Paley asserted that, by analogy, just as a watch requires a watchmaker so too life requires a Creator. He reasoned that, like a watch, organisms display a wide range of features characterized by the precise interplay of complex parts for specific purposes.

According to the Watchmaker analogy:

Watches display design.
Watches are the product of a watchmaker.

Similarly:

Organisms display design.
Therefore, organisms are the product of a Creator.

Facing the Critics

Over the centuries the Watchmaker argument hasn't fared well. Skeptics often point to David Hume's 1779 work *Dialogues Concerning Natural Religion*. This critical analysis of design arguments is considered devastating to Paley's case for the Creator. Hume leveled several criticisms; the foremost centered on the nature of analogical reasoning.

Based on Hume's arguments, skeptics curtly dismissed the Watchmaker argument, maintaining that the two things compared—organisms and watches—were too dissimilar for a good analogy (see chapter 1, p. 30). Hume asserted that the strength of an analogical argument depends on the similarity of the two things compared. He wrote that "whenever you depart, in the least, from the similarity of the cases, you diminish proportionably the evidence; and may at last bring it to a very weak *analogy*, which is confessedly liable to error and uncertainty."[32]

Atheist B. C. Johnson underscored Hume's case by arguing that Paley did not use a strict enough criterion for identifying intelligent design. Paley argued that design is evident when a system contains several parts that work together for a purpose. Johnson, in contrast, says, "We can identify a thing as designed, even when we do not know its purpose, *only* if it resembles the things we make to express our purposes."[33]

Others argued that organisms are not machines, and those who saw them as such took the analogy too far. According to these skeptics, the analogy between machines and living systems was simply an explanatory analogy, an illustration that provided a framework to guide understanding.[34]

The merit of the Watchmaker argument then rests on the questions: Do living systems resemble man-made machines enough to warrant the analogy? And, if so, how strong is this analogy, and can a conclusion reasonably be drawn from it?

Rising from the Dead

The discovery of biomolecular motors and machines inside the cell gives new life to the Watchmaker argument. In many instances, molecular-level biomachinery stands as a strict analog to man-made machinery and represents a potent response to the legitimate criticism leveled by Hume and others, given the state of knowledge at the time. Biomachines found in the cell's interior reveal a diversity of form and function that mirrors the diversity of designs produced by human engineers. The one-to-one relationship between the parts of man-made machines and the molecular components of biomachines is startling. And each new example of a biomotor strengthens Paley's case for the Creator.

Biomotors and machines are not explanatory analogies. The motors and machines described in this chapter are motors and machines by definition. And, because machines stem from the work of a designer, these molecular-level machines must emanate from the work of an Intelligent Designer. The strong, close, and numerous analogies between biological motors and man-made devices logically compel the conclusion that these biomotors, and consequently life's chemistry, are the product of intelligent design.

Nanotechnology's Acclaim

The analogy between molecular motors and man-made machinery finds additional strength in cutting-edge work conducted by researchers developing nanodevices.[35] These molecular-level devices are comprised of precisely arranged atoms and molecules. With dimensions less than 1,000 nanometers (one-billionth of a meter), nanostructures have applications in manufacturing, electronics, medicine, biotechnology, and agriculture among others. But one of the key hurdles preventing nanodevices from becoming a truly viable technology was their inability to power movement.

An important breakthrough was announced at the Sixth Foresight Conference on Molecular Nanotechnology (November 1998). Scientists,

---

Paley's Biochemical Watch

William Paley "pitched his foot against a watch" while "crossing a heath." Yale biochemist Jimin Wang stumbled onto a mechanical molecular clock inside cyanobacteria (photosynthetic blue-green algae) while performing a structural analysis of the Kai proteins.[36] The KaiA, KaiB, and KaiC proteins play an integral role in the circadian oscillation that regulates the metabolic processes of cyanobacteria.

The biochemical activity of this blue-green algae varies periodically in response to the light-dark cycle. When it is dark, certain metabolic activities shut down.

The KaiC protein is key to this cyanobacterial circadian rhythm. When its levels are high inside the cell, the protein represses gene expression. Low levels stimulate gene expression. At night, the KaiC protein forms complexes with the KaiA and KaiB proteins. During the daylight hours, the KaiABC complexes dissociate.

The molecular architecture of the KaiABC complex bears striking similarity to the F_1–F_0 ATPase rotary motor. Six KaiC proteins interact to form a structure similar to the turbine of the F_1–F_0 ATPase rotary motor. Two copies of the KaiA protein interact to form a structure that resembles the rotor of the F_1–F_0 ATPase motor. A spring-loaded mechanism causes the KaiA protein duplex to alternate between two forms (like the opening and closing of a pair of scissors), one that interacts with the KaiC complex channel and one that does not. The KaiB protein functions like a wing nut fastening the KaiA duplex to the bottom of the KaiC complex.

The KaiA duplex rotates within the channel, with the KaiB wing nut controlling the rotation rate of the KaiA rotor. As the KaiA rotor steps through the KaiC channel, a cam sequentially causes changes to each of the KaiC proteins. This mechanical action causes phosphate chemical groups to attach to those proteins. When fully phosphorylated, the KaiC complex dissociates. The formation and dissociation of the KaiABC complex regulates the KaiC levels inside the cell, which in turn controls the cyanobacterial circadian oscillation.

Once the KaiABC complex is assembled, the mechanical clocklike rotary action of the KaiA duplex within the KaiC channel controls its stability through the phosphorylation of the individual KaiC proteins. According to Wang, "The Kai complexes are a rotary clock for phosphorylation, which sets up the destruction pace of the night-dominant Kai complexes and the timely releases of KaiA."[37]

In Paley's words, "This mechanism being observed . . . , the inference, we think, is inevitable, that the watch must have had a maker."[38]

working separately at Cornell University and at the University of Washington in Seattle, "like molecular mechanics . . . [,] have unbolted the motors from their cellular moorings, remounted them on engineered surfaces and demonstrated that they can perform work."[39]

Advancing these earlier feasibility studies, scientists from Cornell University produced a hybrid nanomechanical device powered by the F_1–F_0 ATPase biological molecular motor.[40] The researchers connected F_1–F_0 ATPase to an engineered surface via the enzyme's turbine. They then attached nickel nanopropellers to the motor's rotor. Upon adding ATP—a chemical compound that powers the F_1–F_0 ATPase rotor—the nanopropellers rotated at a velocity of 0.74 to 8.3 revolutions per second.

Sodium azide—an inhibitor of the F_1–F_0 ATPase rotor—halted the nanopropellers' rotation. In the absence of an inhibitor, this rotation typically lasted for at least 2.5 hours before the nanopropellers broke away from the F_1–F_0 ATPase rotor. These molecular motors, co-opted from cells, operated at near 80 percent efficiency in this particular system—far better than humans can achieve with man-made devices.

F_1–F_0 ATPase is not the only molecular motor used by scientists to power nanodevices. Researchers are exploring the feasibility of using the viral DNA packaging motor in gene therapy as a device to deliver DNA to cells with defective genes.[41] Proof-of-principle studies indicate that it is possible to assemble a DNA packaging motor from the components of the viral DNA packaging motor that can drive the translocation of DNA like "driving a bolt with a hex nut."[42] Addition of magnesium ions and ATP caused the imitation motor to rotate, and addition of either the chemical compound EDTA or S-ATP (inhibitors of the motor) halted its rotation.

These two studies powerfully demonstrate that the molecular motors in the cell are literal motors in every sense. Any perceived differences between man-made motors and biomotors evaporate in light of these advances.

This work is just the beginning. Even greater support for the Watchmaker argument will likely accrue with future advances in nanotechnology—particularly as researchers continue to borrow from the superior designs found inside the cell to drive developments in nanotechnology.[43]

The Artist's Expertise

Recent work, described as "science at its very best," provides insight into the superior intelligence of the Designer responsible for the molecular motors found in nature.[44] In the quest to build nanodevices, synthetic chemists have produced molecular switches, gears, valves, shuttles, ratchets, turnstiles, and elevators.[45] These molecular-level devices have obvious utility in nanodevices, but their construction holds additional significance. They represent a significant step towards the "holy grail" of nanotechnology: single-molecule rotary motors capable of rotating in a single direction that can power movement in nanodevices.[46]

Significant steps toward this goal were achieved in 1999 when a team of researchers from Boston College and a collaborative team from the University of Groningen in the Netherlands and Tohuku University in Japan independently designed and synthesized the first single-molecule rotary motors with the capability of spinning in one direction.[47] The rotation of the motors is driven by UV radiation and heat or through chemical energy.

These synthetic molecular motors are the product of careful design and planning. The light- and heat-driven molecular motor made by the team from the universities of Groningen and Tohuku depends upon the "unique combination of axial chirality and the two chiral centers in the molecule" positioned just right in three-dimensional space.[48] Likewise, the molecular motor developed by the team from Boston College is dependent upon molecular chirality, as well as fine-tuning of the molecular substituents.[49]

It is clear these molecular motors did not happen by accident or as the natural outworking of the laws of chemistry and physics. In fact, the chemically driven molecular motor—comprised of only seventy-eight atoms—took over four years to build.[50] In spite of all the effort that went into the preparation of these synthetic molecular motors, both rotary motors rotate in a cumbersome and stepwise fashion. Recently, chemists have prepared even more sophisticated synthetic single-molecule rotary motors capable of changing their direction of rotation in response to chemical cues. Still, these motors are qualitatively no less crude in their operation than the first-generation motors.[51]

The contrast between these synthetic molecular motors designed by some of the finest and most creative organic chemists in the world and the elegance and complexity of molecular motors found in cells is striking. Considering the efforts of scientists working to develop nanoscale devices, the elegance of God's creation on display shows just how superior the brilliance of the Divine Artist and Grand Designer must be.

A Watchmaker Prediction

Many of the cell's molecular devices that should, in principle, be included in the Watchmaker analogy remain unrecognized because the corresponding technology has yet to be developed by human designers. The possibility that advances in human technology will mirror the cell's existing technology leads to the Watchmaker prediction.

If the Watchmaker analogy truly supports design, then it's reasonable to expect that life's biochemical machinery anticipates human technology advances. Recent progress made in nanotechnology already makes significant strides towards making that prediction a reality.

Brownian Ratchets

One of the chief technical hurdles that stands in the path of viable nano-devices is the inability to generate directional movement within nano-machinery. Some researchers have proposed Brownian ratchets as a way around this barrier.[52]

These theoretical devices make use of Brownian motion (see figure 4.9). This phenomenon describes the random zigzag movement of microscopic objects suspended in a liquid or gas. When the sum of forces exerted on a suspended object by the gas or liquid molecules generates a directional force, it causes the particle to move. The forces are short-lived and randomly directed. This causes the particle to move in a zigzag fashion.

Brownian ratchets exploit Brownian motion but use barriers to restrict the motion in a specified direction. These ratchets require energy input to erect and maintain the barriers that prevent motion in unwanted directions. In response to this energy input, Brownian ratchets produce directional movement of microscopic materials—making the ratchets a new generation of potential motors. In short, the components of Brownian ratchets try to wander in every direction. But carefully placed barriers prevent them from going the wrong way.

Recent proof-of-principle experiments demonstrate that devices built around Brownian ratchets may well be possible. This proof-of-principle

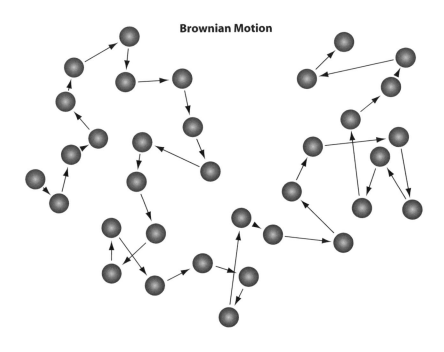

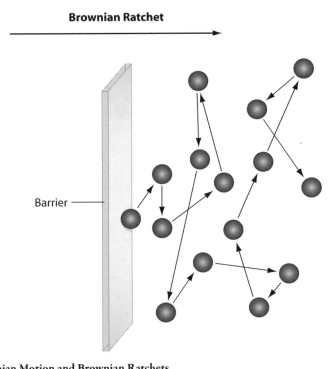

Figure 4.9. Brownian Motion and Brownian Ratchets
This phenomenon describes the random, zigzag movement of microscopic objects
suspended in a liquid or gas. Brownian ratchets rely on barriers to restrict the motion to a
specified direction.

took a significant step toward reality in 1999 when a research team built a device that transports DNA molecules using a Brownian ratchet.[53] These scientists think this DNA transport device can be used to separate DNA fragments, a process required to sequence DNA.

Brownian ratchets are rapidly moving from the theoretical realm to reality. While nanotechnologists strive to develop and implement Brownian ratchet technology in nanodevices, biochemists have already discovered several Brownian ratchets inside the cell. Three examples of these motors are kinesin, BiP, and collagenase.

Kinesin

This molecular motor transports cellular cargo along microtubules that form part of the cell's cytoskeleton.[54] Kinesin's structure resembles two golf clubs with their shafts intertwined around one another in a helical fashion. Attached to kinesin's rodlike region are two lobe-shaped structures that resemble the heads of golf clubs.[55]

The kinesin heads interact with microtubules. The rodlike shaft binds the cellular cargo that kinesin will transport along the microtubules. Kinesin then "walks" along the microtubule with the heads attaching and detaching to the microtubule in an alternating fashion.[56] This motor moves in only one direction.

Biochemists are still attempting to understand how kinesin operates. Recently two biophysicists proposed that the kinesin motor functions as a Brownian ratchet.[57] According to this idea, the kinesin heads randomly diffuse. But once the head binds to the microtubule, it restricts the movement and binding of the other head. This restriction causes kinesin to move in a single direction along the microtubule.

BiP

The BiP protein (also referred to as the Kar2p protein) associated with the endoplasmic reticulum (see chapter 2, p. 40) represents another example of a biochemical Brownian ratchet. BiP plays a role in moving proteins across the endoplasmic reticulum (ER) into its internal space (lumen) for processing and preparation for secretion from the cell (see figure 4.10).

Once produced at the ribosomes associated with the ER, proteins travel through channels in the ER membrane. These channels consist of a

Brownian Ratchet

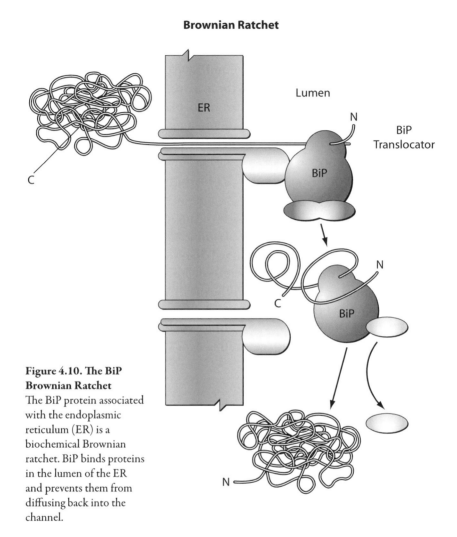

Figure 4.10. The BiP Brownian Ratchet
The BiP protein associated with the endoplasmic reticulum (ER) is a biochemical Brownian ratchet. BiP binds proteins in the lumen of the ER and prevents them from diffusing back into the channel.

conglomeration of several proteins (Sec61p and Sec62/63p). In addition to the channel proteins, BiP is required for protein transport through the ER channels. BiP resides in the ER lumen. Initially, biochemists thought that BiP pulled the proteins through the channel using chemical energy. But, an elegant study published in 1999 demonstrated that BiP operates as a Brownian ratchet.[58]

Instead of pulling proteins through the ER channels, BiP uses chemical energy to bind the protein chains as they passively diffuse through the channel. When BiP binds proteins, it prevents them from diffusing back into the channel. This restricts the proteins' movement to a single direction through the channel.

Collagenase

Biochemists recently identified the protein collagenase MMP-1 as a specialized type of Brownian ratchet. This protein—called a "burnt bridge" Brownian ratchet[59]—breaks down the collagen fibers found in the extracellular space of connective tissues.

The extracellular matrix (ECM) is the region between cells in biological tissues. A complex network of fibers forms scaffolding in the ECM that imparts shape and mechanical resistance to the tissue. Fibers made from the protein collagen are among the most abundant components of the ECM scaffolding. The collagen consists of three elongated protein chains that intertwine to form what biochemists call a triple helix.

From time to time, the scaffolding of the extracellular matrix is remodeled. Existing fibers are broken apart, and new fibers are laid down. Certain disease processes result from improper remodeling of the ECM scaffolding.

Special proteins called matrix metalloproteinases (MMP) break down the ECM collagens. MMP-1 collagenase moves along collagen in a single direction as it degrades the fiber, looking for specific cleavage sites. Diffusion in the reverse direction along the collagen fiber is prevented because cleavage of the fiber destroys the "tracks" (or burns the bridge behind it), preventing reverse migration. MMP-1 collagenase functions as a Brownian ratchet in which directional movement is coupled to the breakdown (proteolysis) of the collagen fiber.

The discovery of biochemical Brownian ratchets strengthens the Watchmaker analogy in two ways. First, it adds to the number of biomolecular machines that are strict analogs to man-made devices. Second, it satisfies the Watchmaker prediction. In other words, life's Brownian ratchets precede and pave the way for the development of man-made Brownian ratchets that could one day become part of nanodevices.

Molecular Motors and the Pattern of Intelligent Design

Chapter 3 described the remarkable overall complexity and organization of the simplest life-forms. Even in its most minimal form, life displays an inherent irreducible complexity. Simplest life also displays a remarkable organization at the molecular level.

This chapter elaborated on some of the details of this molecular complexity and organization—details that reveal the operation of molecular-level machines inside the cell. The cell's machinery logically indicates that life's chemistry stems from intelligent agency. An eerie resemblance between the cell's molecular motors and humanly designed machinery, both in form and function, revitalizes William Paley's Watchmaker argument in a way that addresses the legitimate concerns raised by skeptics over the centuries.

These molecular motors are irreducibly complex, an independent indicator of intelligent design. They would suffer from the same problem as Paley's watch

> if the different parts had been differently shaped from what they are, of a different size from what they are, or placed after any other manner, or in any other order, than that in which they are placed, either no motion at all would have been carried on in the machine, or none which would have answered the use that is now served by it.[60]

Work done in the burgeoning arena of nanoscience and nanotechnology not only highlights the machinelike character of these biomotors, it exposes the elegance and sophistication of their design. The cell's machinery is vastly superior to anything that the best human designers can conceive or accomplish. As a case in point, bacterial flagella operate near 100 percent efficiency.[61] This capability stands in sharp distinction to man-made machines. Electric motors only function at 65 percent efficiency and the best combustion engines only attain a 30 percent efficiency.

The superiority of the cell's molecular machines is consistent with the notion that the intelligent designer is the Creator described in the Bible. It also prompts the question: Is it really reasonable to conclude that these biomotors are the products of blind, undirected physical and chemical processes, when they are far beyond what the best human minds can achieve?

Life's biomolecular motors not only bring to light one of the most remarkable design features inside the cell, they also highlight the Creator's artistry. The elegance and beauty of the cell's machinery cannot be overlooked in the midst of making the case for intelligent design. Its grandeur is even more captivating than the automobile designs that inspire Ken Eberts's fine art.

The next chapter examines another aspect of the cell's biochemical systems that raises some provocative questions about life's origin.

5

WHICH CAME FIRST?

M. C. Escher's woodcuts, lithographs, and mezzotints almost always require a second look. These pieces explore spatial illusions, impossible constructions, and repeating geometric patterns.

Escher's designs contain strong mathematical components. It's no surprise that mathematicians and scientists are drawn to him. Ironically, Escher had no formal training in either discipline. He even failed his high school exams.[1]

Some of this Dutch graphic artist's most well-known works include *Sky and Water*, which plays with shadows and light to transform fish in the water into birds in the sky, and *Ascending and Descending*, in which a line of people simultaneously ascend and descend staircases in a never-ending loop. One of Escher's most fascinating pieces, *Drawing Hands*, depicts a sheet of paper with two "sketched" wrists flat on the page. The two-dimensional wrists transition into three-dimensional hands that appear to be drawing one another.

Drawing Hands exposes a fascinating paradox that plays on the concept of an infinite loop. The two hands appear strictly interdependent—one can't exist without the other. The only way the two hands could arise is if an artist, like Escher, sketches them.

Over the last few decades, biochemists have discovered several chemical operations in the cell that, like *Drawing Hands*, consist of components strictly interdependent on one another. These "chicken-and-egg" systems raise questions about how life's chemistry came about. The molecules that comprise these works of art can't exist apart from each other—unless a Divine Artist sketched them.

A Simultaneous Situation

Human engineers frequently encounter which-comes-first issues when designing systems and processes. The radio frequency identification (RFID) industry illustrates this problem. A chicken-and-egg dilemma confronts manufacturers who consider adopting this technology.

RFID systems employ tags or transponders that emit radio waves. This signal allows the tagged items to be identified automatically. Ideally, this methodology will one day replace bar codes and universal product codes (UPC). The new tags can store much more data and have a diverse range of potential applications from identifying pets to tracking cases and pallets of product in the supply chain.[2]

But many manufacturers resist RFID systems in spite of their potential benefits because of the cost. They won't use the technology until its price drops. And, the price won't drop until RFID technology is widely adopted. In addition, companies that represent one part of the supply chain won't accept the technology until it's widely used by other companies in the rest of the chain.[3]

Resolution to these chicken-and-egg problems for the RFID industry will come only when all parties agree to simultaneously switch to the technology or if they are forced to implement these systems. For example, a mandate from the FDA could require the pharmaceutical industry to employ RFID technology.

Everyday experience teaches that chicken-and-egg systems can come to fruition only through intentional planning and implementation. These systems, therefore, are a potent indicator of intelligent design. Several examples of biochemical chicken-and-egg systems demonstrate why.

Does DNA Draw Proteins or Do Proteins Draw DNA?

DNA houses the information the cell needs to make proteins, which play a role in virtually every cell function. Proteins also help build practically every cellular and extracellular structure (see chapter 2, p. 42). Given this importance, the information housed in DNA defines life's most fundamental operations and structures.

When cells divide and organisms reproduce, DNA and the information it stores is passed on to the daughter cells and their offspring. Biochemical blueprints are conveyed to the next generation through DNA replication. This process generates two "daughter" molecules identical to the "parent" DNA molecule. Once replication occurs, a complex system distributes the two DNA molecules generated by replication between the daughter cells produced during cell division (see figure 5.1).

Biochemists commonly refer to DNA as a self-replicating molecule because its structural properties make it possible to generate two identical daughter molecules from the original parent. In reality, however, DNA cannot replicate on its own.

A Naturalistic Descent

Mutual interdependence of DNA and proteins stands as a major stumbling block for evolutionary explanations of life's origin.[4] Origins-of-life researchers even refer to this conundrum as the chicken-and-egg paradox. Because these two molecules are so complex, scientists don't think DNA and proteins could simultaneously arise from a primordial soup. The existence of DNA apart from proteins and proteins apart from DNA is like a column of people trying to simultaneously ascend and descend a staircase.

The RNA-world hypothesis has been proposed as a resolution to this paradox. This model maintains that RNA preceded DNA and proteins. RNA can simultaneously store information (like DNA) and catalyze chemical reactions (like proteins). So, it's thought that the RNA world eventually evolved into the DNA-protein world of contemporary biochemistry, with RNA currently functioning as an intermediary between DNA and proteins.

While the RNA-world hypothesis rescues the origin-of-life paradigm from the chicken-and-egg paradox on paper, in practical terms it appears largely untenable. Numerous problems abound for the RNA-world hypothesis.[5] For example, it's unlikely that the prebiotic chemical reactions identified in the laboratory for the production of ribose and the nucleobases could take place on early Earth. And, even if these compounds did form, it's unlikely they could assemble into functional RNA molecules. In fact, Leslie Orgel, one of the world's leading origin-of-life researchers, has said, "It would be a miracle if a strand of RNA ever appeared on the primitive Earth."[6]

Even in the face of these serious problems, most origin-of-life scientists are convinced that the RNA world must have existed and paved the way for the DNA-protein world. If it didn't, the chicken-and-egg paradox—from an evolutionary standpoint—cannot be resolved.

Parental DNA

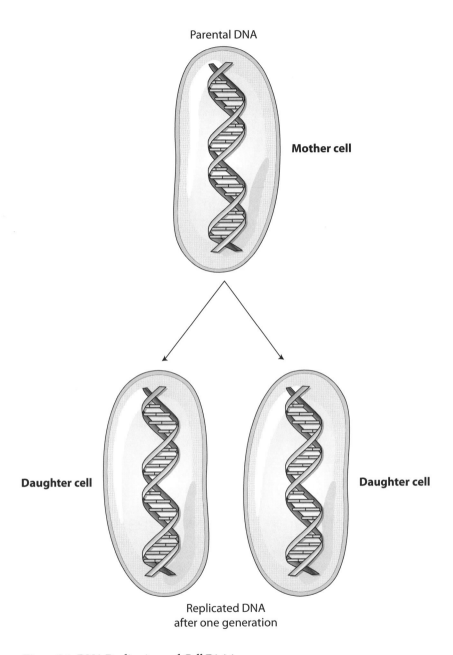

Mother cell

Daughter cell

Daughter cell

Replicated DNA
after one generation

Figure 5.1. DNA Replication and Cell Division
When cells divide, DNA is passed on to the daughter cells. DNA replication generates two
"daughter" molecules identical to the "mother" DNA molecule.

DNA replication requires a myriad of proteins. (Chapter 11 details DNA replication and the role that proteins play in this process.) The synthesis of proteins and the replication of DNA are mutually interdependent. Proteins cannot be produced without DNA, and DNA cannot be produced without proteins—both hands draw each other.

Proteins Make Proteins

When the cell's machinery copies the genetic information stored in the DNA molecule, it sets the stage for protein synthesis (see chapter 2, p. 50). First, a single-stranded polynucleotide messenger RNA (mRNA) molecule (transcription) is assembled using DNA as a template. After processing, mRNA migrates from the nucleus of the cell into the cytoplasm. At the ribosome, mRNA directs the synthesis of protein molecules (translation).

While the details of transcription (taking DNA to mRNA) and translation (taking mRNA to proteins) differ in prokaryotes and eukaryotes, both processes heavily depend upon proteins. In bacteria, mRNA production requires RNA polymerase, a complex protein made from six polypeptide subunits.[7] Biochemists have labeled these subunits: alpha (α), beta (β), beta prime (β′), omega (ω), and sigma (σ). RNA polymerase consists of two α subunits and one each of the β, β′, ω, and σ subunits. It takes five subunits (α, α, β, β′, and ω) to form the core protein.

The RNA polymerase core is capable of synthesizing mRNA on its own but can't recognize the location along the DNA strand where the gene begins. This role is performed by the σ subunit. In fact, several different types of σ subunits exist. Each one recognizes the start site for genes involved in different cellular processes.

In eukaryotic organisms, three different types of RNA polymerase transcribe genes (RNA polymerase I, RNA polymerase II, and RNA polymerase III). Like the bacterial form, eukaryotic RNA polymerases are composed of numerous subunits. However, in eukaryotes, RNA polymerases need transcription factors—proteins that recognize genes and initiate the gene-copying process.

Once mRNA is produced in eukaryotes, it undergoes extensive modification before heading to the ribosome.[8] These modification reactions all involve proteins.

The first set of reactions "caps" one end of mRNA. This capping process begins when an enzyme called guanylyl transferase attaches a chemically modified guanine (called 7-methylguanine) to the first nucleotide in the mRNA strand. After the 7-methylguanine is attached, another enzyme guanine 7-methyl transferase adds methyl groups to the nucleotides in the second and third positions of the mRNA chain.

The next set of reactions modifies the opposite end of the mRNA strand. The poly (A) polymerase protein adds about two hundred adenine nucleotides to the last position of the mRNA molecule to form the poly (A) tail. This tail imparts stability to the mRNA molecule.

The final modification to mRNA, the splicing reactions, also requires proteins. In eukaryotes, the sequences that make up genes consist of stretches of nucleotides that code for the amino acid sequence of polypeptide chains (exons). These exons are interrupted by nucleotide sequences that don't code for anything (introns). After the gene is transcribed, the intron sequences are excised from the mRNA and the exons are spliced together. This process is mediated by an RNA-protein complex called a spliceosome (see figure 5.2).

Once synthesized and processed, mRNA migrates to the ribosome where it directs protein synthesis. Ribosomes are massive complexes composed of proteins and RNA molecules (ribosomal RNA or rRNA).[9]

Though ribosomes of prokaryotes and eukaryotes have the same general structure, they differ in size. Ribosomes consist of two major subunits. The 50S and 30S subunits in prokaryotes combine to form a 70S ribosome. The 60S and 40S subunits in eukaryotes form an 80S ribosome (see figure 5.3).

In prokaryotes, the large subunit contains two rRNA molecules and about thirty different protein molecules. The small subunit consists of a single rRNA molecule and about twenty proteins. The large subunit in eukaryotes is formed by three rRNA molecules that combine with about fifty distinct proteins. Their small subunit consists of a single rRNA molecule and over thirty different proteins.

Researchers have focused extensive effort on understanding the structure of ribosomes and the role of proteins and rRNA in protein synthesis. Amazing progress has been made.[10] The latest work indicates that the production of proteins is ultimately mediated by rRNA.[11] Still, a myriad of proteins that make up ribosomes play an integral structural and functional role, helping mRNA bind to the ribosome and causing the newly formed protein chain to properly fold.[12]

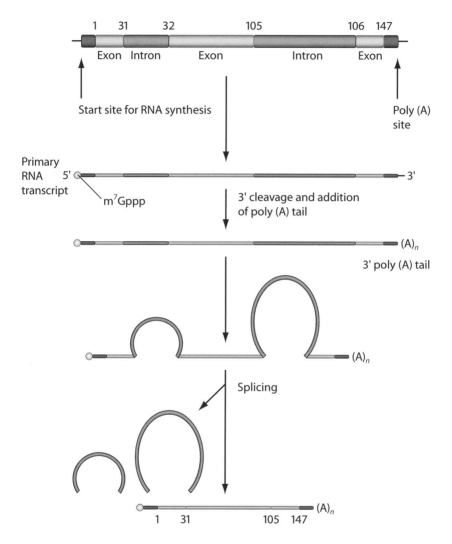

Figure 5.2. mRNA Splicing
In eukaryotes, the DNA sequences that make up genes consist of stretches of nucleotides that code for the amino acid sequence of polypeptide chains (exons) interrupted by nucleotide sequences that don't code for anything (introns). After the gene is copied by assembling the mRNA, a 7-methylguanine (m7Gppp) cap and a poly (A) tail are added. Next, the intron sequences are excised from the mRNA and the exons spliced together by the spliceosome (not shown).

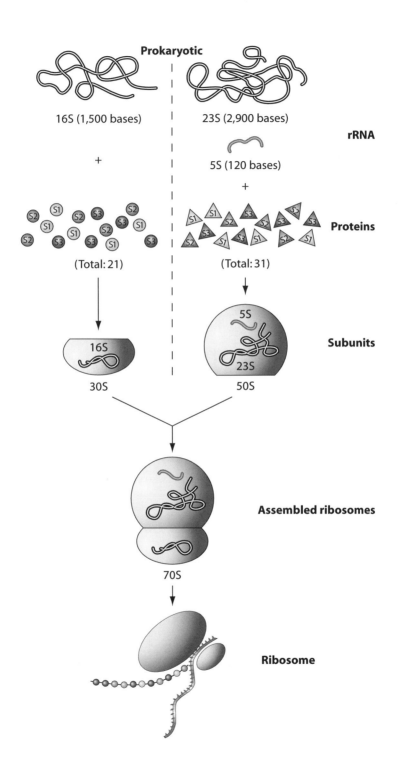

Prokaryotic

16S (1,500 bases)

23S (2,900 bases)

rRNA

5S (120 bases)

+

+

S2 S1 S2 S3 S2
S1 S1
S2 S1 S3 S1 S1
S2 S3 S3 S3 S1

S1 S1 S3 S3 S2 S1
S2 S1 S3 S1 S3 S2 S1

Proteins

(Total: 21)

(Total: 31)

16S

Subunits

5S

23S

30S

50S

70S

Assembled ribosomes

Ribosome

Proteins also play a critical role in the initiation of translation. In both prokaryotes and eukaryotes, proteins called initiation factors help ready the ribosome for protein synthesis by binding to the small subunit.[13] The small subunit and the initiation factors form the pre-initiation complex, which binds mRNA. Once it's bound, the initiation factors dissociate from the small subunit. The initiation complex, in turn, binds the large subunit to form the ribosome. Protein synthesis is now ready to begin.

For protein production to proceed, RNA molecules called transfer RNAs (tRNAs) must bind amino acids, then ferry them to the ribosome.[14] Each of the twenty amino acids used by the cell to form proteins has at least one corresponding tRNA molecule. An activating enzyme (aminoacyl-tRNA synthetase) links each amino acid to its specific tRNA carrier. Each tRNA and amino acid partnership has a corresponding activating enzyme specific to that pair.

Another set of proteins (elongation factors) help usher the amino acid–tRNA pairs to the ribosome and properly position them for protein synthesis.[15] (The role of aminoacyl-tRNA synthetases and elongation factors in protein synthesis is expounded on further in chapter 10.)

This brief and simplified survey of the process of protein production makes clear that proteins cannot be made without proteins. The very proteins that make proteins are made by the processes described—so what came first?

The Art of Protein Folding

Many proteins need the assistance of other proteins to fold into the proper three-dimensional shape after they've been produced at the ribosome. The physicochemical properties of amino acid sequences determine the way that the polypeptide chain folds into its complex three-dimensional shape (see chapter 2, p. 42). In a few cases, polypeptide chains will fold into the proper three-dimensional structure on their own. But, most proteins can't, or if they can, the process is slow and inefficient.

In the cell's environment, improperly folded proteins or proteins that fold slowly and inefficiently represent a potential catastrophe. In the crowded

Figure 5.3. Ribosome Structure
Ribosomes are massive complexes formed from proteins and RNA molecules. The ribosomes of prokaryotes and eukaryotes have the same general structure but differ in size. Ribosomes consist of two major subunits: the 50S and 30S subunits in prokaryotes that combine to form a 70S ribosome and the 60S and 40S subunits in eukaryotes that combine to form an 80S ribosome.

cell, improperly folded proteins tend to aggregate and form massive clumps that gunk up the cell's operations.

To sidestep this potential disaster, virtually every cell throughout the biological realm, from bacteria to humans, relies on a family of proteins called chaperones to encourage efficient and accurate protein folding.

Two types of chaperones exist in most organisms: molecular chaperones and chaperonins.[16] Each category consists of numerous proteins that work cooperatively to assist folding (see figure 5.4). Recent work indicates that parts of the ribosome have chaperone activity helping the newly formed polypeptide chain begin folding.

Once released from the ribosome, some proteins adopt their native three-dimensional structure. Others need more help. Several different

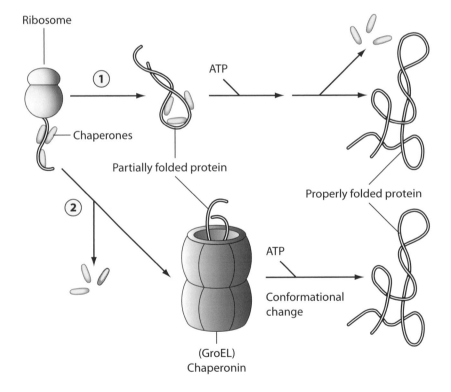

Figure 5.4. Chaperone Activity
Chaperones and chaperonins help polypeptide chains fold once they are released from the ribosome.

chaperones will bind to these polypeptides. They help stabilize the partially folded protein, preventing it from aggregating with other proteins in the cell. When these chaperones debind from the polypeptide chain, it folds into its intended three-dimensional shape.

Other proteins need more help to fold than chaperones can provide. Once the chaperones disassociate from the partially folded polypeptide chain, these proteins are ushered to chaperonins. These large complexes consist of several polypeptide subunits. Perhaps the best understood chaperonin is GroEL-GroES, found in the bacterium *Escherichia coli.*

The GroEL component of the *E. coli* chaperonin consists of fourteen subunits that organize into two ringlike structures that stack on top of one another. The stacked rings form a barrellike ensemble with a large open cavity. A partially folded polypeptide is ushered into the GroEL cavity. Another protein complex, GroES, serves as a cap that covers the GroEL cavity. This cavity provides the optimal environment for protein folding.[17] Once properly folded, the polypeptide chain is released from the GroEL cavity after the GroES lid disassociates from the barrel.

This overview of protein folding highlights the fact that many proteins cannot fold without proteins. Even chaperones and chaperonins require ribosomes, chaperones, and chaperonins to fold.

A Never-Ending Loop

Over the last half-century biochemists have discovered several chemical systems in the cell that, like Escher's *Drawing Hands*, consist of components strictly interdependent on one another. The few examples cited in this chapter represent three of the most central and fundamental activities for life. The "chicken-and-egg" systems of DNA replication, protein synthesis, and protein folding raise questions about how life's chemistry came into existence. Molecules that comprise these operations can't exist apart from one another—unless a Divine Artist created them at the same time.

Human designers and engineers frequently face these kinds of problems. They can be resolved only by the strategic and simultaneous implementation of interdependent components. In like manner, the biochemical chicken-and-egg systems add strength to the biochemical intelligent design analogy. Only the work of a Creator could have put them in place.

Biochemical chicken-and-egg systems represent a special type of irreducible complexity in which the system depends on the system to exist. Like all irreducibly complex systems, significant questions abound about the ability—or inability—of stepwise evolutionary processes to produce them.

The next chapter explores another feature of life's chemistry that points to divine design: the structural and functional fine-tuning and precision of biochemical systems.

6

INORDINATE ATTENTION
TO DETAIL

Sir John Everett Millais (1829–1896) was a childhood prodigy. His immense artistic talent earned him a place in the Royal Academy schools of Great Britain at the extraordinary age of eleven.[1]

As a student at the academy, Millais met William Holman Hunt and Dante Gabriel Rossetti. In 1848, these three men formed the Pre-Raphaelite Brotherhood, which rejected Mannerism. Initially influenced by Raphael, Mannerism dominated art instruction in the academic world during that time. This artistic style created dramatic effects by depicting figures with elongated forms in exaggerated unbalanced poses illuminated by unrealistic lighting.[2]

However, the Pre-Raphaelites desired a return to the abundant details, intense colors, and complex compositions produced before Raphael. They believed that the central purpose of art was to imitate nature and wanted to portray objects with photographic precision.[3] In fact, critics of the Pre-Raphaelites condemned their excessive attention to detail as ugly and eye-jarring. Other reviewers supported their devotion to nature and rejection of contemporary conventions.

Millais paid unusual attention to detail in his paintings, focusing on the beauty and complexity of natural settings. He achieved his first popular success in 1852 with *The Huguenot* and *Ophelia*. The latter work portrays a drowned Ophelia, partially submerged in a gently flowing stream in the midst of idyllic surroundings. Millias's depiction of the natural setting is so dense and elaborate that it inaugurated a new style sometimes described as a type of pictorial ecosystem.

The Pre-Raphaelite movement and Millais have little influence on today's art, which often abandons any attempt to depict reality. Still, the amazing precision and attention to every detail make these works worth seeing.

Meticulous accuracy and the explicit refinement of details also evoke a sense of wonder at life's chemistry. Over the last half-century, scientists have discovered time and again that molecular precision defines biochemical systems. But biochemical fine-tuning far exceeds the best efforts of Millais and the Pre-Raphaelites, highlighting the Creator's exceptional care.

Precision and fine-tuning—hallmark features of intelligent design— dominate the best human design and are often synonymous with exceptional quality. The exacting attention to detail in biochemical systems demonstrates the abilities of a Divine Artist and through analogy strengthens the biochemical intelligent design argument.

A Meticulous Exactness

For the most part, biochemical systems consist of an extensive ensemble of large complex molecules (e.g., proteins, DNA, and RNA). An intimate relationship exists between a biomolecule's structure and its functional role in the cell. Much like an artist uses an assortment of brushes to complete a painting, proteins, DNA, and RNA possess a wide range of molecular architectures that permit them to work in concert with one another to form the cell's structures and carry out all of its biochemical operations (see chapter 2, p. 42). The biochemist's mantra is "structure determines function."

The last half-century of research into the structure-function relationships of biochemical systems has consistently demonstrated that the function of biomolecules critically depends on the exact location and spatial orientation of its chemical constituents. In many instances, function is controlled by just a few chemical groups. For example, substituting a single amino acid in some proteins can have dramatic effects on their function. In other cases, the strict spatial arrangement of a suite of amino acids controls the protein's function. (See the discussion of aquaporins below.)

In addition, the interactions between biomolecules often depend on the exacting placement of chemical groups. For example, in many bio-chemical pathways, proteins bind with each other. These protein-protein interactions are highly specific, occurring only between particular proteins. Recent work, for example, indicates that the specificity of protein binding depends on the exact placement of only a few amino acids located on the three-dimensional surface of the folded protein.[4]

The number of high-precision biochemical systems is far too numer-ous to detail. As each week passes, biochemists report on more and more examples of biochemical fine-tuning in the scientific literature.[5] Looking at a few examples conveys a sense of the remarkable exactness of biochemi-cal systems.

Artistically Detailed Aquaporins

Aquaporins illustrate how advances in biochemical and biophysical methodologies increasingly reveal mounting evidence for design. These integral proteins and the closely related aquaglyceroporins form channels in cell membranes (see chapter 2, p. 45). The channels provide conduits for water—and glycerol and related materials in the case of aquaglyceroporins—to flow in and out of the cell. Aquaporin and aquaglyceroporin channels are unusually selective, transporting only water and glycerol, respectively, across the cell membrane. These protein channels exclude all other materials, even hydrogen ions (protons).[6] This amazing property has, in large mea-sure, motivated biochemists to study the structure-function relationships of aquaporins and aquaglyceroporins over the last decade or so.

For years, several observations suggested that water-conducting pores must exist in cell membranes. But biochemists didn't have the methods to isolate water channels until the early 1990s. The first aquaporin (designated AQP1) was discovered in the cell membrane of red blood cells.

Methods developed to isolate AQP1 and advances in molecular biol-ogy opened up the floodgates of scientific investigation. In short order, biochemists demonstrated that AQP1 was broadly distributed in a wide range of tissues in mammals. Defects in these aquaporins were linked to several diseases.

Researchers also discovered that several distinct aquaporins exist (designated AQP0, AQP2, AQP4, AQP5, AQP6, and AQP8). They identified aquaglyceroporins—the proteins that conduct glycerol and other related compounds—and labeled specific ones (AQP3, AQP7, and AQP9). Aquaporins and aquaglyceroporins have a complex distribution pattern in mammalian tissues, with each tissue type displaying a characteristic set and abundance.[7]

Since then, biochemists have discovered aquaporins in amphibians, insects, plants, and an assortment of microbes. These protein channels appear to be ubiquitous throughout nature, signifying their physiological importance.

Aquaporins reside within the phospholipid bilayer of the cell membrane (see chapter 2, p. 45). Their protein chain folds to form six bilayer-spanning segments. These regions organize within the cell membrane to form an hourglass-like structure. The bilayer-spanning segments form two groups, each containing three membrane-spanning regions, separated by a narrowly constricted area within the membrane. The water channel is housed within this narrow constriction (see figure 6.1).

High resolution X-ray diffraction studies on a variety of aquaporins indicate that the selectivity of these channels depends on (1) the pore size of the channel, (2) the specific identity and precise location of amino acids that line the channel, and (3) the exact orientation of water molecules within the channel.

Biochemists have recently turned their attention to AQPZ, the aquaporin found in the bacterium *E. coli*. This aquaporin proves interesting because it displays an unusually specific and rapid rate of water movement through its channel. Researchers hope that explaining the high selectivity of the AQPZ channel will yield key insights into the structure-function relationships of other aquaporins. Scientists have already discovered that the pore size of the AQPZ channel contributes to its selectivity. A precise diameter allows water to pass through the channel while excluding larger molecular species.[8]

The transport specificity of the AQPZ conduit also stems from precisely balancing the hydrophilic (water-loving) and hydrophobic (water-hating) character of the channel. This balance excludes materials with different physical properties than the channel's. Its hydrophilic character is established by the precise arrangement of the carbonyl chemical groups of eight amino acids (glycine-59, glycine-60, histidine-61, phenylalanine-62,

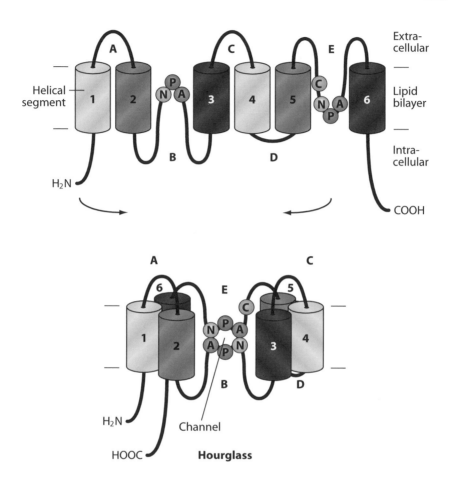

Figure 6.1. Aquaporin Structure
The aquaporin protein chain folds to form six bilayer-spanning segments represented as cylinders in the diagram. The six segments form two groups, each containing three membrane-spanning regions, separated by a narrowly constricted region within the membrane, where the water channel resides.

glutamine-182, glutaric acid-183, serine-184, and valine-185) that line the channel's interior (see figure 6.2 for the chemical structure of amino acid side chains).

These amino acids are brought into proper alignment through the folding of the aquaporin protein chain into an exacting three-dimensional architecture.

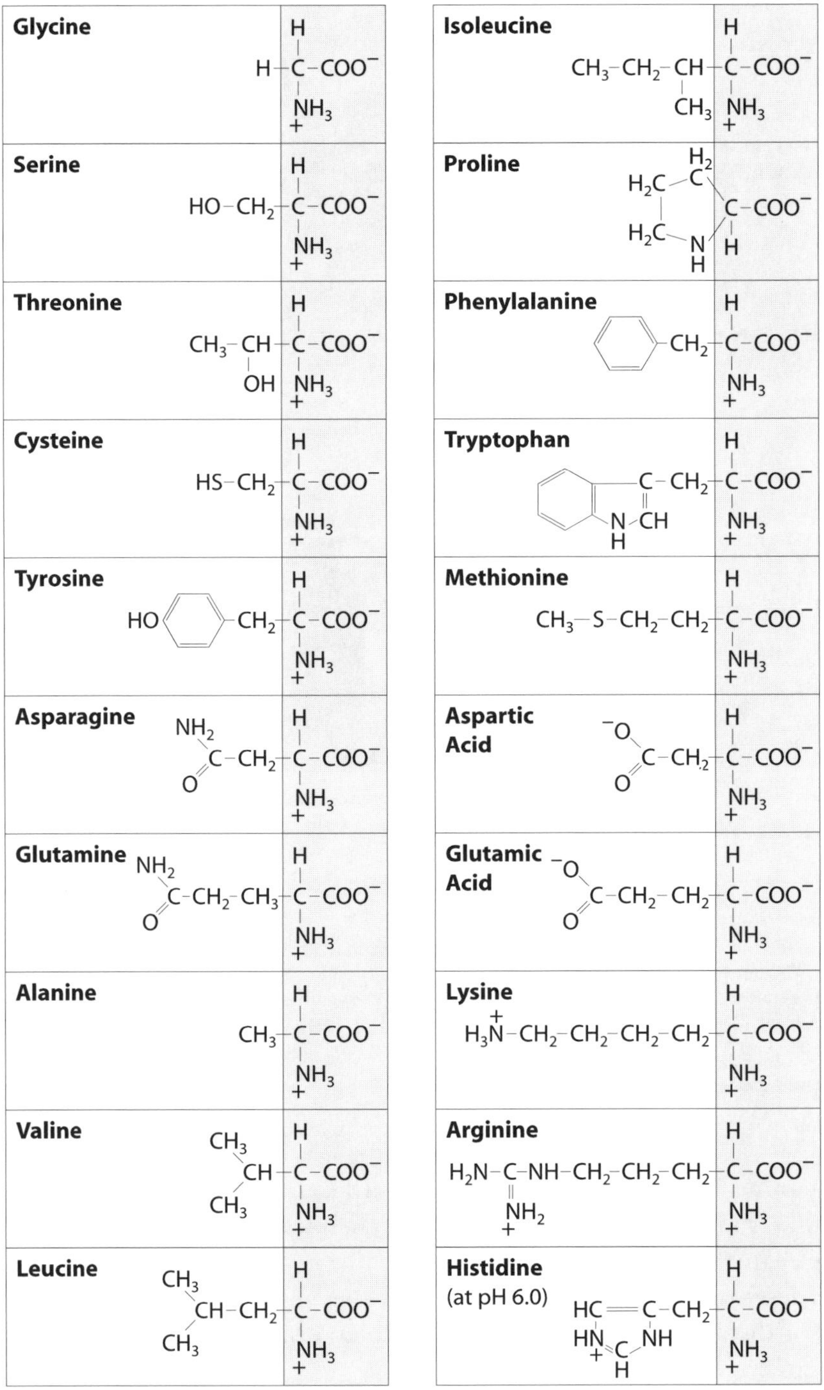

Glycine	$H_3\overset{+}{N}$ structure: H–C(–H)(–NH$_3^+$)–COO$^-$

Glycine	$\text{H}-\overset{\overset{\textstyle H}{\textstyle \mid}}{\underset{\underset{\textstyle \overset{+}{N}H_3}{\textstyle \mid}}{C}}-COO^-$
Serine	$\text{HO}-CH_2-\overset{\overset{\textstyle H}{\textstyle \mid}}{\underset{\underset{\textstyle \overset{+}{N}H_3}{\textstyle \mid}}{C}}-COO^-$
Threonine	$CH_3-\overset{\overset{\textstyle }{\textstyle }}{\underset{\underset{\textstyle OH}{\textstyle \mid}}{CH}}-\overset{\overset{\textstyle H}{\textstyle \mid}}{\underset{\underset{\textstyle \overset{+}{N}H_3}{\textstyle \mid}}{C}}-COO^-$
Cysteine	$\text{HS}-CH_2-\overset{\overset{\textstyle H}{\textstyle \mid}}{\underset{\underset{\textstyle \overset{+}{N}H_3}{\textstyle \mid}}{C}}-COO^-$
Tyrosine	$\text{HO}-\!\langle\!\!\bigcirc\!\!\rangle\!-CH_2-\overset{\overset{\textstyle H}{\textstyle \mid}}{\underset{\underset{\textstyle \overset{+}{N}H_3}{\textstyle \mid}}{C}}-COO^-$
Asparagine	$\overset{\overset{\textstyle NH_2}{\textstyle \mid}}{\underset{\underset{\textstyle O}{\textstyle \parallel}}{C}}-CH_2-\overset{\overset{\textstyle H}{\textstyle \mid}}{\underset{\underset{\textstyle \overset{+}{N}H_3}{\textstyle \mid}}{C}}-COO^-$
Glutamine	$\overset{\overset{\textstyle NH_2}{\textstyle \mid}}{\underset{\underset{\textstyle O}{\textstyle \parallel}}{C}}-CH_2-CH_3-\overset{\overset{\textstyle H}{\textstyle \mid}}{\underset{\underset{\textstyle \overset{+}{N}H_3}{\textstyle \mid}}{C}}-COO^-$
Alanine	$CH_3-\overset{\overset{\textstyle H}{\textstyle \mid}}{\underset{\underset{\textstyle \overset{+}{N}H_3}{\textstyle \mid}}{C}}-COO^-$
Valine	$\overset{\textstyle CH_3}{\underset{\textstyle CH_3}{CH}}-\overset{\overset{\textstyle H}{\textstyle \mid}}{\underset{\underset{\textstyle \overset{+}{N}H_3}{\textstyle \mid}}{C}}-COO^-$
Leucine	$\overset{\textstyle CH_3}{\underset{\textstyle CH_3}{CH}}-CH_2-\overset{\overset{\textstyle H}{\textstyle \mid}}{\underset{\underset{\textstyle \overset{+}{N}H_3}{\textstyle \mid}}{C}}-COO^-$
Isoleucine	$CH_3-CH_2-\overset{\overset{\textstyle }{\textstyle }}{\underset{\underset{\textstyle CH_3}{\textstyle \mid}}{CH}}-\overset{\overset{\textstyle H}{\textstyle \mid}}{\underset{\underset{\textstyle \overset{+}{N}H_3}{\textstyle \mid}}{C}}-COO^-$
Proline	(cyclic: H_2C, H_2C, H_2C, $\overset{H_2}{C}$ ring with N–H) –C(H)–COO$^-$
Phenylalanine	$\langle\!\!\bigcirc\!\!\rangle\!-CH_2-\overset{\overset{\textstyle H}{\textstyle \mid}}{\underset{\underset{\textstyle \overset{+}{N}H_3}{\textstyle \mid}}{C}}-COO^-$
Tryptophan	(indole ring)–C$=$CH / N–H –CH$_2$–$\overset{\overset{\textstyle H}{\textstyle \mid}}{\underset{\underset{\textstyle \overset{+}{N}H_3}{\textstyle \mid}}{C}}$–COO$^-$
Methionine	$CH_3-S-CH_2-CH_2-\overset{\overset{\textstyle H}{\textstyle \mid}}{\underset{\underset{\textstyle \overset{+}{N}H_3}{\textstyle \mid}}{C}}-COO^-$
Aspartic Acid	$\overset{\overset{\textstyle ^-O}{\textstyle \mid}}{\underset{\underset{\textstyle O}{\textstyle \parallel}}{C}}-CH_2-\overset{\overset{\textstyle H}{\textstyle \mid}}{\underset{\underset{\textstyle \overset{+}{N}H_3}{\textstyle \mid}}{C}}-COO^-$
Glutamic Acid	$\overset{\overset{\textstyle ^-O}{\textstyle \mid}}{\underset{\underset{\textstyle O}{\textstyle \parallel}}{C}}-CH_2-CH_2-\overset{\overset{\textstyle H}{\textstyle \mid}}{\underset{\underset{\textstyle \overset{+}{N}H_3}{\textstyle \mid}}{C}}-COO^-$
Lysine	$H_3\overset{+}{N}-CH_2-CH_2-CH_2-CH_2-\overset{\overset{\textstyle H}{\textstyle \mid}}{\underset{\underset{\textstyle \overset{+}{N}H_3}{\textstyle \mid}}{C}}-COO^-$
Arginine	$H_2N-\overset{\overset{\textstyle }{\textstyle }}{\underset{\underset{\textstyle NH_2}{\textstyle \parallel}}{C}}-NH-CH_2-CH_2-CH_2-\overset{\overset{\textstyle H}{\textstyle \mid}}{\underset{\underset{\textstyle \overset{+}{N}H_3}{\textstyle \mid}}{C}}-COO^-$
Histidine (at pH 6.0)	(imidazolium ring: $HC=C$, HN, $\overset{+}{NH}$, C–H) –CH$_2$–$\overset{\overset{\textstyle H}{\textstyle \mid}}{\underset{\underset{\textstyle \overset{+}{N}H_3}{\textstyle \mid}}{C}}$–COO$^-$

Hydrophobic amino acids (valine, phenylalanine, and isoluecine), which line the channel wall, establish the channel's hydrophobicity.[9] Other research teams have likewise noted that the composition, location, and spatial orientation of amino acids forming the channel determine aquaporin specificity for water transport.[10]

Other studies point to the importance of amino acids at the mouth of aquaporin and aquaglyceroporin pores. For example, work on an aquaglyceroporin from the malaria parasite, *Plasmodium falciparum*, pinpointed the importance of interaction between a positively charged amino acid (arginine-196) and a negatively charged one (glutamate-125). Precise bonding of these two amino acid residues enables the pore to transport water along with glycerol through its channel. Replacing glutamate-125 with the amino acid serine all but abolished the permeability of water through the channel of this aquaglyceroporin.[11]

The relationship between aquaporin's structure and function appears to be extremely sensitive. Recent work indicates that the difference between the selectivity of aquaporins and aquaglyceroporins stems from a single amino acid difference in the channel's interior. Aquaglyceroporins have a smaller glycine in place of a larger histidine in the aquaporin pore.[12]

Glycine's smaller size allows larger glycerol molecules to make their way through the channel. Histidine's larger size blocks the movement of glycerol through the pore, yet allows water to freely permeate through aquaporin openings. Substitution of isoleucine for histidine (or glycine) accounts for the unique water conductance profile of the aquaporin AQPM from the archaea, *Methanothermobacter marburgensis*.[13]

Other researchers have noted the importance a single amino acid can play in establishing aquaporin selectivity. For example, a team of United States and Japanese scientists noted that use of an asparagine in place of glycine-57 in the membrane-spanning regions of aquaporins causes AQP6 to function as a conduit for negatively charged chemical species (anions) instead of water or glycerol.[14]

One magnificent property of aquaporins is their ability to conduct water while preventing the flow of hydrogen ions through the channel.

Figure 6.2. Amino Acid Side Groups
The twenty amino acids are used by the cell's machinery to construct proteins. The shaded region of the diagram corresponds to the parts of the molecules that are identical for all amino acids. These parts of the molecules form the backbone of the protein chain. The nonshaded region of the diagram describes the part of the molecules unique to each amino acid. These so-called R groups form the side chains extending from the backbone of the protein molecule.

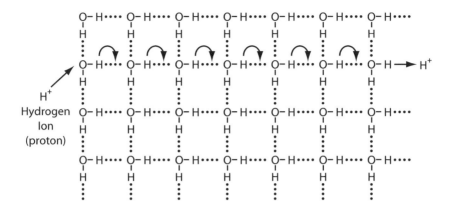

Figure 6.3. Proton Wire

In water, hydrogen ions (or protons) make their way rapidly through water by moving along a "proton wire" formed by a linear arrangement of water molecules. The proton wire pathway is depicted by arrows.

Hydrogen ions are highly mobile in water. But they don't physically migrate through water as other ions do. Instead, hydrogen ions make their way rapidly through water by moving along a "proton wire" formed by a linear arrangement of water molecules (see figure 6.3).[15] In effect, they are passed through water by binding to a water molecule at one end of the wire. That forces a hydrogen ion off of a water molecule at the opposite end of the wire. This movement results from quantum tunneling between the water molecules that constitute the proton wire.

A column of water molecules fills the membrane pores of aquaporins and aquaglyceroporins. In principle, this column should function as a proton wire conducting hydrogen ions. However, recent work explains how aquaporins and aquaglyceroporins keep hydrogen ions from moving through their channels.

An exacting arrangement of water molecules within the channel actually blocks the hydrogen ion flow. Instead of water molecules forming a linear procession with the same orientation throughout the channel—setting up a proton wire—approximately halfway through the channel, the water molecules change orientation breaking the wire. Two asparagines in the middle of the channel mediate the change in orientation of the column of water molecules. This exacting arrangement allows water molecules to freely pass through the aquaporin and aquaglyceroporin channels while hindering the flow of hydrogen ions.

The biochemical fine-tuning of aquaporins appears to exceed the best precision attained by human engineers and designers. Yet, the molecular precision necessary for aquaporins to selectively transport water and glycerin through cell membranes is not unique to these pore-forming proteins. Other membrane channels display the same type of biochemical fine-tuning relying on the precise positioning and spatial orientation of amino acid residues to attain transport specificity.[16]

Carefully Composed Collagen

The structural precision that characterizes proteins is not confined to the exact arrangements and spatial orientation of amino acids. In some proteins, amino acid composition is also fine-tuned. Among these are collagens—the most abundant proteins in the animal kingdom. They are found in the matrix of bone, connective tissue, and skin.

The collagen fibers located in the matrices of tissues are formed from smaller fibrils (see figure 6.4). In turn, these fibrils consist of laterally

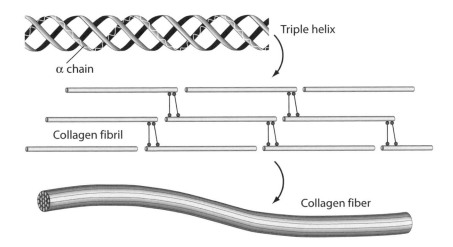

Figure 6.4. Collagen
Collagen molecules are fibrous proteins that consist of three polypeptide chains intertwined around one another to form the collagen triple helix. The triple helices, in turn, associate to form fibrils. These fibrils associate to form much larger collagen fibers.

associated collagen molecules. These molecules are made up of three polypeptide chains intertwined to form the collagen triple helix.[17] The helix requires a highly specific amino acid composition in order to form. In essence, the single polypeptides of collagen are polyproline chains with glycine amino acids interspersed every third position. Because of their small size, the glycine residues allow the polyproline chains to twist into a helical conformation.

Collagen molecules will spontaneously aggregate into fibrils, so they are produced inside the cell in a form that will not self-assemble. This form, pro-collagen, has large globular ends that prevent association of collagen chains. Once produced, the collagen is secreted to the cell's exterior. Then, an enzyme called collagenase cleaves the globular ends from the pro-collagen to form protein chains that can readily aggregate.

Because of collagen's key structural role in animal tissues, biochemists long thought this biomolecule was stable at body temperatures for warm-blooded creatures and at environmental temperatures for cold-blooded animals. To nearly everyone's surprise, however, recent work indicates that the collagen triple helix and fibrils are unstable at body temperatures with the chains spontaneously unfolding from the triple helix arrangement into random coils.[18] Even more surprising is the fact that this instability seems carefully orchestrated by precise adjustments to the collagen amino acid composition.

Biochemists think the instability of the collagen triple helix plays an important role in the assembly of fibrils. The unfolded regions of the collagen triple helix promote the lateral association of the collagen triple helices into the higher order structure of the fibrils. If the triple helix was stable, these associations could not occur. Once the fibrils form, the mutual interaction among the collagen molecules stabilizes the triple helix conformation. The tendency of the collagen helices to unfold also imparts collagen fibrils with elasticity. This property makes the tissues that form tendons and ligaments flexible and able to withstand stresses and strains.

Finally, the unfolded regions are also sites where collagenase enzymes can break down collagen molecules and hence, collagen fibrils. This breakdown allows tissues to undergo dynamic restructuring as animals face ever-changing demands (e.g., due to growth). The exacting amino acid composition imparts collagen with strength and elasticity and allows biochemical machinery to resculpture it as needed.

Perfect Timing

Exact fine-tuning is not limited to the structure of biomolecules. Sometimes the rate of biochemical processes is also meticulously refined. Recent studies indicate that the rate of messenger RNA and protein breakdown, two processes central to the cell's activity, are exquisitely regulated by the cell's machinery.

Shutting Down Production

Messenger RNA (mRNA) plays a central role in protein production (see chapter 2, p. 50, and chapter 5, p. 101). These molecules mediate the transfer of information from the nucleotide sequences of DNA to the amino acid sequences of proteins.

The cell's machinery copies mRNA from DNA only when the cell needs the protein encoded by a particular gene housed in the DNA. When that protein is not needed, the cell shuts down production. This practice is a matter of efficiency. In this way, the cell makes only the mRNAs and consequently the proteins it needs.

Once produced, mRNAs continue to direct the production of proteins at the ribosome. Fortunately, mRNA molecules have limited stability and only exist intact for a brief period of time before they break down. This short lifetime benefits the cell. If mRNA molecules unduly persisted, then they would direct the production of proteins at the ribosome beyond the point the cell needs (see chapter 2, p. 50). Overproduction would not only be wasteful, it would also lead to the coexistence of proteins that carry out opposed functions within the cell. The careful control of mRNA levels is necessary for the cell to have the right amounts of proteins at the right time. Unregulated protein levels would compromise life.

Until recently, biochemists thought regulation of mRNA levels (and hence protein levels) occurred when the cell's transcriptional machinery carefully controlled mRNA production. New research, however, indicates that mRNA breakdown also helps regulate its level.[19]

Prior to this work, biochemists thought that the degradation of mRNA was influenced only by abundance, size, nucleotide sequence, and so forth. However, this perspective was incorrect. The breakdown of mRNA molecules is not random but precisely orchestrated.

Remarkably, messenger RNA molecules, which correspond to proteins that are part of the same metabolic pathways, have virtually identical decay rates. The researchers also found that mRNA molecules, which specify proteins involved in the cell's central activities, have relatively slow breakdown rates. Proteins only needed for transient cell processes are encoded by mRNAs with rapid rates of degradation. The decay of mRNA molecules is not only fine-tuned but also displays an elegant biochemical logic that bespeaks of intelligence.

Tagged for Destruction

Proteins, which play a role in virtually every cell structure and activity, are constantly made—and destroyed—by the cell. Those that take part in highly specialized activities within the cell are manufactured only when needed. Once these proteins have outlived their usefulness, the cell breaks them down into their constitutive amino acids. The removal of unnecessary proteins helps keep the cell's interior free of clutter.

On the other hand, proteins that play a central role in the cell's operation are produced on a continual basis. After a period of time, however, these proteins inevitably suffer damage from wear and tear and must be destroyed and replaced with newly made proteins. It's dangerous for the cell to let damaged proteins linger.

Once a protein is damaged, it's prone to aggregate with other proteins. These aggregates disrupt cellular activities. Protein degradation and turnover, in many respects, are just as vital to the cell's operation as protein production. And, as is the case for mRNAs, protein degradation is an exacting, delicately balanced process.[20]

This complex undertaking begins with ubiquitination. When damaged, proteins misfold, adopting an unnatural three-dimensional shape. Misfolding exposes amino acids in the damaged protein's interior. These exposed amino acids are recognized by E3 ubiquitin ligase, an enzyme that attaches a small protein molecule (ubiquitin) to the damaged protein.[21] Ubiquitin functions as a molecular tag, informing the cell's machinery that the damaged protein is to be destroyed. Severely damaged proteins receive multiple tags.

To the Rescue

Ubiquitination is a reversible process with de-ubiquitinating enzymes removing inappropriate ubiquitin labels. This activity prevents the cell's machinery from breaking down fully functional proteins that may have been accidentally tagged for destruction because E3 ubiquitin ligase occasionally makes mistakes.

A massive protein complex, a proteasome, destroys damaged ubiquitinated proteins, functioning like the cell's garbage can. The overall molecular architecture of the proteasome consists of a hollow cylinder topped with a lid that can exist in either an opened or closed conformation. Protein breakdown takes place within the cylinder's interior. The lid portion of the proteasome controls the entry of ubiquitinated proteins into the cylinder.

The proteasome lid contains de-ubiquitinating activity. If a protein has only one or two ubiquitin tags, it's likely not damaged and the lid will remove the tags rescuing the protein from destruction. The cell's machinery then recycles the rescued protein. If, on the other hand, the protein has several ubiquitin tags, the lid cannot remove them all and shuttles the damaged protein entry into the proteasome cylinder.

The proteasome lid regulates a delicate balance between destruction and rescue, ensuring that truly damaged proteins are destroyed and proteins that can be salvaged escape unnecessary degradation. The cell's protein degradation system, like messenger RNA breakdown, displays fine-tuning and elegant biochemical logic that points to a Creator's handiwork.

Regulating Production

Not only is the breakdown of proteins and messenger RNAs exquisitely fine-tuned, but so is the timing of their production throughout the cell cycle. All cells go through a cycle of activity that begins and ends with mitosis (the process of cell division that yields two daughter cells identical to the mother cell). Once mitosis is completed, cells go through distinct phases of growth and preparation for the next round of cell division.

Biochemists estimate that about 20 percent of genes are turned on (or expressed) only during specific points in the cell cycle. At other times, these genes are turned off. This regulation occurs because the proteins (and other products) encoded by these genes are useful to the cell only at particular intervals during the cell cycle. At other times, they serve no purpose. By producing biomolecules only when they're required, the cell avoids needless waste of resources. This careful control of gene expression and protein production also serves another important function.

Recent work indicates that the regulation in gene expression throughout the cell cycle closely resembles "just-in-time" production and delivery used by manufacturers and builders.[22] When building a home, for example, the construction materials are not all delivered to the job site at once. They are delivered only as needed. This schedule ensures efficient management of resources. It avoids waste and makes things easier to find, keeping the job site uncluttered. Breakage is reduced and errors eliminated that would occur if the wrong materials were inadvertently used because of excess supplies.

The regulation of gene expression occurs in such a way that messenger RNA is continuously produced for those proteins needed at every stage in the cell cycle. Other proteins with transient use to the cell are produced just-in-time and no sooner. As soon as they're no longer needed, production shuts down. This schedule keeps the cell from becoming cluttered with unnecessary proteins and eliminates errors that could occur if proteins are engaged in activities at the inappropriate time by mistake (see chapter 4, p. 74.)

Throughout the course of the cell cycle, gene expression takes place in interdependent waves. Genes coding for proteins needed at the same point in the cell cycle are turned on all together at just the right time and turned off when the cell no longer needs them. When a wave of gene expression is initiated, it produces proteins called transcription factors whose sole function is to turn on or activate genes needed in the ensuing surge of gene expression (see chapter 7, p. 135). It also produces transcription factors whose only role is to turn off genes that code for proteins that were part of the previous wave.

As with messenger RNA and protein degradation, the precision and elegant biochemical logic of messenger RNA and protein production throughout the cell cycle (resembling the best practices of manufacturers and builders) are the types of biochemical features that show the Creator's artistry.

The Painstaking Results

The photographic precision of the Pre-Raphaelite works of art evokes tremendous admiration. This type of concentrated effort also equates with the best possible quality in engineered systems. Exact fine-tuning does not arise by happenstance in either art or engineering. Rather, it results from careful planning and a commitment to execute designs using the best craftsmanship possible.

Such deliberate calibration is a clear indicator of human intelligent design. By analogy the molecular precision and fine-tuning that pervades the design of biochemical systems are potent markers for the work of a Divine Engineer and Artist. No detail is too small to escape the Creator's attention. This fine-tuning defines the structure and compositional makeup of proteins and is very much a key feature of biochemical processes. In fact, the cell cycle, itself, actually depends on the precise timing of biochemical events.

Most remarkable is the apparently extreme nature of this biochemical fine-tuning. It is comparable to the inordinate attention to detail achieved by the Pre-Raphaelite artists and the impressive fine-tuning achieved by top human engineers. The molecular precision—pervasive in nearly all aspects of life's chemical systems—raises questions about the capability of undirected evolutionary processes to achieve such carefully crafted designs (see chapter 14, p. 270). The molecular fine-tuning of biochemical systems is exactly what would be expected if life is the product of a Creator.

The next chapter explores another feature of life's chemistry that points to Divine Design: the structural and functional optimality of biochemical systems.

Theo van Doesburg, *Contra-Composition of Dissonances, XVI* (Reproduced by permission from Haags Gemeentemuseum, The Hague, Netherlands/The Bridgeman Art Library)

7

THE PROPER ARRANGEMENT OF ELEMENTS

Before picking up a brush, many painters spend a lot of time thinking about the best way to position lines, shapes, colors, textures, and so forth to accomplish their purpose. They deliberately arrange elements to create a certain sense of balance.

There are at least three different ways to achieve the desired array of elements in a painting: Symmetric balance refers to a perfectly centered composition or one that employs mirror images. Asymmetric balance describes an off-centered arrangement, or one with an odd, mismatched number of elements. Radial balance is employed when the elements of a piece radiate or swirl around a circular or spiral path.[1]

Artists depend on balance for more than just aesthetic purposes. They use it to communicate moods, emotions, and sentiment and to generate a response in their audience. For example, symmetric balance conveys a sense of elegance or evokes contemplation or a sense of the familiar. Asymmetric balance expresses movement or generates tension. An asymmetric arrangement of elements can also communicate moods like anger, excitement, and joy. Radial balance provides a sense of equilibrium for the viewer.

One artist known for his exceptional use of balance was Piet Mondrian (1872–1944).[2] Through a precise arrangement of red, yellow, blue, or black rectangular forms separated by thick black rectilinear lines, his paintings effuse complexity amidst their simplicity. Mondrian sought to express the utmost awareness of beauty, harmony, and rhythm by carefully positioning the lines, shapes, and colors in his work.

Artists are not alone in their attention to balance. Engineers share similar concerns. In their designs, engineers—like artists—strive to achieve the desired effects by appropriately placing the elements in their compositions. They make careful use of individual components to accomplish a specific purpose or goal. And, as a consequence, their designs are optimized. Balance in an artistic work and in engineered systems requires extensive planning and forethought and, therefore, stands as a hallmark of intelligent design.

Life scientists have discovered that many biochemical systems, like human designs, are ideal for their role in the cell. As with the other characteristics that define life's chemistry, the magnificent array of biochemical systems far exceeds the accomplishments of the finest human engineers and designers in a way befitting a Creator. A few recently discovered examples give a sense of the elegance and molecular balance of life's chemical structures and processes.

Ideal Structures

The last half-century or so of research has yielded remarkable details about the structure and function of a myriad of proteins. Based on these insights, most biochemists would conclude that proteins are structured in the most advantageous way for their specific biochemical roles. So, too, is DNA.

Well-Proportioned Proteins

Amino acids (small subunit molecules) link together in a head-to-tail fashion to form the polypeptide chains that constitute proteins (see chapter 2, p. 42). In principle, these molecules can join up in any possible sequence. Some sequences generate useful proteins. Many yield junk polypeptides that lack function.

The twenty different types of amino acids used to make polypeptides possess a variety of chemical and physical properties (see figure 6.2). Each chain's sequence (primary structure) imparts a specific chemical and physical profile along its length. This physicochemical profile determines how the polypeptide chain folds (secondary and tertiary structures) and in turn the way it interacts (quaternary structure) with other polypeptides to form a functional protein. The sequence ultimately determines the polypeptide's function because the sequence shapes the polypeptide's structure, and structure dictates function (see figure 2.2, p. 44).

Energy efficient. For the protein structures they produce, amino acid sequences appear to be extraordinarily optimized. In a recent study, biochemists from the University of Washington modeled the three-dimensional structure of 108 different proteins starting with random amino acid sequences. They repeatedly varied the sequences looking for protein structures with the least amount of energy. (Minimum-energy structures are the most stable.)

Through this process, the scientists discovered that in virtually all cases, the amino acid sequences that folded into the lowest-energy three-dimensional shapes were nearly identical to the native sequence. They concluded that the most effective amino acid sequence for a given protein structure is closely restricted to sequences highly similar to those found in nature.[3]

Recent studies indicate that protein structure is optimized in a more general sense as well. And, this overall structural optimization represents another example of the impeccable chemical logic that pervades biochemical systems. Biochemists have long known that corresponding proteins from diverse organisms have different amino acid sequences. When compared, some positions in the sequences vary extensively, some differ to a limited extent, and others don't vary at all. Amino acids at these invariable (conserved) positions are regarded as critical to the protein's structure and function. Those amino acids at variable positions are considered relatively unimportant, though they do contribute to the protein's overall three-dimensional shape and in some cases its folding pattern.

New work suggests, however, that the amino acids at variable positions along the polypeptide chain do not differ indiscriminately but appear carefully selected for a number of considerations apart from protein structure and function. For example, several studies show that amino acids used in bacterial proteins have been chosen with metabolic efficiency in mind.[4]

The biosynthesis of amino acids requires the use of the cell's material and energy reserves. Some amino acids are much more metabolically expensive to produce than others. All things being equal, bacteria will use

the metabolically least expensive amino acids, particularly at variable positions. Researchers have noted that this discrimination is especially true for
proteins produced at high levels in the cell. Along these lines, a different
study indicates that whenever possible, free-living organisms minimize the
use of larger, more massive amino acids because of high metabolic costs.[5]

Less is more. Another study reveals an additional aspect of the elegant
chemical logic that undergirds amino acid usage. The cell relies on proteins
to make the amino acids necessary to build proteins. Researchers have shown
by studying several different bacteria that the proteins which manufacture
a particular amino acid are compositionally devoid of that amino acid.[6]

This absence prevents a catch-22 when the cell's reserves become depleted
of a specific amino acid. If that amino acid was a part of the proteins that
in turn synthesize the amino acid, then there would be no way for the cell
to replenish its supply of that amino acid. And that lack would cause the
supply to diminish further and further. The amino acid composition of
proteins appears just right to ensure that the cell can generate the amino
acids it needs at all times.

Building resistance. The variable amino acid positions also make proteins functionally able to withstand mutations to DNA that result in a
change to the protein's amino acid sequence. A recent study on the DNA
repair enzyme, 3-methyladenine DNA glycosylase, illustrates the capacity of
proteins to tolerate amino acid changes. Researchers created three separate
pools of mutated enzymes each consisting of about one hundred thousand
molecules. On average, mutant enzymes in the three groups contained
from two to six amino acid changes. Yet, only 35 percent of these changes
resulted in nonfunctional enzymes.

In other words, 65 percent of amino acid changes leave the function of
3-methyladenine DNA glycosylase unaltered. And, many proteins accrued
multiple amino acid changes without any loss of structure or function.
(These scientists noted that other proteins found in nature also tolerate
amino acid changes to the same extent as this DNA repair enzyme.) Interestingly, conserved amino acid positions appear to be resistant to amino
acid changes, whereas variable positions withstand the changes without
loss of function.[7]

Based on the study of 3-methyladenine DNA glycosylase (and other
proteins), it appears that amino acid composition and sequences of proteins have been maximized to resist the harmful effects of amino acid
changes caused by mutations. This sequence optimization is not a universal

characteristic of proteins, however. Researchers from the University of Michigan have determined that structurally stable proteins designed by human biotechnologists are almost always susceptible to even single amino acid changes.[8] There appears to be something special about the amino acid sequences of proteins found in nature.

Age-resistant. Protein sequences are not only the best possible to resist the harmful effects of amino acid changes. Their structures also appear just right to withstand the damage caused by reactive oxygen species (ROS) in the cell.

ROS such as superoxide (O_2^-), the hydroxy free-radical ($\cdot$OH), and hydrogen peroxide (H_2O_2) are derivatives of molecular oxygen (O_2). The cell's machinery routinely produces these compounds during the normal course of metabolism.[9] ROS randomly and indiscriminately react inside the cell to damage important cell components. For example, ROS attack the molecules that make up the cell's membrane (lipids), proteins, and DNA. And, reactive oxygen species are believed to play a significant role in the aging process.[10]

A recent study by a team of French scientists demonstrated that proteins experienced a heightened level of oxidative damage under conditions that promote the production of defective proteins. These abnormal proteins misfold, rendering them susceptible to oxidation. All things being equal, when the conditions in the cell support the synthesis of properly produced proteins, the level of oxidation plummets. Based on this finding, the researchers concluded that the structures of proteins must be the best possible to avoid damage from oxidation.

Just-Right DNA

Recent studies indicate that, like proteins, the structural features of DNA are also exceptional. DNA consists of two chainlike molecules (polynucleotides) that twist around each other to form the DNA double helix (see chapter 2, p. 48). The cell's machinery forms polynucleotide chains by linking together four different subunit molecules called nucleotides. The nucleotides used to build DNA chains are adenosine (A), guanosine (G), cytidine (C), and thymidine (T) (see figure 2.7, p. 49).

DNA houses the information needed to make all the polypeptides used by the cell. The sequence of nucleotides in DNA strands specifies the sequence of amino acids in polypeptide chains. Scientists refer to this sequence of nucleotides as a gene.

Deliberate sequences. On the surface, there appears to be a problem relating nucleotide sequences to amino acid sequences. Clearly a one-to-one relationship cannot exist between the four nucleotides of DNA and the twenty amino acids used to assemble polypeptides. To overcome this mismatch, the cell uses groupings of three nucleotides (codons) to specify twenty different amino acids. Each nucleotide triplet, or codon, specifies an amino acid.

There are sixty-four possible codons that can be used to specify the twenty amino acids. Because of the excess number, however, more than one codon can correspond to the same amino acid. In fact, up to six different codons specify some amino acids—others are signified by only one. (Chapter 9 discusses the relationship between codons and amino acids in greater detail.)

Because some codons are redundant, the amino acid sequence for a given polypeptide chain can be specified by several different nucleotide sequences. Recent studies indicate that the cell does not randomly make use of redundant codons to specify a particular amino acid in a polypeptide chain. Instead, there appears to be a rationale behind codon usage in genes.

Biochemists have known for some time that highly repetitive nucleotide sequences are unstable and readily mutate. The most common type of mutation to repetitive sequences is the insertion and/or deletion (indels) of one or more nucleotides.

These mutations are devastating. They almost always result in the production of highly defective polypeptide chains. A survey of the genomes from several organisms by researchers at the University of California, San Diego, indicates that codon usage in genes is designed to avoid the type of repetition that leads to unstable sequences.[11] Although the details are beyond the scope of this book, other studies similarly indicate that codon usage in genes is also set up to maximize the accuracy of protein synthesis at the ribosome[12] (see chapter 2, p. 50).

Hand-picked components. The sequence of nucleotides is not the only feature of DNA that is optimized. The components that make up the nucleotides also appear to have been carefully chosen for unsurpassed performance. Nucleotides that form the strands of DNA are complex molecules consisting of both a phosphate moiety and a nucleobase (either adenine, guanine, cytosine, or thymine) joined to a five-carbon sugar (deoxyribose). (See figure 7.1.) In RNA, deoxyribose is replaced with the five-carbon sugar ribose.

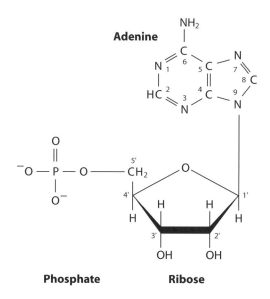

Adenosine 5'-monophosphate (AMP)

Figure 7.1. Nucleotide Structure
The subunit molecules that make up the strands of DNA and RNA consist of both a phosphate moiety and a nucleobase (either adenine, guanine, cytosine, or thymine) joined to a five-carbon sugar (deoxyribose). In RNA, deoxyribose is replaced with the five-carbon sugar ribose.

The backbone of the DNA strand is formed by repeatedly linking the phosphate group of one nucleotide to the deoxyribose unit of another nucleotide. The nucleobases extend as side chains from the backbone of the DNA molecule and serve as interaction points (like ladder rungs) when the two DNA strands align and twist to form the double helix (see figure 7.2).

Scientists have long wondered why the nucleotide subunits of DNA and RNA consist of these particular molecular components (phosphates, adenine, guanine, cytosine, thymine/uracil, deoxyribose, and ribose), because a myriad of sugars and numerous other nucleobases could have conceivably become part of the cell's information storage (DNA) and processing systems (RNA).

For nearly twenty years, biochemists have understood why phosphates are critical to the structures of DNA and RNA.[13] This chemical group is perfectly suited to form a stable backbone for the DNA molecule. Phosphates can form bonds with two sugars at the same time (phosphodiester bonds) to bridge two nucleotides, while retaining a negative charge (see figure

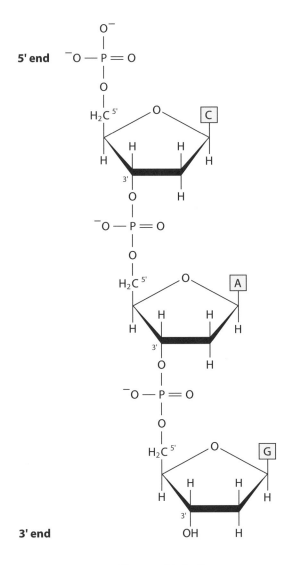

Figure 7.2. DNA Backbone and Side Chains
The backbone of the DNA strand is formed by repeatedly linking the phosphate group of one nucleotide to the deoxyribose unit of another nucleotide.

7.3). Other compounds can form bonds between two sugars but won't retain a negative charge. The negative charge on the phosphate group imparts the DNA backbone with stability protecting it from cleavage by reactive water molecules.

The specific nature of the phosphodiester bonds is also optimized. For example, the phosphodiester linkage that bridges the ribose sugars of RNA could involve the 5′ OH of one ribose molecule with either the 2′ OH or 3′ OH of the adjacent ribose moiety. In nature, RNA exclusively makes use of 5′ to 3′ bonding. A study conducted in the early 1990s explains why life employs these types of bonds. It turns out that 5′ to 3′ linkages impart much greater stability to the RNA molecule than 5′ to 2′ bonds.[14]

Numerous recent studies provide insight as to why deoxyribose and ribose were selected as the sugar molecules that make up the backbones of DNA and RNA. Deoxyribose and ribose are five-carbon sugars that form five-membered rings. Researchers have demonstrated that it's possible to make DNA analogs using a wide range of different sugars that contain four-, five-, and six-carbons that can adopt five- and six-membered rings. But they have shown that these DNA variants have undesirable properties compared to DNA and RNA built with deoxyribose and ribose, respectively (see figure 7.4).

$$(Base)_1 \qquad O \qquad (Base)_2$$
$$| \qquad\qquad || \qquad\qquad |$$
$$(Sugar) - O - P - O - (Sugar) + H_2O$$
$$| $$
$$O^-$$

Figure 7.3. The Phosphodiester Bonds of RNA
Phosphates form bonds with two sugars at the same time (phosphodiester bonds) while retaining a negative charge.

For example, some of these DNA analogs don't form double helices. Others do, but the nucleotide strands interact either too strongly, too weakly, or they display inappropriate selectivity in their associations.[15]

Additionally, other studies show that DNA analogs made from sugars that form 6-membered rings adopt too many structural conformations.[16] This diversity is objectionable. If DNA assumes multiple conformations, then it becomes extremely difficult for the cell's machinery to properly execute DNA replication and repair, as well as transcription. Also researchers have shown that deoxyribose uniquely provides the necessary space within the backbone region of the DNA double helix to accommodate the large nucleobases. No other sugar fulfills this requirement.[17]

For some time, biochemists have understood why deoxyribose was selected for use in DNA and ribose for RNA. The primary role of DNA is information storage. That's why DNA must be a stable molecule. Incorporation of ribose

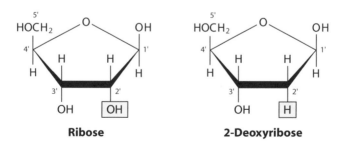

Figure 7.4. Differences between Deoxyribose and Ribose
Deoxyribose and ribose are five-carbon sugars that form five-membered rings. Deoxyribose lacks an OH group at the 2′ position. Ribose possesses a 2′ OH moiety.

in DNA would make this molecule inherently unstable. The 2′ OH of ribose can catalyze the cleavage of the sugar-phosphate backbone of DNA. This is not a concern, however, for deoxyribose because it lacks the 2′ OH group.

However, ribose is well-suited for RNA where some measure of instability is preferable. One of the roles of RNA is to mediate the transfer of information from the nucleotide sequences of DNA to the amino acid sequences of proteins (see chapter 2, p. 50, and chapter 5, p. 101). The cell's machinery copies mRNA from DNA when the cell needs the protein encoded by a particular gene housed in the DNA.

Once produced, mRNAs continue to direct the production of proteins at the ribosome until the cell's machinery breaks down the mRNA molecules (see chapter 6, p. 119). Fortunately, mRNA molecules can exist intact for only a brief period of time, in part because of the breakdown of the sugar-phosphate backbone mediated by the 2′ OH group. The short lifetime of mRNAs serves the cell well. If mRNAs unduly persisted, then these molecules would direct the production of proteins at the ribosome beyond the point needed by the cell.

Like deoxyribose and ribose, the nucleobases (adenine, guanine, cytosine, and thymine/uracil) found in DNA and RNA appear to be the best possible choices. For example, recent research demonstrates that these particular nucleobases display ideal photophysical properties. UV radiation emitted by the sun causes damage to DNA and RNA. The destructive effects of these electromagnetic wavelengths stem in large measure from the absorption of this radiation by the nucleobases.

Even though DNA and RNA routinely experience photophysical damage, it could be far worse. It turns out that the optical properties of the bases found in nature minimize UV-induced damage.[18] These nucleobases maximally absorb UV radiation at the same wavelengths that are most effectively shielded by ozone. Moreover, the chemical structures of the nucleobases of DNA and RNA cause the UV radiation to be efficiently radiated away after being absorbed, limiting the opportunity for damage. (Additional reasons why adenine, guanine, cytosine, and thymine/uracil were selected for use in DNA and RNA are discussed in chapter 8.)

Strategic placement. Biochemists have come to recognize that even the antiparallel arrangement of the nucleotide strands of the DNA molecule is optimal[19] (see chapter 2, p. 48 and figure 2.7). Researchers have demonstrated that DNA analogs with a parallel orientation of nucleotide strands can be prepared in the laboratory. By comparing these novel DNA systems with native DNA, it is clear that aligning the nucleotide strands in an antiparallel fashion leads to greater stability of the DNA double helix found in nature.

The antiparallel arrangement imparts topological and information-storage advantages, as well. The reasons why it does are beyond the scope of this book, but a resource for them can be found in the references.[20]

Processes at Their Peak

Optimal composition is not limited to the structure of proteins and DNA. Researchers have demonstrated that biochemical processes also operate at their ultimate potential. Descriptions of gene regulation and glycolysis make particularly fitting examples of exquisite biochemical composition because both processes are central activities for life.

Gene Regulation

Recent studies indicate that the molecular operations responsible for regulating gene expression are optimized to minimize error. As mentioned earlier, genes are regions along the DNA molecule that specify the production of proteins and other products (see chapter 2, p. 48). Gene structure is complex, broadly consisting of two regions: the protein-coding region and the regulatory region[21] (see figure 7.5).

The protein-coding region contains information needed by the cell's biochemical machinery to produce the polypeptide chain encoded by that gene. The regulatory region, on the other hand, consists of "on/off

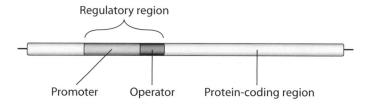

Figure 7.5. Gene Structure
Gene structure broadly consists of two regions: the protein-coding region and the regulatory region. Two key sites exist within the regulatory region of a gene: the promoter and operator.

switches" and "volume control knobs" that control or regulate gene expression. Hence, the regulatory region ultimately dictates the production of the polypeptide chain.

Gene expression plays a central role in coordinating life's biochemical processes. Some genes are "turned on" or expressed nearly all the time. Biochemists refer to these genes as "housekeeping genes" because they specify proteins that are needed virtually all the time to maintain normal cellular operations. Other genes are expressed intermittently, directing the production of proteins only when necessary, either at certain points in the cell cycle or in response to specific environmental effects.

There are two key sites within the regulatory region of a gene: the promoter and the operator. The promoter serves as the binding site for a massive protein complex called RNA polymerase. This enzyme initiates gene expression by producing a messenger RNA molecule that contains a copy of the information found in the protein-coding region of the gene (see chapter 2, p. 50). The messenger RNA molecule eventually makes its way to a subcellular particle or ribosome in the cytoplasm. Once there, messenger RNA directs protein production.

The strength of RNA polymerase binding at the promoter controls the amount of messenger RNA produced and hence the amount of protein generated at the ribosome. In this sense, the promoter functions as a volume control knob of sorts.

The operator also binds proteins. Two different types of proteins— activators and repressors—bind to the operator. As the names imply, activators turn the gene on (or activate it) when they bind, and repressors turn the gene off (or repress it) when they bind. In this way, the operator functions as a type of on/off switch for gene expression.

Debinding of activators can also turn genes on and off. When a repressor debinds, the gene is activated. And, when an activator debinds, the gene is repressed. In other words, genes can be triggered by either activator binding or repressor debinding. And gene activity can be halted by repressor binding or activator debinding.

New work demonstrates that the specific means of regulating individual genes adhere to a precise pattern.[22] Instead of arbitrarily being turned on by activator binding or repressor debinding, genes in high demand are turned on primarily by activator binding. Likewise, instead of randomly being turned off by repressor binding or activator debinding, genes in low demand are turned off mainly by repressor binding.

This pattern of gene regulation keeps errors to a minimum. When unoccupied, undesired regulatory proteins can capriciously bind to a free operator site. Nonspecific binding of activators and repressors causes genes to be expressed at an inappropriate time, leading to mistakes in gene regulation. When occupied, however, unspecified binding cannot occur, ensuring that genes accurately turn on and off at the proper time. This blueprint for gene regulation is optimal, displaying the type of elegant chemical logic expected in the work of an all-wise Creator.

Glycolysis

One of life's most important metabolic pathways, glycolysis, plays a key role in harvesting energy for use in most cells. This biochemical process releases energy from glucose (a six-carbon sugar) by fracturing it into two molecules of pyruvate (a three-carbon compound).[23] The cell captures a portion of this liberated chemical energy and stores it in the chemical bonds of special molecules for later use.

The glycolytic pathway traps energy from glucose breakdown by using it to form ATP (adenosine triphosphate). This molecule has two high-energy chemical bonds. When broken, the energy stored in the high-energy bonds is made available for the cell to use. The forming and breaking of the high energy bonds is like recharging and discharging a battery. The cell couples the breakdown of ATP's high-energy bonds to energy-requiring biochemical processes and activities. In this way, energetically unfavorable processes in the cell become feasible by using the energy stored in ATP (see figure 7.6).

The use of ATP to power the cell's operations displays elegant chemical logic. Biochemists refer to ATP as the cell's energy currency. Instead of inefficiently coupling the breakdown of a large number of different high-energy compounds to a wide range of energetically unfavorable processes in the cell (like a barter-based economy), the cell uses only a few high-energy compounds (like a currency-based economy) to satisfy the multifarious energy demands of the cell.[24]

From an energetics standpoint, the net output of glycolysis is two molecules of ATP for each molecule of glucose broken apart. (Two molecules of NADH [nicotinamide adenine dinucleotide] are also generated for each molecule of glucose. NADH, like ATP, is also an energy-currency molecule that mediates the transfer of electrons between biomolecules in the cell.)

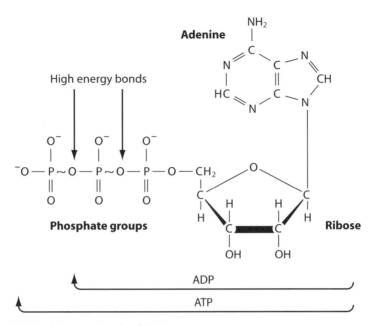

Figure 7.6. High-Energy Bonds of ATP
ATP (adenosine triphosphate) has two high-energy chemical bonds. When broken, the energy stored in the high-energy bonds is made available for the cell to use. When one phosphate bond is broken, the resulting molecule is called ADP (adenosine diphosphate).

Biochemists have long considered glycolytic ATP production to be optimal. The prevailing view has been that the *rate* of ATP production is just right at two ATP molecules/glucose. According to this model, at faster rates the energy yield would fall below two ATP molecules. At slower rates, more ATP molecules/glucose would be generated, but ATP amounts would fall below the minimum *level* needed to satisfy the cell's energy demands.

Recent work indicates that the prevailing view of glycolytic optimization is not entirely correct. The production rate of ATP is not optimal in glycolysis, but the *amount* of ATP produced is. If that's the case, then why isn't the yield of ATP in glycolysis higher? This research demonstrates that any output other than two ATP molecules/glucose negatively impacts the biochemical processes that use ATP.[25]

This molecule sits at the center of a complex web of activities within the cell. For example, in addition to providing energy for cell operations, ATP also regulates metabolic pathways. Production rates that exceed two ATP molecules/glucose would create havoc with other cell processes that use

ATP. Production rates that fall short of two ATP molecules/glucose would fail to yield the maximum amount of energy possible from each glucose molecule. The performance of the glycolytic pathways finds balance between the amount of ATP produced and its global use throughout the cell.

The Just-Right Biochemical Balance

The examples of biochemical optimization described in this chapter are only a small sampling of the optimized designs that make up life's chemistry. Even for those discussed, much more could be written. These few samples were chosen to represent the most important classes of biomolecules (proteins and DNA) and two biochemical processes (gene regulation and glycolysis) central to life.

Artists carefully array the elements in their paintings to achieve a specific effect. Engineers strategically place the parts necessary to optimize their designs. The composition of an artistic piece or of a system operating at optimal capacity doesn't just happen. Piet Mondrian carefully arranged rectangular shapes, lines, and colors in his pieces to achieve the effect he desired. An automotive engineer deliberately crafts and places the parts necessary to make a motor run.

The structures of biomolecules appear carefully constructed as well. Proteins, some of the most important biomolecules, appear to have hand-selected amino acid components and sequences designed to yield structures optimized for stability and production costs. The molecular constituents of DNA also appear to have the just-right chemical properties to produce a stable helical structure capable of storing the information needed for the cell's operation. Only a meticulous Artist could arrange the biochemical elements in such a well-balanced fashion.

Biochemical processes also appear to be intentionally optimized. Gene regulation, one of the most important biochemical activities, displays an exquisite balance in the way that activators and repressors are used to "turn on" and "turn off" genes. And, the production of ATP in one of the cell's most important energy harvesting pathways, glycolysis, appears to be optimized for maximum energy extraction from the fuel molecule glucose in light of the other roles ATP plays in the cell.

The next chapter explores another feature of life's chemistry that points to Divine Design: the information content of biochemical systems.

Islamic scripture in Urdu on a wall (Reproduced by permission from Pankaj & Inky Shah/Gulfimages/Getty Images)

8

THE ARTIST'S HANDWRITING

In the Islamic world, calligraphy is more than just writing with a flourish. It's a form of fine art.[1] In fact, many Muslims hold calligraphers in the highest regard.

Because of Islam's taboo on pictorial representation, calligraphy is both the chief vehicle of artistic expression and an important means of teaching the tenets of the faith. Calligraphy often "illustrates" the Qur'an and adorns the walls and ceilings of mosques. Sometimes calligraphy is purely art with the letters so richly stylized that they are practically illegible. On other occasions calligraphy conveys the Qur'an's declarations. For Muslims, the words of the Qur'an are so treasured that only the best efforts and highest quality are worthy of them.

In the Western world, calligraphy has less to do with art than with elegant penmanship. Instead of appearing in art pieces, so-called modern calligraphy finds its way onto invitations, book covers, and the like. Calligraphy is more than simply expressing sentiments using fancy lettering. This special script communicates a stylized message.

In the West, as in the East, calligraphy associates value with the message being conveyed. The elegant writing that appears on a wedding invitation speaks volumes about the importance of the event. Whether transmitting details for a wedding, or religious ideas, all forms of calligraphy are motivated by a desire to relay highly prized information. Whether an individual reads the Qur'an or receives an invitation, he or she immediately recognizes that someone, somewhere, is responsible for the communication. No matter what form the message takes, the information being conveyed always originates in a mind.

Information can't be separated from the activity of an intelligent agent.[2] And this connection makes this property a potent marker for intelligent design.

Molecular Messages

Over the last forty years, biochemists have learned that the cell's systems are, at their essence, information-based. Proteins and DNA are information-rich molecules. And, like the outpouring from a calligrapher's pen, the structural and functional expressions of molecular-level messages are draped with an artistic elegance and clever logic worthy of an esteemed Writer.

The Protein Pipeline

The description of cellular information begins best with proteins. These molecules form from polypeptides that are made when the cellular machinery links amino acids together in a head-to-tail fashion (see chapter 2, p. 42).

Information theorists maintain that the amino acid sequence of a polypeptide constitutes information.[3] Just as letters form words, amino acids strung together form the "words" of the cell, polypeptides.[4] In language, some letter combinations produce meaningful communication. Others produce gibberish—"words" with no meaning. Amino acid sequences do the same. Some produce functional polypeptides, whereas others produce "junk"—polypeptides that serve no role.[5]

Treating amino acid sequences as information has been a fruitful approach for researchers attempting to characterize the functional utility of different amino acid sequences and understand the origin of proteins.[6] According to information theorist Bernd-Olaf Küppers, the structure of the information found in proteins is identical to the architecture of human language (see table 8.1).[7]

Table 8.1
Cellular Sentences

Language Analog	Proteins	DNA
Character*		Nucleotide
Letter	Amino Acids	Codon
Word	Polypeptides	Gene
Sentence	Protein Complexes	Operon
Paragraph	Biochemical Pathways	Regulon

*Note: Letters are made from characters.

DNA Dishes the Data

Information theorists assert that DNA, like polypeptides, contains instructions. In fact, DNA's chief function is information storage. It houses the directions necessary to make all the polypeptides used by the cell. The polynucleotide chains of DNA form when the cell's machinery links together four different nucleotides: A, G, C, and T (described in chapter 2, p. 48).

The sequence of nucleotides in the DNA strands specifies the sequence of amino acids in polypeptide chains. These coded instructions are called genes. Through the use of genes, DNA stores the messages functionally expressed in the amino acid sequences of polypeptide chains.

According to Küppers, the structure of human language also yields insight into the informative content of DNA. Nucleotides function as characters that build letters and the genes function like words.

On the Information Highway

The "central dogma of molecular biology" describes the "flow" of information inside the cell (see chapter 2, p. 50). This concept describes how information stored in DNA becomes functionally expressed through the amino acid sequences and activity of polypeptide chains as DNA is transcribed to form RNA, and RNA is translated to produce proteins.

Found inside the nucleus of complex cells, DNA compares to the reference section of a library. The books there can be read but cannot be removed. The material stored in these tomes must be copied, or transcribed, before it can be taken from the library. This process is exactly what the cell does.

DNA does not leave the nucleus to direct the synthesis of polypeptide chains. Rather, the cellular machinery copies the gene's contents by assembling another polynucleotide, messenger RNA (mRNA, see chapter 2, p. 50). Transcription occurs as the details in DNA are copied or transcribed into mRNA.

Once assembled, mRNA migrates from the nucleus of the cell into the cytoplasm. At the ribosome, mRNA directs the synthesis of polypeptide chains. The information content of the polynucleotide sequence is translated into the polypeptide amino acid sequence. It's like translating English into Spanish. In other words, the nucleotide language of DNA and RNA is *translated* at the ribosome into the amino acid language of proteins.

The analogical language used by molecular biologists to describe the flow of information in biochemical systems is no accident. According to Küppers, "The analogy between human language and the molecular-genetic language is quite strict. . . . Thus, central problems of the origin of biological information can adequately be illustrated by examples from human language without the sacrifice of exactitude."[8] Biochemical systems are, in fact, information systems. And everyday experience teaches that information only comes from a mind.

Syntax, Semantics, and Pragmatics

The relationship between human and biochemical languages extends beyond the comparisons found in table 8.1. Information theorists recognize multiple dimensions to human information: syntactics, semantics, and pragmatics.[9] And, these properties also apply to biochemical information.

The syntactic component of information refers merely to the ordering of symbols or letters in human language—or for biochemical information, the sequence of nucleotides and amino acids. It has nothing to do with whether the arrangement has meaning. In terms of human language, the letter combinations "cat" and "tca" are equivalent in the syntactic dimension.

The semantic level of information ascribes meaning to the order of symbols, letters, and so forth. This dimension arises because some sequences have meaning (cat) and others don't (tca). The pragmatic level of information recognizes that the meaning of the arrangement depends upon agreement between two parties: the sender and the recipient. Their agreement ascribes meaning to some sequences and not to others. It provides the basis for the recipient of information to respond or take action based on the sender's direction. According to Küppers,

> The identification of a character as a "symbol" presupposes certain prior knowledge . . . in the form of an agreement between sender and recipient. Moreover, semantic information is unthinkable without pragmatic information, because the recognition of semantics *as* semantics must cause some kind of reaction from the recipient.[10]

Biochemical information displays all three dimensions of human communication. The nucleotide sequences of DNA and RNA and the amino acid order of proteins can be described syntactically. But these sequences also have semantic and pragmatic dimensions.

The nucleotide sequences of DNA ultimately specify the amino acid sequences of polypeptides. Amino acid order dictates the three-

---

Biochemical Linguistics

Recent work by a team of chemical engineers and biochemists powerfully highlights the language content and structure of biochemical information.[11] These researchers sought an approach to rationally design novel nonnatural peptide antibiotics.

In the last decade or so, microbiologists and biochemists have discovered that a number of organisms possess relatively small peptides in their skin, saliva, sweat, and so forth. These peptides display antimicrobial activity and appear to be an important part of the immune system.[12] The new antibiotics attract interest because they appear to be active against bacteria that are resistant to the most potent medicines available.

Researchers noticed that these antimicrobial peptides are made from sequence combinations similar to phrases used in language. Based on this insight, the team treated the amino acid sequences of the antimicrobial peptides from a wide range of organisms as a formal language and developed a set of grammatical rules that describe possible arrangements of amino acids in the peptides—just like human grammar permits certain sequences of words and disallows others.

This biochemical grammar consisted of 684 rules. Using these guidelines, the scientists came up with forty-two novel antimicrobial peptides. They displayed antimicrobial activity comparable to the peptides found in nature. Interestingly, the scientists compared their nonnatural peptides with peptides that had the same amino acid compositions but had random sequences. These random peptides lacked activity, just as random use of words in a sentence lacks meaning. Biochemical information appears to be organized in the form of a molecular grammar that bears strong similarity to human languages.

dimensional structure of the polypeptide chain that in turn determines the polypeptide function. Some potential amino acid sequences yield nonfunctional polypeptides, whereas others specify peptides with biologically relevant function. In other words, some amino acid sequences (and hence nucleotide sequences) have meaning to the cell and others do not. And, those meaningful sequences carry out specific activities within the cell.

The semantic content of nucleotide sequences finds pragmatic expression in the activity of polypeptides. In this way, the semantic and pragmatic aspects of biochemical information are inextricably intertwined.

A Sweet Message

While DNA and proteins are typically considered the only information-containing molecules of biochemical systems, recent studies indicate that oligosaccharides house information as well. Oligosaccharides are carbohydrates—a class of biomolecules that consists of compounds composed of carbon, hydrogen, and oxygen in the specific ratio of 1:2:1, respectively.[13]

Carbohydrates typically play important roles in the cell—a few of which are energy storage, the formation of cell structures, mediation of cell-to-cell contact, and regulation of development. They are built from small molecules called sugars. Monosaccharides (mono = one) are carbohydrates composed of a single sugar residue. Glucose and fructose are two monosaccharides familiar to diet-conscious people.

Disaccharides (di = two) consist of two sugars linked together. A familiar example is sucrose, table sugar. It consists of the sugars glucose and fructose combined.

Polysaccharides (poly = many) form when numerous sugars connect. Starch and cellulose are common examples. Both consist of glucose linked into long chains. The difference between starch and cellulose stems from the nature of the linkage between the individual glucose molecules. (For examples of monosaccharides and disaccharides, see figure 8.1.)

Oligosaccharides (oligo = few) form when a handful of sugar molecules are linked together. Frequently, oligosaccharides are attached to proteins associated with the exterior surface of cell membranes and proteins secreted by the cell (see chapter 2, pp. 40 and 45).[14] These oligosaccharides play a structural role, for example, mediating cell-to-cell contact.

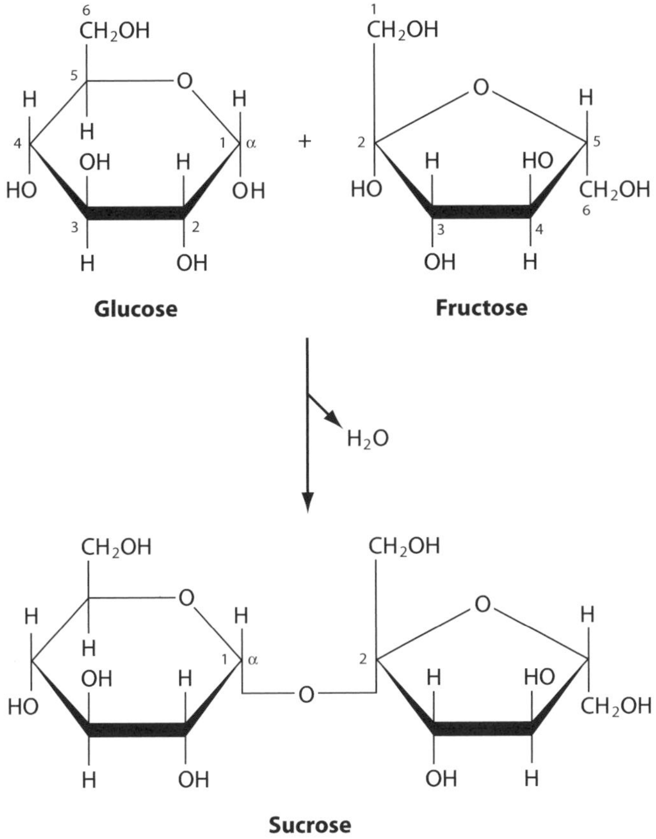

Figure 8.1. Carbohydrate Structures
Glucose and fructose are examples of monosaccharides. Disaccharides consist of two sugars linked together. In this example, sucrose (table sugar) consists of the sugars glucose and fructose linked together.

The structural complexity of oligosaccharides gives them the capacity to house much more information per unit length than DNA, RNA, and proteins. The only basis of information for DNA, RNA, and proteins is the sequence of nucleotides and amino acids. For oligosaccharides, information is not limited just to the sugar sequences. It can also be contained in the variety of chemical substituents that bind to the sugars, the multiple types of bonds that form between sugar subunits, and the branching that occurs along the oligosaccharide chain.[15] For example, the two amino acids glycine and alanine can be linked in two ways: alanine-glycine or glycine-alanine.

Galactose and glucose can be joined together in thirty-six different ways. Each variation represents a unique piece of information.

Oligosaccharides harbor two modes of information: stable and transient.[16] The oligosaccharides carrying stable information remain unaltered after being assembled by the cell's chemical systems. Typically associated with the cell surface, these oligosaccharides are used as a recognition system when the cell interacts with materials in the environment or with other cells.

Those oligosaccharides with transient information are modified by the cell's chemical machinery during the course of biological activity. The cell uses the alterations to report on the status of the protein that binds the oligosaccharide moiety. For example, transient information plays a central role in quality control operations in the endoplasmic reticulum during the process of protein secretion. In this instance, the structure of the oligosaccharides lets the cell's machinery know if the protein chain has been properly folded. (Chapter 10, p. 198 details this process.)

Information-rich biomolecules (proteins, DNA, RNA, and oligosaccharides) and the information-based biochemical systems—central to life's most fundamental activities—strongly indicate that a Divine hand penned life at its most basic level.

Structural Calligraphy

The case for biochemical intelligent design doesn't rest on the mere presence of information in biochemical systems. An incredible chemical "wisdom" displayed in the way the cell's information is crafted shows that it must have been deliberately written.

Gene Organization

The architectural and functional arrangement of genes illustrates the elegant structural properties of biochemical information. A discussion of three textbook examples—operons, alternate splicing, and overlapping genes—highlight this exceptional quality of the cell's genetic information.

Operons. Bacteria's genes are not randomly distributed throughout their genomes. Instead, they are often organized into structural units called operons. Here, the genes are arranged in a contiguous sequence with the end of the first gene juxtaposed to the beginning of the second gene, and so on. These genes code for proteins that work together to achieve a specific metabolic goal.

A classic example of an operon is the *lac* operon found in the bacterium *Eschericia coli* (*E. coli*). This operon was one of the first discovered and characterized (see figure 8.2). Other examples are discussed in most molecular biology textbooks.[17]

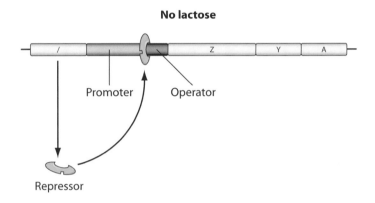

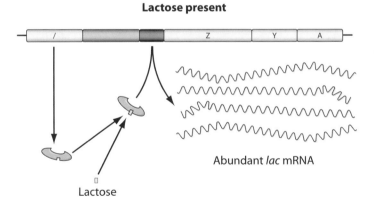

Figure 8.2. The *Lac* Operon
The *lac* operon codes for proteins that help the bacterium *E. coli* metabolize lactose. When lactose is not present, the *lac* repressor protein binds to the operator and the *lac* operon genes are not expressed. When lactose is present, the *lac* operon proteins are produced after the repressor disassociates from the operator.

The *lac* operon codes for proteins that help the cell metabolize lactose. This disaccharide (see p. 146) consists of two sugars—galactose and glucose. Three structural genes and one regulatory gene make up the *lac* operon. One of the structural genes contains the instructions to make the protein β-galactosidase. This protein cleaves lactose into its two constitutive sugars. Another structural gene specifies lactose permease. It helps usher lactose into the cell from the exterior environment. A third structural gene encodes a protein of unknown function, galactoside transacetylase.

Individual gene structure is complex, broadly consisting of two regions: protein coding and regulatory (see figure 7.5, p. 135). The protein-coding region contains information that the cell's biochemical machinery needs to produce the polypeptide chain. The regulatory region controls the expression of the gene and, hence, the polypeptide chain's production.

Within the regulatory region of a gene are two key sites: the promoter and operator. The promoter functions as the binding site for RNA polymerase. This protein complex produces a messenger RNA molecule by reading the information found in the gene. The operator also binds proteins. Two different types of proteins, activators and repressors, bind to the operator. As the names imply, activators turn the gene on when they bind, and repressors turn the gene off.

An operon's regulatory region precedes the structural genes. The operator and promoter of the *lac* operon control the expression of all three structural genes (β-galactosidase, lactose permease, galactoside transacetylase). This operon also contains a regulatory gene (as opposed to the regulatory *region*). It codes for a protein that binds to the *lac* operon operator. The protein is a repressor, and when it binds to the operator it prevents the expression of the *lac* operon structural genes.

This arrangement displays appealing and powerful biochemical logic. Normally, the *lac* repressor protein is bound to the operator and the *lac* operon genes are not expressed. The cell usually doesn't need the *lac* operon proteins, because lactose is not a common nutrient for *E. coli*.

Repression of the *lac* operon benefits the cell because it prevents the wasteful production of unnecessary proteins. Grouping the *lac* operon genes together in a contiguous sequence allows the cell to regulate gene expression with a single repressor.

But, when lactose is present, *lac* operon proteins are produced. The expression of these genes is initiated when this sugar binds to the *lac* repressor causing this protein to dissociate from the operator. Debinding of the *lac* repressor allows RNA polymerase access to the promoter, which consequently leads to the production of the proteins needed to metabolize lactose through the activity of a single repressor.

When RNA polymerase copies operon genes, including those of the *lac* operon, it produces what biochemists call a polycistronic mRNA. (The term *cistron* refers to a region of the DNA that encodes a single polypeptide chain.) Monocistronic (mono = one) mRNA only contains enough information to direct the production of a single polypeptide at the ribosome. Polycistronic (poly = many) mRNA, on the other hand, contains information the ribosome needs to simultaneously produce several polypeptides.

The polycistronic mRNA copied from the *lac* operon simultaneously directs the manufacture of the three proteins needed to metabolize lactose, when lactose is present. This system ensures that *all* the proteins necessary to handle this sugar are produced at appropriate levels and in a timely fashion. Organizing and expressing biochemical information using operons and polycistronic mRNA manifest an impeccable biochemical rationale.

Bumping heads. Until recently, biochemists didn't think that genes found in eukaryotic genomes displayed any type of large-scale structural organization. According to this traditional view, eukaryotic genes are scattered throughout the genome, including those genes that specify the proteins that work together to accomplish a specific biochemical task. Recent work, however, suggests that such random positioning is not the case. Many genes in mammalian genomes are arranged in a head-to-head fashion with the starting points of the genes juxtaposed.[18]

For example, 1,262 pairs of head-to-head genes have been detected in the human genome. Approximately 63 percent of the gene pairs code for proteins that perform related functions and are expressed together. Like the operons in prokaryotes, the head-to-head pairing of genes represents an ordering of the biochemical information in eukaryotic genomes that appears to be undergirded by an elegant molecular logic. According to the researchers who made this discovery, this arrangement "provides an exquisite mechanism of transcriptional regulation based on gene organization."[19]

Alternate splicing. The DNA sequences that make up genes in eukaryotes consist of stretches of nucleotides that specify the amino acid sequence of polypeptide chains (exons), interrupted by nucleotide sequences that don't code for anything (introns). After the gene is copied into an mRNA molecule, the intron sequences are excised and the exons spliced together by a protein-RNA complex known as a spliceosome[20] (see figure 5.2, p. 103, for the splicing process, though spliceosome is not shown).

Splicing is an extremely precise process. Mistakes in splicing are responsible for some human diseases. Medical disorders result because splicing errors fatally distort or destroy information—temporarily stored in mRNA—necessary to assemble polypeptide chains at ribosomes. And improperly produced polypeptides cannot carry out their functional role in the cell. In his textbook *Essentials of Molecular Biology*, George Malacinski points out why proper polypeptide production is critical: "A cell cannot, of course, afford to miss any of the splice junctions by even a single nucleotide, because this could result in an interruption of the correct reading frame, leading to a truncated protein."[21]

Remarkably, in light of this restriction, the spliceosome joins together the same mRNA in different ways to produce a range of functional proteins. This alternate splicing occurs because not all splice sites are necessarily used by the spliceosome.[22] Alternate splicing allows the cell to produce several different proteins from the same mRNA and ultimately from the same gene.

Proteins involved in the splicing process help determine the splicing pattern of mRNA. For example, some proteins bind to splice sites preventing access by the spliceosome. By varying the binding pattern of these proteins, a variety of mRNAs can be produced. The cell also achieves alternate splicing through the use of different promoters associated with the same gene (see chapter 7, p. 135). Each promoter produces an mRNA spliced differently by the spliceosome complex.

Alternate splicing can also be mediated by varying the length of the mRNA's poly(A) tail. Apparently the poly(A) tail helps direct the spliceosome to specific splice junctions along the mRNA strand.

Structuring genes to have noncoding regions (introns) interspersed between coding regions (exons) is an elegant strategy that allows a single gene to simultaneously house the information to produce a range of proteins. Still, given how exacting the splicing process must be and how sensitive it is to errors, that alternate splicing occurs at all is astounding. For the cell to successfully carry out alternate splicing, the nucleotide sequences and the placement of exons have to be carefully orchestrated. And to do that seemingly requires a Divine hand to guide the process. (See Alternate Splicing, p. 153.)

Overlapping genes. In the late 1970s, biochemists studying the bacteriophage *φX174* (a virus that infects the bacterium *E. coli*) made a startling discovery: the genome of this bacteriophage directs the production of more proteins than it should based on the size of its DNA. Researchers resolved this paradox when they demonstrated that some of the $\varphi X174$ genes overlap.[23]

Alternate Splicing: The Word Game

Let's play a game to illustrate how much of a mental challenge it is to properly place splice sites within a gene so genetic information can simultaneously specify several different proteins.

The first step: Identify a word that contains other words, for example, *splendid*. The words *spend*, *lend*, *end*, *lid*, and *did* can be extracted by excising letters and splicing the remaining ones together. The only restriction is that the sequencing of letters can't be altered to extract words from the root word. For example, the words *den* and *slip* cannot be derived from *splendid* because the order of the letters has to be changed to come up with them.

The next step: Come up with arbitrary letter combinations that can be added to the base word so it and other derived words can be uniquely extracted by excising strings of letters and splicing the remaining ones together. For example, **x**'s can be strategically placed to make it possible to yield *splendid* and set the stage to extract *spend*, *lend*, *end*, *lid*, and *did* by alternate splicing:

x*sp*x*l*x*en*x*d*x*id*x (x *sp* x *l* x *en* x *d* x *id* x)

Splendid can be extracted by excising all the **x**'s and splicing together the remaining letters. The **x**'s could have been placed anywhere and the word *splendid* extracted. The placement of **x**'s used above required some planning and forethought, to make it possible to extract the derived words *spend*, *lend*, *end*, *lid,* and *did*.

Now for the part of the game that requires some mental effort. Additional letters need to be inserted into x*sp*x*l*x*en*x*d*x*id*x to make it possible to uniquely extract the derived words. To illustrate, start with *did*.

Then **z**'s could be added as follows:

zx*sp*x*l*x*en*x**z***d***z**x**z**x*id***z**x**z** (**z**x*sp*x*l*x*en*x**z** *d* **z**x**z** *id* **z**x**z**)

By removing any letters bracketed by **z**'s, *did* can be extracted. Yet, a problem arises. This configuration no longer makes it possible to extract *splendid* using the original rule of extracting **x**'s and splicing together the remaining letters. Using that rule leads to:

z x *sp* x *l* x *en* x **z***d***z** x **z***id***z** x **z**

zsplenzdzzidzz

This problem can be rectified by replacing the original rule so that instead of an **x** being excised an **xz** is removed:

xzxz_sp_**xz**_l_**xz**_en_**xz**_d_**xzxz**_id_**xzxz**

xz xz _sp_ **xz** _l_ **xz** _en_ **xz** _d_ **xz xz** _id_ **xz xz**

splendid

This creates a new problem, however. Removing letters bracketed by **z** no longer yields _did_. Instead it generates:

xzxz_sp_**xz**_l_**xz**_en_**xz**_d_**xzxz**_id_**xzxz**

xspxenxx

These problems could be avoided, and the game greatly simplified, by adjusting the rules of the game to allow the participants to specify as many excision and splicing steps as they want in order to extract the desired word. Returning to **z**x_sp_x_l_x_en_**xz**_d_**zxz**_id_**zxz**—if the splicing instructions are to remove both **x**'s and **z**'s, then _splendid_ can be generated while retaining the rule that allows _did_ to be recovered:

z x _sp_ **x** _l_ **x** _en_ **x z** _d_ **z x z** _id_ **z x z**

splendid

zx_sp_x_l_x_en_**xz** _d_ **zxz** _id_ **zxz**

did

Now you can determine what instructions allow other words to be extracted through the excision and splicing process.

This conclusion was quite unsettling. Biochemists considered the relationship "one gene, one protein" to be absolute and a cornerstone of molecular biology. (One reason is discussed below.)[24] Since the work on the bacteriophage _φX174_ genome, biochemists have identified overlapping genes in other viruses as well as in bacteria, insects, fish, and mammals.[25]

It's possible for genes to overlap within the same DNA sequence because the cell's biochemical machinery makes use of reading frames to access the information in DNA. And, each overlapping gene is read using a different reading frame.[26]

The cell's machinery depends upon these reading frames to access information because of the mismatch in the number of nucleotides (four) used by DNA to specify the number of amino acids (twenty) needed to construct proteins. Clearly, there cannot be a 1:1 correspondence between nucleotides in DNA and amino acids in proteins. The cell's biochemical information system overcomes this problem by using short sequence combinations of three nucleotides (called coding triplets or codons) to signify each amino acid.

There are sixty-four possible nucleotide triplets. The cell employs sixty-one codons to specify the twenty amino acids used by the cell to synthesize proteins. Some amino acids are signified by a single codon. Others are connoted by several different codons. The relationship between codons and amino acids is called the genetic code. (Chapter 9 discusses the genetic code and its use in the biochemical intelligent design analogy.)

For the cell's machinery to produce proteins, the information stored in DNA must be copied. The transcribed information resides in molecules of messenger RNA (mRNA). Once assembled in RNA, the information makes its way to the ribosome where it directs the construction of polypeptides (see chapter 2, p. 50). The short model mRNA nucleotide sequence illustrates how the cell uses codons to specify amino acids in polypeptides.

Position: 1 2 3
UCU   CCU GCA AUU CGU AU

If the cell's biochemical apparatus uses a reading frame that starts at the first position (U), the resulting peptide will have the sequence: serine-proline-alanine-isoleucine-arginine because UCU specifies serine, and so on (see table 9.1, p. 172). When the reading frame begins at the second position (C) in the nucleotide sequence, an entirely different peptide is generated with the sequence: leucine-leucine-glutamine-phenylalanine-valine. Shifting the reading frame to the third nucleotide position (U) yields a peptide with the sequence: serine-cysteine-asparagine-serine-tyrosine. (As illustrated in this example, there are only three possible reading frames for a nucleotide sequence.) Simply by shifting the reading frame by one or two nucleotides, a single sequence can encode three very different peptides.

This example makes it possible to see how a single nucleotide sequence could harbor overlapping genes. By using alternate reading frames shifted by one or two nucleotides, the cell's machinery can produce polypeptide chains with radically different amino acid sequences.

In principle, each DNA sequence possesses three reading frames. In most cases only one is used and the nonoverlapping "one gene, one protein" relationship holds. But in some cases two reading frames are used, and two genes overlap onto the same nucleotide sequence.

Because of the genetic code's redundancy, some of the information content of DNA is not used when genes don't overlap. Overlapping genes represent the full use of the information content of DNA.[27] It's no accident, then, that overlapping genes are found in some of the smallest, most compact genomes in nature (viruses and parasitic bacteria like *Mycoplasma genitalium*). Recently researchers discovered evidence that overlapping genes are also abundant in more complex eukaryotic organisms.[28]

The existence of any overlapping genes in nature is remarkable. Typically, when a gene's reading frame shifts as a result of a mutation, it almost always leads to catastrophic results. These so-called frameshift mutations result when nucleotides are accidentally inserted or deleted from a gene. And, as evident in the previous example with the model nucleotide sequence, a frame shift produces a protein with a radically different amino acid sequence as the reading frame moves from the first position to the second or third position.

The mutant protein is almost always nonfunctional junk. Frameshift mutations stand in contrast with substitution mutations, which involve the replacement of one nucleotide for another.

Substitution mutations merely replace one amino acid in the polypeptide chain for another. All other amino acids remain unchanged. Substitution mutations can be catastrophic, but more often than not these types of errors have limited, if any, effect on protein function because the gene's reading frame hasn't changed. (Substitution mutations are discussed in greater detail in chapter 9.)

The existence of overlapping genes points to the intentional activity of a Creator. Another word game helps illustrate why (see "Overlapping Sentence Game," p. 157).[29]

Biochemists have also identified another type of overlapping gene. Instead of the overlap taking place on the same DNA strand, it occurs on opposite strands.[30] To appreciate how remarkable this discovery is, it's

Overlapping Sentence Game

Try coming up with a sentence (or even a word for that matter) that produces another meaningful sentence if the sentence's reading frame shifts by one or two letters. Consider the sentence:

The boy went to the store.

Shift the reading frame one letter:

T heb oyw entt ot hes tore.

A solution to this puzzle is only possible if a judicious, if not ingenious, choice of words is used to construct the sentence. Even so, coming up with an example that works seems almost impossible. Likewise, for genes to overlap on the same nucleotide sequence, particularly in light of the damaging effects of frameshift mutations, a Divine Genius appears necessary.

necessary to understand how genes are typically distributed between the polynucleotide chains of the DNA double helix.

Usually, only one DNA strand harbors a gene. Biochemists call this strand the sense strand. The other strand, aligned opposite the gene, simply serves as a template for DNA replication (see chapter 11, p. 217). This strand is referred to as the nonsense or antisense strand.

A special relationship exists between the nucleotide sequences of the two DNA strands and consequently between the sense and antisense sequences associated with genes. When the DNA strands align, the adenine (A) side chains of one strand always pair with thymine (T) side chains from the other strand. Likewise, guanine (G) always pairs with cytosine (C). Biochemists refer to these relationships as base-pairing rules (see figure 2.7, p. 49).

As a consequence, if biochemists know the sequence of one DNA strand, they can readily determine the sequence of the other strand. The DNA sequences of the two strands are complementary.

Base-pairing rules restrict the nucleotide sequence of the antisense strand. The nucleotide sequence of the sense strand dictates the nucleotide sequence of the antisense strand. Though the sense strand codes for a functional polypeptide, it's highly unlikely that the nucleotide sequence of the antisense strand does. This nucleotide sequence, in principle, specifies an amino acid sequence. However, it's doubtful that the resulting polypeptide could ever adopt a useful configuration because of the strict relationship between a protein's amino acid sequence and its function.

While the purpose of the sense strand's nucleotide sequence is to house the information necessary to produce a functional protein (with full attention given to the relationship between amino acid sequence and function), the purpose of the antisense strand is to serve merely as a placeholder and a template for the sense strand.

In light of this constraint, it's amazing to think that both sense and antisense sequences could simultaneously specify functional proteins under any circumstance. The sequence of the sense strand would have to be carefully written so the complementary sequence of the antisense strand could simultaneously serve as a template for the sense strand and encode an amino acid sequence that could adopt a three-dimensional configuration useful for some cell function. The care, thought, and preplanning required for genes to overlap on opposite DNA strands point to the work of an awe-inspiring biochemical Calligrapher.

DNA Is a Parity Code

Biochemists have long wondered why the nucleobases adenine (A), guanine (G), thymine/uracil (T/U), and cytosine (C) were chosen to be part of DNA's and RNA's structural makeup. At least sixteen other nucleobases could have been selected. For example, experiments designed to simulate the conditions of prebiotic Earth have produced diaminopurine, xanthine, hypoxanthine, and diaminopyrimidine in addition to A, G, T/U, and C.[31] From an evolutionary perspective, any of them could have found their way into DNA's structure.

Recent work by a chemist from Trinity University (Dublin, Ireland) shines new light on this question.[32] When adenine, guanine, thymine, and cytosine are incorporated into DNA, they impart the double helix with a unique structural property that causes the information to behave like a parity code. Computer scientists and engineers use parity codes to minimize errors in the transfer of information (see "Parity Codes," p. 159). None of the other nucleobases give DNA this special quality—only the specific combination of A, G, T, and C.

Every time the cell's machinery transcribes a gene or replicates the DNA molecule (see chapter 11, p. 217), information is transmitted. Because transmission errors have disastrous consequences, error minimization (and

Parity Codes

What is a parity code and how does it detect errors that arise during information transfer? To answer these questions, some appreciation for the way scientists and engineers encode information is essential.

Data commonly consists of numbers, alphabet letters, and special symbols. For computers and digital-data communication hardware to store, read, process, and transmit data, the characters must be represented as binary numbers. Only two digits exist in binary number systems, "1" and "0". (The decimal system uses ten digits—"0 through 9"—to represent quantities.) Binary number systems ideally fit computers and digital-data communication hardware because an electrical pulse or signal corresponds to a 1, and the absence of any signal equates to 0.

Combinations of on-off pulses can be used to represent decimals, letters, and special characters. Information technologists refer to a single on-off pulse as a binary digit or bit. Eight bits are a byte.

Computers usually use either a 7-bit or 8-bit code to represent characters.[33] These 7- or 8-bit sequences are called data units. To detect errors that arise during transmission an additional bit, called a parity bit, is added to the data units.

The value of the parity bit is assigned either a 1 or a 0 depending on if the error-detection scheme is an even or odd parity code. If even, then the value of the parity bit is chosen so the sum of the "on" (1) bits equals an even number. If an odd parity code is employed then the value of the parity bit is selected so that the sum of the "on" bits equals an odd number (see table 8.2).

Errors can occur during data transmission if a 1 is received as a 0, or vice versa. Mistakes can also occur if a bit is lost or dropped. When either problem happens, the sum of "on" bits yields an odd number for an even parity code, and an even number for an odd parity code. When an unexpected sum of "on" bits is tabulated, the transmission's recipient immediately knows an error has occurred.

Table 8.2
Parity Bit Assignment

8 Bit Data Unit	Parity Bit	
	Even	Odd
00000000	000000000	100000000
10100001	110100001	010100001
11010001	011010001	111010001
11111111	011111111	111111111

consequently DNA's parity code) is a critical structure in the cell's information systems.

When the two DNA strands align, the adenine side chains of one strand always pair with thymine side chains from the other strand. Likewise, guanine always pairs with cytosine. When these side chains pair, they form crossbridges between the two DNA strands (see figure 2.7, p. 49). The lengths of the A-to-T and G-to-C crossbridges are nearly identical.

Adenine and guanine are both composed of two rings and thymine and cytosine are composed of one. Each crossbridge consists of three rings.

When A pairs with T, two hydrogen bonds mediate their interaction. Three hydrogen bonds accommodate the interaction between G and C. The specificity of the hydrogen-bonding interactions accounts for the A-to-T and G-to-C base-pairing rules (see figure 8.3).

As noted previously, these base-pairing rules establish the complementary relationship between the nucleotide sequences of the two DNA strands. These complementary sequences play an important role in the transmission of information during DNA replication (see chapter 11, p. 217). Likewise, the base-pairing rules play a critical role when the cell's machinery copies a gene. The nucleotide sequence of the resulting mRNA is complementary to the DNA sequence that harbors the gene.

From time to time base-pairing mistakes can happen. When A-to-T and G-to-C don't properly pair, the wrong information is transmitted. Quality control systems in the cell check for errors that might occur during DNA replication and transcription (see chapter 10).

In addition to these quality control systems, another error-detection system resides within the informational structure of DNA in the form of a parity code.

Each hydrogen bond that links together A-to-T and G-to-C consists of donor chemical groups and acceptor groups. In the DNA informational system, if hydrogen bonds are considered analogous to an electrical pulse in binary number systems, then donor chemical groups can be assigned a 1 and acceptor groups a 0. For example, G would be assigned the bits 011 and C, 100. The parity bits correspond to the ring structure of the nucleobase.

If the nucleobase consists of a single ring, the parity bit is assigned a 1. When the nucleobase possesses two rings, the parity bit assumes a value of 0. The binary representation for G becomes 011, 0 and for C it's 100, 1. Note that the binary depiction for these nucleobases is an even parity code. This arrangement makes it easy to detect transmission errors. Relating the

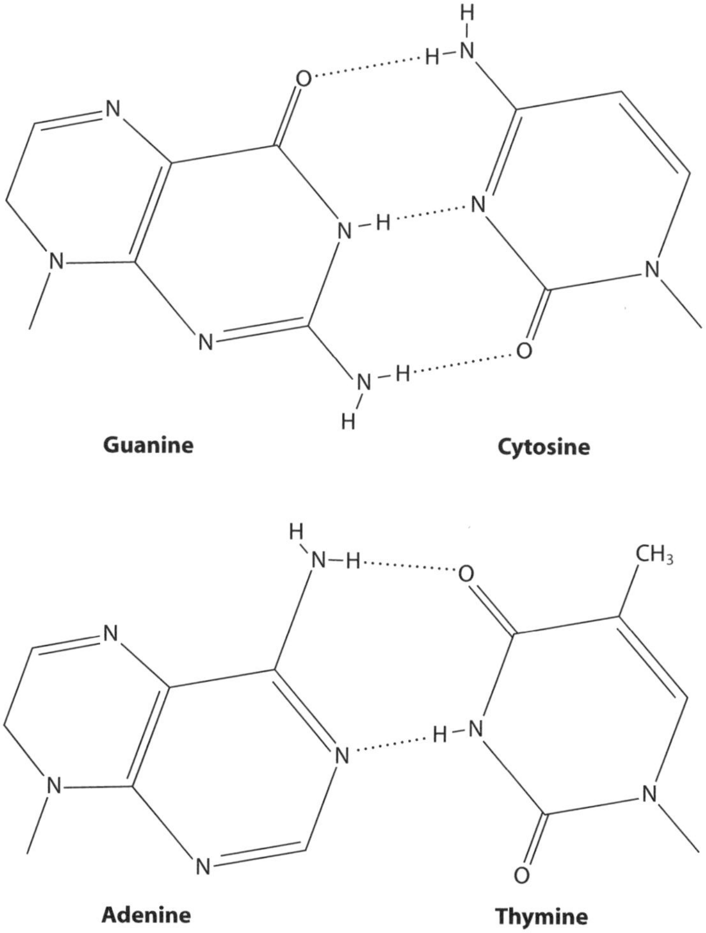

Guanine   **Cytosine**

Adenine   **Thymine**

Figure 8.3. Base-Pairing Rules and the Even Parity Code of DNA
When the two DNA strands align, the Guanine (G) side chains of one strand always pair with Cytosine (C) side chains from the other strand. Likewise, the Adenine (A) side chains from one DNA strand always pair with Thymine (T) side chains from the other strand. When G pairs with C, three hydrogen bonds (shown as dashed lines) mediate the interaction between these two nucleobases. Two hydrogen bonds accommodate the interaction between A and T.

ring structure to the hydrogen bonding patterns between the nucleobases results in an optimal genetic alphabet.

This extraordinary structural property of DNA suggests that a Mind carefully developed the cell's information systems. The even parity code found in DNA is identical to those used in computer hardware and software systems to check for errors when data is transmitted. It's as if an Intelligent Agent hand-selected the nucleobases A, G, T/U, and C to optimize DNA's structure so errors can be readily detected and minimized when any information is transmitted.

Biochemical information also displays other astounding structural characteristics that point to the calligraphy of a Divine Writer. For example, a cell's information systems are organized around a code. In fact, the so-called genetic code defines the cell's information at its most fundamental level. Recently, biochemists have discovered another code—the histone code—at work within the genomes of eukaryotic organisms.

The genetic and histone codes are the focus of the next chapter. But before they are discussed, some provocative advances in nanotechnology—advances inspired by biochemical information systems—deserve some attention.

On the Technology Frontier

Some scholars maintain that biochemical information is not, strictly speaking, information. Instead, they insist that treating the nucleotide sequence of DNA and the amino acid sequence of proteins as information is simply a useful analogy. Rhetorician David Depew questions if evolutionary biologists Richard Dawkins and Daniel Dennet

> would be happy with [the] assumption that genes "contain" information in the same sense that modern computers do, or with the implication that organisms are merely their readouts? This analogy guided the formation of molecular biology. Like many analogies, it generated some good science, and more recently, a biotechnological revolution. But in singling out genes for causal efficacy at the expense of other epigenetic processes it created a scientific myth.[34]

According to these skeptics, application of information theory to problems in molecular biology is predicated on an analogy (albeit a useful one) between biochemical systems, human language, and information schemes. If taken too far, however, this analogy breaks down to the detriment of science and, in this case, the biochemical intelligent design analogy.

But exciting new nano- and biotechnologies—such as DNA computing, DNA encryption, and DNA bar coding—provide justification for the biochemical intelligence argument. These emerging technologies reinforce the notion that biochemical information is indeed information. Their applications make use of data housed in DNA in much the same way that humans would handle information.

DNA Computing

At a fundamental level, all computer operations are based on so-called Turing machines, named for British mathematician Alan Turing. These machines are not real but conceptual in nature. They consist of three components: input, output, and finite control. The input is a stream of data read and transformed by the finite control according to a specific set of rules. A new stream of data results from this transformation, the output.

Input and output data streams consist of sequences of characters called strings. The finite control operates one by one on each character of the input string to generate the output string. These transformations are relatively simple in nature. Complex computations and operations can be affected by linking together several Turing machines, so the output string of one Turing machine becomes the input string of another.

DNA computing had its birth when computer scientist Leonard Adleman recognized that the proteins responsible for DNA replication, repair, and transcription operated as Turing machines.[35] This process treats the nucleotide sequences of DNA as input and output strings. The different chemical, biochemical, and physical processes used to manipulate DNA in the laboratory correspond to the finite control and are used to transform the input DNA sequences into output sequences.[36] Complex operations can be accomplished by linking together simple laboratory operations performed on DNA with the output of one laboratory operation serving as input for the next.

Some operations that can be performed on DNA "strings" include: separating and fusing strands of the DNA double helix; lengthening and shortening individual DNA strands; cutting and linking together DNA molecules; and modifying, multiplying, and reading the DNA nucleotide sequence.[37]

Researchers recognize several advantages to DNA computers.[38] One is the ability to perform a massive number of operations at the same time (in parallel) as opposed to one at a time (serially) which is typically much slower. Second, DNA has the capacity to store an enormous quantity of information. Theoretically one gram of DNA can house as much information as nearly one trillion CDs. And DNA computers operate, in principle, near theoretical capacities with regard to energy efficiency.

The current limitations of DNA computers stem from the chemical nature of the process, namely the inherent incompleteness of chemical reactions and the error prone nature of the biomolecules that operate on DNA.[39] (As discussed in chapter 10, biochemical processes inside test tubes are error prone. Inside the cell, however, "quality control" pathways correct most of these errors when they occur.) Much of the current research effort in DNA computing focuses on overcoming its limitations.[40]

In spite of these difficulties, researchers have already successfully demonstrated a number of applications for DNA computing. This list includes solving directed Hamiltonian-path problems and the knight problem (for a 3 x 3 chessboard).[41] DNA computing has also been used to perform addition (see "Turing Machines and the Watchmaker Analogy" below).[42]

These efforts drive home the point that biochemical systems contain information. It's mind-boggling to think that the information-based activities of biochemical systems, which routinely take place in the cell, can be used to construct computers in a laboratory setting. The direct correspondence between input and output strings with DNA sequences makes

---

Turing Machines and the Watchmaker Analogy

In 1994 Leonard Adleman launched DNA computing when he recognized that the cellular processes operating on DNA functioned as Turing machines.[43] These machines exist only as conceptual entities.

In the mid-1930s, Alan Turing, one of the founders of modern computer science, recognized that the key to solving complex problems computationally was to treat them as a series of simple operations.[44] Each operation has an input, a string of numbers or characters, operated on by a finite control that alters the input to produce an output string. The ensemble is referred to as a Turing machine. The output of the first operation becomes the input of the second operation and so on.

The key point is that Turing machines exist only in human minds, yet inside the cell several actual Turing machines operate on DNA. This reality provides a double analogy for intelligent design. Not only do biochemical Turing machines highlight the informational aspects of DNA, but they also serve as a remarkably profound type of Watchmaker analogy (see chapter 4, p. 85)—except, the analogy is between the conceptual Turing machines in the human mind and the concrete biochemical Turing machines inside the cell.

it clear that DNA is at its essence *information*, contrary to what skeptics say. Molecular-level computers have long been the dream of scientists and engineers because this technology promises large storage capacity, small size, and high speed. By making use of the cell's information systems to build DNA computers, this dream is becoming a reality.

DNA Encryption

During World War II, German spies hid messages as shrunken microdots in what appeared to be harmless letters. They used a technique called steganography—the practice of hiding a message within a message.

Taking their cue, researchers recently invented DNA steganography, in which encrypted messages are embedded within DNA sequences.[45] The genetic letters (nucleotides) of DNA formulate a message in much the same way the letters of the German alphabet did on a shrunken microdot.

The complex nature of DNA sequences prevents anyone who intercepts the DNA encryption from recognizing that a message is present, let alone being able to decode it. To make it possible for the recipient to identify and extract the message, the sender bookends it with specific DNA markers. These marker sequences allow the recipient to "fish out" the encryption and read the message using laboratory techniques. As with DNA computing, DNA steganography highlights the notion that DNA is indeed an information-rich molecule.

DNA Bar Codes

Supermarkets and department stores often use bar codes to facilitate the checkout process. Bar codes present information a computer can scan to rapidly determine the price of items while simultaneously monitoring the store's inventory.

Scientists are currently exploring the bar code concept as a way to identify and track species. DNA bar codes consist of relatively short standardized segments of DNA within the genome unique to a particular species or subspecies in some cases. Biologists have successfully demonstrated that DNA bar codes can be used to identify butterfly, fly, bird, plant, and fungus species.[46]

Other applications have been suggested. One proposal suggests using short synthetic pieces of DNA incorporated into genes as a bar code that allows them to be quickly identified in laboratory experiments.[47] This application differs from species identification. While DNA bar codes used to identify species are naturally part of an organism's genome, scientists use other types of bar codes to track genes. These man-made bar codes are intentionally incorporated into genes by researchers. These synthetic bar codes are much more like the ones used to price items at a supermarket checkout.

The use of DNA as bar codes, again, underscores the informational content of these molecules. DNA computing, steganography, and bar coding all make it clear that treating biochemical information as information goes well beyond a helpful analogy. It is indeed information.

The Writing on the Wall

Human experience consistently teaches that information emanates from intelligence. Whether written in plain or elegant scripts, messages initiate in a mind. In whatever form information takes, it's not limited to communicating ideas, needs, and desires between human minds. Information has become an integral part of modern technology. Designers and engineers routinely develop and refine information systems. Computer technologies, among many other developing innovations, fundamentally depend upon such constructs.

Over the last forty years, biochemists have come to recognize that the cell's biochemical systems are also, at their essence, information-based. Proteins, DNA, and even oligosaccharides are information-rich molecules. By analogy, these discoveries reinforce the biochemical design argument.

It's not the mere presence of information that motivates the case; it's the structure of the information housed in proteins and DNA. The direct analogy between the architecture of human language and the makeup of biochemical systems is startling. Equally provocative is the syntactic, semantic, and pragmatic dimensions of biochemical information that, likewise, correspond to information generated and used by humans in their day-to-day communications and technologies.

The structural elegance of biochemical information also points to the molecular calligraphy penned by a Creator's hand. An awe-inspiring organization of genes in prokaryotes (operons) and eukaryotes (head-to-head orientation of genes, alternate splicing of genes, and overlapping genes) supplies powerful evidence of a deliberate purpose. This structural arrangement contains remarkably sophisticated embellishments and in many cases displays a brilliant logic that relates to functional expression. And, in the case of alternately spliced and overlapping genes, it's difficult to envision how these systems could have originated apart from the meticulous effort of a superior Intelligence.

Random Letters

The evolutionary paradigm currently struggles to account for the vast amount and complexity of biochemical information. Based on current understanding, information-rich molecules can't be assembled by chance processes. And, chemical selection doesn't seem potent enough (as presently conceived) to bridge the gap between a random mixture of free amino acids and even a single functioning polypeptide, let alone the ensemble of proteins needed for life to exist in its most minimal form.

Astronomer Hugh Ross and I describe the difficulties evolutionary models face in trying to explain the origin of biochemical information in our book *Origins of Life*.[48] Although evolutionary biologists hope that a better understanding of the relationship between amino acid sequence and protein structure and function will rescue them from this plight, there is no real reason to think that will happen.

In the face of these concerns, some skeptics assert that application of information theory to problems in molecular biology is merely a helpful analogy between biochemical systems and human language. If taken too far, however, they claim this analogy breaks down.

Complete Sentences

Yet, the assertion that biochemical information is not really information loses potency when new information-based nano- and biotechnologies— like DNA computing, encryption, and bar coding—are considered. These astounding advances profoundly justify the analogy between human language (and information) and biochemical information.

It's no less provocative to think that the cell's systems actually inspired DNA computing. Leonard Adleman, the father of DNA computing, recognized that biochemical information is processed using biomolecular Turing machines. For computer applications, Turing machines exist only in human minds. In the cell, Turing machines are a reality and the means to carry out operations in DNA-based computers.

Perhaps the most remarkable aspect of the cell's information systems is the presence of an even parity code within the structural makeup of DNA. The parity code found in DNA directly corresponds to the parity codes used by computer scientists to minimize error during the transmission of information. DNA's parity code functions in the same way, making it possible for the cell's machinery to recognize when an error has occurred as biochemical information is being replicated or transcribed.

This parity code is only possible if the nucleobases adenine, guanine, thymine (uracil), and cytosine are part of its structure. They seem to have been hand-selected, and DNA's structure appears to have been deliberately optimized to minimize transmission errors (see chapter 7, p. 134). If DNA was assembled with any other nucleobases, its parity code would be lost.

The presence and structural arrangement of information add to the intelligent design analogy. Biochemical systems are irreducibly complex, finely tuned, optimized, and information-based in ways that far surpass the capabilities of the best human designers. Chemically based information systems in the cell make the elegant and stylized flourishes of the divine Calligrapher's pen unmistakable.

The next chapter continues to probe the structural makeup of biochemical information by focusing on the genetic and histone codes. These two aspects of the cell's information systems add even more to the weight of evidence for biochemical design.

9

CELLULAR SYMBOLISM

Artists routinely use symbols to represent emotions, ideas, events, and people. This practice appears to have reached its pinnacle with the Symbolism of the nineteenth century.[1] As much a philosophy and ideology as a school of art, Symbolism was a reaction to naturalism and realism. The movement emerged in France and spread throughout Europe and beyond.

Symbolist painters used spiritual themes, the imagination, and dreams to communicate what they considered truth. Scenes from nature and human experience depicted in esoteric and suggestive ways contained allegorical meaning. However, the more familiar emblems of mainstream iconography were avoided. Instead, Symbolists used obscure and ambiguous images that frequently held personal meaning.

Whether in an art movement or in common everyday experience, the use of symbols involves a type of pictorial code—one that harbors significance and provides a vehicle to communicate ideas. Art uses symbols that may indicate different things to different people. But reliable communication requires the sender and recipient to agree upon a predetermined understanding. This agreement constitutes a code, a set of rules that converts information from one form to another.[2]

Codes can be used when the normal means of communication using ordinary language becomes difficult or impossible. They can also be employed for the sake of brevity. Cable codes (like the Morse code), for instance, convert words into shorter "dashes and dots" that allow information to be sent more quickly and less expensively.

Sometimes the converted information takes on a different form. For example, semaphore flags transmit instructions as a signaler uses a set of rules to transform letters and numbers into flag-waving patterns.

Codes are not limited to art symbols or the various conventions used by humans to communicate under difficult circumstances. Biochemists have discovered a type of symbolism inside the cell in the form of biochemical codes. The genetic code—a set of rules that relays the information stored in the nucleotide sequences of DNA to the amino acid sequences of proteins—is the heart of the cell's information system (see chapter 8, p. 142).

In one of the most significant scientific landmarks in human history, three biochemists—Har Gobind Khorana, Robert W. Holley, and Marshall Warren Nirenberg—deciphered this code. They won the 1968 Nobel Prize in Physiology or Medicine for their tremendous accomplishment. The discovery of the genetic code represents far more than an important scientific milestone. It is one of the most potent evidences for biochemical intelligent design. The following parable shows why.

A Rational Response

A pilot flying his plane over the South Pacific sees an uncharted island in the distance. Deciding to explore, the pilot spirals the plane downward to take a closer look. As the plane descends, he spots large rocks on the island's shore arranged to spell SOS. The pilot then sees a grass hut located farther down the beach. Even before he sees the footprints in the sand, the pilot reaches for the transmitter and radios for help.

Though SOS is not a word, most would agree that the pilot's plea was rational. He easily recognized the universal distress message. The pilot knew the improbability of wind and waves acting on the rocks along the shore to form the right letters.[3] More importantly, based on experience, the pilot understood that the carefully arranged stones communicated meaningful information—they were a code that required an intelligent agent's design and implementation. The island's inhabitant spelled out SOS on the shore with the hope that whoever saw the intentionally placed rocks would know what he meant.

That same type of evidence has been discovered inside the cell (see chapter 8). Biochemical machinery is, at essence, information-based. And, the chemical information in the cell is encoded using symbols.

By itself, this information offers powerful evidence for an Intelligent Designer. But, recent discoveries go one step further. Molecular biologists studying the genetic code's origin have unwittingly stumbled across a "grass hut" in what may be the most profound evidence for intelligent activity—a type of fine-tuning in the code's rules. Just as the hut on the beach helped convince the pilot that someone was using carefully placed rocks to signal for help, the precision of the code adds confirmatory evidence that a mind programmed life's genetic code.

The genetic code's carefully crafted rules supply it with a surprising capacity to minimize errors. These error-minimization properties allow the cell's biochemical information systems to make mistakes and *still* communicate critical information with high fidelity. It's as if the stranded island inhabitant could arrange the rocks in any three letter combination and still communicate his desperate plight.

A Genetic SOS

At first glance, there appears to be a mismatch between the storage and functional expression of information in the cell. Clearly a one-to-one relationship cannot exist between the four different nucleotides of DNA and the twenty different amino acids used to assemble polypeptides. The cell's machinery compensates for this mismatch by using groupings comprised of three nucleotides (codons) to specify the twenty amino acids.[4]

The cell uses a set of rules—the genetic code—to relate these nucleotide triplet sequences to the twenty amino acids used to make polypeptides. Codons represent the fundamental coding units. In the same way the stranded islander used three letters (SOS) to communicate, the genetic code uses three nucleotide "characters" to signify an amino acid.

For all intents and purposes, the genetic code is universal among all living organisms. It consists of sixty-four codons. Because the genetic code only needs to encode twenty amino acids, some of the codons are redundant.

Different codons can code for the same amino acid. In fact, up to six different codons specify some amino acids. A single codon specifies others.

Table 9.1 describes the universal genetic code. It is presented in the conventional way, according to how the information appears in mRNA molecules after the information stored in DNA is transcribed. (In RNA uracil [U] is used instead of thymine [T].)

Table 9.1
The Genetic Code

5′ End	U		C		A		G	
U	UUU	Phe	UCU	Ser	UAU	Tyr	UGU	Cys
	UUC	Phe	UCC	Ser	UAC	Tyr	UGC	Cys
	UUA	Leu	UCA	Ser	UAA	End	UGA	End
	UUG	Leu	UCG	Ser	UAG	End	UGG	Trp
C	CUU	Leu	CCU	Pro	CAU	His	CGU	Arg
	CUC	Leu	CCC	Pro	CAC	His	CGC	Arg
	CUA	Leu	CCA	Pro	CAA	Gln	CGA	Arg
	CUG	Leu	CCG	Pro	CAG	Gln	CGG	Arg
A	AUU	Ile	ACU	Thr	AAU	Asn	AGU	Ser
	AUC	Ile	ACC	Thr	AAC	Asn	AGC	Ser
	AUA	Ile	ACA	Thr	AAA	Lys	AGA	Arg
	AUG	Met(Start)	ACG	Thr	AAG	Lys	AGG	Arg
G	GUU	Val	GCU	Ala	GAU	Asp	GGU	Gly
	GUC	Val	GCC	Ala	GAC	Asp	GGC	Gly
	GUA	Val	GCA	Ala	GAA	Glu	GGA	Gly
	GUG	Val(Start)	GCG	Ala	GAG	Glu	GGG	Gly

The first nucleotide of the coding triplet begins at what biochemists call the 5′ end of the sequence (see chapter 2, p. 48). Each nucleotide in the codon's first position (5′ end) can be read from the left-most column, and the nucleotide in the second position can be read from the row across the top of the table. The nucleotide in each codon's third position (the 3′ end) can be read within each box. For example, the two codons, 5′ UUU and 5′ UUC, that specify phenylalanine (abbreviated Phe) are listed in the box located at the top left corner of the table.

Interestingly, some codons (stop or nonsense codons) don't specify any amino acids. They always occur at the end of the gene informing the protein manufacturing machinery where the polypeptide chain ends. Stop codons serve as a form of "punctuation" for the cell's information system. (For example, UGA is a stop codon.)

Some coding triplets (start codons) play a dual role in the genetic code. These codons not only encode amino acids but also "tell" the cell where a polypeptide begins. For example, the codon GUG not only encodes the amino acid valine, it also specifies the beginning of a polypeptide chain. Start codons function as a sort of "capitalization" for the information system of the cell.

The information content of DNA and proteins—the molecules that ultimately define life's most fundamental structures and processes—leads to the conclusion that an Intelligent Designer must have been responsible for biochemical systems (see chapter 8). The existence of the genetic code makes this conclusion as rational as the pilot's actions when he radioed for a rescue team after spotting the message on the beach.

A Biochemical Grass Hut

The structure of rules for the genetic code reveals even further evidence that it stems from a Creator. A capacity to resist the errors that naturally occur as a cell uses or transmits information from one generation to the next is built into the code. Recent studies employing methods to quantify the genetic code's error-minimization properties indicate that the genetic code's rules have been carefully chosen and finely tuned.

The Potential to Be Washed Away

Why does the genetic code's error-minimization capacity provide such a powerful indicator for intelligent design? Translating the stored information of DNA into the functional information of proteins is the code's chief function. Error minimization, therefore, measures the capability of the genetic code to execute its function.

The failure of the genetic code to transmit and translate information with high fidelity can be devastating to the cell. A brief explanation of the effect mutations have on the cell shows the problem. A mutation refers to any change that takes place in the DNA nucleotide sequence.[5]

Several different types of changes to DNA sequences can occur with substitution mutations being the most frequent. As a result of these mutations, a nucleotide(s) in the DNA strand is replaced by another nucleotide(s). For example, an A may be replaced by a G or a C with a T. When substitutions occur, they alter the codon that houses the substituted nucleotide. And if the codon changes, then the amino acid specified by that codon also changes, altering the amino acid sequence of the polypeptide chain specified by the mutated gene.

This mutation can then lead to a distorted chemical and physical profile along the polypeptide chain. If the substituted amino acid has dramatically different physicochemical properties from the native amino acid, then the polypeptide folds improperly. An improperly folded protein has reduced or even lost function. Mutations can be deleterious because they hold the potential to significantly and negatively impact protein structure and function.

Taking a Closer Look

Simple inspection shows that the genetic code's redundancy is not haphazard but carefully thought out—even more so than a grass hut built beyond the reach of the waves. Deliberate rules were set up to protect the cell from the harmful effects of substitution mutations. For example, six codons encode the amino acid leucine (Leu). If at a particular amino acid position in a polypeptide, Leu is encoded by 5'CUU, substitution mutations in the 3' position from U to C, A, or G produce three new codons—5'CUC, 5'CUA, and 5'CUG, respectively—all of which code for Leu (see table 9.1).

The net effect leaves the amino acid sequence of the polypeptide unchanged. And, the cell successfully avoids the negative effects of a substitution mutation.

Likewise, a change of C in the 5' position to a U generates a new codon, 5'UUU, which specifies phenylalanine, an amino acid with physical and chemical properties similar to Leu. Changing C to an A or a G produces codons that code for isoleucine and valine, respectively. These two amino acids possess chemical and physical properties similar to leucine. Qualitatively, it appears as if the genetic code has been constructed to minimize the errors that could result from substitution mutations.

Calling in the Coordinates

Recently, scientists have worked to quantitatively evaluate the error-minimization capacity of the genetic code. One of the first studies to perform this analysis indicated that the universal genetic code found in nature could withstand the potentially harmful effects of substitution mutations better than all but 0.02 percent (1 out of 5,000) of randomly generated genetic codes with different codon assignments than the one found throughout nature.[6]

This initial work, however, did not take into account the fact that some types of substitution mutations occur more frequently in nature than others. For example, an A-to-G substitution occurs more often than either an A-to-C or an A-to-T mutation. When researchers incorporated this correction into their analysis, they discovered that the naturally occurring genetic code performed better than one million randomly generated genetic codes and that the genetic code in nature resides near the global optimum for all possible genetic codes with respect to its error-minimization capacity.[7] Nature's universal genetic code is truly one in a million!

The genetic code's error-minimization properties are far more dramatic than these results indicate. When the researchers calculated the error-minimization capacity of the one million randomly generated genetic codes, they discovered that the error-minimization values formed a distribution with the naturally occurring genetic code lying outside the distribution (see figure 9.1).[8] Researchers estimate the existence of 10^{18} possible genetic codes possessing the same type and degree of redundancy as the universal genetic code. All of these codes fall within the error-minimization distribution. This means of 10^{18} possible genetic codes few, if any, have an error-minimization capacity that approaches the code found universally throughout nature.

Out of Harm's Way

Some researchers have challenged the optimality of the genetic code.[9] But, the scientists who discovered the remarkable error-minimization capacity of the genetic code have concluded that the rules of the genetic code cannot be accidental.[10] A genetic code assembled through random biochemical events could not possess near ideal error-minimization properties.

Researchers argue that a force shaped the genetic code. Instead of looking to an intentional Programmer, these scientists appeal to natural selection. That is, they believe random events operated on by the forces of natural selection over and over again produced the genetic code's error-minimization capacity.[11]

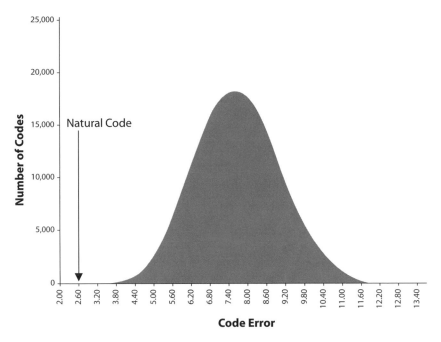

Figure 9.1. Error Minimization Capacity of the Genetic Code
This plot compares the error minimization capacity of the universal genetic code found
in nature with one million random genetic codes. The horizontal axis describes the error-
minimization capacity of the code with lower values corresponding to greater capacity to
withstand error. The vertical axis describes the number of codes. The bell curve represents the
distribution of error-minimization values for the randomly generated genetic codes.

Natural Forces at Work

Even though some researchers think natural selection shaped the genetic
code, other scientific work questions the likelihood that the genetic code
could evolve. In 1968, Nobel laureate Francis Crick argued that the genetic
code could not undergo significant evolution.[12] His rationale is easy to
understand. Any change in codon assignments would lead to changes in
amino acids in *every* polypeptide made by the cell.

This wholesale change in polypeptide sequences would result in a large
number of defective proteins. Nearly any conceivable change to the genetic
code would be lethal to the cell.

The scientists who suggest that natural selection shaped the genetic code are
fully aware of Crick's work. Still they rely on evolution to explain the code's

optimal design because of the existence of nonuniversal genetic codes. While the genetic code in nature is generally regarded as universal, some nonuniversal genetic codes exist—codes that employ slightly different codon assignments. Presumably, these nonuniversal codes evolved from the universal genetic code. Therefore, researchers argue that such evolution is possible.

But, the codon assignments of the nonuniversal genetic codes are nearly identical to those of the universal genetic code with only one or two exceptions. Nonuniversal genetic codes can be thought of as deviants of the universal genetic code.

Does the existence of nonuniversal codes imply that wholesale genetic code evolution is possible? Careful study reveals that codon changes in the nonuniversal genetic codes always occur in relatively small genomes, such as those in mitochondria. These changes involve (1) codons that occur at low frequencies in that particular genome or (2) stop codons.

Changes in assignment for these codons could occur without producing a lethal scenario because only a small number of polypeptides in the cell or organelle would experience an altered amino acid sequence. So it seems limited evolution of the genetic code can take place, but only in special circumstances.[13] The existence of nonuniversal genetic codes does not necessarily justify an evolutionary origin of the amazingly optimal genetic code found in nature.

Is a Timely Rescue Possible?

Even if the genetic code could change over time to yield a set of rules that allowed for the best possible error-minimization capacity, is there enough time for this process to occur?

Biophysicist Hubert Yockey addressed this question.[14] He determined that natural selection would have to explore 1.40×10^{70} different genetic codes to discover the universal genetic code found in nature. The maximum time available for it to originate was estimated at 6.3×10^{15} seconds. Natural selection would have to evaluate roughly 10^{55} codes per *second* to find the one that's universal. Put simply, natural selection lacks the time necessary to find the universal genetic code.

Other work places the genetic code's origin coincidental with life's start. Operating within the evolutionary paradigm, a team headed by renowned origin-of-life researcher Manfred Eigen estimated the age of the genetic code at 3.8 ± 0.6 billion years.[15] Current geochemical evidence places life's first appearance on Earth at 3.86 billion years ago.[16] This timing means that the genetic code's origin coincides with life's start on Earth. It appears as if the genetic code came out of nowhere, without any time to search out the best option.

In the face of these types of problems, some scientists suggest that the genetic code found in nature emerged from a simpler code that employed codons consisting of one or two nucleotides.[17] Over time, these simpler genetic codes expanded to eventually yield the universal genetic code based on coding triplets. The number of possible genetic codes based on one or two nucleotide codons is far fewer than for codes based on coding triplets. This scenario makes code evolution much more likely from a naturalistic standpoint.[18]

One complicating factor for these proposals arises, however, from the fact that simpler genetic codes cannot specify twenty different amino acids. Rather, they are limited to sixteen at most. Such a scenario would mean that the first life-forms had to make use of proteins that consisted of no more than sixteen different amino acids. Interestingly, some proteins found in nature, such as ferredoxins, are produced with only thirteen amino acids. On the surface, this observation seems to square with the idea that the genetic code found in nature arose from a simpler code.

Yet, proteins like the ferredoxins are atypical. Most proteins require all twenty amino acids. This requirement, coupled with recent recognition that life in its most minimal form needs several hundred proteins (see chapter 3), makes these types of models for code evolution speculative at best. The optimal nature of the genetic code and the difficulty accounting for the code's origin from an evolutionary perspective work together to support the conclusion that an Intelligent Designer programmed the genetic code, and hence, life.

Histone's Footprints

Biochemists have recently discovered another code associated with DNA that overlaps the genetic code and plays a key role in gene expression. The rules that define this overlying code are manifested through interactions between DNA and the DNA-binding proteins known as histones.

These globular-shaped proteins organize DNA into chromosomes (see chapter 2, p. 51). In eukaryotes, the DNA molecules found inside the cell's nucleus exist in the form of chromosomes. Each of these highly condensed structures consists of one molecule of DNA associated with a larger number of histone proteins. Histones bind to the DNA at regular intervals along the length of the double helix.

Biochemists have identified five different histone proteins—referred to as H1, H2A, H2B, H3, and H4.[19] Two copies each of the histones H2A, H2B, H3, and H4 interact to form a disk-shaped complex composed of eight protein subunits (an octamer; see figure 9.2). This octamer complex is also known as the histone core.

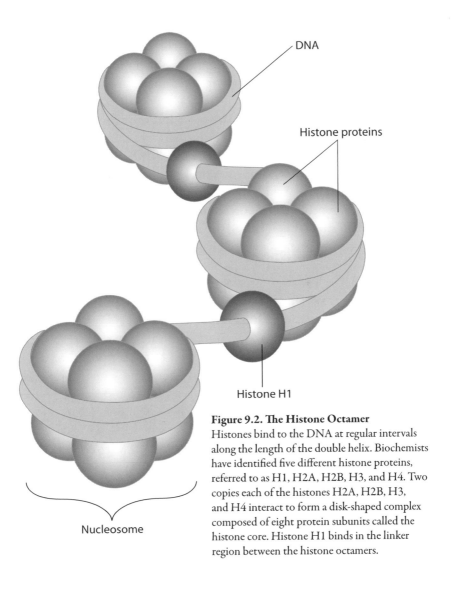

DNA

Histone proteins

Histone H1

Nucleosome

Figure 9.2. The Histone Octamer
Histones bind to the DNA at regular intervals along the length of the double helix. Biochemists have identified five different histone proteins, referred to as H1, H2A, H2B, H3, and H4. Two copies each of the histones H2A, H2B, H3, and H4 interact to form a disk-shaped complex composed of eight protein subunits called the histone core. Histone H1 binds in the linker region between the histone octamers.

At each histone-binding site, the DNA double helix winds around the histone core, sort of like a thread around a spool. Unlike that thread, however, that seems to wind around the spool an endless number of times, the DNA strand wraps around the core only about two-and-one-half full turns. These turns consist of a sequence of about 150 nucleotides.

The complex between the DNA double helix and the histone octamer is a nucleosome (see chapter 2, p. 51). Nucleosomes form the fundamental organizing structure of chromosomes. For each chromosome, nucleosomes occur repeatedly along the length of the DNA molecule to form a supramolecular structure that resembles a string of beads when viewed with an electron microscope. A piece of linker DNA, which varies between about fifteen and fifty-five nucleotides in length, connects the nucleosomes to each other.

In turn, the nucleosomes interact with one another by coiling the "beaded necklace" to form a solenoid. Histone H1 mediates the interactions between the nucleosomes to assemble the solenoid, which further condenses to form higher order structures that comprise the chromosome proper.

The association of DNA with histones plays an important role in regulating gene activity and other important processes like DNA repair. When the DNA double helix wraps around the histone core, the cell's biochemical machinery can't physically get to the genes, blocking transcription, for example.[20]

It's critical that the initiation sites for transcription (promoter sites) reside in the linker regions away from the nucleosomes, so that proteins like RNA polymerase can bind to these DNA regions (see chapters 7, p. 135, and 8, p. 148). Recent studies on the yeast genome indicate that this organization is often the case with nucleosomes positioned to render promoter DNA sequences readily accessible in linker DNA regions.[21] The careful positioning of nucleosomes along the DNA molecule typifies the elegant structural and functional logic that pervades many of the cell's biochemical systems. And this elegance points to the intentional handiwork of a Creator.

So, too, does another study. Researchers from The Weizmann Institute of Science (Israel) demonstrated that histones prefer to bind to specific nucleotide sequences.[22] These sequences impart the DNA double helix with the propensity to bend. This useful property allows the DNA molecule to wrap around the histone core.

Most importantly, the research team demonstrated that the sequence specificity of histone binding to DNA constitutes a code within the genome that dictates the precise positioning of nucleosomes along the DNA molecule. The nucleosome-positioning codes repeat every ten nucleotides along the DNA double helix at the binding site for the histone core. Using this newly discovered code, the scientists from The Weizmann Institute could successfully predict the location of nucleosomes along the length of a DNA molecule.

As with the genetic code, the histone-positioning code suggests the work of an Intelligent Programmer. A code must be deliberately designed. Even more remarkable is the requirement for the genetic and the histone-positioning codes to work in concert with one another. The histone-positioning code overlays the genetic code. These two codes must establish the relationship between the nucleotide sequences of DNA and the amino acid sequences of proteins. At the same time they must precisely position nucleosomes to ensure the proper expression of the information defined by the genetic code.

Foresight and careful planning (the work of an Intelligent Agent) are necessary to get these two codes to work together. If haphazardly constructed, they could easily conflict, disrupting key processes within the cell. Remarkably, the universal genetic code is constructed to harbor overlapping or parallel codes better than the vast majority of other possible genetic codes.[23]

Grasping the Meaning

Great artists often use symbolism to communicate with efficiency and effectiveness. When scrutinized their works often contain messages beyond the obvious that give their works added significance and make them a source of genuine and personal satisfaction.

Sometimes human beings take symbolism a step further and design codes to convey their messages. Such codes require a programmer to establish rules that relate one form of information to another. Life carries that type of code—the genetic code. Its set of rules relate the information stored in the nucleotide sequences of DNA to the amino acid sequences of proteins, and thus, it forms the heart of the cell's information system.

The recent recognition that the genetic code possesses a unique capacity to resist errors caused by mutation imparts the biochemical intelligent design argument with an entirely new level of credibility. Like a giant SOS shaped with letters ablaze, the optimal nature of the genetic code signals that an Intelligent Agent used those rules to start and sustain life.

The fine-tuning that minimizes the likelihood of error indicates that the genetic code cannot be just an accident—happened upon by random biochemical events—nor is it likely the product of undirected evolutionary processes. Genetic code evolution would be catastrophic for the cell.

Remarkably, the genetic code originated at the time when life first appeared on Earth. And, it must have been deliberately programmed. No matter how much time there might have been, the code's complexity makes it virtually impossible that natural selection could have stumbled upon it by accident. Such elaborate rules require forethought and painstaking effort. The message they carry adds an important piece to the analogy that logically compels a Creator's existence and role in life's origin and history.

Chapter 10 reveals even more of the quality control efforts that went into life's design.

10

TOTAL QUALITY

Many art aficionados would love to own a masterpiece, but only a select few have the means to privately enjoy such treasures. Cost simply prohibits most people from being able to afford them.

And yet, reproductions make these paintings widely accessible to millions of people. Through facsimiles—schools, libraries, museums, and individual collectors can procure images of the world's best artwork at a reasonable cost. Everyone benefits.

Fine art reproductions are manufactured in different ways. Expert artists trained in specific art movements, genres, and styles re-create desired masterpieces by hand. But, this technique is time consuming and expensive. And the reproductions are never an exact match. Still, many prefer these copies over other types, such as prints that have a more artificial appearance.

Recent innovations in camera, scanner, software, and ink technologies have overcome most of the problems, however. *Giclée* (a French term pronounced zhee-CLAY) reproductions have made fine art far more available.[1] In this process, a high-resolution printer transfers a digital image onto a canvas or fine art paper. Many connoisseurs are attracted to these prints because the digital image captures every nuance of the original including the most subtle details of lighting, shadowing, and texture.

The resolution exceeds that of traditional lithographs. And, giclée re-creations are relatively inexpensive even in small quantities. Such advantages have helped make these prints well-established fixtures in the fine art community.

A reproduction is only valuable, however, when it's virtually indistinguishable from the original. This requirement makes quality control steps an instrumental part of the manufacturing process—whether a piece is reproduced by an expert artist or sophisticated technology. Before a museum accepts a giclée re-creation, it must go through a rigorous quality assurance process.

After a digital image captures the masterpiece, the reproduction undergoes a proofing procedure to ensure that all aspects of the image (color, detail, brightness, contrast, brush strokes, texture, etc.) correspond exactly to the original. Then, a museum curator further evaluates the giclée. If unacceptable, it is sent back for additional changes until he is satisfied with the reproduction's quality.

This painstaking attention to every imaginable detail mirrors the strict biochemical requirements faced by the cell's machinery that manufactures proteins. For these biomolecules to be usable, they must be exact replicas—high-fidelity copies—of the information housed in the gene sequences of DNA (see chapter 2, p. 48). The cell's protein-manufacturing processes are well-designed to accomplish this task.

Still, from time to time, mistakes happen. And, as is the case for any good manufacturing process, biochemical quality control systems are in place to identify and rectify production errors. Quality assurance checks are also part of other key processes in the cell, like DNA replication, for example.

Avoiding Costly Mistakes

Manufacturing processes often rely on assembly lines to move production units from station to station. Workers, robots, and machinery carefully perform high-precision tasks transforming unrecognizable starting materials and components, one step at a time, into a finished product. Each stage is an engineering marvel that likely took years of research, careful planning, design, and construction to effectively implement.

Some of the most critical and sophisticated steps are not those that directly result in the final product but those that check the quality. These tasks deliberately remove defective products from the production sequence and ensure that no substandard finished product reaches the consumer's hands.

Quality assurance procedures that simply evaluate and reject inferior products at the end of the production line may keep defective items from reaching consumers, but they are costly, inefficient, and of limited value. The best quality control measures intervene throughout the manufacturing process, particularly when mistakes are most likely to occur or are the most costly.

Defective products can then be removed near the point in the manufacturing sequence where the problem occurs and that saves time and resources. Without such intervention, defective units would be carried through to the assembly line's end only to be discarded.

Effective and efficient quality control procedures don't just happen. Rather, they require careful planning and a detailed understanding of the manufacturing process, the product, and the way the consumer will use it. In other words, quality control procedures reflect intelligence and ingenuity and indicate a deliberate, well-designed process.

Scientists compare many of the cell's activities to manufacturing processes. These comparisons provide an important conceptual handle that helps researchers understand the cell's operating systems.

An astounding chemical logic undergirds these complex, well-orchestrated processes. Biochemists have discovered that, just like manufacturing operations designed by human engineers, key cellular processes incorporate a number of quality control checks. Many of them play a central role in cell survival and the cell's ability to propagate from generation to generation.[2] These quality assurance procedures occur at critical junctures in the cell's systems and display remarkable chemical elegance and exquisite fine-tuning.

Describing all the cell's quality control operations is beyond the scope of this book. Therefore, this discussion is limited to some of the quality control procedures associated with the production of one of the cell's most important biochemical products, proteins.

Only the Best

The capacity of the cell's biochemical machinery to make proteins with a high degree of fidelity is critical. Protein ensembles play a role in every cell function and take part in every cell structure (see chapter 2, p. 42).

Wide-scale production of defective proteins would disrupt essential cell activities and result in a distorted cellular architecture.

The problems related to defective protein production extend beyond global disruption of cellular activities. Molecular biologist and physician Michael Denton points out that frequent mistakes in protein production will cause the cell to self-destruct.[3]

The threat of autodestruction stems from the circular nature of protein synthesis. Proteins constitute many components of the cell's protein manufacturing machinery. In other words, the cell uses proteins to make proteins (see chapter 5, p. 101). So, if the protein manufacturing machinery were assembled with defective parts, the cell would fail to accurately manufacture proteins. Such a manufacturing failure would cause protein production systems to become increasingly error-prone with each successive round of protein synthesis. Protein manufacturing systems made up of defective components would be more likely to produce defective proteins. This chain reaction would cascade out of control and quite quickly lead to the cell's self-destruction.

Effective quality assurance procedures must be in place for protein production or life would not be possible.

Manufacturing Instructions

At most production facilities, official documents that contain the manufacturing instructions are housed in a central office where they're formally maintained. The cell does the same. It stores DNA—the master directions for protein production—inside its nucleus. The nucleotide sequence of genes found along the DNA strands specifies the amino acid sequence of proteins, just like manufacturing plans describe the order of production steps for any manufacturing process (see chapter 2, p. 50).

When the time comes to produce a particular protein, the cell's machinery copies these instructions and takes them to the production floor. This reproduction operation results in the assembly of another type of polynucleotide, messenger RNA (mRNA).[4]

A Biochemical Assembly Line

The cell's protein-manufacturing machinery consists of three main components: messenger RNA (mRNA), transfer RNA (tRNA), and ribosomes.

All interact to form an assembly line that generates the polypeptides that constitute proteins.

Messenger RNA

After the manufacturing instructions for protein synthesis have been copied from the DNA (transcription), reviewed, and processed, the newly produced mRNA carries them from the cell's nucleus to the cytoplasm. Once there, the mRNA issues instructions to subcellular particles, the ribosomes, to produce the polypeptides that fold and interact to form proteins[5] (see chapter 2, p. 50). Ribosomes bind and manage the interactions between mRNA and tRNA.[6]

Transfer RNA

Like mRNA, transfer RNA (tRNA) consists of a single RNA strand. Unlike mRNA, tRNA adopts a precise three-dimensional structure critical for its role in protein synthesis.[7] As the single tRNA strand folds to form its three-dimensional shape, four segments of the tRNA strand pair. This union gives tRNA a cloverleaf shape in two dimensions. Bending the clover leaf and twisting the paired regions produces an overall L-shaped architecture. (See figure 10.1.)

Transfer RNAs bind amino acids and carry them to the ribosome.[8] This delivery makes amino acids—the starting materials for protein production—available to the protein synthetic machinery. Each of the twenty amino acids used by the cell to form proteins has at least one corresponding tRNA molecule. An activating enzyme (aminoacyl-tRNA synthetase) links each amino acid to its specific tRNA carrier.

Each tRNA and amino acid partnership has a corresponding activating enzyme specific to that pair. The amino acid binds to one end of the tRNA "L". The other end of the tRNA, the anticodon, "reads" the manufacturing instructions found in mRNA. This anticodon consists of a three-nucleotide sequence that pairs with a codon, a complementary three-nucleotide sequence in mRNA.

The four nucleotides of mRNA, and ultimately DNA, specify the twenty amino acids found in proteins by using groupings of three nucleotides to code for each amino acid.[9] There are sixty-four different codons that correspond to the twenty amino acids involved in protein synthesis. Some of

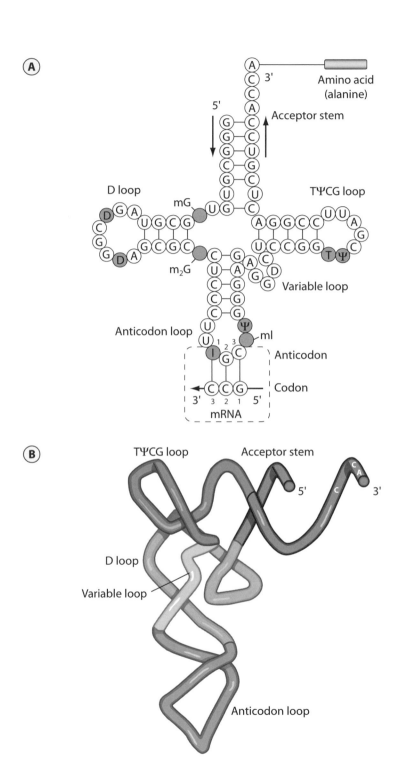

A

A
C 3'
C
A
Amino acid
(alanine)
5'
Acceptor stem
G   C
G   C
G   U
C   G
G   C
U   C
mG U G
D loop   TΨCG loop
D G A   U G C G   A G G C C   U U
C   A
G   U C C G G   G
G D A   G C G C   T Ψ   C
m₂G   C   G   A D
U   A   G
C   C   G
C   C   G Variable loop
C   G
U   U   Ψ
Anticodon loop U   U   ml
                    1 2 3
                    I G C   Anticodon
                                Codon
3' C C G 5'
    3 2 1
        mRNA

B

TΨCG loop   Acceptor stem

                                   C
                                   A
                              5'   C
                                        3'
D loop

Variable loop

Anticodon loop

the sixty-four codons are redundant. That is, they code for the same amino acid. The genetic code (see chapter 9, p. 171) is the set of rules the cell uses to relate nucleotide triplets in mRNA to amino acids in proteins.

Each tRNA's anticodon matches a codon in mRNA. Because each tRNA binds a single and specific amino acid, the codon–anticodon pairs serve as the cellular hardware that implements the manufacturing instructions for protein production.

Ribosomes

These subcellular entities play a central role in protein production by binding and managing interactions between mRNA and tRNA. The chemical reactions that form the bonds that join amino acids together in polypeptide chains are catalyzed or assisted by ribosomes.

Proteins and RNA molecules, called ribosomal RNA (rRNA, see chapter 5, p. 102), form a functional ribosome when two subunits of different sizes combine. In prokaryotes, the large subunit contains two rRNA molecules and about thirty different protein molecules. The small subunit consists of a single rRNA molecule and about twenty proteins. In eukaryotes, the large subunit is formed by three rRNA molecules that combine with around fifty distinct proteins. The small subunit consists of a single rRNA molecule and over thirty different proteins. The rRNAs act as scaffolding that organizes a myriad of ribosomal proteins.

Ribosomes are abundant inside the cell. (A typical bacterium possesses about twenty thousand. They generally comprise one-fourth the total bacterial mass.) These dynamic structures readily self-assemble when mRNA and all of its components are present and disassemble once protein production is complete.

The Manufacturing Process

The ribosome, mRNA, and tRNA molecules work cooperatively to produce proteins. Using an assembly-line process, protein manufacturing machinery forms the polypeptide chains (that constitute proteins) one

Figure 10.1. tRNA Structure
The single tRNA strand folds to form its three-dimensional shape when four segments of tRNA pair. This pairing produces a cloverleaf shape in two dimensions. Bending the clover leaf and twisting the paired regions yields an upside-down L-shaped architecture.

amino acid at a time. This protein synthetic apparatus joins together three to five amino acids per second. Ribosomes, in conjunction with mRNA and tRNAs, assemble the cell's smallest proteins, about one hundred to two hundred amino acids in length, in less than one minute.

When protein synthesis begins, the ribosome complex assembles around mRNA. The rRNAs bind to mRNA and properly position it in the ribosome. This process establishes the proper reading frame (see chapter 8, p. 155). The tRNA–amino acid complex that corresponds to the first amino acid position in the polypeptide chain binds to a site in the ribosome called the P (product) site. The tRNA–amino acid complex corresponding to the second amino acid in the polypeptide chain binds to an adjacent site, the A (accepter) site. The protein synthetic machinery uses the mRNA codon–tRNA anticodon pairing interactions to properly position the tRNA–amino acid adducts. (See figure 10.2.)

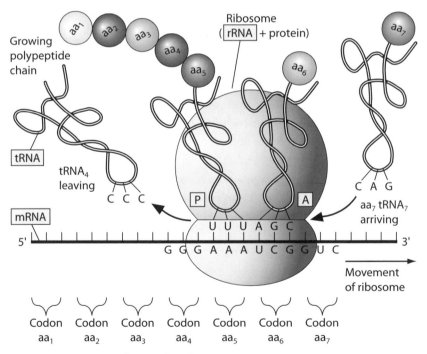

Figure 10.2. Protein Synthesis at the Ribosome
The mechanism of protein synthesis involves the binding of tRNA–amino acid adducts to the A site and the subsequent transfer of the amino acid to the growing polypeptide chain in the P site.

Once positioned in the P and A sites, a region of rRNA in the large subunit (referred to as peptidyl transferase) forms a chemical bond between the first and second amino acids in the polypeptide chain. When this occurs, the amino acid in the P site dissociates from its tRNA. The tRNA in the P site leaves the ribosomes and becomes available to bind another amino acid.

The tRNA in the A site, which has the growing polypeptide chain attached to it, translocates to the P site. And, the tRNA–amino acid complex for the third position in the polypeptide chain enters the A site. Then bond formation, tRNA dissociation, and transfer from A to P site repeats. This entire process occurs over and over again until all the information in the mRNA is read and the entire polypeptide is synthesized. For each step in this assembly-line process, the ribosome complex advances along the mRNA length—one codon at a time.

Quality Control Procedures

As with any well-designed production process, the cell's protein synthetic machinery employs quality assurance protocols. Checkpoints occur at several critical junctures during protein manufacture, including (1) tRNA and rRNA production, (2) mRNA production, (3) amino acid attachment to tRNA, (4) the movement of tRNA to the ribosome, and (5) the positioning of tRNA at the ribosome's A site.

Maintaining the Protein Production Machinery

Biochemists refer to tRNA and rRNA as stable RNAs because these molecules, once produced by the cell's machinery, persist for a long period of time under normal growth conditions. In contrast, mRNA has a high turnover rate (see chapter 6, p. 119).

The biosynthesis of tRNAs and rRNAs is highly accurate. Still, from time to time errors creep into the production process. If left unchecked, defective tRNAs and rRNAs will create havoc for the cell because these molecules are key cogs in the biochemical machinery that manufactures proteins. In any production process, if the machinery that makes the product doesn't work properly, the product either can't be produced or won't be assembled correctly. The stability of these biomolecules further exacerbates the potential damage effected by defective tRNAs and rRNAs because, even if they're flawed, these molecules will persist in the cell. (In contrast, when flawed proteins are accidentally made, the cell's machinery eliminates them.)

In recent years biochemists have discovered the strict quality control governing the production of tRNAs and rRNAs in all cell types.[10] When improperly made, the protein poly(A) polymerase adds several adenine nucleotides to the defective RNAs to form what biochemists call a poly (A) tail (see chapter 5, p. 102). The addition of this poly (A) tail (polyadenylation) flags the faulty RNAs for destruction.[11] Studies on the bacterium *E. coli* show that when mistakes occur in the biosynthesis of tRNA and rRNA, cooperative activity between the proteins RNAase R and PNPase destroys the defective molecules.[12]

If these three enzymes—poly(A) polymerase, RNAase R, PNPase—are inoperable, cell death inevitably occurs. In the process, defective tRNA molecules and rRNA fragments accumulate in the cell and the number of functional ribosomes decreases. Presumably, the defective rRNA molecules disrupt the assembly of working ribosomes.

Placing a quality assurance check at the point of rRNA and tRNA production makes perfect sense. This foresight ensures that the cell's manufacturing machinery is in proper working order before protein production even begins. If this quality control is not in place, the cell's manufacturing floor becomes cluttered with inoperable manufacturing equipment to its detriment.

Recent work indicates that rRNA and tRNA quality control procedures are operable in eukaryotic organisms as well.[13] Just like in the bacterium *E. coli*, flawed tRNA and rRNA molecules are targeted for breakdown by polyadenylation. (In contrast, in eukaryotes the poly (A) tail stabilizes mRNA and directs the splicing operations.) These latest studies suggest that this quality control operation may be a universal feature in the living realm.

Operating at Peak Efficiency

Quality control checkpoints have been discovered at critical junctures in mRNA production, export from the nucleus, and translation at ribosomes.[14] An elegant rationale places quality assurance procedures at these points in protein biosynthesis as well. Before the assembly process even begins, these safeguards generate manufacturing efficiency by ensuring that the protein production machinery will use the correct instructions.

Biochemists recently discovered that RNA polymerases (chapter 5, p. 101)—the protein complexes that synthesize mRNA by copying the information stored in the gene sequences of DNA—use a proofreading mechanism to ensure that mRNA has been accurately transcribed.[15] Messenger RNA, like DNA, is a polynucleotide (see chapter 2, p. 50). Unlike DNA, which consists of two paired polynucleotide strands, mRNA is a single strand. Its nucleobase composition is similar but not identical to DNA. One of the most important differences between DNA and RNA is the use of uridine (U) in place of thymidine (T) in the RNA chains.

RNA polymerases produce mRNA by using a gene's nucleotide sequence, located along the sense strand of the DNA double helix, as a template (see chapter 8, p. 157).[16] RNA polymerases step along the DNA strand and add nucleotides to the mRNA strand one at a time. The nucleotide sequence of the gene dictates each of the nucleotides added to the growing mRNA chain. RNA polymerases rely on the same pairing rules that align the two DNA strands to specify the nucleotide sequence of mRNA.

When the side chain of the DNA template is a C, RNA polymerase adds a G to the growing mRNA strand. If the DNA side chain is a G, RNA polymerase uses a C (because G and C always pair with each other). When the DNA side chain is a T, RNA polymerase incorporates an A into the mRNA chain, and if the RNA polymerase encounters an A, it slots in a U (instead of a T; see figure 10.3).

As mRNA moves along the DNA sense strand adding nucleotides to the mRNA molecule, it constantly checks its work to make sure the correct nucleotide has been added. If an error occurs and the wrong nucleotide becomes incorporated into the mRNA strand, the RNA polymerase removes the incorrect nucleotide, backs up, and repeats the combination step. Biochemists refer to this activity as proofreading. This quality control operation ensures that mRNAs are accurately produced.

In eukaryotes, newly formed mRNA undergoes several processing steps before it leaves the nucleus and makes its way to a ribosome[17] (see chapter 5, p. 102). This processing includes adding a 7-methylguanine "cap" to one end of the mRNA and a poly A "tail" to the other end. Introns (noncoding intervening sequences within a gene) are removed and the remaining exons (the regions of a gene that contain information to make proteins) are spliced together. Biochemists have discovered that if the cell's machinery makes errors in processing mRNA, so-called discard pathways remove flawed mRNA molecules.[18]

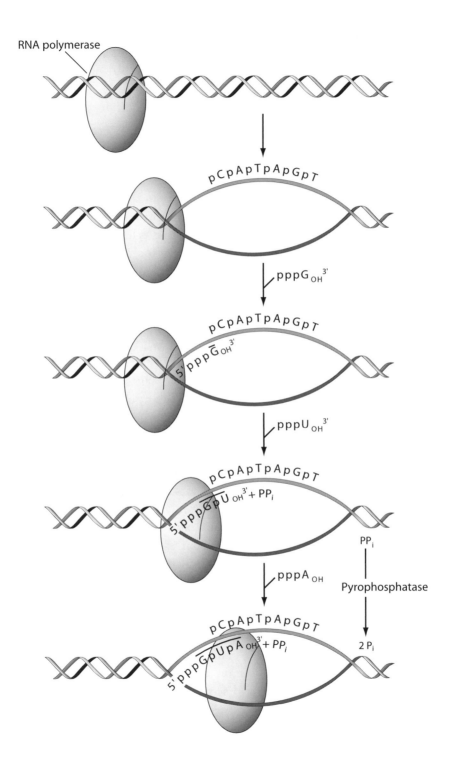

RNA polymerase

pCpApTpApGpT

pCpApTpApGpT

pppG$_{OH}^{3'}$

pCpApTpApGpT
5' ppp$\overline{G}_{OH}^{3'}$

pppU$_{OH}^{3'}$

pCpApTpApGpT
5' ppp$\overline{GpU}_{OH}^{3'}$ + PP$_i$

pppA$_{OH}$

pCpApTpApGpT
5' ppp$\overline{GpUpA}_{OH}^{3'}$ + PP$_i$

PP$_i$

Pyrophosphatase

2 P$_i$

Once processed, mRNA migrates from the cell's nucleus through nuclear pores to the cytoplasm where translation occurs. Another quality assurance checkpoint prevents improperly spliced mRNA from exiting the cell nucleus.[19] This quality control step is accomplished through binding and debinding of proteins to mRNA. When properly spliced, certain proteins that are part of the splicing procedure dissociate from mRNA. If errors occur in splicing, however, these proteins remain attached.

After splicing is completed, other proteins bind to the fully processed mRNA. If not properly spliced, these proteins can't bind to the defective mRNA. When it is associated with the wrong proteins, mRNA isn't granted passage through the nuclear pore, which is how imperfectly processed mRNA is prevented from reaching the ribosome.

Certain types of errors in mRNA production escape detection by the quality control operations in the nucleus. Messenger RNA molecules produced without a stop codon or with a premature stop codon occasionally make their way to the ribosome (see chapter 9, p. 173). Once there, these defective mRNA molecules stall protein production, jamming the ribosome machinery.[20] Several distinct biochemical safeguards are in place to destroy faulty mRNA molecules that clog the ribosomes.[21]

Exact Amino Acid Attachments

A quality control checkpoint also occurs at the step that attaches amino acids to their corresponding tRNA molecules.[22] This energy intensive attachment process, called charging, is highly selective. The error rate for the enzymes that carry out this reaction, aminoacyl-tRNA synthetase (activating enzymes) is about 1 in 3,000.

Activating enzymes achieve this low error rate by correctly binding the appropriate tRNA molecules and amino acids before catalyzing the reaction that joins these two biomolecules together. Proper tRNA binding is readily accomplished because of the chemical differences among the individual tRNAs. The binding of the correct amino acid by activating enzymes, however, is quite remarkable and involves careful biochemical fine-tuning.

The activating enzyme isoleucyl-tRNA synthetase best illustrates the mechanism for selecting the correct amino acid and the fine-tuning

---

Figure 10.3. RNA Polymerase Production of mRNA
RNA polymerases produce mRNA by using a gene's nucleotide sequence as a template. RNA polymerases step along the DNA strand and add nucleotides to the mRNA strand one at a time.

associated with this quality control step. The enzyme is able to effectively discriminate between the amino acids isoleucine and valine. Both have nearly identical chemical and physical properties. Based on the thermodynamics consideration alone, the binding differences between these two amino acids should allow only a 1 in 40 error rate, not a 1 in 3,000. This difference in expected error rate means another mechanism must be at work.

All activating enzymes perform proofreading and editing steps that recognize and delete mischarged amino acids from tRNAs. Activating enzymes proofread and edit through chemical fine-tuning that involves the "just-right" binding to the enzyme's active site (chapter 2, p. 45). Amino acids that are too large can't be accommodated. Those too small become translocated to the enzyme's editing site once the bond between the amino acid and tRNA forms. In the editing site, the enzyme removes the mischarged amino acid from the tRNA and starts all over again.

New work indicates that translocation from the catalytic site to the editing site heavily depends on structural fine-tuning of the activating enzyme.[23] Changing a single amino acid in isoleucyl-tRNA synthetase compromises the enzyme's capacity to edit mischarged tRNAs by disrupting the translocation step.

The proofreading and editing steps are critical. If not executed properly in bacteria, cell growth is inhibited.[24] Faulty proofreading and editing of aminoacyl-tRNA synthetases have been implicated in neurodegenerative diseases.[25]

Separating the Good from the Bad

Recent studies have identified a quality control checkpoint associated with the transport of tRNA–amino acid complexes to the ribosomes.[26] Once charged with an amino acid, tRNAs require a protein, elongation factor Tu (EF-Tu), to escort and position them in the ribosome A site.[27] For some time, biochemists regarded EF-Tu as a passive carrier that indiscriminately bound tRNA–amino acids adducts. These scientists now understand that EF-Tu actively distinguishes properly charged tRNAs from mischarged and uncharged tRNAs.

Biochemists from the University of Colorado at Boulder identified the mechanism EF-Tu employs to discriminate the 20 correctly charged tRNA–amino acid adducts from 380 incorrectly charged ones.[28] The interaction between EF-Tu and properly charged tRNAs is "just right" with binding affinities occurring over a narrow range. Mischarged tRNAs bind to EF-Tu either too weakly or too strongly.

When bound too tight, the mischarged tRNA cannot be released at the ribosome, and if too loose, EF-Tu cannot transport the mischarged tRNA to the ribosome. This finely tuned quality-control system prevents incorrect amino acids from incorporating into polypeptide chains by catching any errors that escape detection by the activating enzyme's editing mechanism.

Less Accuracy Results in Lethal Errors

Collectively, the quality assurance procedures associated with activating enzymes and EF-Tu yield an error rate for protein synthesis on the order of 1 in 10,000 or 100 ppm (parts per million). If the protein manufacturing machinery did not operate with this accuracy, life would not be possible.

The accuracy of protein synthesis can be calculated. The equation $P = (1-E)^n$ expresses the probability for producing a polypeptide chain without error.[29] In this equation P represents the probability for producing an error-free polypeptide, E the error frequency, and n the number of amino acids in the polypeptide chain. An error rate of 1 in 100 is intolerable for the cell. At this frequency, the protein machinery has essentially no chance of producing an error-free polypeptide chain 1,000 amino acids in length and only a 36 percent probability of producing one 300 amino acids long.

An error rate of 1 in 1,000 permits 300-amino-acid-long polypeptide chains to form with an 85 percent error-free probability, but still 1,000-amino-acid-long polypeptide chains would experience only a 37 percent chance of being assembled correctly. At a 1 in 10,000 error rate, polypeptide chains of 1,000 amino acids have a greater than 90 percent chance of correct assembly. Given all this, an error rate of 1 in 10,000 is the minimum protein production efficiency for life to be possible.

An error rate of 1 in 100,000 yields a 99 percent probability of error-free polypeptide assembly for chain lengths 1,000 amino acids long. If this is the case, then why doesn't the protein production machinery include additional quality control steps to push the process accuracy closer to 1 in 100,000?

An error rate of this magnitude would slow down the protein production rate to the point that it becomes harmful to the cell. The error rate of 1 in 10,000 is "just right" to allow for high-fidelity protein synthesis at a rate fast enough to allow cellular chemistry to operate. The design of the protein manufacturing machinery recognizes the trade-offs between accuracy and production time, as does any well-designed production process (see chapter 13, p. 248).

Quality Control in the Endoplasmic Reticulum

A complex system of membrane channels and sacs (see chapter 2, p. 40), the endoplasmic reticulum (ER) is made up of two regions. In the *rough endoplasmic reticulum* ribosomes are associated with the outer surface of the ER membrane. The proteins made by these ribosomes are deposited into the *lumen* (central cavity) of the ER for further biochemical processing. The proteins transported into the lumen will eventually make their way into lysosomes and peroxisomes, become incorporated into the plasma membrane, or be secreted out of the cell.

The processing of proteins in the lumen (posttranslational modification) is quite extensive.[30] Posttranslational modifications include (1) formation and reshuffling of disulfide bonds (these bonds form between the side chains of cysteine amino acid residues within a protein, stabilizing its three dimensional structure), (2) folding proteins into three-dimensional structures, (3) addition and processing of carbohydrate units to form oligosaccharide attachments (see chapter 8, p. 146), (4) cleavage of the protein chains, and (5) assembly of protein complexes. A number of enzymes associated with the ER lumen mediate these posttranslational operations.

Once posttranslation modifications are successfully executed, the fully mature proteins make their way to their final destination.

Error Prone

The complexity and intricacy of the posttranslational modifications that take place within the ER make these processes susceptible to errors. It's not uncommon for proteins in the ER lumen to wind up misfolded or to be improperly assembled because of unbalanced subunit production.

Quality control activities ensure that proteins are properly produced and processed by the rough ER.[31] In fact, many scientists consider the quality assurance procedures of the ER to be the quintessential biochemical quality control systems.[32]

Biochemists have discovered that proteins in the ER lumen experience primary and secondary quality control checks. Primary quality control operations monitor general aspects of protein folding. Secondary quality control activities oversee posttranslational processing unique to specific proteins.

One of the most remarkable features of the ER quality assurance systems is the ability to discriminate between misfolded proteins and partially folded proteins that appear misfolded but are well on their way to adopting their intended three-dimensional architectures. If the quality control operations cannot efficiently make this distinction, it is devastating to the cell. In fact, some diseases have been linked to faulty quality control activities in the ER.[33]

When misfolded proteins escape detection, defective proteins accumulate in the cell. On the other hand, to mistakenly discard proteins in the process of being properly folded would be wasteful.

Inspected By

Biochemists recently discovered that the ER quality control systems use information contained within oligosaccharides (see chapter 8, p. 146) as sensors to monitor the folding status of proteins.[34] This process begins when the ER's machinery attaches an oligosaccharide (abbreviated $Glc_3Man_9GlcNAc_2$) to newly made proteins after they've been manufactured by ribosomes and translocated into the lumen of the ER. Once inside the ER, two Glc units are then trimmed from the oligosaccharide to form $Glc_1Man_9GlcNAc_2$. This modified attachment signifies to the ER's machinery that it's time for chaperones to assist the protein with folding (see chapter 5, p. 105).

Once completed, the remaining Glc residue is cleaved to generate the oligosaccharide $Man_9GlcNAc_2$. This attachment tells the ER's quality control system to scrutinize the newly folded protein for any defects. If improperly folded, the ER's machinery reattaches Glc to the oligosaccharide and sends the protein back to the chaperones for another round of folding.

Moving On Down the Line

Once the protein passes this stage of processing, the ER machinery removes a Man group to generate $Man_8GlcNAc_2$. This marker triggers the ER machinery to send the protein to the Golgi apparatus (see chapter 2,

---

Know When to Fold 'Em

Occasionally, the endoplasmic reticulum's (ER's) machinery becomes overwhelmed with unfolded proteins. This glut can stem from the overproduction of proteins or from errors in the oligosaccharide processing steps that guide the ER's quality control operations.[35] If the cell does not effectively deal with the stress on the machinery, the result is catastrophic. Biochemists think the inordinate accumulation of unfolded proteins in the ER contributes to diseases like cancer and neurodegenerative disorders.[36]

When strained this way, the cell responds with something known as the unfolded protein response (UPR). The UPR represents a form of feedback regulation. When too many unfolded proteins are present in the ER, protein synthesis at the rough ER slows down and mRNA molecules that specify the production of proteins processed through the ER are degraded.[37] The UPR can be compared to a waitress who pours soda pop more slowly as the foam rises to the top of the glass.

The UPR represents one more example of the elegant molecular logic that permeates life's chemistry. It also bespeaks foresight and preplanning, indicators of intelligent design.

---

p. 40). If, however, the quality control system detects any evidence that proteins with the $Man_8GlcNAc_2$ attachment are misfolded, it targets them for destruction. In other words, the quality control systems of the ER continually monitor the folding status of proteins as they're processed. If the structure of the bound oligosaccharide does not match the expected state of the protein, it triggers either a recycling step or a destruction sequence.

If the ER's machinery deems it necessary to destroy a defective protein, the machinery shuttles the protein from the ER lumen to the cell's cytoplasm. This process is referred to as retro-translocation.[38] Once in the cytoplasm, the defective protein becomes coated with the protein ubiquitin and destroyed by the proteasome (see chapter 6, p. 121).

High-Fidelity Copies

To reproduce a masterpiece requires exacting attention to every imaginable detail. Each nuance of the image must exactly correspond to the original.

The strict biochemical requirements faced by the cell's machinery that manufactures proteins reflect the same impeccable quality control. To be usable, each protein must be an exact replica of the information housed in the gene that specifies the protein's amino acid sequence.

Even though the biomolecular pathways responsible for protein production display remarkable complexity and chemical elegance, the inherent nature of these chemical and physical processes inevitably causes mistakes to creep into the operation. The need to detect these problems as soon as possible necessitates quality control procedures as stringent as those in any manufacturing plant.

This biochemical quality assurance further highlights the exceptional ingenuity that defines the cell's chemistry and reinforces the conclusion that life has a supernatural basis. Effective and efficient quality control procedures don't just happen. Rather, they are characterized by intentional foresight. Sound quality control systems require careful planning, a detailed understanding of the manufacturing process, the product, and the way that product will be used. All of these features are evident in the quality control activities in the cell. In protein biosynthesis, the placement of quality assurance checkpoints occurs at strategic stages in the production process in a way that ensures reliable protein production while generating manufacturing efficiency.

This chapter focused on some of the purposeful quality assurance procedures associated with protein biosynthesis. Other biochemical systems rely on quality control activities as well. References for a few examples are noted.[39]

Only a designer who exercises thought and care could be so deliberate as to orchestrate effective quality control procedures—whether for a painting's reproduction or for the operations found within the cell. In this context, the cell's quality assurance systems logically compel the conclusion that life's chemistry emanates from the work of a Grand Engineer—One skilled in making exact reproductions. The biochemical fine-tuning displayed by many of the quality control steps associated with protein production and other operations in the cell adds to this analogy. Such precise attention to detail clearly indicates a supreme intelligence at work (see chapter 6).

As biochemists unveil more and more of the cell's elegant artistry, the evidence for a Creator mounts. The next chapter continues to build the case for biochemical intelligent design by considering repeated use of the same patterns in biochemical systems.

Pablo Picasso, *Portrait of Dora Maar* (Reproduced by permission from © 2008 Estate of Pablo Picasso/ Artists Rights Society [ARS], New York; The Bridgeman Art Library)

11

A Style All His Own

Even the uninitiated can often recognize art by Pablo Picasso, partly because of his worldwide fame. But also because distinct styles and recurring themes characterize his work.

The most easily identifiable paintings come from his Cubist period. Picasso and his friend George Braque invented this school of art around 1910.[1] Cubists fragmented three-dimensional objects and redefined them as a series of interlocking planes.[2]

More sophisticated patrons of the arts may recognize paintings from other stages of Picasso's career. Before inventing Cubism, he went through two periods. During his Blue Period, Picasso produced blue-tinted paintings that depict acrobats, harlequins, prostitutes, beggars, and artists. Orange and pink colors defined Picasso's Rose Period. These paintings generally communicate cheery themes.

Even Picasso's Cubism went through distinct phases. While in his analytical Cubist stage, he analyzed objects by taking them apart. During a stage of synthetic Cubism, he incorporated collages into his paintings.

Picasso is not unique. Every artist identifies with particular schools of art and media of expression. They use colors in characteristic ways and typically portray the same objects and gravitate toward certain themes.

And that makes it possible to associate a piece of art with a particular artist. Each artist has his own style.

Recurring Designs

Artists are not the only ones who create in characteristic ways. Other human designers do as well. Engineers, inventors, and architects typically produce works that reflect their own signature styles. This distinction was certainly the case for Frank Lloyd Wright (1867–1959). Trained as a civil engineer, Wright is considered among America's greatest architects.[3] Known for radical innovations, Wright's houses are characterized by open plans that eliminate walls between rooms.

Like artists who generally gravitate toward the same themes—architects, inventors, and engineers also reuse the same techniques and technologies. Wright did. It was much more prudent and efficient for him to reapply a successful strategy (even one that was unconventional) than to invent a new approach, particularly when confronted with complicated problems that already have solutions.

The tendency of artists and other human designers to revisit the same themes and reuse the same designs provides insight into the way a Creator might work. If human craftsmen made in God's image reuse the same techniques and technologies, it's reasonable to infer that their Creator would do the same. So, if life stems from his hand, then it's reasonable to expect the same designs to repeatedly appear throughout nature. And, those recurring themes will reflect the Divine Artist's signature style.

Identical Accidents?

While repeated occurrences of biochemical designs logically point to a Creator, that's not the case for evolutionary processes. If biochemical systems are the product of evolution, then the same biochemical designs should *not* recur throughout nature.

Chance, "the assumed impersonal purposeless determiner of unaccountable happenings,"[4] governs biological and biochemical evolution at its most fundamental level. Evolutionary pathways consist of a historical sequence of chance genetic changes operated on by natural selection, which also consists of chance components. The consequences are profound. If evolutionary events could be repeated, the outcome would be dramatically different every time. The inability of evolutionary processes to retrace the same path makes it highly unlikely that the same biological and biochemical designs should be repeated throughout nature.

This concept of historical contingency is the theme of evolutionary biologist Stephen J. Gould's book *Wonderful Life*. According to Gould:

> No finale can be specified at the start, none would ever occur a second time in the same way, because any pathway proceeds through thousands of improbable stages. Alter any early event, ever so slightly, and without apparent importance at the time, and evolution cascades into a radically different channel.[5]

To help clarify the idea of historical contingency, Gould used the metaphor of "replaying life's tape." If one could push the rewind button and erase life's history, then let the tape run again, the results would be completely different each time.[6] The very essence of the evolutionary process renders its outcomes nonrepeatable.

Putting the Facts to the Test

Most scientists argue that the design so prevalent in biochemical systems is not true design. It only appears that way, an artifact of evolutionary processes. Accordingly, this apparent biochemical design stems from natural selection operating repeatedly on random genetic changes over vast periods of time to fine-tune biochemical systems.

The idea of historical contingency suggests a way to discriminate between the "appearance of design" and intelligent design. Does contingency account for the patterns observed in the biological realm? If life results exclusively from evolutionary processes, then shouldn't scientists expect to see few, if any, cases in which evolution has repeated itself?[7] However, if life is the product of a Creator, then the same designs should repeatedly appear in biochemical systems.

Molecular Convergence

Over the last decade or so, scientists exploring the origin of biochemical systems have made a series of remarkable discoveries. When viewed from an evolutionary perspective, a number of life's molecules and processes, though virtually identical, appear to have originated independently, multiple times.[8] Evolutionary biologists refer to this independent origin of identical biomolecules and biochemical systems as molecular convergence. According to this concept, these molecules and processes arose separately when different evolutionary pathways converged on the same structure or system.

When molecular biologists first began studying biochemical origins, they expected to find few, if any, instances of molecular convergence.[9] One of the first examples was recognized in 1943 when two distinct forms of the enzyme fructose 1,6-bisphosphate aldolase were discovered in yeast and also in rabbit muscles. From an evolutionary perspective, it appears as if these two enzymes had separate evolutionary histories.[10]

At the time, this result was viewed as an evolutionary oddity. In the past decade, however, the advent of genomics—which now makes it possible to sequence, analyze, and compare the genomes of organisms—has made it evident that molecular convergence is a recurring pattern in nature rather than an exception to the rule. Contrary to expectations, biochemists are uncovering a mounting number of repeated independent biochemical origin events.

Evolutionary biologists recognize five different types of molecular convergence:[11]

1. Functional convergence describes the independent origin of biochemical functionality on more than one occasion.
2. Mechanistic convergence refers to the multiple independent emergences of biochemical processes that use the same chemical mechanisms.
3. Structural convergence results when two or more biomolecules independently adopt the same three-dimensional structure.
4. Sequence convergence occurs when either proteins or regions of DNA arise separately but have identical amino acid or nucleotide sequences, respectively.
5. Systemic convergence is the most remarkable of all. This type of molecular convergence describes the independent emergence of identical biochemical systems.

Table 11.1 lists one hundred recently discovered examples of molecular convergence. This table is neither comprehensive nor exhaustive. It simply calls attention to the pervasiveness of molecular convergence. (Remember, as is true when looking at a particular group of paintings in any gallery, it is fine to skim through them or move on to the next section whenever you're ready.)

Table 11.1
Examples of Molecular Convergence

Example	Reference
RNA	
Small nucleolar RNAs in eukaryotes and archaea	Omer, Arina D., et al. "Homologs of Small Nuclear RNAs in Archaea." *Science* 288 (April 21, 2000): 517–22.
Hammerhead Ribozyme	Salehi-Ashtiani, Kourosh, and Jack W. Szostak. "*In Vitro* Evolution Suggests Multiple Origins for the Hammerhead Ribosome." *Nature* 414 (November 1, 2001): 82–84.
DNA and Genes	
Gene structure of lamprin, elastins, and insect structural proteins	Robson, Paul, et al. "The Structure and Organization of Lamprin Genes: Multiple-Copy Genes with Alternative Splicing and Convergent Evolution with Insect Structural Proteins." *Molecular Biology and Evolution* 17 (November 2000): 1739–52.
Major histocompatibility complex DRB gene sequences in humans and Old and New World monkeys	Kriener, K., et al. "Convergent Evolution of Major Histocompatibility Complex Molecules in Humans and New World Monkeys." *Immunogenetics* 51 (March 2000): 169–78.
Structure and expression of the Ω–crystallin gene in vertebrates and invertebrates	Carosa, Eleonora, et al. "Structure and Expression of the Scallop Ω–Crystallin Gene: Evidence for Convergent Evolution of Promoter Sequences." *Journal of Biological Chemistry* 277 (January 4, 2002): 656–64.
Group I introns in mitochondria and chloroplasts, and hyperthermophilic bacteria	Nesbo, Camillia L., and W. Ford Doolittle. "Active Self-Splicing Group I Introns in 23S rRNA Genes of Hyperthermophilic Bacteria, Derived from Introns in Eukaryotic Organelles." *Proceedings of the National Academy of Sciences, USA* 100 (September 16, 2003): 10806–11.
Flanking sequences to microsatellite DNA in the human genome	Vowles, Edward J., and William Amos. "Evidence for Widespread Convergent Evolution around Human Microsatellites." *PLoS Biology* 2 (August 17, 2004): e199.
Proteins and Enzymes	
Immunoglobulin G-binding proteins in bacteria	Frick, Inga-Maria, et al. "Convergent Evolution among Immunoglobulin G-Binding Bacterial Proteins." *Proceedings of the National Academy of Sciences, USA* 89 (September 15, 1992): 8532–36.
The α/β hydrolase fold of hydrolytic enzymes	Ollis, David L., et al. "The α/β Hydrolase Fold." *Protein Engineering* 5 (April 1992): 197–211.
Peptidases	Rawlings, Neil D., and Alan J. Barrett. "Evolutionary Families of Peptidases." *Biochemical Journal* 290 (February 15, 1993): 205–18.

Myoglobins in humans and gastropods	Suzuki, Tomohiko, H. Yuasa, and Kiyohiro Imai. "Convergent Evolution. The Gene Structure of Sulculus 41 kDa Myoglobin Is Homologous with that of Human Indoleamine Dioxygenase." *Biochimica Biophysica Acta* 1308 (July 31, 1996): 41–48.
Tubulin in eukaryotes and FtsZ in bacteria	Desai, Arshad, and Timothy J. Mitchison. "Tubulin and FtsZ Structures: Functional and Therapeutic Implications." *Bioessays* 20 (July 1998): 523–27.
D-alanine:D-alanine ligase and cAMP-dependent protein kinase	Denessiouk, K. A., et al. "Two 'Unrelated' Families of ATP-Dependent Enzymes Share Extensive Structural Similarities about Their Cofactor Binding Sites." *Protein Science* 7 (May 1998): 1136–46.
Cytokines in vertebrates and invertebrates	Beschin, Alain, et al. "Convergent Evolution of Cytokines." *Nature* 400 (August 12, 1999): 627–28.
Zinc peptidases	Makarova, Kira S., and Nick V. Grishin. "The Zn-Peptidase Superfamily: Functional Convergence after Evolutionary Divergence." *Journal of Molecular Biology* 292 (September 10, 1999): 11–17.
Redox regulation of glucose 6-phosphate dehydrogenase in plants and cyanobacteria	Wendt, Urte K., et al. "Evidence for Functional Convergence of Redox Regulation in G6PDH Isoforms of Cyanobacteria and Higher Plants." *Plant Molecular Biology* 40 (June 1999): 487–94.
MDR ethanol dehydrogenase/acetaldehyde reductase in vertebrates and *Escherichia coli*	Shafqat, Jawed, et al. "An Ethanol-Inducible MDR Ethanol Dehydrogenase/Acetaldehyde Reductase in *Escherichia coli*." *European Journal of Biochemistry* 263 (July 1999): 305–11.
Carbonic anhydrase in bacteria and archaea	Smith, Kerry S., et al. "Carbonic Anhydrase Is an Ancient Enzyme Widespread in Prokaryotes." *Proceedings of the National Academy of Sciences, USA* 96 (December 21, 1999): 15184–89.
Myo-inositol-1–phosphate synthase in eukaryotes, bacteria, and archaea	Bachhawat, N. N., and S. C. Mande. "Complex Evolution of the Inositol-1–Phosphate Synthase Gene among Archaea and Eubacteria." *Trends in Genetics* 16 (March 2000): 111–13.
Myoglobins in eukaryotes and myoglobin-like, heme-containing protein in archaea	Hou, Shaobin, Randy W. Larsen, Dmitri Boudko, Charles W. Riley, et al. "Myoglobin-Like Aerotaxis Transducers in Archaea and Bacteria." *Nature* 403 (February 3, 2000): 540–44.
Calmodulins in vertebrates and cephalochordates	Karabinos, Anton, and Debashish Bhattacharya. "Molecular Evolution of Calmodulin and Calmodulin-Like Genes in the Cephalochordate Branchiostoma." *Journal of Molecular Evolution* 51 (August 2000): 141–48.
Pheromone binding proteins in moths	Willett, Christopher S. "Do Pheromone Binding Proteins Converge in Amino Acid Sequence When Pheromones Converge?" *Journal of Molecular Evolution* 50 (February 2000): 175–83.
DNA Holliday junction resolvases in bacteria and eukaryotic viruses	Garcia, Alonzo D., et al. "Bacterial-Type DNA Holliday Junction Resolvases in Eukaryotic Viruses." *Proceedings of the National Academy of Sciences, USA* 97 (August 1, 2000): 8926–31.
The DNA replication protein, RepA, in Gram-negative bacteria plasmids, archaea, and eukaryotes	Giraldo, Rafael, and Ramón Díaz-Orejas. "Similarities between the DNA Replication Initiators of Gram-Negative Bacteria Plasmids (RepA) and Eukaryotes (Orc4p)/Archaea (Cdc6p)." *Proceedings of the National Academy of Sciences, USA* 98 (April 24, 2001): 4938–43.

Spider silk fibroin sequences	Gatesy, John, et al. "Extreme Diversity, Conservation, and Convergence of Spider Silk Fibroin Sequences." *Science* 291 (March 30, 2001): 2603–5.
Alcohol dehydrogenase in *Drosophila* and medfly, olive fly, and flesh fly	Brogna, Saverio, et al. "The *Drosophila* Alcohol Dehydrogenase Gene May Have Evolved Independently of the Functionally Homologous Medfly, Olive Fly, and Flesh Fly Genes." *Molecular Biology and Evolution* 18 (March 2001): 322–29.
Type II restriction enzymes	Bujnicki, Janusz, Monika Radlinska, and Leszek Rychlewski. "Polyphyletic Evolution of Type II Restriction Enzymes Revisited: Two Independent Sources of Second-Hand Folds Revealed." *Trends in Biochemical Sciences* 26 (January 2001): 9–11.
Heavy metal binding domains of copper chaperones and copper-transporting ATPases	Jordan, I. King, et al. "Independent Evolution of Heavy Metal-Associated Domains in Copper Chaperones and Copper-Transporting ATPases." *Journal of Molecular Evolution* 53 (December 2001): 622–33.
Opsin in vertebrates and invertebrates	Zakon, Harold H. "Convergent Evolution on the Molecular Level." *Brain, Behavior and Evolution* 59, nos. 5–6 (2002): 250–61.
Ionotropic and metabotropic neurotransmitter receptors	Ibid.
Gap junction proteins in invertebrates and vertebrates	Ibid.
Neurotoxins in invertebrates and vertebrates	Ibid.
Anti-β-elimination mechanism in 1 and 10 polysaccharide lyases	Charnock, Simon J., et al. "Convergent Evolution Sheds Light on the Anti-β-Elimination Mechanism in 1 and 10 Polysaccharide Lyases." *Proceedings of the National Academy of Sciences, USA* 99 (September 17, 2002): 12067–72.
α1,4-fucosyltransferase activity in primates	Dupuy, Fabrice, et al. "α1,4-Fucosyltransferase Activity: A Significant Function in the Primate Lineage Has Appeared Twice Independently." *Molecular Biology and Evolution* 19 (June 2002): 815–24.
Aldehyde oxidase into xanthine dehydrogenase two separate times	Rodriguez-Trelles, Francisco, Rosa Tarrio, and Francisco J. Ayala. "Convergent Neofunctionalization by Positive Darwinian Selection after Ancient Recurrent Duplications of the *Xanthine Dehydrogenase* Gene." *Proceedings of the National Academy of Sciences, USA* 100 (November 11, 2003): 13413–17.
RuBisCo-like protein of *Bacillus* in nonphotosynthetic bacteria and archaea and photosynthetic RuBisCo in photosynthetic bacteria	Ashida, Hiroki, et al. "A Functional Link between RuBisCO-Like Protein of *Bacillus* and Photosynthetic RuBisCO." *Science* 302 (October 10, 2003): 286–90.
Active site of creatinine amidohydrolase of *Pseudomonas putida* and hydantoinase-like cyclic amidohydrolases	Beuth, B., K. Niefind, and D. Schomburg. "Crystal Structure of Creatininase from *Pseudomonas putida*: A Novel Fold and a Case of Convergent Evolution." *Journal of Molecular Biology* 332 (September 5, 2003): 287–301.

The insect flight muscle protein arthrin in Diptera and Hemiptera	Schmitz, Stephan, et al. "Molecular Evolutionary Convergence of the Flight Muscle Protein Arthrin in Diptera and Hemiptera." *Molecular Biology and Evolution* 20 (December 2003): 2019–33.
The enzyme, tRNA(m1G37) methyltransferase, in bacteria and archaea	Christian, Thomas, et al. "Distinct Origins of tRNA(m1G37) Methyltransferase." *Journal of Molecular Biology* 339 (June 11, 2004): 707–19.
β-lactam-hydrolyzing function of the B1+B2 and B3 subclasses of metallo-β-lactamases	Hall, Barry, Stephen Salipante, and Miriam Barlow. "Independent Origins of Subgroup B1+B2 and Subgroup B3 Metallo-β-Lactamases." *Journal of Molecular Evolution* 59 (July 2004): 133–41.
Catabolic enzymes for galactitol, and D-tagatose in enteric bacteria	Shakeri-Garakani, et al. "The Genes and Enzymes for the Catabolism of Galactitol, D-Tagatose, and Related Carbohydrates in *Klebsiella oxytoca* M5a1 and Other Enteric Bacteria Display Convergent Evolution." *Molecular Genetics and Genomics* 271 (July 2004): 717–28.
Lipases and GDSL esterases/lipases	Akoh, C. C., et al. "GDSL Family of Serine Esterases/Lipases." *Progress in Lipid Research* 43 (November 2004): 534–52.
Chitosanases	Adachi, Wataru, et al. "Crystal Structure of Family GH-8 Chitosanase with Subclass II Specificity from Bacillus sp. K17." *Journal of Molecular Biology* 343 (October 22, 2004): 785–95.
Plant and cyanobacterial phytochromes	Lamparter, T. "Evolution of Cyanobacterial Plant Phytochromes." *FEBS Letters* 573 (August 27, 2004): 1–5.
The outer membrane protein, OmpA, in *Enterobacteriaceae*	Gophna, U., et al. "OmpA of a Septicemic *Escherichia coli* O78—Secretion and Convergent Evolution." *International Journal of Medical Microbiology* 294 (November 1, 2004): 373–81.
Cardiovascular risk factor, LPA in hedgehogs and primates	Boffelli, D., J. F. Cheng, and E. M. Rubin. "Convergent Evolution in Primates and an Insectivore." *Genomics* 83 (January 2004): 19–23.
Lectin-like activity of cytokines in vertebrates and invertebrates	Beschin, A., et al. "Functional Convergence of Invertebrate and Vertebrate Cytokine-Like Molecules Based on a Similar Lectin-Like Activity." *Progress in Molecular and Subcellular Biology* 34 (2004): 145–63.
Temperature adaptation of A_4-lactate dehydrogenases of Pacific damselfishes	Johns, Glenn C., and George N. Somero. "Evolutionary Convergence in Adaptation of Proteins to Temperature: A_4-Lactate Dehydrogenases of Pacific Damselfishes (*Chromis* spp.)." *Molecular Biology and Evolution* 21 (February 2004): 314–20.
Scorpion and sea anemone toxins that bind to voltage-gated potassium ion channels	Gasparini, S., B. Gilquin, and A. Menez. "Comparison of Sea Anemone and Scorpion Toxins Binding to Kv1 Channels: An Example of Convergent Evolution." *Toxicon* 43 (June 15, 2004): 901–8.
Feruloyl esterase A in microorganisms	Hermoso, J. A., et al. "The Crystal Structure of Feruloyl Esterase A from *Aspergillus niger* Suggests Evolutive Functional Convergence in Feruloyl Esterase Family." *Journal of Molecular Biology* 338 (April 30, 2004): 495–506.

The proofreading domain of the enzyme threonyl-tRNA synthetase in archaea and bacteria	Korencic, Dragana, et al. "A Freestanding Proofreading Domain Is Required for Protein Synthesis Quality Control Archaea." *Proceedings of the National Academy of Sciences, USA* 101 (July 13, 2004): 10260–65.
Protein inhibitors of proteases	Otlewski, Jacek, et al. "The Many Faces of Protease-Protein Inhibitor Interaction." *EMBO Journal* 24 (April 6, 2005): 1303–10.
Alginate lyases	Osawa, Takuo, et al. "Crystal Structure of the Alginate (Poly α-L-Guluronate) Lyase from *Corynebacterium* sp. At 1.2 Å Resolution." *Journal of Molecular Biology* 345 (February 4, 2005): 1111–18.
Defensins from insects and mollusks and ABF proteins in nematodes	Froy, Oren. "Convergent Evolution of Invertebrate Defensins and Nematode Antibacterial Factors." *Trends in Microbiology* 13 (July 2005): 314–19.
Blue and red light photoreceptors in diatoms	Falciatore, Angela, and Chris Bowler. "The Evolution and Function of Blue and Red Light Photoreceptors." *Current Topics in Developmental Biology* 68 (2005): 317–50.
Red light photoreceptors in ferns and green algae	Suetsugu, Noriyuki, et al. "A Chimeric Photoreceptor Gene, NEOCHROME, Has Arisen Twice during Plant Evolution." *Proceedings of the National Academy of Sciences, USA* 102 (September 20, 2005): 13705–9.
Xanthine oxidation in fungus	Cultrone, Antonietta, et al. "Convergent Evolution of Hydroxylation Mechanisms in the Fungal Kingdom: Molybdenum Cofactor-Independent Hydroxylation of Xanthine via α-Ketoglutarate-Dependent Dioxygenases." *Molecular Microbiology* 57, no. 1 (July 2005): 276–90.
The muscle protein troponin C in various insect orders	Herranz, Raúl, Jesús Mateos, and Roberto Marco. "Diversification and Independent Evolution of Troponin C Genes in Insects." *Journal of Molecular Evolution* 60 (January 2005): 31–44.
Structure of immunoglobulin and C type lectin receptors	Feng, Jianwen, et al. "Convergence on a Distinctive Assembly Mechanism by Unrelated Families of Activating Immune Receptors." *Immunity* 22 (April 2005): 427–38.
The placental development syncytin family of proteins in primates and Muridae from separate endogenous retrovirus infections	Dupressoir, Anne, et al. "Syncytin-A and Syncytin-B, Two Fusogenic Placenta-Specific Murine Envelope Genes of Retroviral Origin Conserved in Muridae." *Proceedings of the National Academy of Sciences, USA* 102 (January 18, 2005): 725–30.
Structure and function of *S*-adenosylmethionine-binding proteins	Kozbial, Piotr Z., and Arcady R. Mushegian. "Natural History of *S*-Adenosylmethionine-Binding Proteins." *BMC Structural Biology* 5 (October 14, 2005): art. 19.
2–methylbutyryl-CoA dehydrogenase in potato and short/branched-chain acyl-CoA dehydrogenase in humans	Goetzman, Eric S., et al. "Convergent Evolution of a 2–Methylbutyryl-CoA Dehydrogenase from Isovaleryl-CoA Dehydrogenase in *Solanum tuberosum*." *Journal of Biological Chemistry* 280 (February 11, 2005): 4873–79.
Dynamin-mediated endocytosis in multicellular animals and ciliates	Elde, Nels C., et al. "Elucidation of Clathrin-Mediated Endocytosis in *Tetrahymena* Reveals an Evolutionarily Convergent Recruitment of Dynamin." *PLoS Genetics* 1 (November 4, 2005): e:52.

The animal glycan-recognizing proteins—lectins and sulfated glycosaminoglycan binding proteins—in animals	Varki, Ajit, and Takashi Angata. "Siglecs—The Major Subfamily of I-Type Lectins." *Glycobiology* 16 (January 2006): 1R–27R.
Sodium channel in the electric organ of the mormyriform and gymnotiform electric fishes	Zakon, Harold H., et al. "Sodium Channel Genes and the Evolution of Diversity in Communication Signals of Electric Fishes: Convergent Molecular Evolution." *Proceedings of the National Academy of Sciences, USA* 103 (March 7, 2006): 3675–80.
Clathrin heavy and light chain isoforms in chordates	Wakeham, Diane E., et al. "Clathrin Heavy and Light Chain Isoforms Originated by Independent Mechanisms of Gene Duplication during Chordate Evolution." *Proceedings of the National Academy of Sciences, USA* 102 (May 17, 2005): 7209–14.
Protein-binding receptor that readies proteins for import into the mitochondria of animals and plants	Perry, Andrew J., et al. "Convergent Evolution of Receptors for Protein Import into Mitochondria." *Current Biology* 16 (February 7, 2006): 221–29.
ICP C1 cysteine peptidase inhibitors	Smith, Brian O., et al. "The Structure of *Leishmania mexicana* ICP Provides Evidence for Convergent Evolution of Cysteine Peptidase Inhibitors." *Journal of Biological Chemistry* 281 (March 3, 2006): 5821–28.
TRIM5 anti-retroviral resistance factor in primates and bovines	Si, Zhihai, et al. "Evolution of a Cytoplasmic Tripartite Motif (TRIM) Protein in Cows that Restricts Retroviral Infection." *Proceedings of the National Academy of Sciences, USA* 103 (May 9, 2006): 7454–59.
Protein receptors that bind bitter compounds in humans and chimpanzees	Wooding, Stephen, et al. "Independent Evolution of Bitter-Taste Sensitivity in Humans and Chimpanzees." *Nature* 440 (April 13, 2006): 930–34.
Protoporphyrin (IX) ferrochelatase in prokaryotes and eukaryotes	Shepherd, Mark, Tamara A. Dailey, and Harry A. Dailey. "A New Class of [2Fe-2S]-Cluster-Containing Protoporphyrin (IX) Ferrochelatases." *Biochemical Journal* 397 (July 1, 2006): 47–52.
SPFH (stomatin-prohibitin-flotillin-HflC/K)–like proteins	Rivera-Milla, E., C. A. Stuermer, and E. Málaga-Trillo. "Ancient Origin of Reggie (Flotillin), Reggie-Like, and Other Lipid-Raft Proteins: Convergent Evolution of the SPFH Domain." *Cellular and Molecular Life Sciences* 63, no. 3 (February 2006): 343–57.
Disulfide-rich protein domains	Cheek, S., S. S. Krishna, and N. V. Grishin. "Structural Classification of Small, Disulfide-Rich Protein Domains." *Journal of Molecular Biology* 359 (May 26, 2006): 215–37.
Fatty acid synthases in fungi and animals	Maier, Timm, Simon Jenni, and Nenad Ban. "Architecture of Mammalian Fatty Acid Synthase at 4.5 Å Resolution." *Science* 311 (March 3, 2006): 1258–62; Jenni, Simon, Marc Leibundgut, Timm Maier, and Nenad Ban. "Architecture of a Fungal Fatty Acid Synthase at 5 Å Resolution." *Science* 311 (March 3, 2006): 1263–67.
NAD(P)H:quinone oxidoreductase (NQO)	Vasiliou, Vasilis, David Ross, and Daniel W. Nebert. "Update of the NAD(P)H:Quinone Oxidoreductase (NQO) Gene Family." *Human Genomics* 2 (March 2006): 329–35.

Adenylation activity in BirA, lipoate protein ligase and class II tRNA synthetases	Wood, Zachary A., et al. "Co-Repressor Induced Order and Biotin Repressor Dimerization: A Case for Divergent Followed by Convergent Evolution." *Journal of Molecular Biology* 357 (March 24, 2006): 509–23.
D7 and lipocalin salivary proteins in insects	Calvo, Eric, et al. "Function and Evolution of a Mosquito Salivary Protein Family." *Journal of Biological Chemistry* 281 (January 27, 2006): 1935–42.
Cold shock domain of cold shock proteins in bacteria and higher plants	Nakaminami, Kentaro, Dale T. Karlson, and Ryozo Imai. "Functional Conservation of Cold Shock Domains in Bacteria and Higher Plants." *Proceedings of the National Academy of Sciences, USA* 103 (June 27, 2006): 10122–27.

Biochemical Systems

Bioluminescent systems	Hastings, J. W. "Biological Diversity, Chemical Mechanisms, and the Evolutionary Origins of Bioluminescent Systems." *Journal of Molecular Evolution* 19 (September 1983): 309–21.
Chlorocatechol catabolic pathway in *Rhodococcus opacus* and proteobacteria	Eulberg, Dirk, et al. "Evolutionary Relationship between Chlorocatechol Catabolic Enzymes from *Rhodococcus opacus* 1CP and Their Counterparts in Proteobacteria: Sequence Divergence and Functional Convergence." *Journal of Bacteriology* 180, no. 5 (March 1998): 1082–94.
Nucleotide excision DNA repair in humans and *Escherichia coli*	Petit, C., and A. Sancar. "Nucleotide Excision Repair: From *E. coli* to Man." *Biochimie* 81 (January 2, 1999): 15–25.
DNA replication in bacteria and archaea	Leipe, Detlef D., L. Aravind, and Eugene V. Koonin. "Did DNA Replication Evolve Twice Independently?" *Nucleic Acids Research* 27 (September 1, 1999): 3389–3401.
DNA repair proteins	Aravind, L., D. Roland Walker, and Eugene V. Koonin. "Conserved Domains in DNA Repair Proteins and Evolution of Repair Systems." *Nucleic Acids Research* 27 (March 1, 1999): 1223–42.
Toxin resistance	Zakon, Harold H. "Convergent Evolution on the Molecular Level." *Brain, Behavior and Evolution* 59, nos. 5–6 (2002): 250–61.
Biosurfactants in archaea and bacteria	Maier, Raina M. "Biosurfactants: Evolution and Diversity in Bacteria." *Advances in Applied Microbiology* 52 (2003): 101–21.
Glycolytic pathways in archaea and bacteria	Verhees, Corné H., et al. "The Unique Features of Glycolytic Pathways in Archaea." *Biochemical Journal* 375 (October 15, 2003): 231–46.
Type III and Type IV secretion systems of gram-negative and gram-positive bacteria	Blocker, Ariel, Kaoru Komoriya, and Shin-Ichi Aizawa. "Type III Secretion Systems and Bacterial Flagella: Insights into Their Function from Structural Similarities." *Proceedings of the National Academy of Sciences, USA* 100 (March 18, 2003): 3027–30.
Phosphopantothenate biosynthesis in archaea and bacteria	Genschel, Ulrich. "Coenzyme A Biosynthesis: Reconstruction of the Pathway in Archaea and an Evolutionary Scenario Based on Comparative Genomics." *Molecular Biology and Evolution* 21 (July 2004): 1242–51.

Crassulacean acid metabolism, a specialized form of photosynthesis in the Bromeliaceae family of plants	Crayn, Darren M., Klaus Winter, and J. Andrew C. Smith. "Multiple Origins of Crassulacean Acid Metabolism and the Epiphytic Habit in the Neotropical Family Bromeliaceae." *Proceedings of the National Academy of Sciences, USA* 101 (March 9, 2004): 3703–8.
Alternate splicing of tandem exons in ion-channel genes in humans and *Drosophila melanogaster*	Copley, Richard R. "Evolutionary Convergence of Alternative Splicing in Ion Channels." *Trends in Genetics* 20 (April 2004): 171–76.
Viral capsid structure of viruses that infect archaea, bacteria, and eukarya	Rice, George, et al. "The Structure of a Thermophilic Archaeal Virus Shows a Double-Stranded DNA Capsid Type that Spans All Domains of Life." *Proceedings of the National Academy of Sciences, USA* 101 (May 18, 2004): 7716–20.
Hub-based design of gene regulatory networks	Amoutzias, Gregory D., et al. "Convergent Evolution of Gene Networks by Single-Gene Duplications in Higher Eukaryotes." *EMBO Reports* 5 (March 2004): 274–79.
The two Mg^{2+} metal ion mechanism in protein phosphoryltransferases and RNA phosphoryltransferases	Stahley, Mary R., and Scott A. Strobel. "Structural Evidence for a Two-Metal-Ion Mechanism of Group I Intron Splicing." *Science* 309 (September 2, 2005): 1587–90.
Halophilic biochemical adaptations in bacteria and archaea	Mongodin, E. F., et al. "The Genome of *Salinibacter ruber*: Convergence and Gene Exchange among Hyperhalophilic Bacteria and Archaea." *Proceedings of the National Academy of Sciences, USA* 102 (December 13, 2005): 18147–52.
Regulatory network linking DNA synthesis to cell cycle in yeast and bacteria	Brazhnik, Paul, and John J. Tyson. "Cell Cycle Control in Bacteria and Yeast: A Case of Convergent Evolution?" *Cell Cycle* 5 (March 2006): 522–29.
Biochemical mechanisms for ion regulation in invertebrates	Zanotto, Flavia Pinheiro, and Michele G. Wheatly. "Ion Regulation in Invertebrates: Molecular and Integrative Aspects." *Physiological and Biochemical Zoology* 79 (March/April 2006): 357–62.
Apoptosis and immune response defenses in large nuclear and cytoplasmic DNA viruses of eukaryotes	Iyer, Lakshminarayan M., et al. "Evolutionary Genomics of Nucleo-Cytoplasmic Large DNA Viruses." *Virus Research* 117 (April 2006): 156–84.
Endocannabinoid system	McPartland, John M., et al. "Evolutionary Origins of the Endocannabinoid System." *Gene* 370 (March 29, 2006): 64–74.
Nonuniversal codon usage in the genetic code of arthropod mitochondrial genomes	Abascal, Federico, et al. "Parallel Evolution of the Genetic Code in Arthropod Mitochondrial Genomes." *PLoS Biology* 4 (May 2006): e127.
Xist RNA gene-mediated X chromosome inactivation in eutherian and marsupial mammals	Duret, Laurent, et al. "The *Xist* RNA Gene Evolved in Eutherians by Pseudogenization of a Protein-Coding Gene." *Science* 312 (June 16, 2006): 1653–55.

Currently recognized examples of molecular convergence are likely just the tip of the iceberg. For instance, researchers from Cambridge University (United Kingdom) examined the amino acid sequences of over six hundred peptidase enzymes. (Peptidases are proteins that break down other proteins by cleaving bonds between amino acids.) When viewed from an evolutionary standpoint, these workers discovered that there appear to have been over sixty separate origin events for peptidases. This result stands in sharp contrast to what the researchers expected to find: a handful of peptidase families with separate origins. In many cases, the peptidases appeared to converge on the same enzyme mechanisms and reaction specificities.[12]

Researchers from the National Institutes of Health recently made a similar discovery. These scientists systematically examined protein sequences from 1,709 EC (enzyme commission) classes and discovered that 105 of them consisted of proteins that catalyzed the same reaction, but must have had separate evolutionary origins.[13]

In a separate study, this same team discovered that in at least twelve clear-cut cases the same essential cellular functions were carried out by unrelated enzymes (from an evolutionary vantage point) when the genomes of the bacteria *Mycoplasma genitalium* and *Hemophilus influenzae* were compared.[14] The researchers noted that the genomes of these two microbes are small, close to the size of the minimal gene set (see chapter 3, p. 54). It's quite likely a greater number of convergent systems would be identified if the genomes of more complex organisms were compared.

The explosion in the number of examples of molecular convergence is unexpected if life results from historical sequences of chance evolutionary events. Yet, if life emanates from a Creator, it's reasonable to expect he would use the same designs repeatedly. These creations would give the appearance of multiple independent origin events when viewed from an evolutionary vantage point.

It is beyond the scope of this book to detail each example of molecular convergence. Rather, a discussion of one of the most amazing examples of molecular convergence, the independent origins of DNA replication in bacteria and archaea/eukaryotes, illustrates how remarkable molecular convergence is from an evolutionary standpoint and why it's preferable to view the repeated independent origins of biochemical systems as the work of a Divine Artist who creates with a style all his own.

The Origin of DNA Replication

The process of generating two "daughter" molecules identical to the "parent" DNA molecule—DNA replication—is essential for life. This duplication plays a central role in reproduction, inaugurating the cell-division process. Once replicated, a complex ensemble of enzymes distributes the two newly made DNA molecules between the emerging daughter cells.

Because of its extremely complex nature (described below), most biochemists previously thought DNA replication arose once, prior to the origin of LUCA, the last universal common ancestor. Figure 11.1 shows the relationship between this supposed "organism" and the evolutionary tree of life.

Many biochemists have long regarded the close functional similarity of DNA replication, observed in all life, as evidence for the single origin of DNA replication prior to the emergence of LUCA.

The common features of DNA replication include

1. semiconservative replication,
2. initiation at a defined origin by an origin-replication complex,
3. bidirectional movement of the replication fork,
4. continuous (leading strand) replication for one DNA strand and discontinuous (lagging strand) replication for the other DNA strand,
5. use of RNA primers, and
6. the use of nucleases, polymerases, and ligases to replace RNA primer with DNA (see DNA replication discussion below).

Surprisingly, in 1999 researchers from the National Institutes of Health demonstrated that the core enzymes in the DNA replication machinery of bacteria and archaea/eukaryotes (the two major trunks of the evolutionary tree of life) did not share a common evolutionary origin. From an evolutionary perspective, it appears as if two identical DNA replication systems emerged independently in bacteria and archaea—after these two evolutionary lineages supposedly diverged from the last universal common ancestor.[15] (If evolutionary processes explain the origin of DNA replication, then two *different* systems should exist in archaea and bacteria.)

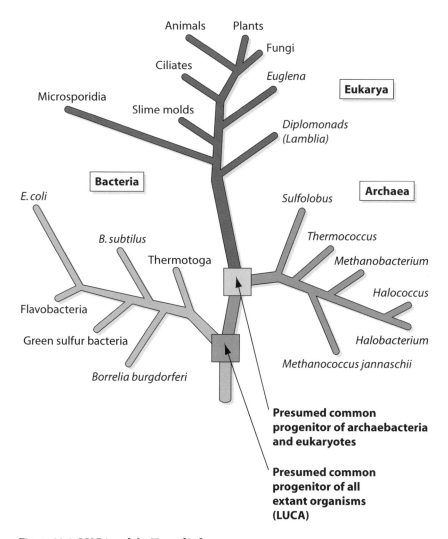

Figure 11.1. LUCA and the Tree of Life
The proposed evolutionary relationship of life's major groups has the domains Archaea and Bacteria diverging separately from the Last Universal Common Ancestor (LUCA).

DNA Replication—A Signature Style

DNA consists of two polynucleotide chains aligned in antiparallel fashion. (The two strands are arranged parallel to one another with the starting point of one strand in the polynucleotide duplex located next to the ending point of the other strand and vice versa. See chapter 2, p. 48.) The paired polynucleotide chains twist around each other forming the well-known DNA double helix. The polynucleotide chains are generated using four different nucleotides: adenosine (A), guanosine (G), cytidine (C), and thymidine (T). (See figure 2.7, p. 49.)

A special relationship exists between the nucleotide sequences of the two DNA strands.[16] These sequences are considered complementary. When the DNA strands align, the A side chains of one strand always pair with T side chains from the other strand. Likewise, the G side chains from one DNA strand always pair with C side chains from the other strand. Biochemists refer to these relationships as base-pairing rules.

As a result of this base pairing, if biochemists know the sequence of one DNA strand, they can readily determine the sequence of the other strand. Base pairing plays a critical role in DNA replication.

Following a Pattern

The nucleotide sequences of the parent DNA molecule function as a template directing the assembly of the DNA strands of the two daughter molecules. It is a semiconservative process because after replication, each daughter DNA molecule contains one newly formed DNA strand and one strand from the parent molecule (see figure 11.2).

Conceptually, template-directed, semiconservative DNA replication entails the separation of the parent DNA double helix into two single strands. According to the base-pairing rules, each strand serves as a template for the cell's machinery to follow as it forms a new DNA strand with a nucleotide sequence complementary to the parent strand. Because each strand of the parent DNA molecule directs the production of a new DNA strand, two daughter molecules result. Each possesses an original strand from the parent molecule and a newly formed DNA strand produced by a template-directed synthetic process.

The Start of It All

DNA replication begins at specific sites along the DNA double helix.

Figure 11.2. Semiconservative DNA Replication
For template-directed, semiconservative DNA replication each strand serves as a template for the cell's machinery to assemble a new DNA strand. Each of the two "daughter" molecules possesses an original strand from the "parent" molecule and a newly formed DNA strand.

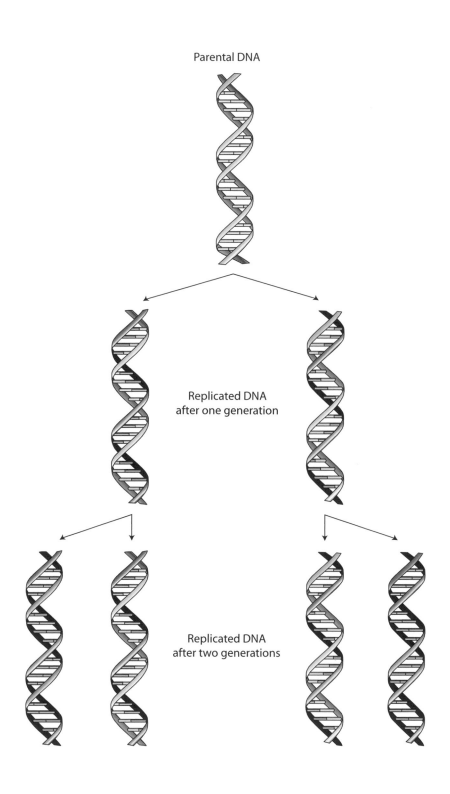

Parental DNA

Replicated DNA
after one generation

Replicated DNA
after two generations

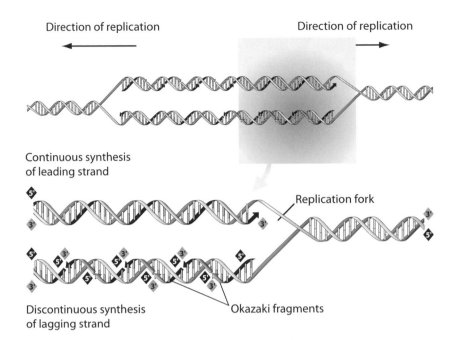

Figure 11.3. DNA Replication Bubble
The replication bubble forms where the DNA double helix unwinds. Because DNA replication proceeds in both directions away from the origin, there are two replication forks within each bubble.

Typically, prokaryotic cells have only a single origin of replication. More complex eukaryotic cells have multiple origins.

The DNA double helix unwinds locally at the origin of replication to produce a replication bubble (see figure 11.3). The bubble expands in both directions from the origin during the course of replication. Once the individual strands of the DNA double helix unwind and are exposed within the replication bubble, they are available to direct the production of the daughter strand. The site where the double helix continuously unwinds is the replication fork. Because DNA replication proceeds in both directions away from the origin, each bubble contains two replication forks.

Moving On

DNA replication can proceed only in a single direction, from the top of the DNA strand to the bottom. Because the strands that form the DNA double helix align in an antiparallel fashion with the top of one strand juxtaposed to the bottom of the other strand, only one strand at each replication fork has the proper orientation (bottom-to-top) to direct the assembly of a new strand in the top-to-bottom direction. For this leading strand, DNA replication proceeds rapidly and continuously in the direction of the advancing replication fork (see figure 11.3).

DNA replication can't proceed along the strand with the top-to-bottom orientation until the replication bubble expands enough to expose a sizeable stretch of DNA. When this happens, DNA replication moves away from the advancing replication fork. It can proceed only a short distance along the top-to-bottom oriented strand before the replication process has to stop and wait for more of the parent DNA strand to be unwound. After a sufficient length of the parent DNA template is exposed the second time, DNA replication can proceed again, but only briefly before it has to stop and wait for more DNA to become available.

The process of discontinuous DNA replication takes place repeatedly until the entire strand is replicated. Each time DNA replication starts and stops, a small fragment of DNA is produced. These pieces of DNA (that eventually comprise the daughter strand) are called Okazaki fragments after the biochemist who discovered them. The discontinuously produced strand is the lagging strand, because DNA replication for this strand lags behind the more rapidly, continuously produced leading strand (see figure 11.3).

One additional point: the leading strand at one replication fork is the lagging strand at the other replication fork because the replication forks at the two ends of the replication bubble advance in opposite directions.

Considering the complexity of DNA replication described up to this point, it's hard to imagine this process evolving once, let alone independently on two separate occasions. But there is even more that makes it difficult to fathom how DNA replication could have occurred by naturalistic processes.

The Protein Palette

An ensemble of proteins is needed to carry out DNA replication (see figure 11.4). Once the origin recognition complex (which consists of several different proteins) identifies the replication origin, a protein called helicase unwinds the DNA double helix to form the replication fork. The

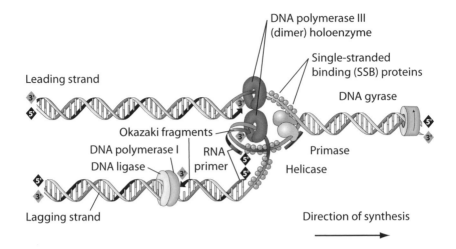

Figure 11.4. The Proteins of DNA Replication
The ensemble of proteins needed to carry out DNA replication include helicase, single-strand binding proteins, the primosome, DNA polymerases, 3'-5' exonuclease, and ligase.

process of helix unwinding introduces torsional stress in the DNA helix downstream from the replication fork. Another protein, gyrase, relieves the stress preventing the DNA molecule from supercoiling, like the cord attached to the telephone receiver after the phone is hung up.

Single-strand binding proteins bind to the DNA strands exposed by the unwinding process. This association keeps the fragile DNA strands from breaking apart.

Once the replication fork is established and stabilized, DNA replication can begin. Before the newly formed daughter strands can be produced, a small RNA primer must be made. The protein that synthesizes new DNA by reading the parent DNA template strand—DNA polymerase—can't start from scratch. It must be primed. A massive protein complex, the primosome, which consists of over fifteen different proteins, produces the RNA primer needed by DNA polymerase.

Primed and Ready to Go

Once primed, DNA polymerase will continuously produce DNA along the leading strand. However, for the lagging strand, DNA polymerase can only generate DNA in spurts to produce Okazaki fragments. Each time

DNA polymerase generates an Okazaki fragment, the primosome complex must produce a new RNA primer.

After DNA replication is completed, the RNA primers are removed from the continuous DNA of the leading strand and the Okazaki fragments that make up the lagging strand. A protein called a 3'-5' exonuclease removes the RNA primers. A different DNA polymerase fills in the gaps created by the removal of the RNA primers. Finally, a ligase protein connects all the Okazaki fragments together to form a continuous piece of DNA out of the lagging strand.

This cursory description of DNA replication clearly illustrates its complexity and intricacies. (Many details were left out.) It's phenomenal to think this biochemical system evolved a single time, let alone twice. There is no obvious reason for DNA replication to take place by a semiconservative, RNA primer-dependent, bidirectional process that depends on leading and lagging strands to produce DNA daughter molecules. Even if DNA replication could have evolved independently on two separate occasions, it's reasonable to expect that functionally distinct processes would emerge for bacteria and archaea/eukaryotes given their idiosyncrasies. But, they did not.

No Other Style Like the Creator's

Considering the complexity of life's chemical systems, pervasive molecular convergence fits uncomfortably within an evolutionary framework. Paleontologist J. William Schopf, one of the world's leading authorities on Earth's early life says,

> Because biochemical systems comprise many intricately interlinked pieces, any particular full-blown system can only arise once.... Since any complete biochemical system is far too elaborate to have evolved more than once in the history of life, it is safe to assume that microbes of the primal LCA [last common ancestor] cell line had the same traits that characterize all its present-day descendents.[17]

The pattern expected by Schopf and other evolutionary biologists is simply not observed at the biochemical level. An inordinate number of examples of molecular convergence have already been discovered. In all likelihood, many more will be identified in the future. Each new instance of molecular convergence makes an evolutionary explanation for life less likely.

Throughout this book, the case for biochemical design has been made by comparing the most salient features of life's chemistry with the hallmark characteristics of human designs. The close analogy between biochemical systems and human designs logically compels one conclusion: life's most fundamental processes and structures reflect the artistry of a Creator. The pervasiveness of molecular convergence—the recurrence of designs—throughout the biological realm adds many more works of art to his portfolio. The Divine Artist creates with a style all his own.

The next chapter shows how he used the biochemistry in the cell to construct a mosaic beyond what humans could begin to imagine.

12

An Elaborate Mosaic

Mosaics made with small pieces of colored glass, stone, or other materials were quite the rage in the ancient world. Homes and buildings throughout Greece, Rome, and North Africa used this decorative art to adorn their interiors. In Rome, elegant floor mosaics distinguished luxurious villas. The walls and ceilings of the Domus Aurea, built for Nero in AD 64, were covered with these intricate designs.[1]

Early Christians adapted the use of mosaics to decorate basilicas with depictions of Christ and biblical scenes. This fourth-century practice inaugurated a long tradition of mosaic art in churches that extended well into the Middle Ages.

In the early 1970s, scientists realized that biochemical mosaics also adorn the surfaces and interior of cells. A montage of hundreds of different phospholipid species and proteins constitute the cell's membranes. Organized into two molecular layers, these membranes form a bilayer (see figures 2.4 and 2.5, p. 47).

At that time, biochemists S. J. Singer and Garth L. Nicolson proposed the fluid mosaic model to describe the structure of cell membranes (see chapter 2, p. 48).[2] This model depicts the bilayer as a two-dimensional fluid composed of a complex mixture of phospholipids. The bilayer acts as both a cellular barrier and a solvent for a variety of different types of integral and peripheral membrane proteins (see figure 2.6, p. 48). According to the fluid mosaic model, membranes are little more than haphazard systems with proteins and lipids freely diffusing laterally throughout the bilayer—at first glance, hardly evidence for the work of a Creator.

Recent advances, however, indicate that the fluid mosaic model is an incomplete depiction. Rather than resembling a chaotic pile of stone or broken glass, the mosaic features of cell membranes much more closely resemble the skillful art form found in Byzantine and Roman churches. Biochemists now acknowledge that cell membranes consist of a careful arrangement of molecular pieces.

This exquisite organization at the molecular level is integral to many functions performed by cell membranes. These supramolecular assemblies also require fine-tuning of their composition to exist as stable structures and carry out key operations. In addition, some biochemists think cell membranes harbor information. These three characteristics (organization, fine-tuning, and information) are part of the intelligent design analogy discussed throughout this book and reveal the meticulous work of a Divine Artist.

A few key advances in membrane biochemistry have transformed the way scientists view cell membranes. These new insights represent a case study of sorts and show how pattern recognition—using the intelligent design template—can be applied to specific features of the cell in order to reveal the work of the Creator.

An Intricate Design

Cell membranes are comprised of phospholipids that possess a wide range of chemical variability. Phospholipid head groups typically consist of a phosphate group bound to a glycerol (glycerin) backbone. That group binds one of several possible compounds that vary in their chemical and physical properties. Frequently, phospholipids are identified by their head group structure. Figure 2.3 (p. 46) shows, as an example, a choline molecule bound to the phosphate head group. Alternatively, phospholipid head groups bind ethanolamine, serine, glycerol, and inositol molecules.

Phospholipids vary in tail length and structure. Their tails are typically long linear hydrocarbon chains linked to the glycerol backbone. The phospholipid hydrocarbon chains are commonly fourteen, sixteen, or eighteen carbon atoms long, but can be as short as twelve and as long as twenty-four. Sometimes one or both of the hydrocarbon chains possesses a permanent kink.

These kinks can occur at different locations along the chain length. (Carbon-carbon double bonds inserted into the hydrocarbon chain cause the kinks.) In addition to phospholipids, the cell membranes of bacteria contain another type of lipid (lipopolysaccharides). The cell boundaries of eukaryotic organisms also consist of several different classes of lipids (such as cholesterol, plasmalogens, sphingolipids, and glycolipids) beyond phospholipids.

Superficially, the complex chaotic lipid compositions of cell membranes appear to reflect a long history of undirected evolutionary events. According to this view, over vast periods of time, a variety of molecules were incorporated into membranes as metabolic pathways that produced the various phospholipids randomly emerged and diversified under the auspices of natural selection.

Recent advances, however, suggest that the seemingly chaotic mix of phospholipids in cell membranes was deliberately planned. This molecular mix is necessary and points to a deep rationale that underlies the membrane's composition.[3]

Using Just the Right Pieces

The variable length and geometry of phospholipids' hydrocarbon chains affect the physical properties of cell membranes. Bilayers composed of phospholipids with short hydrocarbon chains or hydrocarbon chains with kinks possess a fluid, liquidlike interior. On the other hand, cell membranes have solidlike interiors if formed from phospholipids with longer hydrocarbon chains and chains that are straight.[4]

The fluidity of the cell membrane's interior has important biological consequences.[5] The bilayer's physical state regulates the function of integral proteins. Local variations in phospholipid composition also create regions of variable fluidity within the bilayer with some areas more solid and others more liquid. These differences in fluidity help segregate the cell membrane's components into functionally distinct domains within the bilayer. Without a large ensemble of phospholipids, precise regulation of membrane protein activity and creation of functionally distinct domains would be impossible. Phospholipids with a wide-range of hydrocarbon chain lengths and shapes (straight or kinked) make it possible for the cell to precisely adjust bilayer fluidity.

A Living Kaleidoscope

Phospholipids play a critical role in controlling the activity of proteins associated with the cell membranes and, in some instances, those proteins located in the cytoplasm.[6] This control extends beyond simply dictating bilayer fluidity. Phospholipids regulate protein function through direct and highly specific interactions.

Through interactions mediated by the head group, phospholipids with glycerol (PGs) and serine (PSs) attachments bind to target proteins. PGs and PSs are both negatively charged. They also have distinct chemical structures. Both features factor into their association with proteins. PSs play a central role in activating proteins in the cytoplasm that are part of the cell signaling pathways. These pathways alter the cell's metabolism in response to changes taking place outside the cell.

In bacteria, PGs activate some of the proteins involved in (1) replicating DNA, (2) assembling the outer membrane, and (3) moving proteins across cell membranes.

Phospholipids with choline (PCs) and ethanolamine (PEs) as part of their head groups are neutral in charge. Interestingly, these two types of phospholipids have regions both negatively and positively charged. (The charges cancel each other to yield overall electrical neutrality.) PCs and PEs are the major phospholipid components of cell membranes.

Even though PCs and PEs are neutrally charged, their chemical structures differ sufficiently so these two phospholipids play distinct roles in cell membranes.[7] The primary role of PCs is bilayer formation. PEs also function in this capacity. Additionally, PE-rich regions in cell membranes can adopt nonbilayer structures. These nonbilayer phases regulate the activities of some proteins and play a central role in cell division and membrane fusion events. PEs also trigger the activity of membrane proteins that shuttle materials across cell membranes.

Phospholipids are highly involved in a litany of biochemical processes. As biochemist William Dohan notes, "The wide range of processes in which specific involvement of phospholipids have been documented explains the need for diversity in phospholipid structure and why there are so many membrane lipids."[8] Far from reflecting the aimlessness of evolutionary processes, the complexity of cell membranes appears intentional. Each phospholipid is an essential part of the biochemical mosaic that adorns the cell's surfaces.

Baked in the Creator's Kiln

Other evidence substantiates the belief that the compositional makeup of cell membranes is no accident. One of the universal features that defines all cell membranes is their unilamellar structure. In other words, cell membranes are made up of a single bilayer.

The structure of cell membranes stands in sharp contrast to the behavior of bilayers made from pure phospholipids. Purified phospholipids spontaneously form bilayers in water environments. Instead of forming unilamellar bilayers, however, phospholipids assemble into stacks of bilayers (multilamellar bilayers), or alternatively, they form spherical structures that consist of multiple bilayer sheets.[9] (These structures resemble an onion, with each layer corresponding to one of the bilayers in the stack.) These aggregates only superficially resemble the cell membrane's structure that consists of a single bilayer, not bilayer stacks (see figure 12.1).

Phospholipids can be manipulated by researchers to form structures composed of only a single bilayer. These particular aggregates arrange into a hollow spherical structure called liposomes or unilamellar vesicles. However, they are considered physically unstable and last only for a limited lifetime.[10] Liposomes readily fuse with one another and revert to multilamellar sheets or vesicles.[11]

In other words, apart from cell membranes, phospholipids spontaneously assemble into multibilayer sheets. So how can cell membranes consist of a single bilayer phase? National Institutes of Health researcher Norman Gershfeld explained that single bilayer phases, similar to those that constitute cell membranes, can be permanently stable but only under unique conditions.[12] (Chemists refer to phenomena that occur under a unique set of conditions as critical phenomena.)

Formation of single bilayer vesicles occurs only at a specific critical temperature. At this temperature, pure phospholipids spontaneously transform from either multiple bilayer sheets or unstable liposomes into stable single

Multibilayer Sheet

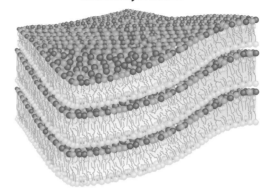

Multibilayer Vesicle

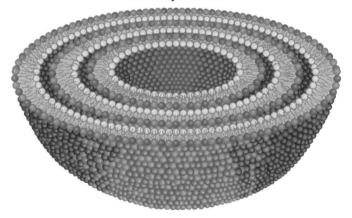

Liposome

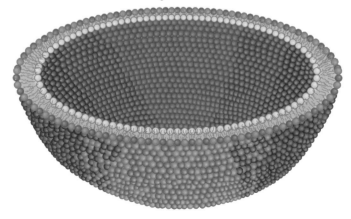

bilayers.[13] Above or below this temperature, the unilamellar phase collapses into multilamellar structures. The critical temperature varies depending on the specific chemical makeup of the phospholipids. In the case of bilayers formed from a mixture of phospholipids, the critical temperatures depend on the bilayers' specific phospholipid composition.[14]

Gershfeld and his team made some interesting observations along these lines. They noted that phospholipids extracted from rat and squid nervous system tissue assemble into single bilayer structures at critical temperatures that correspond to the physiological temperatures of these two organisms.[15]

The team also observed that for the cold-blooded sea urchin *L. pictus*, the membrane composition of the earliest cells in the embryo varies in response to the environment's temperature. In these cases, changes in phospholipid composition allowed the bilayers to adopt a unilamellar phase at a critical temperature that corresponded to the environmental conditions.[16] In addition, Gershfeld's group noted that the bacterium *E. coli* also adjusts its cell membrane phospholipid composition to maintain a single bilayer phase as growth temperature varies.[17]

These studies highlight the biological importance of the critical bilayer phenomena. So does other research that indicates how devastating it is for life when cell membranes deviate from critical conditions. Gershfeld identified a correlation between the rupture of human red blood cells (hemolysis) and incubation at temperatures exceeding 37°C (the normal human body temperature). Transformation of the cell membrane from a single bilayer to multiple bilayer stacks accompanies the red blood cells' hemolysis—a loss of the cell membrane's critical state.[18]

Gershfeld and his collaborators even provided some evidence that cell membrane defects at the sites of neurodegeneration may play a role in Alzheimer's disease.[19] Presumably, collapse of the cell membrane's single bilayer state into a multiple bilayer condition stems from altered membrane phospholipid composition.

The work of Gershfeld's team provides further evidence that cell membranes are carefully crafted structures that appear to be the product of a Creator's painstaking handiwork. It indicates that cell membranes are highly

---

Figure 12.1. Bilayer Assemblies
A segment of a multilamellar bilayer sheet and a cutaway of a multilamellar vesicle are depicted. These structures spontaneously form when phospholipids are added to water. Researchers can induce phospholipids to form structures composed of only a single bilayer in the laboratory. A cutaway of a unilamellar vesicle or liposome is shown.

fine-tuned molecular structures dependent on an exacting set of physical and chemical conditions.

Each Piece Placed by Hand

The fine-tuning of cell membrane lipid compositions does more than stabilize the single bilayer phase. One recent study demonstrates that it also appears to critically influence the interactions between cell membranes and proteins.

A team of Russian scientists, exploring the role that phospholipids play when the cell's machinery inserts proteins into membranes, discovered that successful insertion of the protein colicin E (a bacterial toxin) requires a fairly exacting phospholipid composition.[20] Introduction of colicin E into bilayers requires PG levels between 25 and 30 percent.

PGs bear a negative charge that sets up an electrical potential at the membrane's surface. This potential plays a key role in the insertion process. If the surface potential varies outside a narrow range of values, protein insertion doesn't properly take place. This restrictive range of values occurs only for specific concentrations of PGs.

Surface potential depends on the salt concentration in the environment. The researchers noted that as they changed the salinity, the PG concentrations in the membranes had to vary accordingly to maintain the just-right surface potential for protein insertion to take place.

Interestingly, the content of negatively charged phospholipids (PGs and PSs) in most membranes is between 25 and 30 percent.[21] In fact, most bacteria adjust the level of PGs in their membranes in response to changes in the salinity of the growth medium. These observations suggest that the compositional fine-tuning of phospholipids needed for the import of colicin E into bilayers may be a general requirement for the insertion of most membrane proteins.

An Astonishing Arrangement

For nearly a quarter of a century, the fluid mosaic model provided the guiding framework for scientists to interpret biochemical phenomena associated with cell membranes. But over time discoveries continue to mount that suggest this model is incomplete, perhaps even in some ways inaccurate. In recent years, biochemists have revised the fluid mosaic model, recognizing that cell membranes display far more organization than originally conceived by Singer and Nicolson.[22]

Meaningful Biochemical Messages

Biochemists and information theorists typically think of DNA, RNA, proteins, and more recently, oligosaccharides as harboring information (see chapter 8, p. 142). These biomolecules are made of subunit molecules linked together to form chains. Four different subunits (nucleotides) make DNA and RNA, and twenty different subunits (amino acids) compose proteins. Oligosaccharides consist of linear and branched monosaccharide chains.

Just as specific sequences of letters form words, certain sequences of nucleotides, amino acids, and monosaccharides strung together form the biochemical "words" of the cell. In language, some letter combinations produce meaningful words and others produce gibberish. The same is true for the subunit sequences of DNA, RNA, proteins, and oligosaccharides. Some produce functional biomolecules, whereas others produce "junk" that serves no role inside the cell.

Recently, a team of computational biologists from Israel demonstrated that information can also be housed and transferred in the form of complex chemical mixtures with highly specific molecular compositions.[23] The researchers explicitly applied this idea to lipid aggregates and even argued from an evolutionary standpoint that the first protocells consisted of micelles comprised exclusively of a diverse ensemble of lipids.[24]

According to their hypothesis, in much the same way as the basilica mosaics contained meaning in their biblical scenes, these first protocells harbored information within the aggregate's lipid composition. These lipid aggregates replicated and transferred information to the next generation whenever they split in two. It's believed this process occurred by the addition of compounds to the lipid aggregates. These ensembles eventually grew so large that the conglomerate became unstable and divided. According to this model, over time the information housed in the specific lipid compositions gave way to information-rich biomolecules like RNA and eventually DNA and proteins.

This imaginative explanation for life's start has received limited acceptance among origin-of-life researchers. Still, the idea that lipid mixtures can harbor information raises an important question: Do cell membranes house information in their phospholipid compositions?

The functional necessity of extensive phospholipid diversity and the high-precision compositions of phospholipids needed to stabilize and assemble cell membranes suggest that these structures do indeed contain information. As computational biologists Daniel Segré and his colleagues point out, "When present day cells divide, they too transmit considerable elements of compositional information (including specific gamuts of lipids, proteins and RNA) which are 'inherited' from the mother cell."[25]

Biochemists still consider cell membranes to be a molecular mosaic. But, instead of viewing them as a chaotic mixture of freely diffusing components, scientists regard the cell's boundaries as dynamically structured, displaying a hierarchy of order. This newly found order bespeaks of a Creator.

Using Different Shapes and Sizes

Recent studies provide strong support for the idea that there are localized regions of order and organization within bilayers in the immediate vicinity of membrane proteins. For nearly thirty years, biochemists suspected that integral proteins had close association with some phospholipids in cell membranes. For example, when membrane proteins are isolated from cell membranes, they are often co-purified with specific phospholipid species.

Biochemists speculated that these co-purified compounds were annular or boundary lipids that formed a ring about one molecular-layer thick around the integral proteins.[26] Traditionally these scientists viewed this lipid ring as dynamic. They thought that individual phospholipids "hop" on and off the protein, exchanging with phospholipids in the "bulk" bilayer.

But now, biochemists can directly visualize annular phospholipids in association with membrane proteins. One of the few studies along these lines examined the structure of aquaporin 0 isolated from the lenses of sheep eyes (see chapter 6, p. 111).[27] Researchers noted that this protein had a tightly bound layer of phospholipids surrounding it. The tight association between the protein and the head groups of the phospholipids appears to be mediated by specific interactions.

Scientists also noticed that the hydrocarbon chains of the lipids—aligned along the protein's axis—followed the contour of the protein's surface. In some cases, the hydrocarbon chains were straight, other times they were kinked or bent. The net effect was to produce a uniform lipid casing around the protein.

This study suggests that the annular lipids are much more intimately associated with integral proteins than originally thought. This close, nearly permanent association is critical for membrane stability. It allows the integral protein to "fit" into the bilayer without creating defects from imperfect packing between it and the lipid components. These defects would make the membrane "leaky," a detrimental condition for the cell.

Artistic Asymmetry

Even before Singer and Nicolson proposed the fluid mosaic model, life scientists recognized that the inner and outer surfaces of cell membranes performed different functions. Biochemists quickly determined that these functional differences stem from distinct protein and phospholipid compositions in the inner and outer leaflets of membrane bilayers. Because the inner and outer monolayers differ in composition, structure, and function, biochemists refer to cell membranes as asymmetric.[28]

The asymmetry of cell membranes reflects long-range order. Ironically, membrane asymmetry has always been part of the fluid mosaic model, even though this paradigm primarily views cell membranes as chaotic rather than organized. The asymmetry of proteins and phospholipids is established by complex biochemical processes when cell membranes are assembled. This asymmetry is actively maintained by the cell's machinery during the membrane's lifetime.[29] (Discussion of these processes is beyond the scope of this book.)

Protein asymmetry consists of the specific orientation of integral proteins that span the bilayer and differences in the composition of peripheral proteins in the inner and outer monolayers. This asymmetry allows cell membranes to

1. transport materials in a single direction,
2. detect changes in the environment outside the cell,
3. perform specific chemical operations inside the cell, and
4. stabilize the cell membranes through interactions between the cytoskeletal proteins and the interior surface of the bilayer.

The asymmetric distribution of phospholipids in the inner and outer leaflets of the cell membrane is highly variable, differing from membrane to membrane. But, it is not random. For example, the plasma membrane that surrounds the cell typically has markedly higher levels of PSs, PEs, and PIs in the inner leaflet and higher levels of PCs and sphingomyelins in the outer monolayer. The inner membranes of mitochondria usually have greater amounts of PCs and PEs in the outer monolayer and higher levels of PIs and cardiolipin in the inner leaflet. The membranes of the Golgi apparatus (see chapter 2, p. 40) have higher concentrations of PEs, PCs, and PSs in the membrane surface in contact with the cytoplasm and greater amounts of PIs and sphingomyelins on the membrane surface in contact with the Golgi's interior.[30]

Phospholipid asymmetry, like protein asymmetry, has important biological consequences. Differences in phospholipid composition lead to variations in the charge, permeability, and fluidity of inner and outer leaflets of the membranes. These compositional differences also play an important role in the ability of each monolayer to support and regulate the activity of proteins associated with the membrane.

Super Organized

The discovery of annular lipids and compositional asymmetry by biochemists in the early days of the fluid mosaic model represented a small foreshadowing of what was to come. Over the last decade or so, life scientists have come to recognize that ordering and organization are hallmark features of cell membranes.[31] These membranes are highly organized, consisting of numerous structurally and functionally discrete domains. The domains, in turn, appear to be arranged into supradomains, reflecting a hierarchy of order and organization. The membrane domains are made of distinct lipid and protein compositions that dictate each domain's unique functional role.

Biochemists have discovered a special type of domain in cell membranes, called lipid rafts.[32] These domains are solidlike regions of the membrane that "float" in more fluid regions, like a raft on the sea. Typically, lipid rafts are enriched in cholesterol and another class of lipids called sphingomyelins. Presumably, interactions between the lipid head groups maintain the structural integrity of the lipid raft.

Specific types of proteins are associated with lipid rafts, typically those involved in signal transduction. High levels of protein receptors are embedded in lipid rafts. These receptors bind molecules in the environment and, in turn, initiate biochemical pathways that elicit a response by the cell to changes in its surroundings. Lipid rafts also appear to play a role in secretion of vesicles by the Golgi apparatus.

The ordering and organization of the cell membranes—carefully arranged for the myriad functions they perform—appears intentionally thought out. But is it?

Where Did This Wondrous Masterpiece Come From?

Finely-tuned phospholipid compositions, an extensive molecular-level organization, and the likelihood that cell membranes harbor information beg the question, Can the biochemical marvel of cell membranes be accounted for apart from a Creator?

For most biochemical systems and characteristics, a fundamental lack of knowledge and insight prevent a rigorous assessment of proposed evolutionary explanations. In other words, it's not possible to say whether evolutionary processes can generate specific aspects of life's chemistry.

But, this limitation is not a consideration for assessing the origin of cell membranes. Origin-of-life researchers have focused enough attention on the problem of membrane origins to permit vigorous evaluation of the likelihood that unguided evolutionary pathways produced them. The origin of cell membranes has to be one of the first steps in life's emergence. Researchers assume, for the most part, that once membrane components form or appear on early Earth, they readily self-assembled to form the first cell membranes.[33] To explain this origin, and along with it the emergence of the first cell, most investigators simply attempt to identify compounds—likely present on early Earth—with the potential to spontaneously assemble into bilayer structures.

These scientists also look to define mechanisms in which bilayer structures can encapsulate more complex self-replicating molecules and acquire properties that resemble those of contemporary cell membranes such as transport and energy transduction.

Art Supplies

In the quest to identify bilayer-forming molecules, origin-of-life investigators have discovered several chemical routes that produce both simple amphiphilic compounds consisting of a single long hydrocarbon chain and more complex phospholipids.[34] In spite of this, the origin-of-life community hotly debates the likelihood of these chemical pathways occurring on the early Earth.[35]

In the face of the questions that surround the prebiotic synthesis of amphiphilic compounds, some researchers appeal to extraterrestrial materials falling onto the early Earth to explain the source of bilayer-forming compounds.[36] Analysis of carbon-containing meteorites (carbonaceous

chondrites), like the Murchison, initially indicated the presence of compounds consisting of long hydrocarbon chains. However, subsequent analysis demonstrated that these compounds more than likely resulted from
terrestrial contamination.[37]

Recent laboratory experiments rejuvenate support for an extraterrestrial
source of amphiphilic materials on early Earth.[38] Scientists from NASA
Ames Research Center, the SETI Institute, and the University of California, Santa Cruz, demonstrated that irradiating simulated cometary and
interstellar ice with UV light produces a complex mixture of compounds
that includes bilayer-forming materials. Presumably, delivery of these materials to early Earth provided the compounds needed to form the first
cell membranes.

One Piece at a Time

Even though phospholipids are the dominant lipid species of contemporary cell membranes, origin-of-life researchers think that simpler lipids
assembled to form the first bilayers.

Amphiphilic compounds with "water-loving" and "water-hating" regions
all form aggregates when added to water (see chapter 2, p. 46). These aggregates take on a variety of forms depending on the amphiphile's molecular
structure.[39] Phospholipids with two long hydrocarbon chains can form
bilayers. Amphiphilic compounds with a single long hydrocarbon chain
generally form spherical structures referred to as micelles (see figure 12.2).
Origin-of-life researchers don't regard micelles as having importance in
forming the first protocells.

In spite of their tendency to form micelles, some single-chain amphiphilic
compounds form bilayers under highly specific solution (pH, for example) conditions and temperatures when mixed with the right materials.[40]
Origin-of-life researchers regard these results as key to explaining the first
appearance of cell membranes.

The results increase in significance in light of the observation that lipid-
like materials extracted from the Murchison meteorite form bilayer structures under specific solution conditions.[41] Similar bilayer structures also
form from extracts of simulated cometary and interstellar ice irradiated
with UV light.[42] Researchers point to these compounds as possibly the first
cell membrane components and as evidence that the materials necessary to
form the first protocells' boundary structures were present on early Earth.

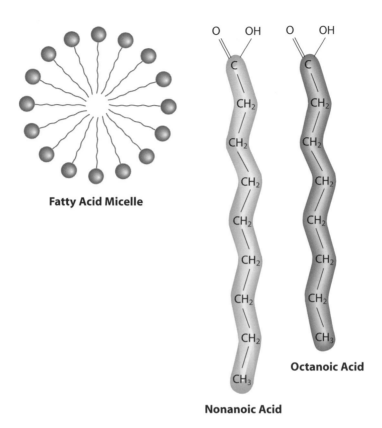

Fatty Acid Micelle

Octanoic Acid

Nonanoic Acid

Figure 12.2. Fatty Acids and Micelles
A cutaway of a micelle is shown. Amphiphilic compounds with a single long hydrocarbon chain, like octanoic and nonanoic acids, usually will form these spherical structures when added to water.

They also argue that these results indicate the ease with which bilayers can spontaneously form once the right components appear.

A Work of Nature's Art?

Origin-of-life investigators speculate that when bilayer-forming compounds appeared on early Earth, cycles of dehydration and rehydration at the intertidal zones of islands might have encapsulated large self-replicating molecules (proteins, DNA, and RNA) and smaller subunit molecules within the bilayer's confines. Support for this idea comes, scientists claim, from experiments showing that bilayer vesicles formed from structurally specific phospholipids encapsulated DNA during drying and subsequent water addition.[43]

Researchers presume that once bilayer vesicles containing encapsulated self-replicating molecules formed, they could carry out the necessary chemical processes to sustain self-replicating activity, grow, self-reproduce, and acquire transport and energy transduction capabilities.[44]

Lipid bilayers are generally impermeable to the types of molecules needed to maintain the activity of encapsulated self-replicators. In spite of this, a few origin-of-life researchers have shown that if the chain length of the lipids that form the bilayers is carefully adjusted, enough of the compounds needed to sustain the self-replicator can pass through the bilayer.[45]

The studies that pertain to cell membrane origins seem to reinforce the view that cell membranes readily self-assembled on the early Earth. Once formed, these primitive bilayers also seemingly could acquire the functional attributes of contemporary biological membrane systems. Yet, this conclusion is a bit premature.

An Unskilled Composition?

While the work on the origin of cell membranes has been taking place, other research designed to characterize the structure of lipid aggregates and determine the principles governing cell membrane biophysics suggests that evolutionary models for the origin of biological membranes are oversimplified. The emerging tenets of membrane biophysics demand a more convoluted and intricate pathway than that conceived by the evolutionary origin-of-life community. It's an incredibly arduous process to go from simple lipid molecules to the bilayers found in contemporary cell membrane systems. The next section illustrates some of the problems for what researchers think was the first step in the evolution of cell membranes.

Origin-of-life researchers think that the primitive membranes of the first cells were composed of aromatic hydrocarbons mixed with octanoic and nonanoic acid. (Octanoic acid consists of a linear carbon chain of eight carbon atoms in length and nonanoic acid involves a linear carbon chain nine carbon atoms long. See figure 12.2.) Bilayer-forming extracts from the Murchison meteorite include these compounds.

Neither octanoic nor nonanoic acid would likely have occurred at levels significant enough, however, for origin-of-life scenarios. Researchers have recovered only extremely low levels of these compounds from the Murchison meteorite.[46] Additionally, the level of individual amphiphilic species decreases exponentially with increasing chain length.[47] While extraterrestrial infall could potentially deliver octanoic and nonanoic acid to early Earth, the levels would be far too low to participate in primitive membrane structures. Octanoic and nonanoic acids can form bilayer structures only at relatively high concentrations.[48]

In addition to the concentration requirements, octanoic and nonanoic acids also require exacting environmental conditions. These compounds can only form bilayers at highly specific pHs.[49] Octanoic and nonanoic bilayers become unstable if the solution pH deviates from near neutral values. The solution temperature is also critical for bilayer stability.[50] Another complication is the solution salt level. Research shows that model primitive membranes fall apart in the presence of salt. These structures only display stability in pure water.[51]

Octanoic and nonanoic bilayer stability also requires the "just-right" molecular companions. Inclusion of nonanol (a nine-carbon alcohol) extends the pH range for nonanoic bilayers.[52] Bilayer stability results from specific interactions between the nonanoic acid head group and nonanol. Such stability only occurs when nonanol is present at specific levels within the nonanoic bilayers.

To date, no studies have been conducted on the long-term stability of octanoic and nonanoic bilayers. Quite possibly octanoic and nonanoic acid bilayers lack long-term stability under conditions that allow these compounds to form bilayers. Regardless, the strict requirements necessary for bilayer formation make it unlikely that these compounds could have ever contributed to the formation of the first cell's membranes.

Formation of nonanoic acid bilayers (or bilayers comprised of any amphiphile with a single hydrocarbon chain) is improbable because several "just-right" conditions must be simultaneously met. Should a bilayer structure form, any environmental fluctuations or compositional deviations would cause it to destabilize and revert to micelle structures.

The instability of primitive bilayers in salt is perhaps most problematic. It is difficult to imagine any aqueous location on early Earth free of salt. In fact, primitive bilayer stability would have been compromised at salt levels far less than those found in Earth's oceans today. And, early Earth's oceans were one and a half to two times more salty.[53] That condition makes the emergence of primitive membranes even less likely.

The exacting requirements for primitive bilayer assembly also make it unlikely these structures could encapsulate a self-replicator via dehydration-hydration cycles. Once dehydrated, unless the "just-right" conditions existed upon rehydration, the bilayers could not reform.

In fact, a recent survey of the scientific literature shows that every step in the proposed pathway from prebiotic amphiphilic compounds to contemporary cell membranes strictly depends on exacting compositional and environmental factors.[54] These stringent requirements make it unlikely that cell membranes could have emerged under the conditions of early Earth.

Acknowledging the Creator

The zenith of Byzantine art occurred between the ninth and eleventh centuries. Some of the world's most beautiful mosaics were produced during that time. The mosaics of the Hagia Sophia in Constantinople include a wall covered with one of the most famous. *Emperor Kneeling before Christ* depicts an emperor acknowledging Jesus Christ as Lord and Savior.[55]

Unlike this highly valued mosaic, however, the first depictions of cell membranes portrayed them as little more than haphazard disorganized systems with proteins and lipids freely diffusing laterally throughout the bilayer formed by phospholipids. In the early 1970s, cell membranes were described as a fluid mosaic.

Advances over the last thirty-five years, however, dramatically changed how scientists think about cell membranes. Biochemists now understand the cell's boundaries as highly structured, highly organized systems that display local ordering in the vicinity of membrane proteins (annular lipids) and long-range ordering (membrane asymmetry, membrane domains, and lipid rafts). In the 1980s and early 1990s, Norman Gershfeld's team demonstrated that cell membranes require extraordinary fine-tuning of their phospholipid composition to exist as stable unilamellar structures. More recent work indicates that a high-precision phospholipid composition appears necessary for membrane proteins to be inserted into bilayers during cell membrane assembly.

Only in recent years have biochemists come to appreciate why such a complex ensemble of phospholipids make up cell membranes. Instead of reflecting the outworking of a history of undirected evolutionary processes, the seemingly chaotic mix of phospholipids in cell membranes is quite necessary and points to a rationale that undergirds the membrane's composition. Phospholipids do more than form the cell membrane's bilayer. They control the bilayer's physical properties and play a key role in regulating the activity of proteins associated with the membrane. Some biochemists have even suggested that cell membranes harbor information.

The hallmark features of cell membranes are the same features found on the wall of the churches in Constantinople. This artwork consists of the careful, well-thought-out choice of stone and glass pieces deliberately organized and arranged in a precise way to yield a specific depiction of Christ. In this sense, that mosaic conveys the information the artist wanted to communicate to its viewers.

When the features of cell membranes are viewed through the grid of the intelligent design template, they continue to build a powerful weight-of-evidence case for biochemical intelligent design. Cell membranes supply an excellent case study of how pattern recognition can be used to interpret new biochemical insights as additional support for the Creator's handiwork. It takes a brilliant mind to produce the complex pieces that communicate a powerful message. Only a Divine Mind could put them together in such a way that they came to life.

13

COLORING OUTSIDE THE LINES

Not all the world's art treasures hang on museum walls. Some are affixed to refrigerator doors. Drawings and paintings produced by small hands won't usually command much of a price at an auction, but for proud parents the artistic renderings of their children are priceless.

Works of art reflect the ability and sophistication of the artists that produce them. Art created by little ones doesn't compare with the work of the world's masters. Though adorable, the musings of children reflect their lack of experience, skill, and perhaps even talent. On the other hand, masterpieces are widely appreciated because they express the artist's immense insight, originality, and depth of emotion.

Like art, the characteristics of life's chemical systems reflect the identity and capability of their maker. As demonstrated through analogical comparisons in previous chapters, many biochemical systems display an elegance that points to a Creator.

Still, most evolutionary biologists reject the notion of intelligent design, partly because of the apparent defects and faulty designs of some biochemical systems.[1] These imperfections represent potentially powerful disanalogies (see chapter 1, p. 31) weakening the conclusion that life's chemistry is the work of a Creator. Sometimes, for skeptics, life's chemistry more closely resembles a child's drawing than a magnificent masterpiece.

The Problem of Imperfections

Most scientists acknowledge the appearance of design in biochemical systems but argue that it's not true design. Rather, they claim this characteristic is an artifact of evolutionary processes that stems from natural selection operating repeatedly on random inheritable variations over vast periods of time to produce and fine-tune biochemical systems.

Like a small child coloring outside the lines of a picture—blind, undirected, chance processes of evolution are just as likely to produce "jury-rigged" structures as they are to produce fine-tuned structures. The likelihood of these makeshift outcomes led the late evolutionary biologist Stephen Jay Gould to argue in his classic essay *The Panda's Thumb* that biological imperfections would "win no prize in an engineering derby."[2] Instead, they make a compelling case for evolution. From an evolutionary standpoint, if a "design" somehow works—even imperfectly—there is no impetus for it to further evolve.

For Gould, "odd arrangements and funny solutions are the proof of evolution—paths that a sensible God would never tread but that a natural process, constrained by history, follows perforce."[3] In other words, even though biochemical systems are replete with elegant design features, the assortment of imperfections in life's chemistry undermines the case for biochemical intelligent design. From an evolutionist viewpoint, an all-powerful, all-knowing Designer would never scribble so haphazardly.

But, Bad Designs Can Be Good

Careful consideration suggests that imperfections may not be as big a problem for the biochemical intelligent design analogy as they appear at first glance. Perhaps a Creator's intentional activity can explain suboptimal biochemical systems.

From Better to Worse

Some bad designs are truly less-than-perfect. From an intelligent design perspective, they merely reflect the unavoidable consequences of the laws of nature instituted by the Creator. For instance, this universe and all it contains, including life, is subject to the second law of thermodynamics (entropy). When optimal biochemical systems experience this law's unrelenting effects, they tend toward disorder. Over time, flaws creep in, and the decay becomes permanent when it leads to changes in the nucleotide sequences of DNA.

Mutations. Chemical and physical insults to DNA inevitably cause abnormalities. So do errors made by the cell's machinery during DNA replication. The cell possesses machinery that can repair this damage, but sometimes errors occur and the repair is not completely effective. Then the nucleotide sequence of DNA becomes permanently altered.[4]

Biochemists have identified numerous types of mutations. For example, substitutions replace one nucleotide in the DNA sequence with another. Insertions add nucleotides to the DNA sequence and deletions remove them.

Gene mutations are seldom beneficial because they alter the information contained in the gene and cause the structure of the protein specified by that gene to become distorted (see chapter 9, p. 173). This structure-altering effect makes most mutations harmful, although sometimes their effect can be neutral.

When deleterious mutations occur, natural selection often prevents their propagation to the next generation because they often compromise the fitness and reproductive success of the organism experiencing the altered DNA sequence. Still, natural selection is not always diligent. Sometimes mildly harmful mutations escape notice. Over time, the accumulation of these damaging mutations can transform an optimally designed biochemical system into one with substandard performance.

Less than peak performance. Nonuniversal genetic codes (discussed in chapter 9, p. 177) supply an excellent example of how mutations and other natural processes degrade optimal systems—in this case, the universal genetic code that is optimized to withstand errors caused by substitution mutations. Deviants of the universal genetic code, nonuniversal genetic codes arise when changes occur in tRNA molecules in such a way that the assignments of stop codons or low frequency codons are altered (see chapter 10, p. 187).

Compared to the universal code, these nonuniversal codes do not possess the same capacity to withstand mutational error. The processes that generate nonuniversal codes transform a highly optimized masterpiece into a system that appears far less deliberate. The "new" codon assignments may not be design defects but ultimately the consequence of the second law of thermodynamics. The appearance of a faulty design

---

The Second Law of Thermodynamics

Even though the second law of thermodynamics causes systems to tend toward disorder, its operation is absolutely necessary for life to be possible. The effects of entropy leads to the "downhill" flow of energy that makes it possible for cells to carry out *all* of their metabolic abilities. Entropy also drives the formation of cell membranes, the precise folding of proteins, and the assembly of the DNA double helix. From an intelligent design perspective, the second law of thermodynamics reflects the providential care of the Creator. The decay associated with the second law appears to be an unavoidable trade-off.

---

doesn't necessarily indicate an evolutionary origin but may instead reflect the effects of entropy superimposed on once optimal biochemical systems.

Planned That Way

Engineers who invent complex systems often face trade-offs and must purposely design some components to be suboptimal in order to achieve the maximum overall performance. In fact, if a system consists of finite resources and must accomplish numerous objectives, then the system must represent a compromise. Inevitably its objectives will compete with one another. Any attempt to maximize performance in one area will degrade performance in others.

When confronted with trade-offs, the engineer carefully manages them in such a way as to achieve optimal performance for the system *as a whole*. And this overall efficiency can be accomplished only by intentionally suboptimizing individual aspects of the system's design.[5]

The conflict between performance and robustness is a specific trade-off often encountered. Usually high performance systems do not do well under a wide range of conditions. To address this compromise, engineers frequently design systems to underperform, enabling those systems to operate under a variety of conditions.

Given the trade-offs, this idea makes sense within the context of the biochemical intelligent design argument—in some instances, suboptimal designs result from the Creator's intent. They may not be disanalogies that militate against intelligent design at all. Instead suboptimal designs round out the comparison between man and his Maker.

Lack of Understanding

Life's chemistry is complex. Biochemists lack detailed understanding of the structure and functional behavior of most biochemical systems, even those that have been the subject of focused investigation. Rarely do biochemists understand how a specific process interacts with others inside the cell, let alone globally throughout the organism.

When evolutionary biologists label a biochemical system "imperfect," they do so largely from ignorance. Any claim that a certain aspect of life's chemistry exemplifies poor design is largely based on a scientist's authority, not a comprehensive understanding of that system and its interrelationship to other biomolecular processes. All too often biochemists gain new insight into the operation of a so-called imperfect biochemical system only to discover another marvelous illustration of the elegant designs that define life's chemistry.

Based on current knowledge, however, some systems truly appear to be poorly designed. Limited knowledge about these systems doesn't permit the case for biochemical intelligent design to be made. These seemingly faulty designs, however, provide an opportunity to scientifically test the biochemical intelligent design hypothesis. If life is indeed the product of a Creator, then new discoveries should yield insights that transform these biochemical aberrations into remarkable works of art.

From Funny to Fantastic

A few representative examples such as glycolysis, bilirubin production, uric acid metabolism, junk DNA, and genetic redundancy show how time can produce the kind of scientific advance that rehabilitates the image of biochemical systems that at one time or other acquired the reputation as bad designs.

Glycolysis

One of life's most important metabolic pathways, glycolysis plays a key role in harvesting energy for use by most cells. This biochemical process fractures six-carbon sugar glucose into two molecules of pyruvate, a three-carbon compound. The cell captures a portion of the chemical energy released by glucose breakdown for later use. Some organisms further break down pyruvate to yield even more energy.[6]

Early on in the glycolytic pathway, glucose is transformed into another six-carbon sugar, fructose 6-phosphate, through a sequence of chemical reactions that involve the addition of a phosphate group and a rearrangement of the glucose molecule. Fructose 6-phosphate is then converted into fructose 1,6-bisphosphate by adding a phosphate group.

The process uses some of the cell's energy reserves. Because it takes energy to generate energy from glucose breakdown, biochemists refer to the generation of fructose 1,6-bisphosphate from glucose as the "pump-priming" reaction.

Phosphofructokinase is the protein that converts fructose 6-phosphate into fructose 1,6-bisphosphate. The cell controls glycolysis by regulating phosphofructokinase activity. In other words, the cell can turn glycolysis on and off by activating or inhibiting phosphofructokinase. The cell can also change the gylcolytic rate by increasing or decreasing the activity of this protein.[7] Phosphofructokinase is somewhat analogous to an on-off light switch with a dimmer knob.

Regulating glycolysis via phosphofructokinase represents elegant biochemical logic because this protein catalyzes an energy-consuming step. By shutting down glycolysis before the cell uses energy to prime the glycolytic pathway, the cell avoids wasting energy.

Once the reaction catalyzed by phosphofructokinase takes place, there is no turning back. The cell has committed valuable energy stores to glycolysis. Stopping glycolysis before the cell makes this commitment conserves the cell's energy resources and makes them available for other processes.

A futile cycle. In sharp contrast to the elegant phosphofructokinase regulation of glycolysis is the back conversion of fructose 1,6-bisphosphate to fructose 6-phosphate. This reaction is catalyzed by the protein fructose 1,6-bisphosphatase. This chemical conversion undoes the work of phosphofructokinase, throwing away the energy that the cell used to convert fructose 6-phosphate to fructose 1,6-bisphosphate. Just like a toddler quickly undoes a mother's hard work shortly after she cleans the house.

The paired reactions catalyzed by phosphofructokinase and fructose 1,6-bisphosphatase are known as a futile cycle. These two proteins cause fructose 6-phosphate and fructose 1,6-bisphosphate to endlessly cycle back and forth wasting the cell's energy resources. Historically, biochemists have regarded this futile cycle as an imperfection produced by evolutionary processes.[8]

Greater understanding. Discovering the way these two reactions relate to each other, however, has changed the mind of most biochemists. The futile cycle associated with glycolysis actually plays a critical role in regulating this key pathway by amplifying the biochemical signals that activate and inhibit the breakdown of glucose. A hypothetical futile cycle in which compound A gets converted to compound B and compound B converts back to A shows how this works.

Suppose the conversion of A to B occurs at a rate of 100 molecules per second and B to A occurs at 90 molecules per second. The overall conversion rate of A to B is 10 molecules per second. Increasing the rate of the forward reaction by 10 percent and decreasing the reverse reaction rate by 10 percent results in an overall increase in the production of A from 10 molecules per second to 29 molecules per second. If the futile cycle didn't exist, however, and there was no reverse reaction, an increase in the production of A by 10 percent merely increases the flux from 10 to 11 molecules per second (see figure 13.1). Without the futile cycle, the cell lacks a quick and sensitive response to changes in its energy requirements.

Another function for futile cycles is heat production. By cycling back and forth between fructose-6-phosphate and fructose-1,6-bisphosphate, the cell's chemical energy is converted into heat, which helps provide organisms with necessary warmth.

Even though the futile cycle of glycolysis appears to be a metabolic imperfection, more comprehensive understanding of this operation within the context of the cell's chemistry reveals this process to be an elegant design feature.

Bilirubin

Biochemists would never enter the metabolic pathways that break down hemoglobin's components in any show featuring masterpieces. (Hemoglobin is the oxygen-transporting protein found in red blood cells.) This critical degradation process employs seemingly unnecessary steps, consumes extensive amounts of energy, and generates a toxic end product (bilirubin).

Hemoglobin consists of four protein chains that interact to form a tetrameric (tetra = four, mer = unit) conglomerate. A complex ring system (the heme group) that includes an iron atom associates with the hemoglobin tetramer. The heme group binds oxygen serving as the "business" part of hemoglobin.[9]

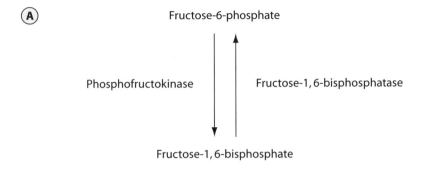

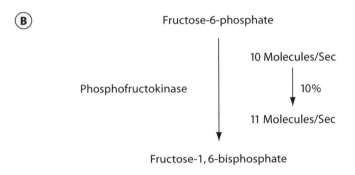

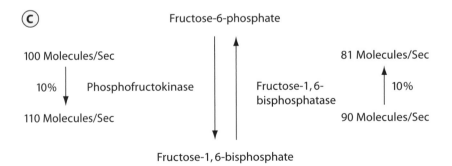

Figure 13.1. The Futile Cycle of Glycolysis
This futile cycle actually plays a critical role in regulating glycolysis by amplifying the biochemical signals that activate and inhibit glycolysis.

When red blood cells die, the spleen's biochemical pathways degrade the red blood cell's contents (including hemoglobin). Parts of the hemoglobin are recycled and parts are eliminated from the body. The protein chains are broken down into their constitutive amino acids, which find new use. So does the iron atom. The heme ring, on the other hand, is eliminated.

Prior to elimination, an enzyme (heme oxygenase) converts the heme ring into a linear molecule, biliverdin, in an energy-intensive process. For birds and reptiles, the process stops here. Biliverdin is water-soluble and readily excreted from the body of these animals.

In mammals, however, another enzyme (biliverdin reductase) converts biliverdin to bilirubin in a process that also uses energy. That's where the problems begin.

A futile cycle. Because bilirubin lacks appreciable water solubility, it cannot be readily eliminated until blood serum albumin carries it to the liver. Once there, an enzyme adds two sugar groups to the bilirubin (a process that also requires substantial energy) making it water-soluble and suitable for elimination.[10]

In other words, mammals employ several seemingly unnecessary energy-intensive steps to convert biliverdin (a compound easily eliminated) into bilirubin (a molecule that can't be secreted). Further compounding the inefficiency is the back conversion of bilirubin into biliverdin. This reversion readily occurs in the presence of oxygen and reactive oxygen species (ROS), ever-present in the cell. The energy used to convert biliverdin to bilirubin is wasted and the process has to be repeated—sometimes again and again.

Lastly, bilirubin is toxic. This compound causes jaundice, brain damage, and other disorders.[11] On the surface, heme degradation appears ill-conceived—something expected for a product of evolution, not for a God whose creation would stay within the well-defined lines of perfection.

Greater understanding. Researchers from Johns Hopkins University, however, recently made a series of discoveries that demonstrate elegant artistry in all aspects of bilirubin metabolism.[12] It turns out bilirubin is an effective antioxidant that reacts with oxygen and ROS. This property protects the cell from oxidative damage, the destruction caused by ROS when these compounds indiscriminately react with biomolecules.

That explains bilirubin's formation. Its water insolubility, a detriment for elimination, causes bilirubin to partition into the cell membrane. In this location bilirubin guards the membrane components from harmful reactions with oxygen. As for the futile cycle, the reversion of bilirubin back to biliverdin allows the cell to regenerate bilirubin each time after it detoxifies oxygen and ROS—again and again. This cycle amplifies bilirubin's antioxidative potential. Bilirubin eliminates ten thousand times its level of oxygen and ROS. These compounds are highly destructive if left unchecked in the cell.

This new discovery makes it untenable to view bilirubin metabolism as a senseless process, an imperfection produced by evolution. Rather, these pathways make sense. Bilirubin metabolism stands as impressive "biotechnology" that buffers the cell's structures against the harmful effects of oxidative compounds.

Uric Acid Metabolism

Kidney stones develop in one out of ten people during their lifetime and account for nearly ten out of one thousand hospital admissions.[13] These mineral deposits can result whenever a chemical imbalance occurs in the kidney. The type of stone that forms depends upon the exact nature of that imbalance and reflects different etiologies. Calcium oxalate stones result from dehydration or excess levels of oxalate (found in certain vegetables, nuts, berries, chocolate, and tea[14]) in the diet. On the other hand, sodium urate stones stem from an inborn error in metabolism that leads to excessive production of uric acid.[15]

As a normal metabolic activity, the cell turns over biomolecules, continually replacing "older" molecules with newly synthesized ones. This turnover allows cells to maintain their structural and functional integrity. The cell recycles most of the adenine and guanine generated from the breakdown of nucleotides (the building blocks of DNA and RNA) through salvage pathways, but it targets a significant portion of adenine and guanine for breakdown and secretion in the form of uric acid.[16]

In blood serum, uric acid possesses low solubility. This condition causes it to readily precipitate out in the kidney and urinary tract when dehydration occurs or when the body generates an excessive amount (which can occur if the enzymes of the salvage pathway are defective).[17]

A flawed process. Except for primates, all mammals further metabolize uric acid to a more soluble derivative. Evolutionary biologists think the enzymes responsible for this transformation were lost in the evolutionary process that led to primates.[18] For evolutionists, the elimination of adenine and guanine in the form of uric acid is the type of evidence that makes a potent case for evolution, because it appears to be a poor design.[19]

Why would an all-powerful and all-knowing Creator put in place such an imperfect biochemical process—one that leaves human beings susceptible to kidney stones and other disorders, like gout? Evolutionists maintain that the adenine and guanine elimination pathways represent nothing more than an evolutionary "kludge" job, an imperfection that barely suffices, not the Creator's exacting handiwork.

Greater understanding. Evolutionists who adopt this perspective, however, fail to consider uric acid's full range of metabolic properties. This compound is a potent antioxidant that scavenges the chemically corrosive hydroxyl free radical, singlet oxygen, and superoxide anion, all produced by the metabolic pathways the cell uses to harvest chemical energy.[20] The maximal levels of uric acid in the blood serum, though precariously poised to precipitate as stones in the urinary tract, help prevent cancer and may contribute to long human life spans. For other mammals, the conversion of uric acid to more soluble forms before elimination deprives them of a key antioxidant and limits the length of their lives.

When considered more broadly, it's been discovered that the primate adenine and guanine elimination pathways reflect an elegant design that finds an important use for a waste product. There's a trade-off, however. If an inborn metabolic error occurs in the salvage pathway enzymes or if one eats an unbalanced diet, then kidney stones (and gout) can result—a small price to pay for cancer prevention and longer life expectancies.

Junk DNA

Many evolutionary biologists regard "junk" DNA as one of the most potent pieces of evidence for biological evolution.[21] According to this view, junk DNA results when undirected biochemical processes and random molecular and physical events transform a functional DNA segment into a useless molecular artifact. This segment remains part of an organism's genome solely because of its attachment to functional DNA.

Junk DNA persists from generation to generation.[22] The amount varies from organism to organism, ranging from 30 percent to nearly 100 percent of an organism's genome.[23]

Evolutionary biologists highlight the fact that in many instances identical segments of "junk" DNA appear in a wide range of related organisms.

Frequently these segments share the same genome location. For evolutionists, this pattern clearly indicates that these organisms also shared an ancestor.

Accordingly, scientists believe that the junk segment arose prior to the time those organisms diverged from their common predecessor.[24] Skeptical of other explanations, evolutionists wonder why a Creator would purposely introduce nonfunctional junk DNA at the exact location in the genomes of different, but seemingly related organisms.

Numerous classes of junk DNA have been identified. The most widely recognized include pseudogenes, endogenous retroviruses, and LINE and SINE sequences.

Pseudogenes. Evolutionary biologists consider pseudogenes to be the dead remains of once functional genes. According to this view, severe mutations destroyed the capacity of the cell's machinery to "read" and process the information in these genes. Still, pseudogenes possess tell-tale signatures that allow molecular biologists to recognize them as genes, albeit nonfunctional.[25]

Several classes of pseudogenes have been identified (see figure 13.2). *Unitary pseudogenes*, a relatively rare type, occur as single copies in an organism's genome.[26] These pseudogenes arise when a functional gene experiences such severe mutations that it's rendered nonfunctional. The loss of this gene presumably doesn't compromise the organism's fitness if it engages in a lifestyle that largely makes the gene unnecessary.

Duplicated pseudogenes are the largest pseudogene class. Molecular biologists suggest that these DNA segments arose when one or more genes underwent duplication in the genome. Afterwards, the copies experienced severe mutations that rendered them unrecognizable as a functional gene by the cell's machinery. Loss of duplicated gene function has little, if any, effect on an organism's fitness because an intact functional copy still exists.[27]

As conceived by molecular biologists, the pathway that produces *processed pseudogenes* is quite complex. The mechanism that generates them overlaps with the one used by the cell's machinery to make proteins.

Genes contain the information the cell needs for this process. As the first step in protein synthesis, the cell's machinery copies the gene in the form of RNA, a biomolecule class that structurally resembles DNA. The RNA message migrates to a subcellular particle, a ribosome. Once there, the cell's machinery "reads" the information stored in the RNA message to form the protein encoded by messenger RNA.[28]

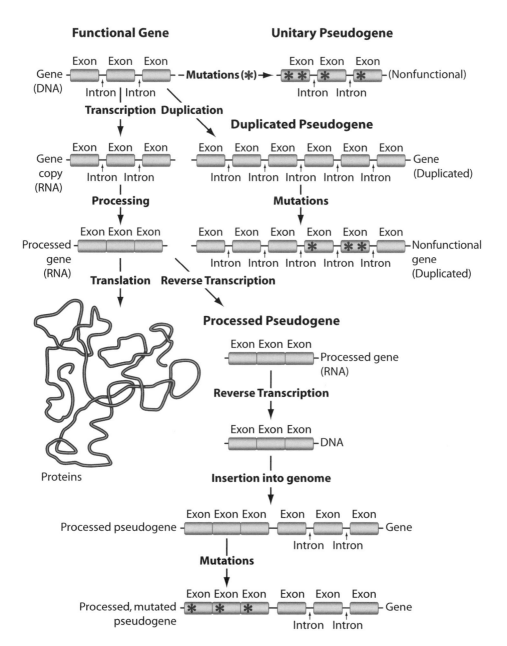

Figure 13.2. Pseudogenes

Evolutionary biologists consider pseudogenes to be the dead, useless remains of once functional genes. Molecular biologists recognize three classes of pseudogenes: unitary, duplicated, and processed.

Before the RNA message migrates to the ribosome, the cell's machinery alters it in several ways. These changes include removing segments in the message that correspond to noncoding regions found in the gene (introns), splicing together the RNA segments that correspond to the gene-coding regions (exons), and modifying and making additions to the ends of the RNA molecule.[29]

Processed pseudogenes are thought to arise when the reverse transcriptase enzyme generates DNA from the processed RNA message. Once produced and inserted back into the genome, processed pseudogenes resemble the genes from which they originate. Yet they also contain telltale signs of having been processed. These pseudogenes are nonfunctional because they lack the regions surrounding the functional genes that initiate the production of the RNA message.[30]

Endogenous retroviruses. These retroviruses are permanently incorporated into the host organism's genome. Like all viruses, retroviruses consist of protein capsules that house genetic material (either DNA or RNA).

Viruses infect organisms by invading specific cell types of their hosts. Once viruses attach to the target cell's surface, they inject their genetic material into the healthy cell. Then the viral genetic material exploits the cell's machinery to produce more viral genetic material and proteins, which combine forming new viral particles. When the newly formed viruses escape from the host cell, the infection cycle repeats.[31]

Instead of DNA, RNA is the genetic material used by retroviruses. After it is injected into the host cell, reverse transcriptase uses the retroviral RNA to make DNA. This newly made DNA can then direct the production of new retroviral particles.[32] (HIV, the virus responsible for AIDS, is a retrovirus.)

The DNA copy of the retroviral genetic material can become incorporated into the host cell's genome. If the retroviral DNA suffers severe mutations, the retrovirus becomes disabled. When this happens, the retrovirus DNA presumably remains nonfunctional in the host genome and is referred to as an endogenous retrovirus.[33]

SINEs and LINEs. These two types of noncoding DNA are known as transposable elements—pieces of DNA that jump around the genome or transpose. In the process of moving around, transposable elements direct the cell's machinery to make additional copies and consequently increase the number of these elements.[34]

SINEs (short interspersed nuclear elements) and LINEs (long interspersed nuclear elements) belong to a class of transposable elements called retroposons. Molecular biologists believe SINEs and LINEs duplicate and move around the genome through an RNA intermediate and the work of reverse transcriptase.

Making a difference. Junk DNA at one time represented an insurmountable challenge to the biochemical intelligent design argument and appeared to make an ironclad case for evolution. Now, recent advances suggest otherwise. Much to the surprise of scientists, junk DNA has function.

Based on the characteristics possessed by pseudogenes, few molecular biologists would have ever thought junk DNA plays any role in the cell's operation. However, several recent studies unexpectedly identified functions for both duplicated and processed pseudogenes. Some duplicated pseudogenes help regulate the expression of their corresponding genes.[35] And, many processed pseudogenes code for functional proteins.[36]

The scientific community is also well on its way to establishing functional roles for endogenous retroviruses and their compositional elements. Recent advances indicate that this class of noncoding DNA regulates gene expression and helps the cell ward off retroviral infections by disrupting the assembly of retroviruses after they take over the cell's machinery.[37]

As with pseudogenes and endogenous retroviruses, molecular biologists now recognize that the SINE DNA found in the genomes of a wide range of organisms plays an important part in regulating gene expression and offers protection when the cell becomes distressed.[38] Researchers have also identified another potential function for SINEs—regulation of gene expression during the course of development.

SINEs possess regions that the cell's machinery methylates (attaches the methyl chemical functional group). This process turns genes off. Depending on the tissue type, SINEs display varying patterns of DNA methylation. These diverse patterns implicate SINEs in the differential gene expression that occurs during development.[39]

Much in the same way the scientific community acknowledges function for SINE DNA, molecular biologists now recognize that LINEs critically regulate gene expression. For example, researchers have identified a central role for LINE DNA in X chromosome inactivation.[40] This inactivation occurs in healthy females to compensate for duplicate genes found on the two X chromosomes.[41] (Females have two X chromosomes. Males have an X and a Y chromosome.) The inactivation of one set of X chromosomal genes ensures proper levels of gene expression in females. If X chromosome inactivation doesn't occur, genetic disorders result.[42]

The scientific community now thinks LINE DNA controls monoallelic gene expression, a situation in which only one of the two genes inherited from both parents is used.[43] This process completely "turns off" the other gene.

Many scientists now maintain that even though they can't directly identify functional roles for many classes of noncoding DNA, these DNA segments must be functional because so many distantly related or unrelated organisms share them.[44] Scientists reason that these noncoding DNA classes must serve in a critical capacity. If they didn't, mutations would readily accrue in them. These noncoding DNA segments must have resisted change, otherwise mutations would have rendered them nonfunctional. And, that would have been harmful to the organism.

Genetic Redundancy

Many biochemists consider duplicate biochemical systems to be yet another example of a bad design. From an evolutionary standpoint, redundant systems arise as the result of random gene duplication events. This repetition appears senseless and unnecessary, something an all-powerful, all-knowing Creator would never do.

However, sometimes engineers intentionally design systems with duplicate components. On this basis, it could be argued that biochemical redundancy is a good design feature. These systems would, in principle, buffer against the harmful effects of mutations. If mutations disable one of the system's components, then another copy of that component is available to take its place.

But in contrast to biochemical systems—which appear to be haphazardly redundant—redundancy in human designs is not aimless. It is well thought out. Because of cost and efficiency concerns, engineers introduce redundant components into their designs judiciously, limiting them to only those parts critical for the system's operation.

Typically only one of the redundant components operates at a time. It functions as the primary system while the other provides backup. The backup system kicks into operation only when the primary system fails. Engineers refer to this type of system as a responsive backup circuit.

Redundant biochemical systems didn't appear to display the same exquisite operational control as human designs, at least not until a team of geneticists from Israel recently published their work on gene regulation.[45]

These researchers examined the gene regulation patterns for duplicated genes and noted that, more often than not, they functioned as a responsive backup circuit, just like those found in human designs. In other words, these scientists discovered that only one of the duplicated genes was active. The other was down regulated or turned off. It became active only if the primary gene became mutated.

In light of this discovery, it's difficult to maintain that biochemical redundancy is a bad design. Rather, duplicate systems appear to have the same purpose and function as redundancies in human designs.

Deliberate Scribbles

In some instances biochemical systems appear to be purposely suboptimized to balance trade-offs. A few representative examples such as protein synthesis, the carbon fixation reaction of photosynthesis, and the interplay between the motor proteins kinesin and dynein highlight how intentional suboptimization leads to an overall optimal performance for critical biochemical systems.

Protein Synthesis

The production of a myriad of proteins inside the cell occurs at structures called ribosomes (see chapter 2, p. 39). They assemble each protein chain by linking together twenty different amino acid building blocks in a unique combination. The amino acid sequence then dictates, in part, the way each protein chain "folds" into the precise three-dimensional structure that determines its function.[46]

Highly inefficient. Researchers have recently come to recognize that cells employ a wasteful process when producing proteins. Roughly 30 percent of all proteins synthesized must be degraded by the cell because they are improperly made.[47] Anyone with experience in manufacturing would agree that a production process with a 30 percent defect rate needs much improvement.

These problems challenge the notion that a Creator produced life's chemistry. However, the seemingly wasteful process of protein synthesis actually plays a critical role in the ability of the immune system to respond rapidly to viral infections.

After proteins outlive their usefulness to the cell or become damaged in the process of carrying out their cellular function, they are degraded. Their breakdown occurs in a highly orchestrated fashion catalyzed by a large protein complex called a proteasome.[48] Degradation releases the protein's amino acids and makes them available for use in the production of new proteins.

In addition to recycling amino acids, the cell also uses small protein fragments produced during the breakdown process to communicate to the immune system what's happening inside the cell. The cell incorporates these protein-degradation fragments into a complex assembly of molecules known as the class 1 major histocompatibility complex (MHC). The MHC eventually makes its way to the cell surface. Once there, the MHC presents the protein fragments to the immune system.[49]

These protein fragments inform the immune system when viruses infect cells. Upon infection, viral particles invade the cell and take over the cellular machinery. Viral DNA directs the production of viral proteins. Some of these proteins are eventually degraded and subsequently presented to the immune system via the class 1 MHC. In this way, the immune system "knows" when cells fall victim to a viral infection (see figure 13.3).

A new discovery. Scientists once believed the cell used only aged viral proteins to produce the complexes that signal the immune system of a viral infection. This limitation creates a dilemma. If the cell waits until viral proteins age, the immune response can't be rapid enough to destroy the infected cell before the virus invasion gets too far along.

Researchers have found, however, that defective proteins produced by the ribosome are degraded immediately after their production by proteasomes.[50] The defective protein fragments then make their way to the cell surface as part of the class 1 MHC. As soon as a viral infection occurs, the immune system becomes aware of the presence of viral particles inside the cell through the production of defective viral proteins.

This cutting-edge discovery reveals elegant design in the inefficiency of protein synthesis. The high level of defective proteins produced by the cell allows for an efficient immune response to viral infection—the perfect plan of a Master who colors inside the lines.

Rubisco

Perhaps the most important chemical reaction in nature is the addition of carbon dioxide to the five-carbon sugar ribulose 1,5-bisphosphate. (This

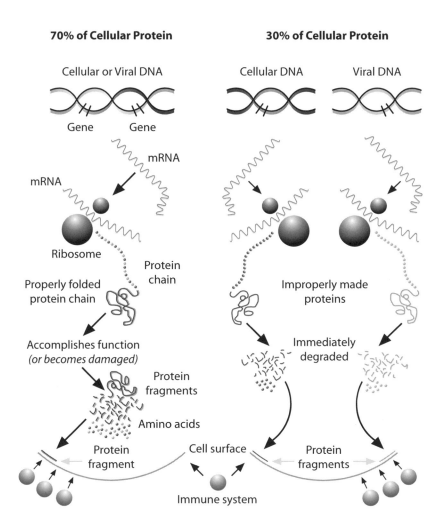

70% of Cellular Protein

Cellular or Viral DNA

Gene   Gene

mRNA

mRNA

Ribosome

Properly folded
protein chain

Protein
chain

Accomplishes function
(or becomes damaged)

Protein
fragments

Amino acids

Protein
fragment

30% of Cellular Protein

Cellular DNA   Viral DNA

Improperly made
proteins

Immediately
degraded

Cell surface

Protein
fragments

Immune system

Figure 13.3. Two Metabolic Fates of Proteins
The cell incorporates the protein-degradation fragments into a complex assembly of
molecules called the class 1 major histocompatibility complex (MHC). At the cell surface
the MHC presents the protein fragments to the immune system. The inefficiency of protein
synthesis allows for a highly efficient immune response to viral infection.

process is referred to as the carbon fixation reaction of photosynthesis.)
This chemical transformation, which is the first step in the so-called dark
reactions of photosynthesis, sustains virtually every life-form in Earth's
surface biosphere. In the dark reaction, these two compounds produce a

transiently existing six-carbon species that breaks down into two three-carbon compounds. Once formed, these three-carbon entities get swept away by a series of reactions that ultimately yield six-carbon sugars, the foodstuff at the base of the food chain.[51]

Highly inefficient. The protein that catalyzes the addition of carbon dioxide to ribulose 1,5-bisphosphate is rubisco (ribulose 1,5-bisphosphate carboxylase/oxygenase). Because of its central role in photosynthesis and its primary importance in ecosystems, rubisco is the most abundant protein in nature. In spite of its significance, rubisco has acquired the reputation among biochemists as a wasteful enzyme.

The rubisco-catalyzed reaction of carbon dioxide and ribulose 1,5-bisphosphate proceeds slowly. Prone to errors, rubisco confuses molecular oxygen for carbon dioxide, further compounding its inefficiency. When rubisco makes this mistake, oxygen combines with ribulose 1,5-bisphosphate to form unwanted compounds. Photorespiration, an undesired process, detracts from the carbon fixation reaction that inaugurates the dark reactions of photosynthesis, necessitating many more copies of rubisco than would be required if this enzyme operated with greater efficiency.[52]

Such wastefulness has prompted some biochemists to focus their efforts on developing genetically engineered plants with novel forms of rubisco that would operate with greater efficacy than those found in nature. The hope is that these genetically modified plants would boost food production around the world.

A new discovery. Recent work by scientists from Australia, however, is changing the way biochemists view rubisco.[53] These researchers point out that rubisco's slow turnover and struggles to discriminate between molecular oxygen and carbon dioxide stem from the small linear and symmetric nonpolar nature of both gases. In other words, rubisco's confusion is not its fault, but rather results from the inherent chemical nature of the two gases. To overcome this confusion, rubisco uses the chemical intermediate that forms during the process that adds carbon dioxide to ribulose 1,5-bisphosphate (the transition state complex) to indirectly discriminate between carbon dioxide and oxygen.

This indirect discrimination has unavoidable consequences, however. It slows down the carbon fixation reaction. The reason for the slow down has to do with the similarity between the transition state complex and the six-carbon compound produced by the carbon fixation reaction. This similarity makes it more difficult for rubisco to release the product once it forms at the enzyme's catalytic site, hindering the rate of chemical conversion. The bottom line: Rubisco faces a trade-off between rate of reaction and discrimination between the gases.

A survey of rubiscos from a variety of plants reveals a pattern that stems from this trade-off. Rubiscos exposed to an environment with a relatively low carbon dioxide-to-oxygen ratio bind the transition state complex more tightly in order to distinguish carbon dioxide from oxygen. By contrast, rubiscos in an environment with higher carbon dioxide-to-oxygen ratios bind the transition state complex more loosely. This difference in binding dictates reaction rate. Rubiscos in a low carbon dioxide-to-oxygen environment convert carbon dioxide and ribulose 1,5-bisphosphate into a six-carbon compound at a relatively slow rate. Rubiscos in relatively high carbon dioxide-to-oxygen environments complete the carbon fixation reaction more rapidly.

Based on this pattern, the researchers from Australia concluded that rubiscos found throughout nature are perfectly optimized for their environments and the slow carbon fixation reaction is a necessary trade-off for this enzyme to make the difficult discrimination between carbon dioxide and molecular oxygen. These workers conclude that "despite appearing sluggish and confused, most rubiscos may be near-optimally adapted to their different gaseous and thermal environments."[54]

In other words, biochemists likely can't improve upon the elegant design of the rubiscos found in nature. This enzyme no longer deserves the reputation as a poorly designed product of evolutionary processes; rather, its deliberate design adds the necessary depth to an amazing work of art.

Dynein and Kinesin

The molecular motors dynein and kinesin transport cellular cargo along microtubules (see chapter 4, pp. 81 and 93).[55] Part of the cell's cytoskeleton, microtubules display polarity with "plus" and "minus" ends. Microtubules form an astrallike structural array within the cell. Their minus ends cluster near the nucleus at the center of the cell. The plus ends locate to the cell's peripheral regions.

Dynein and kinesin transport cellular cargo along microtubules in single and opposite directions. These motor proteins recognize microtubule polarity and use the directional nature of the cytoskeletal elements to move materials either toward or away from the cell's center. Kinesin moves cargo toward the plus ends of microtubules at the cell's periphery. Its structural simplicity makes kinesin a highly efficient and robust transporter.

Highly inefficient. Dynein moves materials toward the minus ends located near the cell's nucleus. In contrast to kinesin, dynein's greater structural complexity makes this motor cumbersome and inefficient by comparison. On this basis, dynein appears to be best explained as the imperfect product of evolutionary process, not the work of a Creator.

A new discovery. Recent work paints a different picture of dynein's operation.[56] Though kinesin is simple and efficient, its simplicity limits the cell's ability to regulate its activity. Kinesin can only exist in two functional states, either fully active or fully inactive. Dynein's complexity, on the other hand, provides the cell with several means to dynamically tune its activity. This motorized carrier can speed up or slow down depending on the cell's needs.

From a design standpoint, a trade-off between efficiency and the cell's ability to regulate motor activity exists for dynein and kinesin. These molecular motors both appear optimally designed for allowing the motors to function individually and cooperatively in a variety of cellular situations.

Perfect Imperfections

Biomolecular imperfections represent potentially devastating disanalogies for the biochemical intelligent design argument. The abundant elegant designs that characterize life's chemical systems, which seemingly make such a strong case for a Creator, are often overshadowed by poorly performing biochemical systems. Bad biochemical designs are unworthy of intelligent agency.

According to evolutionary biologists, the blind undirected processes of evolution can just as readily account for good designs through the repeated action of natural selection on random genetic variation. But evolutionary processes are also just as likely to generate "jury-rigged" structures. Biochemical imperfections seem to indicate the amateurish scribbling of happenstance, not the intentional expertise of an all-powerful, all-knowing Designer.

But, imperfections may not be as big a problem for the biochemical intelligent design argument as they first appear. Rather than representing disanalogies that mitigate against the biochemical intelligent design argument, suboptimal biochemical designs could result from the outworkings of the second law of thermodynamics. Entropy introduces defects into elegantly designed biochemical systems through genetic mutations.

And, some poor designs are not really bad at all. Instead, these seemingly poor designs actually add to the list of analogical features shared by human designs and the Creator. Any engineer who designs a complex multiobjective system faces trade-offs and must carefully introduce suboptimal features in order to achieve overall performance.

This important design principle, relied on by human engineers, appears in living color in the cell's chemistry. Recent advances have made it possible for biochemists to identify trade-offs in a number of biochemical systems.

Prior to these new insights, scientists considered many of these systems to be cumbersome and inefficient—certainly not the work of the all-powerful, all-knowing Creator described in the Bible. All too often, evolutionary biologists quickly pronounced sentence on the quality of life's biomolecular designs without fully understanding their structure, function, and interrelationship to other biochemical processes. This misjudgment clearly has been the case for so-called junk DNA sequences.

The recognition that several examples of bad biochemical design are, in fact, optimal neutralizes one of the most potent challenges against biochemical intelligent design. These discoveries also make it distinctly possible that when other biochemical imperfections are more fully understood, they too may reveal themselves to be perfect.

The next chapter pulls together the components of the Creator's artistry in the cell to more fully reveal his masterpiece.

14

THE MASTERPIECE
AUTHENTICATED

An exhibit opened on May 3, 2004, that caused quite a stir in the art world. The Mitchell-Innes and Nash gallery in New York City unveiled part of a collection that had never before been displayed—a 1970 album of twenty-six drawings and watercolors created by a ninety-one-year-old Picasso.[1]

Throughout his life Picasso developed such sketchbooks. Now his family controls most of them and limits their access. The so-called Berggruen Album (named for art dealer Heinz Berggruen) provides a rare and intimate glimpse into the art and thoughts of Picasso. Put together over the span of about seven days, Picasso produced about four works per day and carefully dated each one.

Nature's sketchbook compiled by the day-to-day research efforts of biochemists, biophysicists, and molecular biologists over the last half-century also reveals remarkable insights into the work of its Creator. This process marks a continuous unveiling of the biochemical masterpiece. With each new discovery, life's most fundamental structures and activities continue to generate a stir in the scientific world and beyond.

Life—A Magnificent Masterpiece

The sheer beauty and artistry of life's chemical systems is undeniable. So, too, is the appearance of design. For those who regard this glorious treasure as the handiwork of a Creator, the page-by-page details supplied by researchers provide a rare and intimate glimpse into the art and thoughts of the Divine Master.

Even scientists who maintain that undirected processes (natural selection operating iteratively on random genetic change) produced the elegant chemical systems in the living realm find this *appearance* of biochemical design awe-inspiring.[2]

Careful consideration of the hallmark characteristics of biochemical systems suggests the work of a Mastermind. The few pages from the sketch pad made available in this book were carefully selected and organized to cast the intuition of design into a formal argument.

Rather than relying on a single biochemical feature (like irreducible complexity) to argue for a Creator's role in life's origin, the case for biochemical intelligent design is erected upon a weight of evidence argument. Each feature, in and of itself, points to the work of a Creator. And collectively, the individual strands of evidence intertwine and mutually support one another to make the case that much more compelling.

Skeptics are within their rights to regard a single piece of evidence or a single line of reasoning as marginal in its support for intelligent design. However, if a litany of diverse evidence exists, it becomes less tenable to reject a supernatural basis for life as unfounded.

Can Evolution Explain Life's Chemical Picture?

When attempting to make any scientific case, all the evidence should be examined to come to the most valid conclusion. The fact that evolutionary explanations have been offered to account for life's elegant chemical systems can't be ignored. For example, some scientists claim that biochemical fine-tuning and optimization result when the forces of natural selection operate iteratively on random genetic variation over eons of time to precisely hone the structural and functional features of life's chemistry.

Origin-of-life researchers maintain that information-rich biomolecules, like DNA and proteins, emerged under the influence of chemical selection. According to this idea, it's not just random processes alone that explain the origin of information-harboring molecules. Rather, the intrinsic chemical and physical properties of subunit molecules (amino acids and nucleotides, for example) and the resulting physicochemical features of information-containing polymers (proteins, DNA, and RNA) efficiently guided random processes and led to the emergence of biochemical information systems over vast periods of time.

Evolutionary Stepping Stones

Evolutionary biologists also claim that irreducibly complex systems (and chicken-and-egg systems) did not have to arise all at once but could emerge in a stepwise fashion.[3] According to this model, the biomolecules of irreducibly complex biochemical systems originally played other roles in the cell and were later recruited or co-opted, one-by-one, to be part of transitional systems that eventually led to the irreducibly complex systems of contemporary biochemical operations.

For instance, some evolutionary biologists claim that the bacterial flagellum (see chapter 4, p. 71) evolved from the type III secretion apparatus through the process of co-option.[4] Pathogenic bacteria use the type III secretion system to export proteins into the cells of the host organism. The molecular architecture of the type III secretion system closely resembles the part of the flagellum embedded in the bacterial cell envelope.[5]

Speculation has the first flagellum arising from the merger of the type III secretion apparatus and a filamentous protein system. Presumably, both structures provided the microbe with prior services, neither of which had anything to do with motility. These evolutionary explanations have not gone unchallenged, however.

Evolution's critics point out that these explanations seem plausible, but only on the surface. In essence, they are no more than evolutionary "just-so" stories.[6] Invariably, the naturalistic scenarios proposed to account for the origin of irreducibly complex systems are highly speculative and lack any type of detailed mechanistic undergirding. This problem is clearly the case for all the evolutionary explanations offered to account for the emergence of the bacterial flagellum. Biologists Mark Pallen and Nicholas Matzke state that

> the flagellar research community has scarcely begun to consider how these systems have evolved. This neglect probably stems from a reluctance to engage in the "armchair speculation" inherent in building evolutionary models.[7]

Compounding the speculative nature of the evolutionary explanations for the origin of the bacterial flagellum is the nagging problem of which came first: the flagellum or the type III secretion machine. According to Milton Saier, a biologist from the University of California, San Diego, insufficient information exists to determine from an evolutionary framework whether (1) the type III secretion apparatus came first or (2) the bacterial flagellum came first, or (3) both structures evolved from the same precursor system.[8] If evolutionary analyses indicate that the type III secretion machine emerged from the flagellum, it thoroughly undermines the co-option explanation.

On the other hand, the type III secretion system—the proposed evolutionary stepping stone to the bacterial flagellum—is an irreducibly complex structure. It's an elegant machine that, like many other biomolecular machines, bears an uncanny resemblance to humanly crafted devices. In other words, the type III secretion machinery, in and of its own right, evinces biochemical intelligent design. Further evidence for intelligent design comes from the recognition that highly similar flagellar systems appear to have emerged independently (from an evolutionary perspective) in bacteria and archaea.[9] This remarkable example of convergence fits awkwardly within an evolutionary context but makes perfect sense if a Creator repeatedly employed the same blueprint when he made flagellar systems in archaea and bacteria (see chapter 11).

Evolutionary biologists own the burden of proof. If irreducibly complex systems do, indeed, have an evolutionary origin, the scientific community must provide a detailed mechanistic accounting for each step in the sequence of molecular events that yielded the system. Additionally, they must demonstrate that this sequence of steps could have happened in the available time and with the resources at its disposal.

It's not enough to merely propose a chronology of events that "may have happened" or "most likely took place." Yet, virtually every evolutionary explanation for irreducibly complex biochemical systems is littered with these types of qualifiers.[10]

Is the Probability Probable?

As for the origin of information-rich biomolecules, evoking chemical selection as a mechanistic explanation for the origin of proteins and nucleic acids—like DNA and RNA—again, at a surface level seems plausible. But as astronomer Hugh Ross and I show in our book *Origins of Life*, chemical selection seems to play a minor, almost negligible, role in the formation of information-containing molecules. For all intents and purposes, the formation of biochemical information systems is a probability problem. And based on what's currently known, it appears superastronomically improbable for the essential gene set to emerge through natural means alone.[11]

Still, this probability analysis is incomplete because the fundamental relationships among sequence, structure, and function for proteins and DNA are still not known. When these relationships are better understood, it may turn out that it is much easier for mechanistic processes to generate information-rich molecules. But these future insights could also make the probabilities of producing functional biomolecules even more remote. The bottom line: Current knowledge about the capability of evolutionary processes is insufficient to either establish or rule out an evolutionary origin of biochemical information systems.

What Are the Odds?

While it's impossible at this point in time to calculate the probability of functional biomolecules like proteins emerging through natural means, scientists can rigorously assess the likelihood that the genetic code arose through natural processes. Simply put, there does not appear to be enough time for evolutionary processes to stumble upon the universal genetic code—a code that displays exceptional levels of design in terms of its error-minimization capacity (see chapter 9, p. 174) and its ability to harbor overlapping codes.

Biophysicist Hubert Yockey determined that natural selection would have to explore 1.40×10^{70} different genetic codes to discover the universal genetic code found in nature. Yockey estimated 6.3×10^{15} seconds is the maximum time available for the code to originate. Natural selection would have to evaluate roughly 10^{55} codes per *second* to find the universal genetic code.[12] The universal genetic code that defines biochemical information doesn't appear to have an evolutionary origin.

The origin of cell membranes has to be one of the first steps in the origin of life. These structures play critical biochemical roles.

Even though biochemists and biophysicists have identified plausible pathways that could produce the first components of primitive cell membranes and have uncovered physicochemical processes that could, in principle, have yielded the vesicles, they have ultimately failed to explain the origin of cell membranes. Numerous experiments demonstrate that every step in the proposed pathway from prebiotic amphiphilic compounds to contemporary cell membranes strictly depends on exacting compositional and environmental factors.[13] These stringent requirements make it unlikely that cell membranes could ever emerge on early Earth—unless guided by the hand of an intelligent being.

The proposed evolutionary explanations for fine-tuning and optimization of biochemical systems in no way invalidate the case for biochemical intelligent design. These two elegant design features of biochemical systems are precisely what can be expected if life is the product of a Creator. According to the late evolutionary biologist Stephen Jay Gould, "Textbooks like to illustrate evolution with examples of optimal design. . . . But ideal design is a lousy argument for evolution, for it mimics the postulated action of an omnipotent creator."[14]

According to Gould, the optimal design of biochemical systems could point equally to the work of a Creator or evolutionary fine-tuning. However, Gould as well as other evolutionary biologists think the seemingly bad designs in nature make an unequivocal case for an evolutionary explanation for life's origin and history. The blind undirected chance processes of evolution are just as likely to produce "jury-rigged" structures as they are to produce fine-tuned structures. Evolutionists claim that even though biochemical systems are replete with elegant design features, the assortment of imperfections in life's chemistry undermines the case for biochemical intelligent design. An all-powerful, all-knowing Designer would never produce such faulty work.

Can Disanologies Be Explained?

When employing analogical reasoning, the ways in which the compared system, events, or objects differ must be considered (see chapter 1, p. 31). Biochemical imperfections match the expected pattern for evolution and potentially represent powerful disanalogies, wreaking havoc on the conclusion that life's chemistry is the work of a Creator.

Yet, imperfections may not be as big a problem for the biochemical intelligent design argument as they appear on the surface (see chapter 12). Faulty designs could result from the outworkings of the second law of thermodynamics that introduces defects into elegantly designed biochemical systems through genetic mutations.

And, some bad designs may not be bad at all. Seemingly poor designs may represent the intentional actions of the Creator. When engineers design finite multiobjective complex systems, they face trade-offs and must carefully introduce suboptimal features in order to achieve overall optimal performance.

This important design principle, relied on by human engineers, appears to be in full effect in the cell's chemistry. Recent advances have made it possible for biochemists to identify trade-offs in a number of biochemical systems. Prior to these new insights, biochemists considered many of these systems cumbersome and inefficient. All too often, evolutionary biologists are quick to pronounce sentence on the quality of life's biomolecular designs without fully understanding their structure, function, and interrelationship to other biochemical processes.

The recognition that several examples of bad biochemical design are, in fact, optimal neutralizes one of the most potent challenges against biochemical intelligent design. Such discoveries make it distinctly possible that other biochemical imperfections may actually be perfect when more fully understood. Instead of representing disanalogies that mitigate against the biochemical intelligent design argument, suboptimal biochemical designs actually add to the list of analogical features shared with human designs. Just as human designers intentionally introduce suboptimal features in their designs to achieve overall optimality, so too does the Creator (see chapter 13, p. 248).

Is There a Consistent Style?

The idea of historical contingency championed by Stephen Jay Gould provides another way to discriminate between the "appearance of design" and intelligent design. Does contingency account for the patterns observed in the biological realm?[15]

If life results exclusively from evolutionary processes, then scientists should expect to see few, if any, cases in which evolution repeated itself. Chance governs biological and biochemical evolution at its most fundamental level. Evolutionary pathways consist of a historical sequence of chance genetic changes operated on by natural selection, which also consists of chance components. The consequences are profound. If evolutionary events could be repeated, the outcome would be dramatically different every time.

If life is the product of a Creator, however, then the same designs should repeatedly appear in biochemical systems. Human engineers routinely reuse the same techniques and technologies.

Over the course of the last decade or so, scientists exploring the origin of biochemical systems have discovered that a number of life's molecules and processes, though virtually identical, appear to have originated independently, multiple times (see chapter 11).

Evolutionary biologists refer to the independent origin of identical biomolecules and biochemical systems as molecular convergence. Repeated creations would give the appearance of multiple independent origin events when viewed from an evolutionary vantage point. So the explosion in the number of examples of molecular convergence is unexpected if life resulted from historical sequences of chance evolutionary events. Yet, if life emanated from a Creator, it is reasonable to expect that he used the same designs repeatedly as he created.

Reasoning to the Best Explanation for Life

The highly speculative, proposed evolutionary scenarios for life's chemistry don't necessarily weaken the case for biochemical intelligent design. Even in light of these evolutionary explanations, the defining features of biochemical systems are precisely what would be expected if life is the product of a Creator. This line of thinking is an example of what philosophers refer to as abductive reasoning.[16]

Commonly used by scientists to evaluate hypotheses, abductive reasoning takes the following form:

X is observed.
If Y were true, then X would be expected.
There is good reason to believe that Y is true.

In the case of biochemical systems:

Design is observed in biochemical systems.
If life stemmed from the direct work of a Creator, the elegant design of
    biochemical systems would be expected.
There is good reason to believe that life is the product of a Creator.

In other words, the same reasoning process that scientists use, day in and day out, to evaluate a hypothesis rationally and logically leads to the expectation that life, at its most fundamental level, stemmed from a Creator's handiwork.

Making the Case for a Divine Artist

Arguments for intelligent design typically fall into one of two categories: those that rely on probabilities and those based on analogies. In the biochemical arena, probability arguments primarily focus on the inability (or at least the claimed inability) of natural mechanistic processes to generate the information-rich biomolecules (DNA and proteins, for example) central to life's chemical systems.

The Problems with Probabilities

This book has avoided probability arguments for two reasons. Based on current understanding, the case for biochemical intelligent design is unattainable through the use of probabilities. Biochemists lack the necessary understanding of the relationship between amino acid sequences and protein structure and function. Without this critical knowledge, it's impossible to determine the likelihood, one way or the other, of evolutionary processes spawning the information-based systems of life's systems.

In addition, at their very essence, probability-based design arguments are negative in scope. Instead of making a positive case for the specific features found in nature, probability arguments fixate on what natural processes can or can't do. In the end, this approach proves nothing because a negative can't be proven.

Even Dembski's explanatory filter (see chapter 1, p. 25) depends upon probabilities (or more appropriately, improbabilities). Though this technique is touted as a method that positively detects the work of an intelligent agent in nature, it considers a feature in the natural realm to be the product of intentional design only *after* natural processes are demonstrated incapable of generating that feature. As with all probability arguments, the explanatory filter is ultimately a commentary on what natural mechanisms can or can't do. And this insight can never be achieved apart from an omniscient viewpoint.

An Analogical Analysis

In the tradition of William Paley's Watchmaker analogy (see chapter 4, p. 85), this book makes the case for biochemical intelligent design based on analogical reasoning. Many have considered this approach ineffective based on the work of philosopher David Hume (1711–1776) and myriad others who came after him. Critics of analogical reasoning rightfully reacted against weak or poorly constructed analogies and justifiably rejected the conclusions drawn from them.

This rejection, however, doesn't mean that it is impossible to make a logically compelling case for intelligent design based on analogy. Rather, it sets up the imperative to properly and carefully employ analogical thinking (see chapter 1, p. 31).

One effective form of analogical reasoning, particularly commonplace in science, is pattern recognition. For instance, analytical chemists routinely use pattern recognition to identify unknown chemical compounds by comparing the physical, chemical, and spectral properties for a series of known standards with those of an unknown substance. These scientists feel confident they can identify an unknown compound when its characteristics closely match those of a known chemical entity. This approach can only succeed, however, if the researchers have a predetermined pattern available to compare against the unknown material.

Likewise, it's necessary to define ahead of time an intelligent design pattern that can be used as a template to compare with life's chemistry for successful use of this technique. If life is the product of a Creator, then the defining features of biochemical systems should line up with the intelligent design template. If it is not, then the defining characteristics will be different.

Unfortunately, no universal pattern for intelligent design is currently known. The only unequivocal example available to construct the template is the behavior of human designers. But it may not be legitimate to generalize human behavior into a set of criteria that universally describes the activity of *any* intelligent designer. Human designers could very well create in an anomalous fashion.

This problem was circumvented by linking the behavior of human designers to the activities of the Intelligent Agent responsible for creating life. This book identifies that Creator as the God of the Old and New Testaments. The biblical account of humanity's origin establishes the desired connection between human designers and their Maker. The Genesis 1 creation account (and Genesis 5) teaches that God created human beings, male and female, in his image.[17] This declaration implies that humans bear a similarity to God, at least in some ways.[18]

Just as God is a Creator, so too human beings (who bear his image) are minicreators. This resemblance implies that the hallmark characteristics of humanly produced systems will mirror those of divinely designed systems, if the Divine Artist is the God described in the Bible. The expectation, however, is that the hallmark characteristics of man-made systems would, at best, imperfectly reflect divine design. As a corollary to this idea, the cell's chemical systems should be clearly superior to anything produced by the best human designers.

The analogical comparison used to argue for biochemical intelligent design is an integral part of day-to-day decision making. Analogical reasoning is not neat and tidy. Its conclusions are not certain, but instead they depend upon a weight of evidence. Properly employed, analogical thinking can produce sound conclusions. In general, the conclusions drawn from analogies engender increasing confidence as the number of comparisons and the number of relevant similarities for each increases.

The Weight of Evidence

The examples discussed throughout this book reveal some of the defining features of life's chemical systems that correspond to the distinctive characteristics of systems designed by humans. A summary of the features from these systems tips the scales in favor of creation authenticating the masterpiece.

Irreducible complexity. As highlighted in Behe's *Darwin's Black Box*, biochemical systems typically are irreducibly complex. They are composed of numerous components, all of which must be present for the system to have any function at all. Many man-made systems are also irreducibly complex; therefore, this feature indicates intelligent design.

Chicken-and-egg systems. Which came first? Many biochemical systems are made up of components that mutually require each other for all the components to be produced. For example, ribosomes make proteins, yet, in turn, are formed from proteins. So proteins can't be made without ribosomes, and ribosomes can't be made without proteins. The mutual interdependence of the components of many biochemical systems signifies intelligent design.

Fine-tuning. Many biochemical structures and activities depend on the precise location and orientation of atoms in three-dimensional space. Man-made systems often require a high-degree of precision to function. Fine-tuning reflects intelligent design.

Optimization. Many biochemical structures and activities are designed to carry out a specific activity while operating at peak performance. Man-made systems often are planned in the same way. Optimization demonstrates the work of an Intelligent Agent.

Biochemical information systems. Information comes from intelligence. At their essence, the cell's biochemical systems are information-based. The presence of information in the cell, therefore, must emanate from an Intelligent Designer.

Structure of biochemical information. The evidence for intelligent design goes beyond the mere existence of information-based biochemical systems. Biochemical information displays provocative structural features, such as language structure and the organization and regulation of genes, that also point to the work of a Creator.

Biochemical codes. The information-based biochemical systems of the cell employ encoded information. The genetic code, the histone code, and even the parity code of DNA are three examples. The encoded information of the cell requires an Intelligent Designer to generate it.

Genetic code fine-tuning. The rules that comprise the genetic code are better designed than any conceivable alternative code to resist errors that occur as the genetic code translates stored information into functional information. This fine-tuning strongly indicates that a superior Intelligence designed the genetic code. The universal genetic code also has been optimized to house multiple parallel codes.

Quality control. Designed processes incorporate quality control systems to ensure the efficient and reproducible production of quality product. Many biochemical systems employ sophisticated quality control processes and consequently reflect the work of an Intelligent Designer.

Molecular convergence. Several biochemical systems and/or biomolecules isolated from different organisms are structurally, functionally, and mechanistically identical. These biochemical systems have independent origins. Given these systems' complexity, it is unwarranted to conclude that blind random natural processes independently produced them. Rather, molecular convergence reflects the work of a single Creator that employs a common blueprint to bring these systems into existence.

Strategic redundancy. Engineers frequently design systems with redundancy, particularly for those components that play a critical role in the operation of the system. When engineers incorporate duplicate parts into their designs, the redundant components form a responsive backup circuit. Many duplicated genes in genomes operate as a responsive backup circuit, reflecting the work of a Creator.

Trade-offs and intentional suboptimization. When engineers design complex systems, they often face trade-offs and must purposely design components in the system to be suboptimal in order to achieve overall optimal performance. Many biochemical systems display evidence of intentional suboptimization to balance trade-offs pointing to the work of a Divine Engineer.

In light of these criteria, it is significant that so many disparate characteristics of life's chemistry bear an uncanny resemblance to human designs. And for each category that is part of the biochemical intelligent design analogy, numerous examples abound in cells—far more than could be described in this work. In a sense, the information presented grossly understates the case for biochemical intelligent design.

Piling On Extra Pounds

Many additional provocative aspects of life's chemistry also signify the work of a Creator. These features are not necessarily a formal part of the biochemical intelligent design analogy yet are very much a part of the case for divine artistry. Some of the features specifically discussed add to the increasing weight of evidence for a Creator.

Life's minimum complexity. Life in its bare minimal form is remarkably complex. Minimal life seems irreducibly complex. There appears to be a lower bound of several hundred genes, below which life cannot be pushed and still be recognized as "life." In *Darwin's Black Box*, Behe demonstrated that individual biochemical systems are irreducibly complex. In its totality, life appears that way as well.

Molecular-level organization of simplest life. Over the last decade or so, microbiologists have come to recognize that prokaryotes (the simplest life-forms) display an exquisite spatial and temporal organization at the molecular level. Common experience teaches that it takes thought and intentional effort to carefully organize a space for functional use. By analogy, the surprising internal organization of prokaryotic cells bespeaks of intelligent design.

Exquisite molecular logic. Often, the design and operation of biochemical systems are remarkably clever. Many aspects of life's chemistry display an eerie though appealing molecular logic that indicates a Creator's wisdom.

Preplanning. Planning ahead indicates purpose and reflects design. Many biochemical processes, like the assembly of the bacterial flagellum, consist of a sequence of molecular events and chemical reactions. Often the initial steps or initial structures of the pathways elegantly anticipate the pathway's final steps. Biochemical preplanning points to divine intentionality in life's chemistry.

Molecular motors. Individual proteins and protein complexes literally are direct structural and functional analogs to machines made by humans. These molecular motors revitalize the Watchmaker argument for a Creator's existence.

Cell membranes. These structures, which establish the cell's external and internal boundaries, require precise chemical compositions to form stable structures. Cell membranes also display exquisite organization that includes asymmetric inner and outer surfaces, dynamic structural and functional domains, and many specialized embedded machines.

The designs of biochemical systems inspire human designs. Some of the most important advances in nanoscience and nanotechnology come from insight gained from life's chemical operations. Apart from this insight, researchers struggle to discover, let alone implement, the principles needed to build molecular devices. The fact that biochemical systems can inspire human design indicates that life's chemistry was produced by the One who made humankind.

Man can't do it better. Frequently, humans fail in their attempts to duplicate the cell's complex and elegant chemical processes in the laboratory. When humans mimic biochemical processes, they find that their best efforts are cumbersome and lead to crude and inefficient systems. It doesn't seem reasonable to believe that blind random processes can account for the elegance of life's chemistry when the best researchers utilizing state-of-the-art technology can't produce even remotely comparable systems.

A Profound Implication

This book makes the case for biochemical design by comparing the most salient features of life's chemistry with the hallmark characteristics of human designs. The close match between biochemical systems and the pattern for intelligent design based on the behavior of human designers logically compels the conclusion that life's most fundamental processes and structures stem from the work of a Divine Designer.

The significance of the biochemical intelligent design argument extends beyond the conclusion that life's chemistry represents the work of a Divine Being. It displays the handiwork of the God described in the Old and New Testaments. The close analogy between the qualities of human and biochemical designs is quite provocative and points to a resonance between the human mind and the Divine Mind responsible for creating biochemical systems. This connection finds explanation in the biblical text, which declares that humans are made in God's image. The biochemical intelligent design analogy viewed in the context of Scripture supports the notion that humans were made to be in a relationship with the Creator.

EPILOGUE

Though it stands on its own, *The Cell's Design* is a sequel to *Origins of Life*, a book I coauthored with astronomer Hugh Ross. In it, we explored how the first life-forms (eubacteria and archaea) on Earth came into existence and presented a way to test those beginnings as a creation event. We also made the case that life's origins are miraculous and presented the first-ever scientifically testable creation model for life's beginnings, part of Reasons To Believe's creation model research program.[1] (Reasons To Believe [RTB] is a think tank devoted to exploring the connection between the frontiers of science and Christianity.)

This effort represents a new approach in the creation/evolution controversy, one that directly responds to the concern raised by many scientists who contend that creation is not science, because it cannot be falsified.

The RTB creation model is based on the biblical descriptions of God's creative work found in Scripture. The ongoing process of building the creation model starts by collating the biblical data from the major accounts and individual scriptural passages that describe God's creative actions. Once interpreted, the biblical data is recast in scientific terms rendering the biblical creation account testable. Biblical statements about God's creative activity are subjected to experimental validation. They also lead to predictions regarding future scientific discoveries.

This approach makes creation a scientific endeavor. Creation becomes testable and falls within the domain of science. The model's predictions delineate the features we'd expect to see in the record of nature—God's fingerprints—if the creation model has validity.

The biblical text inspires the creation model's tenets and constrains the overall model. However, within these constraints, the model finds considerable freedom for adjustments and fine-tuning as scientists and theologians make new discoveries.

The RTB creation model for the origin of life comes primarily from Genesis 1:2, Psalm 104:5–6, and Deuteronomy 32:10–11.[2] Based on these passages, the model predicts that (1) life appears early in Earth's history while our planet was still in its primordial state, (2) life originated and persisted through the hostile conditions of early Earth, (3) life originated abruptly on Earth, and (4) Earth's first life displays complexity. Remarkably, the latest advances in origin-of-life research continue to substantiate these predictions.[3]

The RTB origins-of-life model makes other important predictions. One of the most significant is that life's chemistry displays hallmark characteristics of intelligent design. *The Cell's Design* demonstrates how this important prediction finds satisfaction in the latest advances in biochemistry.

Within the context of the RTB origin-of-life creation model, the biochemical evidence for design goes beyond a mere inference to testable predictions based on intelligent causation. And in that context, RTB's model places creation squarely within the domain of science.

NOTES

Introduction A Rare Find

1. Robert P. Wolff, *About Philosophy*, 2nd ed. (Englewood Cliffs, NJ: Prentice-Hall, 1981), 193–97.

2. Fazale Rana and Hugh Ross, *Origins of Life: Biblical and Evolutionary Models Face Off* (Colorado Springs: NavPress, 2004), 13–15; Joe Aguirre, "Biochemistry and the Bible: Collaborators in Design," *Facts for Faith*, no. 3, third quarter 2000, 34–41.

3. Richard Dawkins, *The Blind Watchmaker: Why the Evidence of Evolution Reveals a Universe without Design* (New York: Norton, 1996), 1.

4. See, for example, Michael J. Behe, *Darwin's Black Box: The Biochemical Challenge to Evolution* (New York: Free Press, 1996).

5. Francis Crick, *What Mad Pursuit* (New York: Basic Books, 1988), 138.

6. "A Scientific Dissent from Darwinism," Discovery Institute, February 2007, http://www.discovery.org/scripts/viewDB/filesDB-download.php?command=download&id=660.

7. Behe, *Darwin's Black Box*, 39.

8. For example, Bruce H. Weber, "Biochemical Complexity: Emergence or Design?" *Rhetoric & Public Affairs* 1 (1998): 611–16; Philip Kitcher, "Born-Again Creationism," in *Intelligent Design Creationism and Its Critics: Philosophical, Theological and Scientific Perspectives*, ed. Robert T. Pennock (Cambridge, MA: MIT Press, 2001), 257–87; Matthew J. Brauer and Daniel R. Brumbaugh, "Biology Remystified: The Scientific Claims of the New Creationists," in *Intelligent Design Creationism and Its Critics*, 289–334.

9. Michael J. Behe, William A. Dembski, and Stephen C. Meyer, *Science and Evidence for Design in the Universe* (San Francisco: Ignatius, 2000), 133–49.

Chapter 1 Masterpiece or Forgery?

1. For more details, see Mark Harris's website, The Picasso Conspiracy, http://web.org.uk/picasso/Welcome.html (accessed February 6, 2007).

2. Guillermo Gonzalez and Jay W. Richards, *The Privileged Planet: How Our Place in the Cosmos Is Designed for Discovery* (Washington, DC: Regnery, 2004), 293–311.

3. William A. Dembski, *The Design Inference: Eliminating Chance through Small Probabilities* (New York: Cambridge University Press, 1998). For a lay level discussion of the ideas found in *The Design*

Inference, see William A. Dembski, *Intelligent Design: The Bridge between Science and Theology* (Downers Grove, IL: InterVarsity, 1999).

4. Dembski, *Intelligent Design*, 122–52.

5. Ibid., 139–44.

6. Ibid., 146–49.

7. Michael J. Behe, *Darwin's Black Box: The Biochemical Challenge to Evolution* (New York: Free Press, 1996), 39–48.

8. Philosophers Branden Fitelson, Christopher Stephens, and Elliott Sober have raised questions about the validity of the explanatory filter as a design detection system. Part of their criticism is that the application of the explanatory filter requires omniscience. See Branden Fitelson, Christopher Stephens, and Elliott Sober, "How Not to Detect Design—Critical Notice: William A. Dembski, *The Design Inference*," *Philosophy of Science* 66 (September 1999): 472–88, reprinted in Robert T. Pennock, ed., *Intelligent Design Creationism and Its Critics: Philosophical, Theological, and Scientific Perspectives* (Cambridge, MA: MIT Press, 2001), 597–615. It should be noted that Dembski has replied to the concerns raised by Fitelson, Stephens, and Sober and some of the concerns raised by other critics. See William A. Dembski, *No Free Lunch: Why Specified Complexity Cannot Be Purchased without Intelligence* (Lanham, MD: Roman & Littlefield, 2002).

9. For a popular level treatment of this idea, see Christian de Duve's *Vital Dust: Life as a Cosmic Imperative* (New York: Basic Books, 1995).

10. For a recent critique of evolutionary explanations for life's origin, see Fazale Rana and Hugh Ross, *Origins of Life: Biblical and Evolutionary Models Face Off* (Colorado Springs: NavPress, 2004).

11. Dembski, *Intelligent Design*, 127.

12. Genesis 1:26–27: "Then God said, 'Let us make man in our image, in our likeness, and let them rule over the fish of the sea and the birds of the air, over the livestock, over all the earth, and over all the creatures that move along the ground.' So God created man in his own image, in the image of God he created him; male and female he created them." Genesis 5:1–2: "This is the written account of Adam's line. When God created man, he made him in the likeness of God. He created them male and female and blessed them. And when they were created, he called them 'man.'"

13. C. John Collins, *Science and Faith: Friends or Foes?* (Wheaton: Crossway, 2003), 124–27; Kenneth Richard Samples, "The Historic Christian View of Man," in *A World of Difference* (Grand Rapids: Baker, 2007), 171–88.

14. Millard J. Erickson, *Christian Theology*, 2nd ed. (Grand Rapids: Baker, 1998), 517–36; Wayne Grudem, *Systematic Theology: An Introduction to Biblical Doctrine* (Grand Rapids: Zondervan, 1994), 442–50.

15. Much of the material for this discussion comes from Patrick J. Hurley's book, *A Concise Introduction to Logic*, 6th ed. (Belmont, CA: Wadsworth, 1997), 493–592.

16. Romans 1:20: "For since the creation of the world God's invisible qualities—his eternal power and divine nature—have been clearly seen, being understood from what has been made, so that men are without excuse."

Chapter 2 Mapping the Territory

1. "Picture Gallery: Johannes Vermeer 'van Delft,'" Kunsthistorisches Museum Vienna, http://www.khm.at/system2E.html?/staticE/page242.html (accessed August 25, 2005).

2. Anna Oliver, "The Use of Maps in Contemporary Art," (MA diss., Cardiff School of Art, 2001–2003), http://www.annao.pwp.blueyonder.co.uk/text_dissertation.htm#art.

3. Ibid.

4. Details about the cell's structural and chemical makeup can be found in any introductory biology textbook. For this chapter, the book consulted was Karen Arms and Pamela S. Camp, *Biology*, 3rd ed. (Philadelphia: Saunders College Publishing, 1987).

5. Denyse O'Leary, "Cool Animations: The World inside the Cell," April 17, 2007, The ID Report, http://www.arn.org/blogs/index.php/2/2007/04/21/cool_animations_the_world_inside_the_cel.

Chapter 3 The Bare Essentials

1. "Cubism," *Answers.com*, http://www.answers.com/Cubism (accessed September 16, 2005).

2. "Minimalism," *Answers.com*, http://www.answers.com/minimalism (accessed September 16, 2005).

3. Robert D. Fleischmann et al., "Whole-Genome Random Sequencing and Assembly of *H. influenzae* Rd," *Science* 269 (July 28, 1995): 496–512.

4. Don Cowan, "Use Your Neighbor's Genes," *Nature* 407 (September 28, 2000): 466–67; Andreas Ruepp et al., "The Genome Sequence of the Thermoacidophilic Scavenger *Thermoplasma acidiphilum*," *Nature* 407 (September 28, 2000): 508–13; Gerard Deckert et al., "The Complete Genome of the Hyperthermophilic Bacterium *Aquifex aeolicus*," *Nature* 392 (March 26, 1998): 353–58; Alexei I. Slesarev et al., "The Complete Genome of Hyperthermophile *Methanopyrus kandleri AV19* and Monophyly of Archaeal Methanogens," *Proceedings of the National Academy of Sciences, USA* 99 (April 2, 2002): 4644–49; Virginia Morell, "Life's Last Domain," *Science* 273 (August 23, 1996): 1043–45; Carol J. Bult et al., "Complete Genome Sequence of the Methanogenic Archaeon, *Methanococcus jannaschii*," *Science* 273 (August 23, 1996): 1058–73; Elizabeth Pennisi, "Microbial Genomes Come Tumbling In," *Science* 277 (September 5, 1997): 1433; Karen E. Nelson et al., "Evidence for Lateral Gene Transfer between Archaea and Bacteria from Genome Sequence of *Thermotoga maritima*," *Nature* 399 (May 27, 1999): 323–29; O. Fütterer et al., "Genome Sequence of *Picrophilus torridus* and Its Implications for Life Around pH 0," *Proceedings of the National Academy of Sciences, USA* 101 (June 15, 2004): 9091–96; Stephen J. Giovannoni et al., "Genome Streamlining in a Cosmopolitan Oceanic Bacterium," *Science* 309 (August 19, 2005): 1242–45; Jean-F. Tomb et al., "The Complete Genome Sequence of the Gastric Pathogen *Helicobacter pylori*," *Nature* 388 (August 7, 1997): 539–47; Joseph J. Ferretti et al., "Complete Genome Sequence of an M1 Strain of *Streptococcus pyogenes*," *Proceedings of the National Academy of Sciences, USA* 98 (April 10, 2001): 4658–63; Kathleen M. Scott et al., "The Genome of Deep-Sea Vent Chemolithoautotroph *Thiomicrospira crunogena* XCL-2," *PLoS Biology* 4 (November 14, 2006), doi:10.1371/journal.pbio.0040383, http://biology.plosjournals.org/perlserv/?request=get-document&doi=10.1371%2Fjournal.pbio.0040383.

5. Giovannoni et al., "Genome Streamlining," 1242–45.

6. For example, see: Harold Huber et al., "A New Phylum of Archaea Represented by a Nanosized Hyperthermophilic Symbiont," *Nature* 417 (May 2, 2002): 63–67; Yan Boucher and W. Ford Doolittle, "Something New Under the Sea," *Nature* 417 (May 2, 2002): 27–28; Elizabeth Waters et al., "The Genome of *Nanoarchaeum equitans*: Insights into Early Archaeal Evolution and Derived Parasitism," *Proceedings of the National Academy of Sciences, USA* 100 (October 28, 2003): 12984–88; André Goffeau, "Life with 482 Genes," *Science* 270 (October 20, 1995): 445–46; Claire M. Fraser et al., "The Minimal Gene Complement of *Mycoplasma genitalium*," *Science* 270 (October 20, 1995): 397–403; Ralf Himmelreich et al., "Complete Sequence Analysis of the Genome of the Bacterium *Mycoplasma pneumoniae*," *Nucleic Acids Research* 24 (November 15, 1996): 4420–49; Fleischmann et al., "Whole-Genome Random Sequencing and Assembly of *H. influenzae* Rd," 496–512; Sara Islas et al., "Comparative Genomics and the Gene Complement of a Minimal Cell," *Origins of Life and Evolution of the Biosphere* 34 (February 2004): 243–56.

7. Colin Patterson, *Evolution*, 2nd ed. (Ithaca, NY: Comstock, 1999), 23.

8. Alexis Dufresne et al., "Genome Sequence of the Cyanobacterium *Prochlorococcus marinus* SS120, A Nearly Minimal Oxyphototrophic Genome," *Proceedings of the National Academy of Sciences, USA* 100 (August 19, 2003): 10020–25; Gabrielle Rocap et al., "Genome Divergence in Two *Prochlorococcus* Ecotypes Reflects Oceanic Niche Differentiation," *Nature* 424 (August 28, 2003): 1042–47; Jonathan A. Eisen et al., "The Complete Genome Sequence of *Chlorobium tepidum* TLS, A Photosynthetic, Anaerobic, Green-Sulfur Bacterium," *Proceedings of the National Academy of Sciences, USA* 99 (July 9, 2002): 9509–14; Yasukazu Nakamura et al., "Complete Genome Structure of the Thermophilic Cyanobacterium *Thermosynechococcus elongatus* BP-1," *DNA Research* 9 (August 31, 2002): 123–30.

9. Pennisi, "Microbial Genomes Come Tumbling In," 1433.

10. Goffeau, "Life with 482 Genes," 445; Fraser et al., "Minimal Gene Complement," 397–403; J. Travis, "Small Wonder: Microbial Hitchhiker Has Few Genes," *Science News* 161 (May 4, 2002): 275;

Huber et al., "New Phylum of Archaea," 63–67; Boucher and Doolittle, "Something New Under the Sea," 27–28; Waters et al., "Genome of *Nanoarchaeum equitans*," 12984–88.

11. Craig M. Stephens and Michael T. Laub, "Microbial Genomics: All That You Can't Leave Behind," *Current Biology* 13 (July 15, 2003): R571–R573.

12. Arcady R. Mushegian and Eugene V. Koonin, "A Minimal Gene Set for Cellular Life Derived by Comparison of Complete Bacterial Genomes," *Proceedings of the National Academy of Sciences, USA* 93 (September 17, 1996): 10268–73.

13. Nikos Kyrpides, Ross Overbeek, and Christos Ouzounis, "Universal Protein Families and the Functional Content of the Last Universal Common Ancestor," *Journal of Molecular Evolution* 49 (October 1999): 413–23.

14. J. Kirk Harris et al., "The Genetic Core of the Universal Ancestor," *Genome Research* 13 (March 2003): 407–12; Eugene Koonin, "Comparative Genomics, Minimal Gene-Sets and the Last Universal Common Ancestor," *Nature Reviews Microbiology* 1 (November 2003): 127–36.

15. Jack Maniloff, "The Minimal Cell Genome: 'On Being the Right Size,'" *Proceedings of the National Academy of Sciences, USA* 93 (September 17, 1996): 10004–6; Mitsuhiro Itaya, "An Estimation of Minimal Genome Size Required for Life," *FEBS Letters* 362 (April 10, 1995): 257–60; Clyde A. Hutchinson III et al., "Global Transposon Mutagenesis and a Minimal *Mycoplasma* Genome," *Science* 286 (December 10, 1999), 2165–69; Brian J. Akerley et al., "A Genome-Scale Analysis for Identification of Genes Required for Growth or Survival of *Haemophilus influenzae*," *Proceedings of the National Academy of Sciences, USA* 99 (January 22, 2002): 966–71; Yinduo Ji et al., "Identification of Critical Staphylococcal Genes Using Conditional Phenotypes Generated by Antisense RNA," *Science* 293 (September 21, 2001): 2266–69; R. Allyn Forsyth et al., "A Genome-Wide Strategy for the Identification of Essential Genes in *Staphylococcus aureus*," *Molecular Microbiology* 43, no. 6 (March 2002): 1387–400; S. Y. Gerdes et al., "Experimental Determination and System Level Analysis of Essential Genes in *Escherichia coli* MG1655," *Journal of Bacteriology* 185, no. 19 (October 2003): 5673–84; Michael A. Jacobs et al., "Comprehensive Transposon Mutant Library of *Pseudomonas aeruginosa*," *Proceedings of the National Academy of Sciences, USA* 100 (November 25, 2003): 14339–44; John I. Glass et al., "Essential Genes of a Minimum Bacterium," *Proceedings of the National Academy of Sciences, USA* 103 (January 10, 2006): 425–30; Nicole T. Liberati et al., "An Ordered, Nonredundant Library of *Pseudomonas aeruginosa* Strain PA14 Transposon Insertion Mutants," *Proceedings of the National Academy of Sciences, USA* 103 (February 21, 2006): 2833–38.

16. Rosario Gil et al., "Extreme Genome Reduction in *Buchnera* spp.: Toward the Minimal Genome Needed for Symbiotic Life," *Proceedings of the National Academy of Sciences, USA* 99 (April 2, 2002): 4454–58; Vicente Perez-Brocal et al., "A Small Microbial Genome: The End of a Long Symbiotic Relationship?" *Science* 314 (October 13, 2006): 312–13; Siv G. E. Andersson, "The Bacterial World Gets Smaller," *Science* 314 (October 13, 2006): 259–60.

17. Rosario Gil et al., "The Genome Sequence of *Blochmannia floridanus*: Comparative Analysis of Reduced Genomes," *Proceedings of the National Academy of Sciences, USA* 100 (August 5, 2003): 9388–93.

18. Atsushi Nakabachi et al., "The 160-Kilobase Genome of the Bacterial Endosymbiont *Carsonella*," *Science* 314 (October 13, 2006): 267.

19. The genome sizes of viruses are extremely small. These parasites, however, are not useful to assess life's minimal complexity because they are not "living" organisms. Viruses cannot reproduce on their own, extract energy from the environment, or engage in metabolism.

20. Carl Zimmer, "Tinker, Tailor: Can Ventor Stitch Together a Genome from Scratch?" *Science* 299 (February 14, 2003): 1006–7.

21. Jeronimo Cello, Aniko V. Paul, and Eckard Wimmer, "Chemical Synthesis of Poliovirus cDNA: Generation of Infectious Virus in the Absence of Natural Template," *Science* 297 (August 9, 2002): 1016–18; Hamilton O. Smith et al., "Generating a Synthetic Genome by Whole Genome Assembly: φX174 Bacteriophage from Synthetic Oligonucleotides," *Proceedings of the National Academy of Sciences, USA* 100 (December 23, 2003): 15440–45; Sarah J. Kodumal et al., "Total Synthesis of Long DNA Se-

quences: Synthesis of a Contiguous 32-kb Polyketide Synthase Gene Cluster," *Proceedings of the National Academy of Sciences, USA* 101 (November 2, 2004): 15573–78.

22. M. Castellanos, D. B. Wilson, and M. L. Shuler, "A Modular Minimal Cell Model: Purine and Pyrimidine Transport and Metabolism," *Proceedings of the National Academy of Sciences, USA* 101 (April 27, 2004): 6681–86; M. Scott Long et al., "Dynamic Microcompartmentation in Synthetic Cells," *Proceedings of the National Academy of Sciences, USA* 102 (April 26, 2005): 5920–25.

23. Vincent Noireaux and Albert Libchaber, "A Vesicle Bioreactor as a Step Toward an Artificial Cell Assembly," *Proceedings of the National Academy of Sciences, USA* 101 (December 21, 2004): 17669–74.

24. David Deamer, "A Giant Step Towards Artificial Life?" *Trends in Biotechnology* 23 (July 2005): 336–38.

25. Ibid.

26. Lucy Shapiro and Richard Losick, "Protein Localization and Cell Fate in Bacteria," *Science* 276 (May 2, 1997): 712–18; Richard Losick and Lucy Shapiro, "Changing Views on the Nature of the Bacterial Cell: From Biochemistry to Cytology," *Journal of Bacteriology* 181 (July 1999): 4143–45; Lucy Shapiro and Richard Losick, "Dynamic Spatial Regulation in the Bacterial Cell," *Cell* 100 (January 7, 2000): 89–98; Lucy Shapiro, Harley H. McAdams, and Richard Losick, "Generating and Exploiting Polarity in Bacteria," *Science* 298 (December 6, 2002): 1942–46; Zemer Gitai, "The New Bacterial Cell Biology: Moving Parts and Subcellular Architecture," *Cell* 120 (March 11, 2005): 577–86.

27. Shapiro and Losick, "Protein Localization," 712–18.

28. Michaela E. Sharpe and Jeff Errington, "Upheaval in the Bacterial Nucleoid: An Active Chromosome Segregation Mechanism," *Trends in Genetics* 15 (February 1, 1999): 70–74; Gideon Scott Gordon and Andrew Wright, "DNA Segregation in Bacteria," *Annual Review of Microbiology* 54 (October 2000): 681–708; David J. Sherratt, "Bacterial Chromosome Dynamics," *Science* 301 (August 8, 2003): 780–85; Patrick H. Viollier et al., "Rapid and Sequential Movement of Individual Chromosomal Loci to Specific Subcellular Locations during Bacterial DNA Replication," *Proceedings of the National Academy of Sciences, USA* 101 (June 22, 2004): 9257–62.

29. Joe Pogliano et al., "Multicopy Plasmids Are Clustered and Localized in *Escherichia coli*," *Proceedings of the National Academy of Sciences, USA* 98 (April 10, 2001): 4486–91.

30. Katherine P. Lemon and Alan D. Grossman, "Localization of Bacterial DNA Polymerase: Evidence for a Factory Model of Replication," *Science* 282 (November 20, 1998): 1516–19; Richard Losick and Lucy Shapiro, "Bringing the Mountain to Mohammed," *Science* 282 (November 20, 1998): 1430–31.

31. Sherry C. Wang and Lucy Shapiro, "The Topoisomerase IV ParC Subunit Colocalizes with the *Caulobacter* Replisome and Is Required for Polar Localization of Replication Origins," *Proceedings of the National Academy of Sciences, USA* 101 (June 22, 2004): 9251–56.

32. Ken Begg, "Ring of Bright Metal," *Nature* 354 (November 14, 1991): 109–10; Erfei Bi and Joe Lutkenhaus, "FtsZ Ring Structure Associated with Division in *Escherichia coli*," *Nature* 354 (November 14, 1991): 161–64.

33. Danielle N. Margalit et al., "Targeting Cell Division: Small-Molecule Inhibitors of FtsZ GTPase Perturb Cytokinetic Ring Assembly and Induce Bacterial Lethality," *Proceedings of the National Academy of Sciences, USA* 101 (August 10, 2004): 11821–26.

34. Petra Anne Levin, Iren G. Kurtser, and Alan D. Grossman, "Identification and Characterization of a Negative Regulator of FtsZ Ring Formation in *Bacillus subtilis*," *Proceedings of the National Academy of Sciences, USA* 96 (August 17, 1999): 9642–47; Christine Jacobs and Lucy Shapiro, "Bacterial Cell Division: A Moveable Feast," *Proceedings of the National Academy of Sciences, USA* 96 (May 25, 1999): 5891–93; Xuan-Chuan Yu and William Margolin, "FtsZ Ring Clusters in *min* and Partition Mutants: Role of Both the Min System and the Nucleoid in Regulating FtsZ Ring Localization," *Molecular Microbiology* 32, no. 2 (April 1999): 315–26; David M. Raskin and Piet A. J. de Boer, "Rapid Pole-to-Pole Oscillation of a Protein Required for Directing Division to the Middle of *Escherichia coli*," *Proceedings of the National Academy of Sciences, USA* 96 (April 27, 1999): 4971–76; Debabrata RayChaudhuri, G. Scott Gordon, and Andrew Wright, "Protein Acrobatics and Bacterial Cell Polarity," *Proceedings of the National Academy of Sciences, USA* 98 (February 13, 2001): 1332–34; Xiaoli Fu et al., "The MinE

Ring Required for Proper Placement of the Division Site Is a Mobile Structure that Changes Its Cellular Location During the *Escherichia coli* Division Cycle," *Proceedings of the National Academy of Sciences, USA* 98 (January 30, 2001): 980–85.

35. Zemer Gitai and Lucy Shapiro, "Bacterial Cell Division Spirals into Control," *Proceedings of the National Academy of Sciences, USA* 100 (June 24, 2003): 7423–24.

36. Zemer Gitai, "The New Bacterial Cell Biology: Moving Parts and Subcellular Architecture," *Cell* 120 (March 11, 2005): 577–86.

37. Yu-Ling Shih, Trung Le, and Lawrence Rothfield, "Division Site Selection in *Escherichia coli* Involves Dynamic Redistribution of Min Proteins within Coiled Structures That Extend between the Two Cell Poles," *Proceedings of the National Academy of Sciences, USA* 100 (June 24, 2003): 7865–70.

38. Cheryl A. Kerfeld et al., "Protein Structures Forming the Shell of Primitive Bacterial Organelles," *Science* 309 (August 5, 2005): 936–38.

39. Michael J. Behe, *Darwin's Black Box: The Biochemical Challenge to Evolution* (New York: Free Press, 1996)

40. Fazale Rana and Hugh Ross, *Origins of Life: Biblical and Evolutionary Models Face Off* (Colorado Springs: NavPress, 2004), 159–68.

Chapter 4 Such a Clean Machine

1. "Ken Eberts," *VisionArt*, http://www.solarshadingsystems.com/galleries/artist_popup.asp?artist_ ID=23 (accessed November 18, 2005).

2. Michael Polanyi, "Life Transcending Physics and Chemistry," *Chemical and Engineering News* 45 (August 21, 1967): 54–66; Michael Polanyi, "Life's Irreducible Structure," *Science* 160 (June 21, 1968): 1308–12.

3. Michael J. Behe, *Darwin's Black Box: The Biochemical Challenge to Evolution* (New York: Free Press, 1996), 69–73.

4. David F. Blair, "How Bacteria Sense and Swim," *Annual Review of Microbiology* 49 (October 1995): 489–520.

5. David F. Blair, "Flagellar Movement Driven by Proton Translocation," *FEBS Letters* 545 (June 12, 2003): 86–95; Christopher V. Gabel and Howard C. Berg, "The Speed of the Flagellar Rotary Motor of *Escherichia coli* Varies Linearly with Protonmotive Force," *Proceedings of the National Academy of Sciences, USA* 100 (July 22, 2003): 8748–51.

6. For example, a cursory survey of the prestigious journal *Nature* over the last several years turns up the following papers: Scott A. Lloyd et al., "Structure of the C-Terminal Domain of FliG, a Component of the Rotor in the Bacterial Flagellar Motor," *Nature* 400 (July 29, 1999): 472–75; William S. Ryu, Richard M. Berry, and Howard C. Berg, "Torque-Generating Units of the Flagellar Motor of *Escherichia coli* Have a High Duty Ratio," *Nature* 403 (January 27, 2000): 444–47; Fadel A. Samatey et al., "Structure of the Bacterial Flagellar Hook and Implication for the Molecular Universal Joint Mechanism," *Nature* 431 (October 28, 2004): 1062–68; Yoshiyuki Sowa et al., "Direct Observation of Steps in Rotation of the Bacterial Flagellar Motor," *Nature* 437 (October 6, 2005): 916–19.

7. Matti Saraste, "Oxidative Phosphorylation at the *Fin de Siècle*," *Science* 283 (March 5, 1999): 1488–93.

8. Hiroyuki Noji, "The Rotary Enzyme of the Cell: The Rotation of F1-ATPase," *Science* 282 (December 4, 1998): 1844–45; William S. Allison, "F_1-ATPase: A Molecular Motor that Hydrolyzes ATP with Sequential Opening and Closing of Catalytic Sites Coupled to Rotation of Its γ Subunit," *Accounts of Chemical Research* 31 (December 1998): 819–26; Hiroyuki Noji and Masasuke Yoshida, "The Rotary Machine in the Cell, ATP Synthase," *Journal of Biological Chemistry* 276 (January 19, 2001): 1665–68.

9. Vinit K. Rastogi and Mark E. Girvin, "Structural Changes Linked to Proton Translocation by Subunit *c* of the ATP Synthase," *Nature* 402 (November 18, 1999): 263–68; Joachim Weber and Alan E. Senior, "ATP Synthesis Driven by Proton Transport in F_1–F_0–ATP Synthase," *FEBS Letters* 545 (June 12, 2003): 61–70; Wolfgang Junge and Nathan Nelson, "Nature's Rotary Electromotors," *Science* 308 (April 29, 2005): 642–44.

10. E. J. Boekema et al., "Visualization of a Peripheral Stalk in V-Type ATPase: Evidence for the Stator Structure Essential to Rotational Catalysis," *Proceedings of the National Academy of Sciences, USA* 94 (December 1997): 14291–93; E. J. Boekema et al., "Connecting Stalks in V-Type ATPase," *Nature* 401 (September 2, 1999): 37–38; Junge and Nelson, "Nature's Rotary Electromotors," 642–44; Takeshi Murata et al., "Structure of the Rotor of the V-Type Na$^+$-ATPase from *Enterococcus hirae*," *Science* 308 (April 29, 2005): 654–59.

11. Shoko Kawasaki-Nishi et al., "Proton Translocation Driven by ATP Hydrolysis in V-ATPases," *FEBS Letters* 545 (June 12, 2003): 76–85.

12. F. Xavier Gomis-Ruth et al., "The Bacterial Conjugation Protein TrwB Resembles Ring Helicases and F$_1$-ATPase," *Nature* 409 (February 1, 2001): 637–41.

13. I. Tato et al., "TrwB, the Coupling Protein Involved in DNA Transport during Bacterial Conjugation, Is a DNA-Dependent ATPase," *Proceedings of the National Academy of Sciences, USA* 102 (June 7, 2005): 8156–61.

14. Shimon Schuldiner, "The Ins and Outs of Drug Transport," *Nature* 443 (September 14, 2006): 156–57; Markus A. Seeger et al., "Structural Asymmetry of AcrB Trimer Suggests a Peristaltic Pump Mechanism," *Science* 313 (September 1, 2006): 1295–98; Satoshi Murakami et al., "Crystal Structures of a Multidrug Transporter Reveal a Functionally Rotating Mechanism," *Nature* 443 (September 14, 2006): 173–79.

15. For an accessible discussion of peristaltic pumps, see Wikipedia contributors, "Peristaltic Pump," *Wikipedia, The Free Encyclopedia*, http://en.wikipedia.org/wiki/Peristaltic_pump (accessed August 31, 2006).

16. S. Kalir et al., "Ordering Genes in a Flagella Pathway by Analysis of Expression Kinetics from Living Bacteria," *Science* 292 (June 15, 2001): 2080–83; Gavin S. Chilcott and Kelly T. Hughes, "Coupling of Flagellar Gene Expression to Flagellar Assembly in *Salmonella enterica* Serovar Typhimurium and *Escherichia coli*," *Microbiology and Molecular Biology Reviews* 64 (December 2000): 694–708.

17. Alan A. Simpson et al., "Structure of the Bacteriophage φ29 DNA Packaging Motor," *Nature* 408 (December 7, 2000): 745–50; Douglas E. Smith et al., "The Bacteriophage 29 Portal Motor Can Package DNA against a Large Internal Force," *Nature* 413 (October 18, 2001): 748–52.

18. Michael J. Pelczar Jr., E. C. S. Chan, and Merna Foss Pelczar, *Elements of Microbiology* (New York: McGraw-Hill, 1981), 180–212.

19. Thorsten Hugel et al., "Experimental Test of Connector Rotation during DNA Packaging into Bacteriophage φ29 Capsids," *PLoS Biology* 5 (March 2007): e59.

20. Ibid.

21. Steven M. Block, "Fifty Ways to Love Your Lever: Myosin Motors," *Cell* 87 (October 18, 1996): 151–57; Roger Cooke, "The Actomyosin Engine," *FASEB Journal* 9 (May 1995): 636–42.

22. For example, James D. Jontes, Elizabeth M. Wilson-Kubalek, and Ronald A. Milligan, "A 32° Tail Swing in Brush Border Myosin I on ADP Release," *Nature* 378 (December 14, 1995): 751–53; Michael Whittaker et al., "A 35-Å Movement of Smooth Muscle Myosin on ADP Release," *Nature* 378 (December 14, 1995): 748–51; Jeffery T. Finer, Robert M. Simmons, and James A. Spudich, "Single Myosin Molecule Mechanics: Piconewton Forces and Nanometre Steps," *Nature* 368 (March 10, 1994): 113–19; Roberto Dominguez et al., "Crystal Structure of a Vertebrate Smooth Muscle Myosin Motor Domain and Its Complex with Essential Light Chain: Visualization of the Pre-Power Stroke State," *Cell* 94 (September 4, 1998): 559–71; A. F. Huxley, "Support for the Lever Arm," *Nature* 396 (November 26, 1998): 317–18; Yoshikazu Suzuki et al., "Swing of the Lever Arm of a Myosin Motor at the Isomerization and Phosphate-Release Steps," *Nature* 396 (November 26, 1998): 380–83; Ian Dobbie et al., "Elastic Bending and Active Tilting of Myosin Heads During Muscle Contraction," *Nature* 396 (November 26, 1998): 383–87; Fumi Kinose et al., "Glycine 699 Is Pivotal for the Motor Activity of Skeletal Muscle Myosin," *Journal of Cell Biology* 134, no. 4 (August 1996): 895–909; Thomas P. Burghardt et al., "Tertiary Structural Changes in the Cleft Containing the ATP Sensitive Tryptophan and Reactive Thiol Are Consistent with Pivoting of the Myosin Heavy Chain at Gly699," *Biochemistry* 37 (June 2, 1998): 8035–47; Katalin Ajtai et al., "Trinitrophenylated Reactive Lysine Residue in Myosin Detects

Lever Arm Movement during the Consecutive Steps of ATP Hydrolysis," *Biochemistry* 38 (May 18, 1999): 6428–40; J. E. T. Corrie et al., "Dynamic Measurement of Myosin Light-Chain-Domain Tilt and Twist in Muscle Contraction," *Nature* 400 (July 29, 1999): 425–30; Josh E. Baker et al., "A Large and Distinct Rotation of the Myosin Light Chain Domain Occurs upon Muscle Contraction," *Proceedings of the National Academy of Sciences, USA* 95 (March 17, 1998): 2944–49; Susan Lowey, Guillermina S. Waller, and Kathleen M. Trybus, "Skeletal Muscle Myosin Light Chains Are Essential for Physiological Speeds of Shortening," *Nature* 365 (September 30, 1993): 454–56.

23. Stephen M. King, "The Dynein Microtubule Motor," *Biochimica et Biophysica Acta (BBA) / Molecular Cell Research* 1496 (March 17, 2000): 60–75.

24. Richard B. Vallee and Peter Hook, "A Magnificent Machine," *Nature* 421 (February 13, 2003): 701–2; Stan A. Burgess et al., "Dynein Structure and Power Stroke," *Nature* 421 (February 13, 2003): 715–18.

25. R. A. Cross, "Molecular Motors: Dynein's Gearbox," *Current Biology* 14 (May 4, 2004): R355–56; Roop Mallik et al., "Cytoplasmic Dynein Functions as a Gear in Response to Load," *Nature* 427 (February 12, 2004): 649–52.

26. Patrick Cramer et al., "Architecture of RNA Polymerase II and Implications for the Transcription Mechanism," *Science* 288 (April 28, 2000): 640–49.

27. Joan Weliky Conaway and Ronald C. Conaway, "Light at the End of the Channel," *Science* 288 (April 28, 2000): 632–33.

28. Katharine Sanderson, "Crystallography Grabs Chemistry Nobel: Structural Determination of RNA Polymerase Unlocked Secrets of Cells," *news@nature.com*, October 4, 2006, doi:10.1038/news061002-7, http://www.nature.com/news/2006/061002/full/news061002-7.html.

29. Jonathan B. Vivona and Zvi Kelman, "The Diverse Spectrum of Sliding Clamp Interacting Proteins," *FEBS Letters* 546 (July 10, 2003): 167–72; Gregory D. Bowman, Mike O'Donnell, and John Kuriyan, "Structural Analysis of a Eukaryotic Sliding DNA Clamp-Clamp Loader Complex," *Nature* 429 (June 17, 2004): 724–30; Spencer Campbell and Anthony Maxwell, "The ATP-Operated Clamp of Human DNA Topoisomerase IIα: Hyperstimulation of ATPase by 'Piggy-Back' Binding," *Journal of Molecular Biology* 320 (July 5, 2002): 171–88.

30. Brett W. Lennon, Charles H. Williams Jr., and Martha L. Ludwig, "Twists in Catalysis: Alternating Conformations of *Escherichia coli* Thioredoxin Reductase," *Science* 289 (August 18, 2000): 1190–94.

31. William Paley, *Natural Theology; or, Evidences of the Existence and Attributes of the Deity Collected from the Appearances of Nature*, 12th ed. (1802; Weybridge, Surrey, UK: printed by S. Hamilton, 1809), 1–3.

32. David Hume, "*Dialogues Concerning Natural Religion*," in *Classics of Western Philosophy*, ed. Steven M. Cahn, 3rd ed. (1779; repr., Indianapolis: Hackett, 1990), 880. Hume makes this point through a fictional character.

33. B. C. Johnson, *The Atheist Debater's Handbook* (Buffalo: Prometheus Books, 1981), 45.

34. David Depew, "Intelligent Design and Irreducible Complexity: A Rejoinder," *Rhetoric and Public Affairs* 1, no. 4 (1998): 571–78.

35. Robert F. Service, "Borrowing from Biology to Power the Petite," *Science* 283 (January 1, 1999): 27–28.

36. Jimin Wang, "Recent Cyanobacterial Kai Protein Structures Suggest a Rotary Clock," *Structure* 13 (May 2005): 735–41.

37. Ibid.

38. Paley, *Natural Theology*, 3.

39. Service, "Borrowing from Biology," 27–28.

40. Ricky K. Soong et al., "Powering an Inorganic Nanodevice with a Biomolecular Motor," *Science* 290 (November 24, 2000): 1555–58.

41. Peixuan Guo, "Bacterial Virus φ29 DNA-Packaging Motor and Its Potential Applications in Gene Therapy and Nanotechnology," *Methods in Molecular Biology* 300 (January 2005): 285–324.

42. Ibid.

43. Joe Alper, "Chemists Look to Follow Biology Lead," *Science* 295 (March 29, 2002): 2396–97; Nadrian C. Seeman and Angela M. Belcher, "Emulating Biology: Building Nanostructures from the Bottom Up," *Proceedings of the National Academy of Sciences, USA* 99 (April 30, 2002): 6451–55; George M. Whitesides, "The Once and Future Nanomachine," *Scientific American*, September 2001, 78–83.

44. Corinna Wu, "Molecular Motors Spin Slowly but Surely," *Science News* 156 (September 11, 1999): 165.

45. See, for example, Jovica D. Badjić et al., "A Molecular Elevator," *Science* 303 (March 19, 2004): 1845–49; David I. Gittins et al., "A Nanometre-Scale Electronic Switch Consisting of a Metal Cluster and Redox-Addressable Groups," *Nature* 408 (November 2, 2000): 67–69; Thoi D. Nguyen et al., "A Reversible Molecular Valve," *Proceedings of the National Academy of Sciences, USA* 102 (July 19, 2005): 10029–34; Thomas C. Bedard and Jeffrey S. Moore, "Design and Synthesis of Molecular Turnstiles," *Journal of the American Chemical Society* 117 (November 1, 1995): 10622–71; T. Ross Kelly, Imanol Tellitu, and José Pérez Sestelo, "In Search of Molecular Ratchets," *Angewandte Chemie* 36 (September 17, 1997): 1866–68; Richard A. Bissell et al., "A Chemically and Electrochemically Switchable Molecular Shuttle," *Nature* 369 (May 12, 1994): 133–37; Peter R. Ashton et al., "Acid-Base Controllable Molecular Shuttles," *Journal of the American Chemical Society* 120 (November 25, 1998): 11932–42.

46. See, for example, Jonathan Clayden and Jennifer H. Pink, "Concerted Rotation in a Tertiary Aromatic Amide: Towards a Simple Molecular Gear," *Angewandte Chemie* 37 (August 3, 1998): 1937–39; Anne Marie Schoevaars et al., "Toward a Switchable Molecular Rotor: Unexpected Dynamic Behavior of Functionalized Overcrowded Alkenes," *Journal of Organic Chemistry* 62 (July 25, 1997): 4943–48.

47. T. Ross Kelly, Harshani De Silva, and Richard A. Silva, "Unidirectional Rotary Motion in a Molecular System," *Nature* 401 (September 9, 1999): 150–52; Nagatoshi Komura et al., "Light-Driven Monodirectional Molecular Rotor," *Nature* 401 (September 9, 1999): 152–55.

48. Komura et al., "Molecular Rotor," 152–55.

49. Kelly, De Silva, and Silva, "Rotary Motion," 150–52.

50. Anthony P. Davis, "Synthetic Molecular Motors," *Nature* 401 (September 9, 1999): 120–21.

51. José V. Hernández, Euan R. Kay, and David A. Leigh, "A Reversible Synthetic Rotary Molecular Motor," *Science* 306 (November 26, 2004): 1532–37; Stephen P. Fletcher et al., "A Reversible, Unidirectional Molecular Rotary Motor Driven by Chemical Energy," *Science* 310 (October 7, 2005): 80–82; Jay Siegel, "Inventing the Nanomolecular Wheel," *Science* 310 (October 7, 2005): 63–64.

52. Joel S. Bader et al., "DNA Transport by a Micromachined Brownian Ratchet Device," *Proceedings of the National Academy of Sciences, USA* 96 (November 9, 1999): 13165–69.

53. Ibid.

54. Ronald D. Vale, "The Molecular Motor Toolbox for Intracellular Transport," *Cell* 112 (February 21, 2003): 467–80.

55. For example, Deborah B. Stone, Rex P. Hjelm, and Robert A. Mendelson, "Solution Structures of Dimeric Kinesin and Ncd Motors," *Biochemistry* 38 (April 20, 1999): 4938–47.

56. For example, Wei Hua et al., "Coupling of Kinesin Steps to ATP Hydrolysis," *Nature* 388 (July 24, 1997): 390–93; Karel Svoboda et al., "Direct Observation of Kinesin Stepping by Optical Trapping Interferometry," *Nature* 365 (October 21, 1993): 721–27; Yasushi Okada and Nobutaka Hirokawa, "A Processive Single-Headed Motor: Kinesin Superfamily Protein KIF1A," *Science* 283 (February 19, 1999): 1152–57.

57. R. Dean Astumian and Imre Derényi, "A Chemically Reversible Brownian Motor: Application to Kinesin and Ncd," *Biophysical Journal* 77 (August 1999): 993–1002.

58. Kent E. S. Matlack et al., "BiP Acts as a Molecular Ratchet during Posttranslational Transport of Prepro-α Factor Across the ER Membrane," *Cell* 97 (May 28, 1999): 553–64.

59. Saveez Saffarian et al., "Interstitial Collagenase Is a Brownian Ratchet Driven by Proteolysis of Collagen," *Science* 306 (October 1, 2004): 108–11.

60. Paley, *Natural Theology*, 2.

61. Kazuhiko Kinosita Jr. et al., "A Rotary Molecular Motor That Can Work at Near 100% Efficiency," *Philosophical Transactions of the Royal Society* B 355 (April 29, 2000): 473–89.

Chapter 5 Which Came First?

1. "Biography of M. C. Escher," The M. C. Escher Company B. V., http://www.mcescher.com/ (accessed January 11, 2006); World of Escher, http://www.worldofescher.com/ (accessed January 11, 2006).

2. Wikipedia contributors, "Radio-Frequency Identification," *Wikipedia, The Free Encyclopedia*, http://en.wikipedia.org/wiki/Radio_frequency_identification (accessed June 24, 2006).

3. "The Chicken or the Egg?" *RFID Journal*, http://www.rfidjournal.com/article/article-print/2261/-1/1 (accessed June 22, 2006).

4. Iris Fry, *The Emergence of Life on Earth: A Historical and Scientific Overview* (New Brunswick, NJ: Rutgers University Press, 2000), 100–101.

5. Fazale Rana and Hugh Ross, *Origins of Life: Biblical and Evolutionary Models Face Off* (Colorado Springs: NavPress, 2004), 109–21.

6. Leslie Orgel quoted in ibid., 115.

7. Alan G. Atherly, Jack R. Girton, and John F. McDonald, *The Science of Genetics* (Fort Worth: Saunders College Publishing, 1999): 315–21.

8. Ibid., 321–28.

9. Harvey Lodish et al., *Molecular Cell Biology*, 4th ed. (New York: Freeman, 2000): 125–27.

10. For example, see Graeme L. Conn et al., "Crystal Structure of a Conserved Ribosomal Protein-RNA Complex," *Science* 284 (May 14, 1999): 1171–74; Jamie H. Cate et al., "X-Ray Crystal Structures of 70S Ribosome Functional Complexes," *Science* 285 (September 24, 1999): 2095–2104; Gloria M. Culver et al., "Identification of an RNA-Protein Bridge Spanning the Ribosomal Subunit Interface," *Science* 285 (September 24, 1999): 2133–35; William M. Clemons Jr. et al., "Structure of a Bacterial 30S Ribosomal Subunit at 5.5 Å Resolution," *Nature* 400 (August 26, 1999): 833–40; Nenad Ban et al., "Placement of Protein and RNA Structures into a 5 Å-Resolution Map of the 50S Ribosomal Subunit," *Nature* 400 (August 26, 1999): 841–47; Sultan C. Agalarov et al., "Structure of the S15, S6, S18-rRNA Complex: Assembly of the 30S Ribosome Central Domain," *Science* 288 (April 7, 2000): 107–12; Nenad Ban et al., "The Complete Atomic Structure of the Large Ribosomal Subunit at 2.4 Å Resolution," *Science* 289 (August 11, 2000): 905–20; Brian T. Wimberly et al., "Structure of the 30S Ribosomal Subunit," *Nature* 407 (September 21, 2000): 327–39; Andrew P. Carter et al., "Functional Insights from the Structure of the 30S Ribosomal Subunit and Its Interactions with Antibiotics," *Nature* 407 (September 21, 2000): 340–48; Marat M. Yusupov et al., "Crystal Structure of the Ribosome at 5.5 Å Resolution," *Science* 292 (May 4, 2001): 883–96.

11. Thomas R. Cech, "The Ribosome Is a Ribozyme," *Science* 289 (August 11, 2000): 878–79; Poul Nissen et al., "The Structural Basis of Ribosome Activity in Peptide Bond Synthesis," *Science* 289 (August 11, 2000): 920–30; Gregory W. Muth, Lori Ortoleva-Donnelly, and Scott A. Strobel, "A Single Adenosine with a Neutral pK_a in the Ribosomal Peptidyl Transferase Center," *Science* 289 (August 11, 2000): 947–50.

12. For example, John Dresios, Panagiotis Panopoulos, and Dennis Synetos, "Eukaryotic Ribosomal Proteins Lacking a Eubacterial Counterpart: Important Players in Ribosomal Function," *Molecular Microbiology* 59 (March 2006): 1651–63.

13. Lodish et al., *Molecular Cell Biology*, 128–37.

14. Ibid., 120–25.

15. Ibid., 130–32.

16. Ibid., 62–64; Elke Deuerling and Bernd Bukau, "Chaperone-Assisted Folding of Newly Synthesized Proteins in the Cytosol," *Critical Reviews in Biochemistry and Molecular Biology* 39 (October–December 2004): 261–77.

17. Yun-Chi Tang et al., "Structural Features of the GroEL-GroES Nano-Cage Required for Rapid Folding of Encapsulated Protein," *Cell* 125 (June 2, 2006): 903–14.

Chapter 6 Inordinate Attention to Detail

1. Wikipedia contributors, "John Everett Millais," *Wikipedia, The Free Encyclopedia*, http://en.wikipedia.org/wiki/Millais (accessed June 21, 2006).

2. Wikipedia contributors, "Mannerism," *Wikipedia, The Free Encyclopedia*, http://en.wikipedia.org/wiki/Mannerism (accessed June 22, 2006).

3. Wikipedia contributors, "Pre-Raphaelite Brotherhood," *Wikipedia, The Free Encyclopedia*, http://en.wikipedia.org/wiki/Pre-Raphaelite_Brotherhood (accessed June 22, 2006).

4. Deepa Rajamani et al., "Anchor Residues in Protein-Protein Interactions," *Proceedings of the National Academy of Sciences, USA* 101 (August 3, 2004): 11287–92.

5. Some recently discovered examples of biochemical fine-tuning can be found at http://www.reasons.org/ as part of the *Today's New Reason To Believe* (*TNRTB*) feature. Some examples that have appeared recently under the *TNRTB* banner include: Won-Ho Cho et al., "CDC7 Kinase Phosphorylates Serine Residues Adjacent to Acidic Amino Acids in Minichromosome Maintenance 2 Protein," *Proceedings of the National Academy of Sciences, USA* 103 (August 1, 2006): 11521–26; Daniel F. Jarosz et al., "A Single Amino Acid Governs Enhanced Activity of DinB DNA Polymerases on Damaged Templates," *Science* 439 (January 12, 2006): 225–28; William H. McClain, "Surprising Contribution to Amino-acylation and Translation of Non-Watson-Crick Pairs in tRNA," *Proceedings of the National Academy of Sciences, USA* 103 (March 21, 2006): 4570–75; Kobra Haghighi et al., "A Mutation in the Human Phospholamban Gene, Deleting Arginine 14, Results in Lethal, Hereditary Cardiomyopathy," *Proceedings of the National Academy of Sciences, USA* 103 (January 31, 2006): 1388–93; Surajit Ganguly et al., "Melatonin Synthesis: 14-3-3-Dependent Activation and Inhibition of Arylalkylamine N-Acetyltransferase Mediated by Phosphoserine-205," *Proceedings of the National Academy of Sciences, USA* 102 (January 25, 2005): 1222–27; Yohei Kirino et al., "Specific Correlation between the Wobble Modification Deficiency in Mutant tRNAs and the Clinical Features of a Human Mitochondrial Disease," *Proceedings of the National Academy of Sciences, USA* 102 (May 17, 2005): 7127–32; Yoshie Hanzawa, Tracy Money, and Desmond Bradley, "A Single Amino Acid Converts a Repressor to an Activator of Flowering," *Proceedings of the National Academy of Sciences, USA* 102 (May 24, 2005): 7748–53; Stefan Trobro and Johan Åqvist, "Mechanism of Peptide Bond Synthesis on the Ribosome," *Proceedings of the National Academy of Sciences, USA* 102 (August 30, 2005): 12395–400; Tianbing Xia et al., "RNA-Protein Recognition: Single-Residue Ultrafast Dynamical Control of Structural Specificity and Function," *Proceedings of the National Academy of Sciences, USA* 102 (September 13, 2005): 13013–18; A. J. Rader et al., "Identification of Core Amino Acids Stabilizing Rhodopsin," *Proceedings of the National Academy of Sciences, USA* 101 (May 11, 2004): 7246–51; Rajamani et al., "Anchor Residues," 11287–92; Lina Salomonsson et al., "A Single-Amino Acid Lid Renders a Gas-Tight Compartment within a Membrane-Bound Transporter," *Proceedings of the National Academy of Sciences, USA* 101 (August 10, 2004): 11617–21; Gianguido Coffa and Alan R. Brash, "A Single Active Site Residue Directs Oxygenation Stereospecificity in Lipoxygenases: Stereocontrol Is Linked to the Position of Oxygenation," *Proceedings of the National Academy of Sciences, USA* 101 (November 2, 2004): 15579–84; Isabel Martinez-Argudo, Richard Little, and Ray Dixon, "A Crucial Arginine Residue Is Required for a Conformational Switch in NifL to Regulate Nitrogen Fixation in *Azotobacter vinelandii*," *Proceedings of the National Academy of Sciences, USA* 101 (November 16, 2004): 16316–21; Oded Danziger et al., "Conversion of the Allosteric Transition of GroEL from Concerted to Sequential by the Single Mutation Asp-155 → Ala," *Proceedings of the National Academy of Sciences, USA* 100 (November 25, 2003): 13797–802; Hu Pan et al., "Structure of tRNA Pseudouridine Synthase TruB and Its RNA Complex: RNA Recognition through a Combination of Rigid Docking and Induced Fit," *Proceedings of the National Academy of Sciences, USA* 100 (October 28, 2003): 12648–53; Yoshimitsu Kuwabara et al., "Unique Amino Acids Cluster for Switching from the Dehydrogenase to Oxidase Form of Xanthine Oxidoreductase," *Proceedings of the National Academy of Sciences, USA* 100 (July 8, 2003): 8170–75. This sampling represents the tip of the iceberg. Countless examples of biochemical fine-tuning are littered throughout the scientific literature.

6. Mario Borgina et al., "Cellular and Molecular Biology of the Aquaporin Water Channels," *Annual Review of Biochemistry* 68 (July 1999): 425–58.

7. Ibid.

8. David F. Savage et al., "Architecture and Selectivity in Aquaporins: 2.5 Å X-Ray Structure of Aquaporin Z," *PLoS Biology* 1, no. 3 (December 22, 2003): doi:10.1371/journal.pbio.0000072, http://biology.plosjournals.org/perlserv/?request=get-document&doi=10.1371/journal.pbio.0000072.

9. Ibid.

10. See, for example, Bert L. de Groot and Helmut Grubmüller, "Water Permeation across Biological Membranes: Mechanism and Dynamics of Aquaporin-1 and GlpF," *Science* 294 (December 14, 2001): 2353–57; William E. C. Harries et al., "The Channel Architecture of Aquaporin 0 at a 2.2-Å Resolution," *Proceedings of the National Academy of Sciences, USA* 101 (September 28, 2004): 14045–50.

11. Eric Beitz et al., "Molecular Dissection of Water and Glycerol Permeability of the Aquaglyceroporin from *Plasmodium falciparum* by Mutational Analysis," *Proceedings of the National Academy of Sciences, USA* 101 (February 3, 2004): 1153–58.

12. John K. Lee et al., "Structural Basis for Conductance by the Archaeal Aquaporin AqpM at 1.68 Å," *Proceedings of the National Academy of Sciences, USA* 102 (December 27, 2005): 18932–37.

13. Ibid.

14. Kun Liu et al., "Conversion of Aquaporin 6 from an Anion Channel to a Water-Selective Channel by a Single Amino Acid Substitution," *Proceedings of the National Academy of Sciences, USA* 102 (February 8, 2005): 2192–97.

15. Peter R. Bergethon and Elizabeth R. Simons, *Biophysical Chemistry: Molecules to Membranes* (New York: Springer-Verlag, 1990), 253–57.

16. Some examples include: Nicolás Reyes and David C. Gadsby, "Ion Permeation through the Na^+, K^+-ATPase," *Nature* 443 (September 28, 2006): 470–74; Eric Gouaux and Roderick MacKinnon, "Principles of Selective Ion Transport in Channels and Pumps," *Science* 310 (December 2, 2005): 1461–65; Francis I. Valiyaveetil et al., "Glycine as a D-Amino Acid Surrogate in the K^+-Selectivity Filter," *Proceedings of the National Academy of Sciences, USA* 101 (December 7, 2004): 17045–49; Lei Zheng et al., "The Mechanism of Ammonia Transport Based on the Crystal Structure of AmtB of *Escherichia coli*," *Proceedings of the National Academy of Sciences, USA* 101 (December 7, 2004): 17090–95; Sheila E. Unkles et al., "Two Perfectly Conserved Arginine Residues Are Required for Substrate Binding in a High-Affinity Nitrate Transporter," *Proceedings of the National Academy of Sciences, USA* 101 (December 14, 2004): 17549–54; Yong Zhao, Todd Scheuer, and William A. Caterall, "Reversed Voltage-Dependent Gating of a Bacterial Sodium Channel with Proline Substitutions in the S6 Transmembrane Segment," *Proceedings of the National Academy of Sciences, USA* 101 (December 21, 2004): 17873–78; Tinatin I. Brelidze, Xiaowei Niu, and Karl L. Magleby, "A Ring of Eight Conserved Negatively Charged Amino Acids Doubles the Conductance of BK Channels and Prevents Inward Rectification," *Proceedings of the National Academy of Sciences, USA* 100 (July 22, 2003): 9017–22.

17. Lubert Stryer, *Biochemistry*, 3rd ed. (New York: W. H. Freeman, 1988), 261–74.

18. E. Leikina et al., "Type I Collagen Is Thermally Unstable at Body Temperature," *Proceedings of the National Academy of Sciences, USA* 99 (February 5, 2002): 1314–18; Anton V. Persikov and Barbara Brodsky, "Unstable Molecules Form Stable Tissues," *Proceedings of the National Academy of Sciences, USA* 99 (February 5, 2002): 1101–3.

19. Yulei Wang et al., "Precision and Functional Specificity in mRNA Decay," *Proceedings of the National Academy of Sciences, USA* 99 (April 30, 2002): 5860–65; Jonathan A. Bernstein et al., "Global Analysis of mRNA Decay and Abundance in *Escherichia coli* at Single-Gene Resolution Using Two-Color Fluorescent DNA Microarrays," *Proceedings of the National Academy of Sciences, USA* 99 (July 23, 2002): 9697–9702.

20. Michael H. Glickman and Noam Adir, "The Proteasome and the Delicate Balance between Destruction and Rescue," *PLoS Biology* 2 (January 20, 2004): doi:10.1371/journal.pbio.0020013, http://biology.plosjournals.org/perlserv/?request=get-document&doi=10.1371%2Fjournal.pbio.0020013.

21. Stryer, *Biochemistry*, 794–95.

22. Linda L. Breeden, "Periodic Transcription: A Cycle within a Cycle," *Current Biology* 13 (January 8, 2003): R31–R38.

Chapter 7 The Proper Arrangement of Elements

1. Shelley Esaak, "Balance," *About.com*, http://arthistory.about.com/cs/glossaries/g/b_balance.htm (accessed June 22, 2006).

2. Wikipedia contributors, "Piet Mondrian," *Wikipedia, The Free Encyclopedia*, http://en.wikipedia .org/wiki/Piet_Mondrian (accessed July 11, 2006).

3. Brian Kuhlman and David Baker, "Native Protein Sequences Are Close to Optimal for Their Structures," *Proceedings of the National Academy of Sciences, USA* 97 (September 12, 2000): 10383–88.

4. Hiroshi Akashi and Takashi Gojobori, "Metabolic Efficiency and Amino Acid Composition in the Proteomes of *Escherichia coli* and *Bacillus subtilis*," *Proceedings of the National Academy of Sciences, USA* 99 (March 19, 2002): 3695–3700; Hiroshi Akashi, "Metabolic Economics and Microbial Proteome Evolution," *Bioinformatics* 19, suppl. 2 (October 2003): ii15; Esley M. Heizer Jr. et al., "Amino Acid Cost and Codon-Usage Biases in 6 Prokaryotic Genomes: A Whole-Genome Analysis," *Molecular Biology and Evolution* 23 (September 2006), doi:10.1093/molbev/msl029, http://mbe.oxfordjournals.org/ cgi/content/full/23/9/1670.

5. Hervé Seligmann, "Cost-Minimization of Amino Acid Usage," *Journal of Molecular Evolution* 56 (February 2003): 151–61.

6. Rui Alves and Michael A. Savageau, "Evidence of Selection for Low Cognate Amino Acid Bias in Amino Acid Biosynthetic Enzymes," *Molecular Microbiology* 56, no. 4 (May 2005): 1017–34.

7. Haiwei H. Guo, Juno Choe, and Lawrence A. Loeb, "Protein Tolerance to Random Amino Acid Change," *Proceedings of the National Academy of Sciences, USA* 101 (June 22, 2004): 9205–10.

8. Darin M. Taverna and Richard A. Goldstein, "Why Are Proteins So Robust to Site Mutations?" *Journal of Molecular Biology* 315 (January 2002): 479–84.

9. Sandeep Raha and Brian H. Robinson, "Mitochondria, Oxygen Free Radicals, Disease and Ageing," *Trends in Biochemistry* 25 (October 1, 2000): 502–8.

10. Robert Arking, *The Biology of Aging: Observations and Principles*, 2nd ed. (Sunderland, MA: Sinauer, 1998), 398–414.

11. Martin Ackermann and Lin Chao, "DNA Sequences Shaped by Selection for Stability," *PLoS Genetics* 2 (February 2006): e22.

12. Hiroshi Akashi, "Synonymous Codon Usage in *Drosophila melanogaster*: Natural Selection and Translational Accuracy," *Genetics* 136 (March 1994): 927–35; Xuhua Xia, "How Optimized Is the Translational Machinery in *Escherichia coli*, *Salmonella typhimurium* and *Saccharomyces cerevisiae*?" *Genetics* 149 (May 1998): 37–44; Marco Archetti, "Selection on Codon Usage for Error Minimization at the Protein Level," *Journal of Molecular Evolution* 59 (September 2004): 400–15; Eduardo P. C. Rocha, "Codon Usage Bias from tRNA's Point of View: Redundancy, Specialization, and Efficient Decoding for Translation Optimization," *Genome Research* 14 (November 2004): 2279–86.

13. F. H. Westheimer, "Why Nature Chose Phosphates," *Science* 235 (March 6, 1987): 1173–78.

14. Ryszard Kierzek, Liyan He, and Douglas H. Turner, "Association of 2'–5' Oligoribonucleotides," *Nucleic Acids Research* 20 (April 11, 1992): 1685–90.

15. Albert Eschenmoser, "Chemical Etiology of Nucleic Acid Structure," *Science* 284 (June 25, 1999): 2118–24.

16. Eveline Lescrinier, Matheus Froeyen, and Piet Herdewijn, "Difference in Conformational Diversity between Nucleic Acids with a Six-Membered 'Sugar' Unit and Natural 'Furanose' Nucleic Acids," *Nucleic Acids Research* 31 (June 15, 2003): 2975–89.

17. Gaspar Banfalvi, "Why Ribose Was Selected as the Sugar Component of Nucleic Acids," *DNA and Cell Biology* 25 (March 2006):189–96.

18. Jean-Marc L. Pecourt, Jorge Peon, and Bern Kohler, "Ultrafast Internal Conversion of Electronically Excited RNA and DNA Nucleotides in Water," *Journal of the American Chemical Society* 122 (September 27, 2000): 9348–49.

19. Reiner Veitia and Chris Ottolenghi, "Placing Parallel Stranded DNA in an Evolutionary Context," *Journal of Theoretical Biology* 206 (September 2000): 317–22.

20. Ibid.

21. George M. Malacinski, *Essentials of Molecular Biology*, 4th ed. (Boston: Jones and Bartlett, 2003), 223–83.

22. Guy Shinar et al., "Rules for Biological Regulation Based on Error Minimization," *Proceedings of the National Academy of Sciences, USA* 103 (March 14, 2006): 3999–4004.

23. Lubert Stryer, *Biochemistry*, 3rd ed. (New York: Freeman, 1988), 349–96.

24. Ibid., 315–30.

25. Alicia Esteban del Valle and J. Carlos Aledo, "What Process Is Glycolytic Stoichiometry Optimal For?" *Journal of Molecular Evolution* 62 (April 2006): 488–95.

Chapter 8 The Artist's Handwriting

1. Wikipedia contributors, "Calligraphy," *Wikipedia, The Free Encyclopedia*, http://en.wikipedia.org/wiki/Calligraphy (accessed July 13, 2006); Wikipedia contributors, "Islamic Calligraphy," *Wikipedia, The Free Encyclopedia*, http://en.wikipedia.org/wiki/Arabic_calligraphy (accessed July 12, 2007); Wikipedia contributors, "Sheikh Hamdullah," *Wikipedia, The Free Encyclopedia*, http://en.wikipedia.org/wiki/Sheikh_Hamdullah (accessed July 12, 2006).

2. Peter Kreeft, *Fundamentals of the Faith: Essays in Christian Apologetics* (San Francisco: Ignatius, 1988), 25–26.

3. Bernd-Olaf Küppers, *Information and the Origin of Life* (Cambridge, MA: MIT Press, 1990), 6–27.

4. See, for example, Michael Denton, *Evolution: A Theory in Crisis* (Bethesda, MD: Adler & Adler, 1986), 308–25; Walter L. Bradley and Charles B. Thaxton, "Information and the Origin of Life," in *The Creation Hypothesis: Scientific Evidence for an Intelligent Designer*, ed. J. P. Moreland (Downers Grove, IL: InterVarsity, 1994), 188–90.

5. Harvey Lodish et al., *Molecular Cell Biology*, 4th ed. (New York: Freeman, 2000), 257.

6. Hubert P. Yockey, *Information Theory, Evolution, and the Origin of Life* (New York: Cambridge University Press, 2005); Hubert P. Yockey, *Information Theory and Molecular Biology* (Cambridge: Cambridge University Press, 1992); Küppers, *Information and the Origin of Life*.

7. Küppers, *Information and the Origin of Life*, 24–25.

8. Ibid., 23.

9. Ibid., 31–56.

10. Ibid., 32–33.

11. Christopher Loose et al., "A Linguistic Model for the Rational Design of Antimicrobial Peptides," *Nature* 443 (October 19, 2006): 867–69.

12. Michael Zasloff, "Antimicrobial Peptides of Multicellular Organisms," *Nature* 415 (January 24, 2002): 389–95.

13. Biochemists use the general formula $C_nH_{2n}O_n$ (where *n* can be any number) to represent carbohydrates.

14. See, for example, Lubert Stryer, *Biochemistry*, 3rd ed. (New York: Freeman, 1988), 343–46.

15. Mark A. Lehrman, "Oligosaccharide-Based Information in Endoplasmic Reticulum Quality Control and Other Biological Systems," *Journal of Biological Chemistry* 276 (March 23, 2001): 8623–26.

16. Ibid.

17. See, for example, George M. Malacinski, *Essentials of Molecular Biology*, 4th ed. (Boston: Jones and Bartlett, 2003), 233–47.

18. Yuan-Yuan Li et al., "Systematic Analysis of Head-to-Head Gene Organization: Evolutionary Conservation and Potential Biological Relevance," *PLoS Computational Biology* 2 (July 2006): e74.

19. Ibid.

20. Alan G. Atherly, Jack R. Girton, and John F. McDonald, *The Science of Genetics* (Fort Worth: Saunders College Publishing, 1999), 321–28.

21. Malacinski, *Essentials of Molecular Biology*, 261–65.

22. Ibid.

23. B. G. Barrell, G. M. Air, and Clyde A. Hutchison III, "Overlapping Genes in Bacteriophage φX174," *Nature* 264 (November 4, 1976): 34–41; M. Smith et al., "DNA Sequence at the C Termini of the Overlapping Genes A and B in Bacteriophage φX174," *Nature* 265 (February 24, 1977): 702–5; Frederick Sanger et al., "Nucleotide Sequences of Bacteriophage φX174 DNA," *Nature* 265 (February 24, 1977): 687–89.

24. Gina B. Kolata, "Overlapping Genes: More Than Anomalies?" *Science* 196 (June 10, 1977): 1187–88.

25. Denis C. Shaw et al., "Gene *K*, A New Overlapping Gene in Bacteriophage G4," *Nature* 272 (April 5, 1978): 510–15; Walter Fiers et al., "Complete Sequence of SV40 DNA," *Nature* 273 (May 11, 1978): 113–20; Charlotte A. Spencer, R. Daniel Gietz, and Ross B. Hogdetts, "Overlapping Transcription Units in the DOPA Decarboxylase Region of *Drosophilia*," *Nature* 322 (July 17, 1986): 279–81; Jacek M. Jankowski et al., "In Vitro Expression of Two Proteins from Overlapping Reading Frames in a Eukaryotic DNA Sequence," *Journal of Molecular Evolution* 24 (December 1986): 61–71; Maya Shmulevitz et al., "Sequential Partially Overlapping Gene Arrangement in the Tricistronic S1 Genome Segments of Avian Reovirus and Nelson Bay Reovirus: Implications for Translation Initiation," *Journal of Virology* 76 (January 2002): 609–18; Yoko Fukuda, Takanori Washio, and Masaru Tomita, "Comparative Study of Overlapping Genes in the Genomes of *Mycoplasma genitalium* and *Mycoplasma pneumoniae*," *Nucleic Acids Research* 27 (April 15, 1999): 1847–53; Paul R. Cooper et al., "Divergently Transcribed Overlapping Genes Expressed in Liver and Kidney and Located in the 11p15.5 Imprinted Domain," *Genomics* 49 (April 1, 1998): 38–51; Marilyn Kozak, "Extensively Overlapping Reading Frames in a Second Mammalian Gene," *EMBO Reports* 2 (September 2001): 768–69; Martin Klemke, Ralph H. Kehlenbach, and Wieland B. Huttner, "Two Overlapping Reading Frames in a Single Exon Encode Interacting Proteins—A Novel Way of Gene Usage," *EMBO Journal* 20 (July 16, 2001): 3849–60.

26. Malacinski, *Essentials of Molecular Biology*, 177–78.

27. Yockey, *Information Theory, Evolution*, 85–92.

28. Wen-Yu Chung et al., "A First Look at ARFome: Dual-Coding Genes in Mammalian Genomes," *PLoS Computational Biology* 3 (May 18, 2007): e91.

29. The rules of the "Overlapping Sentence Game" do not correspond exactly to overlapping genes because of the redundancy of the genetic code in which several codons can specify the same amino acids. This situation would be equivalent to words in English having multiple spellings.

30. John P. Adelman et al., "Two Mammalian Genes Transcribed from Opposite Strands of the Same DNA," *Science* 235 (1987): 1514–17; Mariano Labrador et al., "Molecular Biology: Protein Encoding by Both DNA Strands," *Nature* 409 (February 22, 2001): 1000.

31. Stanley L. Miller, "The Endogenous Synthesis of Organic Compounds," in *The Molecular Origins of Life: Assembling Pieces of the Puzzle*, ed. André Brack (New York: Cambridge University Press, 1998), 59–85.

32. Dónall A. Mac Dónaill, "A Parity Code Interpretation of Nucleotide Alphabet Composition," *Chemical Communications*, no. 18 (September 21, 2002): 2062–63; Dónall A. Mac Dónaill, "Why Nature Chose A, C, G and U/T: An Error-Coding Perspective of Nucleotide Alphabet Composition," *Origins of Life and Evolution of the Biosphere* 33 (October 2003): 433–55.

33. Robert A. Stern and Nancy Stern, *An Introduction to Computers and Information Processing*, 2nd ed. (New York: Wiley & Sons, 1985), 124–36.

34. David Depew, "Intelligent Design and Irreducible Complexity: A Rejoinder," *Rhetoric & Public Affairs* 1 (1998): 571–78.

35. Leonard M. Adleman, "Computing with DNA," *Scientific American*, August 1998, 54–61.

36. Ibid.

37. Gheorghe Paun, Grzegorz Rozenberg, and Arto Salomaa, *DNA Computing: New Computing Paradigms* (Berlin: Springer-Verlag, 1998), 19–41.

38. Paun, Rozenberg, and Salomaa, *DNA Computing*, 1–6; Adleman, "Computing with DNA," 54–61.

39. Ivars Peterson, "Computing with DNA: Getting DNA-Based Computers Off the Drawing Board and Into the Wet Lab," *Science News* 150 (July 13, 1996): 26–27.

40. Charles Seife, "Molecular Computing: RNA Works Out Knight Moves," *Science* 287 (February 18, 2000): 1182–83; Dirk Faulhammer et al., "Molecular Computation: RNA Solutions to Chess Problems," *Proceedings of the National Academy of Sciences, USA* 97 (February 15, 2000): 1385–89; Anthony G. Frutos et al., "Demonstration of a Word Design Strategy for DNA Computing on Surfaces," *Nucleic Acids Research* 25 (December 1, 1997): 4748–57; Anthony G. Frutos, Lloyd M. Smith, and Robert M. Corn, "Enzymatic Ligation Reactions of DNA 'Words' on Surfaces for DNA Computing," *Journal of the American Chemical Society* 120 (October 14, 1998): 10277–82; Adrian Cho, "DNA Computing: Hairpins Trigger an Automatic Solution," *Science* 288 (May 19, 2000): 1152–53; Kensaku Sakamoto et al., "Molecular Computation by DNA Hairpin Formation," *Science* 288 (May 19, 2000): 1223–26.

41. Leonard M. Adleman, "Molecular Computation of Solutions to Combinatorial Problems," *Science* 266 (November 11, 1994): 1021–24; Seife, "Molecular Computing," 1182–83; Faulhammer et al., "Molecular Computation," 1385–89.

42. Frank Guarnieri, Makiko Fliss, and Carter Bancroft, "Making DNA Add," *Science* 273 (July 12, 1996): 220–23.

43. Adleman, "Computing with DNA," 54–61.

44. Paun, Rozenberg, and Salomaa, *DNA Computing*, 65–70.

45. Catherine Taylor Clelland, Viviana Risca, and Carter Bancroft, "Hiding Messages in DNA Microdots," *Nature* 399 (June 10, 1999): 533–34.

46. Paul D. N. Hebert et al., "Ten Species in One: DNA Barcoding Reveals Cryptic Species in the Neotropical Skipper Butterfly *Astraptes fulgerator*," *Proceedings of the National Academy of Sciences, USA* 101 (October 12, 2004): 14812–17; Paul D. N. Herbert et al., "Identification of Birds through DNA Barcodes," *PLoS Biology* 2 (October 2004): e312; W. John Kress et al., "Use of DNA Barcodes to Identify Flowering Plants," *Proceedings of the National Academy of Sciences, USA* 102 (June 7, 2005): 8369–74; M. Alex Smith et al., "DNA Barcodes Reveal Cryptic Host-Specificity within the Presumed Polyphagous Members of a Genus of Parasitoid Flies (Diptera: Tachinidae)," *Proceedings of the National Academy of Sciences, USA* 103 (March 7, 2006): 3657–62; Mehrdad Hajibabaei et al., "DNA Barcodes Distinguish Species of Tropical Lepidoptera," *Proceedings of the National Academy of Sciences, USA* 103 (January 24, 2006): 968–71; Keith A. Seifert et al., "Prospects for Fungus Identification Using *CO1* DNA Barcodes, with *Penicillium* as a Test Case," *Proceedings of the National Academy of Sciences, USA* 104 (March 6, 2007): 3901–6.

47. Robert G. Eason et al., "Characterization of Synthetic DNA Bar Codes in *Saccharomyces cerevisiae* Gene-Deletion Strains," *Proceedings of the National Academy of Sciences, USA* 101 (July 27, 2004): 11046–51.

48. Fazale Rana and Hugh Ross, *Origins of Life: Biblical and Evolutionary Models Face Off* (Colorado Springs: NavPress, 2004), 135–141.

Chapter 9 Cellular Symbolism

1. Wikipedia contributors, "Symbolism (Arts)," *Wikipedia, The Free Encyclopedia*, http://en.wikipedia.org/wiki/Symbolism_(arts) (accessed August 28, 2006).

2. Wikipedia contributors, "Code," *Wikipedia, The Free Encyclopedia*, http://en.wikipedia.org/wiki/Code (accessed September 1, 2006).

3. Peter Kreeft, *Fundamentals of the Faith: Essays in Christian Apologetics* (San Francisco: Ignatius, 1988), 25–26.

4. Harvey Lodish et al., *Molecular Cell Biology*, 4th ed. (New York: Freeman, 2000), 117–20.

5. Lubert Stryer, *Biochemistry*, 3rd ed. (New York: Freeman, 1988), 675–76.

6. David Haig and Laurence D. Hurst, "A Quantitative Measure of Error Minimization in the Genetic Code," *Journal of Molecular Evolution* 33 (November 1991): 412–17.

7. Gretchen Vogel, "Tracking the History of the Genetic Code," *Science* 281 (July 17, 1998): 329–31; Stephen J. Freeland and Laurence D. Hurst, "The Genetic Code Is One in a Million," *Journal of Molecular*

Evolution 47 (September 1998): 238–48; Stephen J. Freeland et al., "Early Fixation of an Optimal Genetic Code," *Molecular Biology and Evolution* 17 (April 2000): 511–18.

8. Freeland and Hurst, "Genetic Code," 238–48.

9. Massimo Di Giulio, "The Origin of the Genetic Code," *Trends in Biochemical Sciences* 25 (February 1, 2000): 44; Massimo Di Giulio and Mario Medugno, "The Level and Landscape of Optimization in the Origin of the Genetic Code," *Journal of Molecular Evolution* 52 (April 2001): 372–82; Massimo Di Giulio, "A Blind Empiricism against the Coevolution Theory of the Origin of the Genetic Code," *Journal of Molecular Evolution* 53 (December 2001): 724–32.

10. J. Gregory Caporaso, Michael Yarus, and Robin D. Knight, "Error Minimization and Coding Triplet/Binding Site Associations Are Independent Features of the Canonical Genetic Code," *Journal of Molecular Evolution* 61 (November 2005): 597–607; Stephen J. Freeland, Tao Wu, and Nick Keulmann, "The Case for an Error Minimizing Standard Genetic Code," *Origin of Life and Evolution of the Biosphere* 33 (October 2003): 457–77; Stephen J. Freeland, Robin D. Knight, and Laura F. Landweber, "Measuring Adaptation within the Genetic Code," *Trends in Biochemical Sciences* 25 (February 1, 2000): 44–45; Stephen J. Freeland and Laurence D. Hurst, "Load Minimization of the Genetic Code: History Does Not Explain the Pattern," *Proceedings of the Royal Society of London* B 265 (November 7, 1998): 2111–19; Terres A. Ronneberg, Laura F. Landweber, and Stephen J. Freeland, "Testing a Biosynthetic Theory of the Genetic Code: Fact or Artifact?" *Proceedings of the National Academy of Sciences, USA* 97 (December 5, 2000): 13690–95; Ramin Amirnovin, "An Analysis of the Metabolic Theory of the Origin of the Genetic Code," *Journal of Molecular Evolution* 44 (May 1997): 473–76.

11. Robin D. Knight, Stephen J. Freeland, and Laura F. Landweber, "Selection, History and Chemistry: The Three Faces of the Genetic Code," *Trends in Biochemical Sciences* 24 (June 1, 1999): 241–47.

12. F. H. C. Crick, "The Origin of the Genetic Code," *Journal of Molecular Biology* 38 (December 1968): 367–79.

13. Syozo Osawa et al., "Evolution of the Mitochondrial Genetic Code. I. Origin of AGR Serine and Stop Codons in Metazoan Mitochondria," *Journal of Molecular Evolution* 29 (September 1989): 202–7; Dennis W. Schultz and Michael Yarus, "On Malleability in the Genetic Code," *Journal of Molecular Evolution* 42 (May 1996): 597–601; Eörs Szathmáry, "Codon Swapping as a Possible Evolutionary Mechanism," *Journal of Molecular Evolution* 32 (February 1991): 178–82.

14. Hubert P. Yockey, *Information Theory and Molecular Biology* (Cambridge: Cambridge University Press, 1992), 180–83.

15. Manfred Eigen et al., "How Old Is the Genetic Code? Statistical Geometry of tRNA Provides an Answer," *Science* 244 (May 12, 1989): 673–79.

16. For a comprehensive list of references to the scientific literature, see Fazale Rana and Hugh Ross, "An Early or Late Appearance?" in *Origins of Life: Biblical and Evolutionary Models Face Off* (Colorado Springs: NavPress, 2004), 63–79 and notes.

17. Yockey, *Information Theory*, 184–96; Alfonso Jimenez-Sanchez, "On the Origin and Evolution of the Genetic Code," *Journal of Molecular Evolution* 41 (December 1995): 712–16; Huan-Lin Wu, Stefan Bagby, and Jean van den Elsen, "Evolution of the Genetic Triplet Code via Two Types of Doublet Codons," *Journal of Molecular Evolution* 61 (July 2005): 54–64.

18. Yockey, *Information Theory*, 184–96.

19. Lodish, *Molecular Cell Biology*, 321–27.

20. Ibid., 384–90.

21. Guo-Cheng Yuan et al., "Genome-Scale Identification of Nucleosome Positions in *S. cerevisiae*," *Science* 309 (July 22, 2005): 626–30; Edward A. Sekinger, Zarmik Moqtaderi, and Kevin Struhl, "Intrinsic Histone-DNA Interactions and Low Nucleosome Density Are Important for Preferential Accessibility of Promoter Regions in Yeast," *Molecular Cell* 18 (June 10, 2005): 735–48; Fatih Ozsolak et al., "High-Throughput Mapping of the Chromatin Structure of Human Promoters," *Nature Biotechnology* 25 (February 2007): 244–48; Ben Wong et al., "Characterization of Z-DNA as a Nucleosome-Boundary Element in Yeast *Saccharomyces cerevisiae*," *Proceedings of the National Academy of Sciences, USA* 104 (February 13, 2007): 2229–34.

22. Eran Segal et al., "A Genomic Code for Nucleosome Positioning," *Nature* 442 (August 17, 2006): 772–78.

23. Shalev Itzkovitz and Uri Alon, "The Genetic Code Is Nearly Optimal for Allowing Additional Information within Protein-Coding Sequences," *Genome Research* 17 (April 2007): 405–12.

Chapter 10 Total Quality

1. Wikipedia contributors, "Giclée," *Wikipedia, The Free Encyclopedia*, http://en.wikipedia.org/wiki/Giclee (accessed December 14, 2006).

2. Stella M. Hurtley, "Frontiers in Cell Biology: Quality Control," *Science* 286 (December 3, 1999): 1881; Lars Ellgaard, Maurizio Molinari, and Ari Helenius, "Setting the Standards: Quality Control in the Secretory Pathway," *Science* 286 (December 3, 1999): 1882–88; Sue Wickner, Michael R. Maurizi, and Susan Gottesman, "Posttranslational Quality Control: Folding, Refolding, and Degrading Proteins," *Science* 286 (December 3, 1999): 1888–93; Michael Ibba and Dieter Söll, "Quality Control Mechanisms During Translation," *Science* 286 (December 3, 1999): 1893–97; Tomas Lindahl and Richard D. Wood, "Quality Control by DNA Repair," *Science* 286 (December 3, 1999): 1897–1905.

3. Michael Denton, *Evolution: A Theory in Crisis* (Bethesda, MD: Adler & Adler, 1986), 264–68.

4. Harvey Lodish et al., *Molecular Cell Biology*, 4th ed. (New York: Freeman, 2000), 111–16.

5. Ibid., 125–34.

6. Lubert Stryer, *Biochemistry*, 3rd ed. (New York: Freeman, 1988), 746–64.

7. Ibid., 739–42.

8. Ibid., 733–35.

9. Lodish et al., *Molecular Cell Biology*, 117–20.

10. Murray P. Deutscher, "Degradation of Stable RNA in Bacteria," *Journal of Biological Chemistry* 278 (November 14, 2003): 45041–44; Murray P. Deutscher, "Degradation of RNA in Bacteria: Comparison of mRNA and Stable RNA," *Nucleic Acids Research* 34 (February 2006): 659–66.

11. Deutscher, "Degradation of Stable RNA," 45041–44; Deutscher, "Degradation of RNA in Bacteria," 659–66.

12. Zhongwei Li et al., "RNA Quality Control: Degradation of Defective Transfer RNA," *EMBO Journal* 21 (March 1, 2002): 1132–38; Zhuan-Fen Cheng and Murray P. Deutscher, "Quality Control of Ribosomal RNA Mediated by Polynucleotide Phosphorylase and RNase R," *Proceedings of the National Academy of Sciences, USA* 100 (May 27, 2003): 6388–6393.

13. Letian Kuai et al., "Polyadenylation of rRNA in *Saccharomyces cerevisiae*," *Proceedings of the National Academy of Sciences, USA* 101 (June 8, 2004): 8581–86; Štěpánka Vaňáčová et al., "A New Yeast Poly(A) Polymerase Complex Involved in RNA Quality Control," *PLoS Biology* 3 (June 2005): e189; Sujatha Kadaba, Xuying Wang, and James T. Anderson, "Nuclear RNA Surveillance in *Saccharomyces cerevisiae*: Trf4p-Dependent Polyadenylation of Nascent Hypomethylated tRNA and an Aberrant Form of 5S rRNA," *RNA* 12 (March 2006): 508–21; Shimyn Slomovic et al., "Polyadenylation of Ribosomal RNA in Human Cells," *Nucleic Acids Research* 34 (July 2006): 2966–75.

14. Lynne E. Maquat and Gordon G. Carmichael, "Quality Control of mRNA Function," *Cell* 104 (January 26, 2001): 173–76.

15. Nikolay Zenkin, Yulia Yuzenkova, and Konstantin Severinov, "Transcript-Assisted Transcriptional Proofreading," *Science* 313 (July 28, 2006): 518–20; Patrick Cramer, "Self-Correcting Messages," *Science* 313 (July 28, 2006): 447–48.

16. Alan G. Atherly, Jack R. Girton, and John F. McDonald, *The Science of Genetics* (Fort Worth: Saunders College Publishing, 1999), 315–21.

17. Ibid.

18. See, for example, Cécile Bousquet-Antonelli, Carlo Presutti, and David Tollervey, "Identification of a Regulated Pathway for Nuclear Pre-mRNA Turnover," *Cell* 102 (September 15, 2000): 765–75; Maquat and Carmichael, "Quality Control," 173–76; Laura Milligan et al., "A Nuclear Surveillance Pathway for mRNAs with Defective Polyadenylation," *Molecular and Cellular Biology* 25 (November 2005): 9996–10004.

19. See, for example, Maquat and Carmichael, "Quality Control," 173–76; Zhaolan Zhou et al., "The Protein Aly Links Pre-Messenger-RNA Splicing to Nuclear Export in Metazoans," *Nature* 407 (September 21, 2000): 401–4.

20. For example, Maquat and Carmichael, "Quality Control," 173–76.

21. As a case in point, see David Tollervey, "RNA Lost in Translation," *Nature* 440 (March 23, 2006): 425–26; Meenakshi K. Doma and Roy Parker, "Endonucleolytic Cleavage of Eukaryotic mRNAs with Stalls in Translation Elongation," *Nature* 440 (March 23, 2006): 561–64; Audrey Stevens et al., "β-Globin mRNA Decay in Erythroid Cells: UG Site-Preferred Endonucleolytic Cleavage That Is Augmented by a Premature Termination Codon," *Proceedings of the National Academy of Sciences, USA* 99 (October 1, 2002): 12741–46; Joshua T. Mendell, Colette M. J. ap Rhys, and Harry C. Dietz, "Separable Roles for rent1/hUpf1 in Altered Splicing and Decay of Nonsense Transcripts," *Science* 298 (October 11, 2002): 419–22.

22. Stryer, *Biochemistry*, 735–37; Ibba and Söll, "Quality Control Mechanisms," 1893–97.

23. Anthony C. Bishop, Tyzoon K. Nomanbhoy, and Paul Schimmel, "Blocking Site-to-Site Translocation of Misactivated Amino Acid by Mutation of a Class I tRNA Synthetase," *Proceedings of the National Academy of Sciences, USA* 99 (January 22, 2002): 585–90.

24. Jamie M. Bacher, Valérie de Crécy-Lagard, and Paul R. Schimmel, "Inhibited Cell Growth and Protein Functional Changes from an Editing-Defective tRNA Synthetase," *Proceedings of the National Academy of Sciences, USA* 102 (February 1, 2005): 1697–1701.

25. Jeong Woong Lee et al., "Editing-Defective tRNA Synthetase Causes Protein Misfolding and Neurodegeneration," *Nature* 443 (September 7, 2006): 50–55.

26. Ibba and Söll, "Quality Control Mechanisms," 1893–97.

27. Stryer, *Biochemistry*, 754–55.

28. Frederick J. LaRiviere, Alexey D. Wolfson, and Olke C. Uhlenbeck, "Uniform Binding of Aminoacyl-tRNAs to Elongation Factor Tu by Thermodynamic Compensation," *Science* 294 (October 5, 2001): 165–68; Michael Ibba, "Discriminating Right from Wrong," *Science* 294 (October 5, 2001): 70–71.

29. Stryer, *Biochemistry*, 756.

30. Lodish et al., *Molecular Cell Biology*, 696–722.

31. Ari Helenius, "Quality Control in the Secretory Assembly Line," *Philosophical Transactions of the Royal Society of London* B 356 (February 28, 2001): 147–50; Christopher M. Cabral, Yan Liu, and Richard N. Sifers, "Dissecting Glycoprotein Quality Control in the Secretory Pathway," *Trends in Biochemical Sciences* 26 (October 2001): 619–24; Roberto Sitia and Ineke Braakman, "Quality Control in the Endoplasmic Reticulum Protein Factory," *Nature* 426 (December 18, 2003): 891–94.

32. Ellgaard, Molinari, and Helenius, "Setting the Standards," 1882–88.

33. Helenius, "Quality Control," 147–50; Cabral, Liu, and Sifers, "Dissecting Glycoprotein Quality Control," 619–24; Sitia and Braakman, "Quality Control," 891–94.

34. Cabral, Liu, and Sifers, "Dissecting Glycoprotein Quality Control," 619–24; Mark A. Lehrman, "Oligosaccharide-Based Information in Endoplasmic Reticulum Quality Control and Other Biological Systems," *Journal of Biological Chemistry* 276 (March 23, 2001): 8623–26.

35. Lehrman, "Oligosaccharide-Based Information," 8623–26.

36. Jean Marx, "A Stressful Situation," *Science* 313 (September 15, 2006): 1564–66.

37. David Ron, "Stressed Cells Cope with Protein Overload," *Science* 313 (July 7, 2006): 52–53; Julie Hollien and Jonathan S. Weissman, "Decay of Endoplasmic Reticulum-Localized mRNAs during the Unfolded Protein Response," *Science* 313 (July 7, 2006): 104–7.

38. See, for example, Brendan N. Lilley and Hidde L. Ploegh, "A Membrane Protein Required for Dislocation of Misfolded Proteins from the ER," *Nature* 429 (June 24, 2004): 834–40; Yihong Ye et al., "A Membrane Protein Complex Mediates Retro-Translocation from the ER Lumen into the Cytosol," *Nature* 429 (June 24, 2004): 841–47; Brendan N. Lilley and Hidde L. Ploegh, "Multiprotein Complexes that Link Dislocation, Ubiquitination, and Extraction of Misfolded Proteins from the Endoplasmic Reticulum Membrane," *Proceedings of the National Academy of Sciences, USA* 102 (October 24, 2005): 14296–301.

39. See, for example, Christopher M. Dobson, "Protein Folding and Misfolding," *Nature* 426 (December 18, 2003): 884–90; Alfred L. Goldberg, "Protein Degradation and Protection against Misfolded or Damaged Proteins," *Nature* 426 (December 18, 2003): 895–99; Dennis J. Selkoe, "Folding Proteins in Fatal Ways," *Nature* 426 (December 18, 2003): 900–904; Wickner, Maurizi, and Gottesman, "Posttranslational Quality Control," 1888–93; Lindahl and Wood, "Quality Control," 1897–1905.

Chapter 11 A Style All His Own

1. Wikipedia contributors, "Pablo Picasso," *Wikipedia, The Free Encyclopedia*, http://en.wikipedia.org/wiki/Pablo_Picasso (accessed May 24, 2006).

2. "Cubism," *Answers.com*, http://www.answers.com/cubism (accessed September 16, 2006).

3. "Wright, Frank Lloyd," *The Columbia Encyclopedia*, http://education.yahoo.com/reference/encyclopedia/entry/Wright-FL (accessed June 8, 2006).

4. "Chance," *Merriam-Webster's Collegiate Dictionary*, 11th ed., Merriam-Webster, 2007, http://unabridged.merriam-webster.com/ (accessed November 9, 2007).

5. Stephen J. Gould, *Wonderful Life: The Burgess Shale and the Nature of History* (New York: Norton, 1989), 51.

6. Ibid., 48.

7. John Cafferky, *Evolution's Hand: Searching for the Creator in Contemporary Science* (Toronto: eastendbooks, 1997), 66–69.

8. See, for example, Russell F. Doolittle, "Convergent Evolution: The Need to Be Explicit," *Trends in Biochemical Sciences* 19 (January 1994): 15–18; Eugene V. Koonin, L. Aravind, and Alexy S. Kondrashov, "The Impact of Comparative Genomics on Our Understanding of Evolution," *Cell* 101 (June 9, 2000): 573–76; Harold H. Zakon, "Convergent Evolution on the Molecular Level," *Brain, Behavior and Evolution* 59, nos. 5–6 (2002): 250–61.

9. Michael Y. Galperin, D. Roland Walker, and Eugene V. Koonin, "Analogous Enzymes: Independent Inventions in Enzyme Evolution," *Genome Research* 8 (August 1998): 779–90.

10. Ibid.

11. Doolittle, "Convergent Evolution," 15–18.

12. Neil D. Rawlings and Alan J. Barrett, "Evolutionary Families of Peptidases," *Biochemical Journal* 290 (February 15, 1993): 205–18.

13. Galperin, Walker, and Koonin, "Analogous Enzymes," 779–90.

14. Eugene V. Koonin, Arcady R. Mushegian, and Peer Bork, "Non-Orthologous Gene Displacement," *Trends in Genetics* 12 (September 1996): 334–36.

15. Detlef D. Leipe, L. Aravind, and Eugene V. Koonin, "Did DNA Replication Evolve Twice Independently?" *Nucleic Acids Research* 27 (September 1, 1999): 3389–3401.

16. The material for this section was taken from Alan G. Atherly, Jack R. Girton, and John F. McDonald, *The Science of Genetics* (Fort Worth: Saunders College Publishing, 1999), 256–77.

17. J. William Schopf, "When Did Life Begin?" in *Life's Origin: The Beginnings of Biological Evolution*, ed. J. William Schopf (Berkeley: University of California Press, 2002), 163.

Chapter 12 An Elaborate Mosaic

1. Wikipedia contributors, "Mosaic," *Wikipedia, The Free Encyclopedia*, http://en.wikipedia.org/wiki/Mosaic (accessed April 17, 2007).

2. S. J. Singer and Garth L. Nicolson, "The Fluid Mosaic Model of the Structure of Cell Membranes," *Science* 175 (February 18, 1972): 720–31.

3. W. Dohan, "Molecular Basis for Membrane Phospholipid Diversity: Why Are There So Many Lipids?" *Annual Review of Biochemistry* 66 (July 1997): 199–232.

4. Miles D. Houslay and Keith K. Stanley, *Dynamics of Biological Membranes: Influence on Synthesis, Structure and Function* (New York: John Wiley & Sons, 1982), 51–65.

5. Ibid., 105–25.

6. Dohan, "Molecular Basis," 199–232.

7. Ibid.

8. Ibid.

9. Danilo D. Lasic, "The Mechanism of Vesicle Formation," *Biochemical Journal* 256 (November 15, 1988): 1–11.

10. Ibid.

11. See, for example, Barry L. Lentz, Tamra J. Carpenter, and Dennis R. Alford, "Spontaneous Fusion of Phosphatidylcholine Small Unilamellar Vesicles in the Fluid Phase," *Biochemistry* 26 (August 25, 1987): 5389–97.

12. Norman L. Gershfeld, "The Critical Unilamellar Lipid State: A Perspective for Membrane Bilayer Assembly," *Biochimica et Biophysica Acta* 988 (December 6, 1989): 335–50.

13. See, for example, Norman L. Gershfeld et al., "Critical Temperature for Unilamellar Vesicle Formation in Dimyristoylphosphatidylcholine Dispersions from Specific Heat Measurements," *Biophysical Journal* 65 (September 1993): 1174–79.

14. Norman L. Gershfeld, "Spontaneous Assembly of a Phospholipid Bilayer as a Critical Phenomenon: Influence of Temperature, Composition, and Physical State," *Journal of Physical Chemistry* 93 (June 29, 1989): 5256–61.

15. Lionel Ginsberg, D. L. Gilbert, and Norman L. Gershfeld, "Membrane Bilayer Assembly in Neural Tissue of Rat and Squid as a Critical Phenomenon: Influence of Temperature and Membrane Proteins," *Journal of Membrane Biology* 119 (January 1991): 65–73.

16. K. E. Tremper and Norman L. Gershfeld, "Temperature Dependence of Membrane Lipid Composition in Early Blastula Embryos of *Lytechinus pictus*: Selective Sorting of Phospholipids into Nascent Plasma Membranes," *Journal of Membrane Biology* 171 (September 1, 1999): 47–53.

17. A. J. Jin et al., "A Singular State of Membrane Lipids at Cell Growth Temperatures," *Biochemistry* 38 (October 5, 1999): 13275–78.

18. Norman L. Gershfeld and M. Murayama, "Thermal Instability of Red Blood Cell Membrane Bilayers: Temperature Dependence of Hemolysis," *Journal of Membrane Biology* 101 (December 1988): 67–72.

19. Lionel Ginsberg, John H. Xuereb, and Norman L. Gershfeld, "Membrane Instability, Plasmalogen Content, and Alzheimer's Disease," *Journal of Neurochemistry* 70 (June 1998): 2533–38.

20. Stanislav D. Zakharov et al., "Tuning the Membrane Surface Potential for Efficient Toxin Import," *Proceedings of the National Academy of Sciences, USA* 99 (June 25, 2002): 8654–59.

21. Dohan, "Molecular Basis," 199–232.

22. G. Vereb et al., "Dynamic, Yet Structured: The Cell Membrane Three Decades after the Singer-Nicolson Model," *Proceedings of the National Academy of Sciences, USA* 100 (July 8, 2003): 8053–58; Donald M. Engelman, "Membranes Are More Mosaic than Fluid," *Nature* 438 (December 1, 2005): 578–80.

23. Daniel Segré and Doron Lancet, "Composing Life," *EMBO Reports* 1 (September 2000): 217–22; Daniel Segré, Dafna Ben-Eli, and Doron Lancet, "Compositional Genomes: Prebiotic Information Transfer in Mutually Catalytic Noncovalent Assemblies," *Proceedings of the National Academy of Sciences, USA* 97 (April 11, 2000): 4112–17.

24. Daniel Segré et al., "The Lipid World," *Origins of Life and the Evolution of the Biosphere* 31 (February 2001): 119–45.

25. Ibid.

26. Houslay and Stanley, *Dynamics of Biological Membranes*, 98–105.

27. Tamir Gonen et al., "Lipid-Protein Interactions in Double-Layered Two-Dimensional AQP0 Crystals," *Nature* 438 (December 1, 2005): 633–38.

28. Houslay and Stanley, *Dynamics of Biological Membranes*, 152–205.

29. Philippe F. Devaux, "Static and Dynamic Lipid Asymmetry in Cell Membranes," *Biochemistry* 30 (February 5, 1991): 1163–73.

30. Houslay and Stanley, *Dynamics of Biological Membranes*, 152–205.

31. G. Vereb et al., "Dynamic, Yet Structured," 8053–58; Donald M. Engelman, "Membranes," 578–80.

32. Kai Simons and Elina Ikonen, "Functional Rafts in Cell Membranes," *Nature* 387 (June 5, 1997): 569–72; Deborah A. Brown and Erwin London, "Functions of Lipid Rafts in Biological Membranes," *Annual Review of Cell and Developmental Biology* 14 (November 1998): 111–36.

33. Geoffrey Zubay, *Origins of Life on the Earth and in the Cosmos*, 2nd ed. (San Diego: Academic Press, 2000), 371–76.

34. Ibid., 347–50; Arthur L. Weber, "Origin of Fatty Acid Synthesis: Thermodynamics and Kinetics of Reaction Pathways," *Journal of Molecular Evolution* 32 (February 1991): 93–100; Ahmed I. Rushdi and Bernd R. T. Simoneit, "Lipid Formation by Aqueous Fischer-Tropsch-Type Synthesis over a Temperature Range of 100 to 400°C," *Origins of Life and Evolution of the Biosphere* 31 (February 2001): 103–18; William R. Hargreaves, S. Mulvihill, and David W. Deamer, "Synthesis of Phospholipids and Membranes in Prebiotic Conditions," *Nature* 266 (March 3, 1977): 78–80; M. Rao, J. Eichberg, and J. Oró, "Synthesis of Phosphatidylcholine under Possible Primitive Earth Conditions," *Journal of Molecular Evolution* 18 (May 1982): 196–202; M. Rao, J. Eichberg, and J. Oró, "Synthesis of Phosphatidylethanolamine under Possible Primitive Earth Conditions," *Journal of Molecular Evolution* 25 (May 1987): 1–6.

35. Stanley L. Miller and Jeffrey L. Bada, "Submarine Hot Springs and the Origin of Life," *Nature* 334 (August 18, 1998): 609–11; Nils G. Holm and Eva M. Andersson, "Hydrothermal Systems," in *The Molecular Origins of Life: Assembling Pieces of the Puzzle*, ed. André Brack (Cambridge: Cambridge University Press, 1998), 86–99; Charles B. Thaxton, Walter L. Bradley, and Roger L. Olsen, *The Mystery of Life's Origin: Reassessing Current Theories* (Dallas: Lewis and Stanley, 1984), 56, 177–78.

36. David W. Deamer, Elizabeth Harang Mahon, and Giovanni Bosco, "Self-Assembly and Function of Primitive Membrane Structures," in *Early Life on Earth: Nobel Symposium No. 84*, ed. Stefan Bengtson (New York: Columbia University Press, 1994), 107–123; David W. Deamer, "Membrane Compartments in Prebiotic Evolution," in *The Molecular Origins of Life: Assembling Pieces of the Puzzle*, ed. André Brack (Cambridge: Cambridge University Press, 1998), 189–205.

37. John R. Cronin, "Clues from the Origin of the Solar System: Meteorites," in *The Molecular Origins of Life: Assembling Pieces of the Puzzle*, ed. André Brack (Cambridge: Cambridge University Press, 1998), 119–46.

38. Jason P. Dworkin et al., "Self-Assembling Amphiphilic Molecules: Synthesis in Simulated Interstellar/Precometary Ices," *Proceedings of the National Academy of Sciences, USA* 98 (January 30, 2001): 815–19; Ron Cowen, "Life's Housing May Come from Space," *Science News*, February 3, 2001, 68.

39. J. N. Israelachvili, S. Marcelja, and R. G. Horn, "Physical Principles of Membrane Organization," *Quarterly Review of Biophysics* 13 (May 1980): 121–200.

40. William R. Hargreaves and David W. Deamer, "Liposomes from Ionic, Single-Chain Amphiphiles," *Biochemistry* 17 (September 5, 1978): 3759–68.

41. Deamer, Mahon, and Bosco, "Self-Assembly," 107–23; Deamer, "Membrane Compartments," 189–205; David W. Deamer and R. M. Pashley, "Amphiphilic Components of the Murchison Carbonaceous Chondrite: Surface Properties and Membrane Formation," *Origins of Life and Evolution of the Biosphere* 19 (January 1989): 21–38; David W. Deamer, "Boundary Structures Are Formed by Organic Components of the Murchison Carbonaceous Chondrite," *Nature* 317 (October 31, 1985): 792–94.

42. Dworkin et al., "Self-Assembling Amphiphilic Molecules," 815–19.

43. Deamer, Mahon, and Bosco, "Self-Assembly," 107–23; David W. Deamer and Gail L. Barchfeld, "Encapsulation of Macromolecules by Lipid Vesicles under Simulated Prebiotic Conditions," *Journal of Molecular Evolution* 18 (May 1982): 203–6; David W. Deamer, "The First Living Systems: A Bioenergetic Perspective," *Microbiology and Molecular Biology Reviews* 61 (June 1997): 239–61.

44. Deamer, Mahon, and Bosco, "Self-Assembly," 107–23; Deamer, "Membrane Compartments," 189–205.

45. Deamer, "Membrane Compartments," 189–205.

46. Deamer, Mahon, and Bosco, "Self-Assembly," 107–23; Deamer, "Membrane Compartments," 189–205.

47. James G. Lawless and George U. Yuen, "Quantification of Monocarboxylic Acids in the Murchison Carbonaceous Meteorite," *Nature* 282 (November 22, 1979): 396–98.

48. Deamer, Mahon, and Bosco, "Self-Assembly," 107–23; Deamer, "Membrane Compartments," 189–205.

49. Deamer, "Boundary Structures," 792–94.

50. Hargreaves and Deamer, "Liposomes," 3759–68.

51. Matt Kaplan, "A Fresh Start: Life May Have Begun Not in the Sea but in Some Warm Little Freshwater Pond," *New Scientist*, May 11, 2002, 7.

52. Charles L. Apel, David W. Deamer, and Michael N. Mautner, "Self-Assembled Vesicles of Mono-carboxylic Acids and Alcohols: Conditions for Stability and for the Encapsulation of Biopolymers," *Biochimica et Biophysica Acta* 1559 (February 10, 2002): 1–9.

53. Kaplan, "Fresh Start," 7.

54. Jacquelyn A. Thomas and F. R. Rana, "The Influence of Environmental Conditions, Lipid Composition, and Phase Behavior on the Origin of Cell Membranes," *Origins of Life and Evolution of Biospheres* 37 (June 2007): 267–85.

55. Wikipedia contributors, "Mosaic," http://en.wikipedia.org/wiki/Mosaic.

Chapter 13 Coloring Outside the Lines

1. See, for example, Edward J. Behrman, George A. Marzluf, and Ronald Bentley, "Evidence from Biochemical Pathways in Favor of Unfinished Evolution Rather than Intelligent Design," *Journal of Chemical Education* 81 (July 2004): 1051–52.

2. Stephen Jay Gould, *The Panda's Thumb: More Reflections in Natural History* (New York: Morton, 1980), 24.

3. Ibid., 20–21.

4. Roderic D. M. Page and Edward C. Holmes, *Molecular Evolution: A Phylogenetic Approach* (Malden, MA: Blackwell Science, 1998), 63–65; Wen-Hsiung Li, *Molecular Evolution* (Sunderland, MA: Sinauer Associates, 1997), 23–30.

5. Private correspondence with Dr. Mark Wharton, November 28, 2005. Dr. Wharton holds a PhD in aerospace engineering from the Georgia Institute of Technology and has worked for the NASA Marshall Space Flight Center since 1990. He is an internationally recognized expert in the control of structures and is the principal investigator of the International Space Station experiment.

6. Lubert Stryer, *Biochemistry*, 3rd ed. (New York: Freeman, 1988), 349–96.

7. Ibid., 359–61.

8. Ibid., 442–44.

9. Ibid., 150–71.

10. Ibid., 596–97.

11. David A. Greenberg, "The Jaundice of the Cell," *Proceedings of the National Academy of Sciences, USA* 99 (December 10, 2002): 15837–39.

12. Sylvain Doré et al., "Bilirubin, Formed by Activation of Heme Oxygenase-2, Protects Neurons against Oxidative Stress Injury," *Proceedings of the National Academy of Sciences, USA* 96 (March 2, 1999): 2445–50; David E. Baranano et al., "Biliverdin Reductase: A Major Physiologic Cytoprotectant," *Proceedings of the National Academy of Sciences, USA* 99 (December 10, 2002): 16093–98.

13. "Kidney Stones," *ehealthMD*, http://www.ehealthmd.com/library/kidneystones/KS_whatis .html (accessed October 5, 2007).

14. "Kidney Stones," Urology Channel, Healthcommunities.com, http://www.urologychannel.com/ kidneystones/index.shtml (accessed March 11, 2003).

15. Stryer, *Biochemistry*, 619–22.

16. Ibid.

17. Urology channel, http://www.urologychannel.com/kidneystones/index.shtml.

18. Stryer, *Biochemistry*, 619–22.

19. Gould, *The Panda's Thumb*, 19–26.

20. Stryer, *Biochemistry*, 619–22.

21. Edward E. Max, "Plagiarized Errors and Molecular Genetics: Another Argument in the Evolution-Creation Controversy," TalkOrigins Archive, May 5, 2003, http://www.talkorigins.org/faqs/molgen/ (accessed August 12, 2003).

22. Li, *Molecular Evolution*, 395–99.

23. Ibid., 379–84.

24. Max, "Plagiarized Errors and Molecular Genetics," http://www.talkorigins.org/faqs/molgen/.

25. Page and Holmes, *Molecular Evolution*, 56–57.

26. Max, "Plagiarized Errors and Molecular Genetics," http://www.talkorigins.org/faqs/molgen/.

27. Page and Holmes, *Molecular Evolution*, 56–57.

28. Harvey Lodish et al., *Molecular Cell Biology*, 4th ed. (New York: Freeman, 2000), 62–65.

29. Ibid., 410–22.

30. Page and Holmes, *Molecular Evolution*, 56–57.

31. Michael J. Pelczar Jr., E. C. S. Chan, and Merna Foss Pelczar, *Elements of Microbiology* (New York: McGraw-Hill, 1981), 180–212.

32. Alan G. Atherly, Jack R. Girton, and John F. McDonald, *The Science of Genetics* (Fort Worth: Saunders College Publishing, 1999), 597–604.

33. Page and Holmes, *Molecular Evolution*, 80–85.

34. Ibid.

35. See, for example, Sergei A. Korneev, Ji-Ho Park, and Michael O'Shea, "Neuronal Expression of Neural Nitric Oxide Synthase (nNOS) Protein Is Supressed by an Antisense RNA Transcribed from an NOS Pseudogene," *Journal of Neuroscience* 19 (September 15, 1999): 7711–20; Shinji Hirotsune et al., "An Expressed Pseudogene Regulates the Messenger-RNA Stability of Its Homologous Coding Gene," *Nature* 423 (May 1, 2003): 91–96; Evgeniy S. Balakirev and Francisco J. Ayala, "Pseudogenes: Are They 'Junk' or Functional DNA?" *Annual Review of Genetics* 37 (December 2003): 123–51; Shinji Hirotsune et al., "Addendum: An Expressed Pseudogene Regulates the Messenger-RNA Stability of Its Homologous Coding Gene," *Nature* 426 (November 6, 2003): 100.

36. Esther Betrán et al., "Evolution of the *Phosphoglycerate mutase* Processed Gene in Human and Chimpanzee Revealing the Origin of a New Primate Gene," *Molecular Biology and Evolution* 19 (May 2002): 654–63; Örjan Svensson, Lars Arvestad, and Jens Lagergren, "Genome-Wide Survey for Biologically Functional Pseudogenes," *PLoS Computational Biology* 2 (May 5, 2006): e46; Nicolas Vinckenbosch, Isabelle Dupanloup, and Henrik Kaessmann, "Evolutionary Fate of Retroposed Gene Copies in the Human Genome," *Proceedings of the National Academy of Sciences, USA* 103 (February 28, 2006): 3220–25.

37. Jerzy Jurka, "Subfamily Structure and Evolution of the Human L1 Family of Repetitive Sequences," *Journal of Molecular Evolution* 29 (December 1989): 496–503; Atherly, Girton, and McDonald, *Science of Genetics*, 597–608; for example, Greg Towers et al., "A Conserved Mechanism of Retrovirus Restriction in Mammals," *Proceedings of the National Academy of Sciences, USA* 97 (October 24, 2000): 12295–99; Jonathan P. Stoye, "An Intracellular Block to Primate Lentivirus Replication," *Proceedings of the National Academy of Sciences, USA* 99 (September 3, 2002): 11549–51; Caroline Besnier, Yasuhiro Takeuchi, and Greg Towers, "Restriction of Lentivirus in Monkeys," *Proceedings of the National Academy of Sciences, USA* 99 (September 3, 2002): 11920–25; Theodora Hatziioannou et al., "Restriction of Multiple Divergent Retroviruses by Lv1 and Ref1," *EMBO Journal* 22 (February 3, 2003): 385–94; Clare Lynch and Michael Tristem, "A Co-Opted *gypsy*-Type LTR-Retrotransposon Is Conserved in the Genomes of Humans, Sheep, Mice, and Rats," *Current Biology* 13 (September 2, 2003): 1518–23; Vera Schramke and Robin Allshire, "Hairpin RNAs and Retrotransposon LTRs Effect RNAi and Chromatin-Based Gene Silencing," *Science* 301 (August 22, 2003): 1069–74; Wenhu Pi et al., "The LTR Enhancer of ERV-9 Human Endogenous Retrovirus Is Active in Oocytes and Progenitor Cells in Transgenic Zebrafish and Humans," *Proceedings of the National Academy of Sciences, USA* 101 (January 20, 2004): 805–10; Catherine A. Dunn, Patrik Medstrand, and Dixie L. Mager, "An Endogenous Retroviral Long Terminal Repeat Is the Dominant Promoter for Human β1,3–Galactosyltransferase 5 in the Colon," *Proceedings of the National Academy of Sciences, USA* 100 (October 28, 2003): 12841–46; François Mallet et al., "The

Endogenous Retroviral Locus ERVWE1 Is a Bona Fide Gene Involved in Hominoid Placental Physiology," *Proceedings of the National Academy of Sciences, USA* 101 (February 10, 2004): 1731–36.

38. Wen-Man Liu et al., "Cell Stress and Translational Inhibitors Transiently Increase the Abundance of Mammalian SINE Transcripts," *Nucleic Acids Research* 23 (May 25, 1995): 1758–65; Tzu-Huey Li et al., "Physiological Stresses Increase Mouse Short Interspersed Element (SINE) RNA Expression In Vivo," *Gene* 239 (November 1, 1999): 367–72; Richard H. Kimura, Prabhakara V. Choudary, and Carl W. Schmid, "Silk Worm Bm1 SINE RNA Increases Following Cellular Insults," *Nucleic Acids Research* 27 (August 15, 1999): 3380–87; Wen-Ming Chu et al., "Potential Alu Function: Regulation of the Activity of Double-Stranded RNA-Activated Kinase PKR," *Molecular and Cellular Biology* 18 (January 1998): 58–68.

39. Wen-Man Liu et al., "Alu Transcripts: Cytoplasmic Localisation and Regulation by DNA Methylation," *Nucleic Acids Research* 22 (March 25, 1994): 1087–95; Wen-Man Liu and Carl W. Schmid, "Proposed Roles for DNA Methylation in *Alu* Transcriptional Repression and Mutational Inactivation," *Nucleic Acid Research* 21 (March 25, 1993): 1351–59; Carol M. Rubin et al., "Alu Repeated DNAs Are Differentially Methylated in Primate Germ Cells," *Nucleic Acids Research* 22 (November 25, 1994): 5121–27; Igor N. Chesnokov and Carl W. Schmid, "Specific Alu Binding Protein from Human Sperm Chromatin Prevents DNA Methylation," *Journal of Biological Chemistry* 270 (August 4, 1995): 18539–42; Utha Hellmann-Blumberg et al., "Developmental Differences in Methylation of Human Alu Repeats," *Molecular and Cellular Biology* 13 (August 1993): 4523–30.

40. Jeffrey A. Bailey et al., "Molecular Evidence for a Relationship Between LINE-1 Elements and X Chromosome Inactivation: The Lyon Repeat Hypothesis," *Proceedings of the National Academy of Sciences, USA* 97 (June 6, 2000): 6634–39; Christine Moulton Clemson et al., "The X Chromosome Is Organized into a Gene-Rich Outer Rim and an Internal Core Containing Silenced Nongenic Sequences," *Proceedings of the National Academy of Sciences, USA* 103 (May 16, 2006): 7688–93.

41. Edith Heard, Philippe Clerc, and Philip Avner, "X-Chromosome Inactivation in Mammals," *Annual Review of Genetics* 31 (December 1997): 571–610.

42. Jack J. Pasternuk, *An Introduction to Human Molecular Genetics: Mechanisms of Inherited Diseases* (Bethesda, MD: Fitzgerald Science, 1999), 31–32.

43. Elena Allen et al., "High Concentrations of Long Interspersed Nuclear Element Sequence Distinguish Monoallelically Expressed Genes," *Proceedings of the National Academy of Sciences, USA* 100 (August 23, 2003): 9940–45.

44. Lynch and Tristem, "Co-Opted *gypsy*-Type LTR-Retrotransposon," 1518–23; Matthew P. Hare and Stephen R. Palumbi, "High Intron Sequence Conservation across Three Mammalian Orders Suggest Functional Constraints," *Molecular Biology and Evolution* 20 (June 2003): 969–78; J. W. Thomas et al., "Comparative Analyses of Multi-Species Sequences from Targeted Genomic Regions," *Nature* 424 (August 14, 2003): 788–93; Nicholas J. Kaplinsky et al., "Utility and Distribution of Conserved Noncoding Sequences in the Grasses," *Proceedings of the National Academy of Sciences, USA* 99 (April 30, 2002): 6147–51; Emmanouil T. Dermitzakis et al., "Evolutionary Discrimination of Mammalian Conserved Non-Genic Sequences (CNGs)," *Science* 302 (November 7, 2003): 1033–35; Gill Bejerano et al., "Ultraconserved Elements in the Human Genome," *Science* 304 (May 28, 2004): 1321–25; Michael Kamal, Xiaohiu Xie, and Eric S. Lander, "A Large Family of Ancient Repeat Elements in the Human Genome Is under Strong Selection," *Proceedings of the National Academy of Sciences, USA* 103 (February 21, 2006): 2740–45; Eliot C. Bush and Bruce T. Lahn, "Selective Constraint on Noncoding Regions of Hominid Genomes," *PLoS Computational Biology* 1 (December 16, 2005): e73.

45. Ran Kafri, Melissa Levy, and Yitzhak Pilpel, "The Regulatory Utilization of Genetic Redundancy through Responsive Backup Circuits," *Proceedings of the National Academy of Sciences, USA* 103 (August 1, 2006): 11653–58.

46. Lodish et al., *Molecular Cell Biology*, 62–65.

47. Ulrich Schubert et al., "Rapid Degradation of a Large Fraction of Newly Synthesized Proteins by Proteasomes," *Nature* 404 (April 13, 2000): 770–74.

48. Michael Gross, *Travels to the Nanoworld: Miniature Machinery in Nature and Technology* (New York: Plenum Trade, 1999), 86–90.

49. Eric Pamer and Peter Cresswell, "Mechanisms of MHC Class I-Restricted Antigen Processing," *Annual Review of Immunology* 16 (April 1998): 323–58; Kenneth L. Rock and Alfred L. Goldberg, "Degradation of Cell Proteins and the Generation of MHC Class I-Presented Peptides," *Annual Review of Immunology* 17 (April 1999): 739–79.

50. Hansjörg Schild and Hans-Georg Rammensee, "Perfect Use of Imperfection," *Nature* 404 (2000): 709–10; J. Travis, "Trashed Proteins May Help Immune System," *Science News* 157 (2000): 245; Eric A. J. Reits et al., "The Major Substrates for TAP *in vivo* Are Derived from Newly Synthesized Proteins," *Nature* 404 (2000): 774–78.

51. Robert C. Bohinski, *Modern Concepts in Biochemistry*, 4th ed. (Boston: Allyn and Bacon, 1983), 373–80.

52. Ibid.

53. Guillaume G. B. Tcherkez, Graham D. Farquhar, and T. John Andrews, "Despite Slow Catalysis and Confused Substrate Specificity, All Ribulose Bisphosphate Carboxylases May Be Nearly Perfectly Optimized," *Proceedings of the National Academy of Sciences, USA* 103 (May 9, 2006): 7246–51.

54. Ibid.

55. Ronald D. Vale, "The Molecular Motor Toolbox for Intracellular Transport," *Cell* 112 (February 1, 2003): 467–80; Stephen M. King, "The Dynein Microtubule Motor," *Biochimica et Biophysica Acta (BBA)/Molecular Cell Research* 1496 (March 17, 2000): 60–75.

56. Roop Mallik and Steven P. Gross, "Molecular Motors: Strategies to Get Along," *Current Biology* 14 (November 23, 2004): R971–82.

Chapter 14 The Masterpiece Authenticated

1. Natasha Gural, "A Revealing Look at Picasso's Last Years," *Boston Globe*, May 5, 2004.

2. See, for example, Ursula Goodenough, *The Sacred Depths of Nature* (New York: Oxford University Press, 1998).

3. See, for example, Kenneth R. Miller, *Finding Darwin's God: A Scientist's Search for Common Ground between God and Evolution* (New York: Cliff Street Books, 1999), 129–64.

4. See, for example, Mark J. Pallen and Nicholas J. Matzke, "From *The Origin of Species* to the Origin of Bacterial Flagella," *Nature Reviews Microbiology* 4 (October 2006): 784–90; Renyi Liu and Howard Ochman, "Stepwise Formation of the Bacterial Flagellar System," *Proceedings of the National Academy of Sciences, USA* 104 (April 24, 2007): 7116–21.

5. See, for example, Ariel Blocker, Kaoru Komoriya, and Shin-Ichi Aizawa, "Type III Secretion Systems and Bacterial Flagella: Insights into Their Function from Structural Similarities," *Proceedings of the National Academy of Sciences, USA* 100 (March 18, 2003): 3027–30.

6. The phrase "just-so" refers to Rudyard Kipling's *Just-So Stories*. This book, first published in 1902, contains mythical accounts of how various natural phenomena came about like "How the Whale Got His Throat," "How the Leopard Got His Spots," and "How the Camel Got His Hump," to name a few. This phrase is also an academic term used to describe ad hoc, unverifiable, unfalsifiable narrative accounts of how some organism or biological trait came into existence.

7. Pallen and Matzke, "*Origin of Species* to the Origin of Bacterial Flagella," 784–90.

8. Milton H. Saier Jr., "Evolution of Bacterial Type III Protein Secretion Systems," *Trends in Microbiology* 12 (March 2004): 113–15.

9. Sonia L. Bardy, Sandy Y. M. Ng, and Ken F. Jarrell, "Prokaryotic Motility Structures," *Microbiology* 149 (February 2003): 295–304.

10. Michael J. Behe, *Darwin's Black Box: The Biochemical Challenge to Evolution* (New York: Free Press, 1996), 165–86.

11. Fazale Rana and Hugh Ross, *Origins of Life: Biblical and Evolutionary Models Face Off* (Colorado Springs: NavPress, 2004), 159–68.

12. Hubert P. Yockey, *Information Theory and Molecular Biology* (Cambridge: Cambridge University Press, 1992), 180–83.

13. Jacquelyn A. Thomas and F. R. Rana, "The Influence of Environmental Conditions, Lipid Composition, and Phase Behavior on the Origin of Cell Membranes," *Origins of Life and Evolution of Biospheres* 37 (June 2007): 267–85.

14. Stephen Jay Gould, *The Panda's Thumb: More Reflections in Natural History* (New York: Norton, 1980), 20.

15. John Cafferky, *Evolution's Hand: Searching for the Creator in Contemporary Science* (Toronto: eastendbooks, 1997), 66–69.

16. For a good discussion of abductive reasoning and its relationship to the inference of the best explanation, see Stephen C. Meyer, "Modern Science and the Return of the 'God Hypothesis,'" in *Science and Christianity: Four Views*, ed. Richard F. Carlson (Downers Grove, IL: InterVarsity Press, 2000), 127–74.

17. Genesis 1:26–27; 5:1–2 (see chap. 1, n. 12).

18. Kenneth Richard Samples, "The Historic Christian View of Man," in *A World of Difference* (Grand Rapids: Baker, 2007), 171–88.

Epilogue

1. For an overview, see Hugh Ross, *Creation as Science: A Testable Model Approach to End the Creation/Evolution Wars* (Colorado Springs: NavPress, 2006).

2. Genesis 1:2: "Now the earth was formless and empty, darkness was over the surface of the deep, and the Spirit of God was hovering over the waters." Psalm 104:5–6: "He set the earth on its foundations; it can never be moved. You covered it with the deep as with a garment; the waters stood above the mountains." Deuteronomy 32:10–11: "In a desert land he found him, in a barren and howling waste. He shielded him and cared for him; he guarded him as the apple of his eye, like an eagle that stirs up its nest and hovers over its young, that spreads its wings to catch them and carries them on its pinions."

3. Fazale Rana and Hugh Ross, *Origins of Life: Biblical and Evolutionary Models Face Off* (Colorado Springs: NavPress, 2004), 35–46.

GLOSSARY

actin. The protein that constitutes microfilaments, one of three types of filaments that make up the cytoskeleton.

activators. Proteins that bind to the operator. Activators turn a gene on when they bind.

adenine. One of four nucleobases found in DNA and RNA.

adenosine (A). One of four nucleotides used to build DNA chains. The other three are cytidine, guanosine, and thymidine.

amino acid. An organic compound that has both amino (NH_2) and carboxyl (COOH) groups. Amino acids join together in a chainlike fashion to form proteins.

amphiphilie. A chemical compound in which part of its molecular structure is water-soluble and part is water-insoluble. Cell membranes consist of amphiphilic materials.

anion. A negatively charged chemical specie.

anticodon. Each tRNA's anticodon matches a codon in mRNA. The codon–anticodon pairs are part of the cellular hardware that implements the manufacturing instructions for protein production.

antioxidant. Any compound that protects biochemical systems from the harmful effects of oxygen or reactive oxygen species by reacting with them and converting these compounds into benign materials.

314

antiparallel. Refers to the alignment of two polynucleotide chains. The two strands are arranged parallel to one another with each starting point of a strand in the polynucleotide duplex located next to the ending point of the other strand.

antisense strand. One of two strands in a DNA double helix. It normally does not harbor a gene but simply serves as a template for DNA replication. The other strand is known as the sense strand.

aquaglyceroporins. Proteins that form channels in cell membranes that provide conduits for glycerol and related materials to flow in and out of the cell.

aquaporins. Proteins that form channels in cell membranes that provide conduits for water to flow in and out of the cell.

archaea. One of life's three domains. Bacteria-like microorganisms comprise archaea. While these microbes superficially resemble bacteria, they are genetically and biochemically distinct. Some origin-of-life researchers think that archaea were the first organisms to emerge on Earth.

ATP (adenosine triphosphate). The cell uses this compound as a source of chemical energy to drive the operation of cellular processes.

ATPases. A class of proteins that break down ATP, an energy-storing molecule within the cell.

autotrophs. Chemoautotrophs and photoautotrophs are the two types of autotrophs. Autotrophs survive by generating the organic materials they need using inorganic compounds or light as energy sources.

bacteria. One of life's major domains consisting of single-celled organisms that lack a nucleus and other organelles.

base-pairing rules. Rules that establish the complementary relationship between the nucleotide sequences of the two DNA strands.

bilayer. The sheet that is spontaneously formed by phospholipids when added to water. When organized into a bilayer, phospholipid molecules align into two monolayers with the phospholipid tails of one monolayer contacting the phospholipid tails of its companion monolayer.

biochemistry. The study of the chemical processes and compounds that constitute life.

biomolecule. A molecule that is found in living organisms or plays an important role in life processes.

biosynthesis. The production of life molecules by biochemical systems.

bottom-up approach. An approach to account for the origin of life from an evolutionary standpoint. The bottom-up approach starts with simple chemical systems and seeks to identify pathways that lead to increased complexity, culminating in the first life-form.

Brownian motion. The random, zigzag movement of microscopic objects suspended in a liquid or gas. This motion stems from the net force exerted on the suspended object by the gas or liquid molecules.

Brownian ratchet. A device that restricts Brownian motion using a barrier to power directional movement. Brownian ratchets require energy input to erect and maintain the barriers that prevent motion in unwanted directions.

carbonaceous chondrites. Carbon-containing meteorites, like the Murchison meteorite.

carbohydrate. A biomolecule that consists of carbon, hydrogen, and oxygen in the specific ratio of 1:2:1, respectively. Carbohydrates include sugars, starches, and celluloses.

catalyze. To facilitate a chemical reaction.

cell. The fundamental unit of life and the smallest entity that can be considered "life." All organisms consist of one or more cells.

cell membrane. The outer layer of the cell (comprised of lipids and proteins), which protects the cell's inner parts from the cell's surroundings while allowing materials to enter and exit the cell.

cellulose. A large sugar molecule that consists of glucose subunits. The cell wall in plants is composed of cellulose.

central dogma of molecular biology. This concept describes the flow of information inside the cell. Information stored in DNA is copied to form a messenger RNA molecule (transcription). This molecule, in turn, directs the formation of proteins at ribosomes (translation).

centromere. The central region of the chromosome. This region plays a role in separating chromosomes during cell division.

chemoautotroph. A type of autotroph. Chemoautotrophs use chemical energy extracted from the environment as an energy source to produce organic materials.

chromosome. Complexes formed from a single DNA molecule and histone proteins. Chromosomes are found in the nucleus of eukaryotic organisms.

codon. The fundamental unit of the genetic code. Codons consist of groupings of three nucleotides. Codons are used to specify the twenty different amino acids used to make proteins.

complementary. Refers to the sequences of the two polynucleotide chains that make up the DNA double helix. Because of the base-pairing rules (A pairs with T, and G pairs with C), the sequence of one polynucleotide chain dictates the sequence of the other chain.

cyanobacteria. A group of bacteria with the capacity for photosynthesis. Cyanobacteria are also called blue-green algae.

cytidine (C). One of four nucleotides used to build DNA chains. The other three are adenosine, guanosine, and thymidine.

cytoplasm. Forms the cell's internal matrix and is made up of water, salts, and organic molecules.

cytosine. One of four nucleobases found in DNA and RNA.

cytoskeleton. A fibrous network of proteins that form the cell's internal structural framework. It assembles and disassembles at various locales with the cytoplasm as needed. The cytoskeleton is made of three filaments: microtubules, intermediate filaments, and microfilaments.

daughter cells. Two cells produced during cell division, with DNA identical to the parent cell.

disaccharide. A carbohydrate that consists of two sugars linked together. Table sugar (sucrose) is an example.

disulfide bond. A bond formed between the side chains of cysteine amino acid residues within a protein, stabilizing its three-dimensional structure.

DNA. The cell's genetic material, which consists of two polynucleotide chains that twist around each other to form the double helix. Polynucleotide chains are made by linking four subunit molecules called nucleotides. The four nucleotides are adenosine, cytidine, guanosine, and thymidine—abbreviated as A, C, G, and T, respectively.

DNA polymerase. An enzyme that duplicates DNA molecules during cell replication.

DNA replication. The biochemical process that generates two "daughter" molecules identical to the "parent" DNA molecule.

domain. All of life is divided into one of three domains: Eubacteria, Archaea, or Eukarya.

double helix. Describes the molecular topology of a DNA molecule.

electron micrograph. The image produced by an electron microscope.

endogenous retrovirus. Presumably nonfunctional retroviral DNA that has become permanently incorporated into the host organism's genome.

entropy. The measure of energy quality and disorder of a system.

enzyme. A protein that catalyzes or assists a chemical process.

essential genome size. The number of distinct genes necessary to sustain the minimal metabolic and structural requirements for life.

eubacteria. One of life's three domains. These organisms are single-celled and lack internal structures such as a nucleus.

eukarya. One of life's three domains comprised of organisms that possess a nucleus as part of their cellular makeup. Eukarya includes one-celled protists and multicellular fungi, plants, and animals.

eukaryote. One of two types of cells. It contains internal membrane systems, a nucleus, organelles, a cytoskeleton, and other components that organize the cell contents at the subcellular and even molecular level.

evolution. Biological changes that occur in populations of organisms through time.

evolutionary pathways. The proposed sequence of changes that transforms an ancestral population into a novel group.

evolutionary tree of life. A treelike diagram showing proposed evolutionary interrelationships among various species or other biological groups believed to have a common ancestor.

exon. Nucleotide sequence in a gene that codes for part of the amino acid sequence of polypeptide chains.

explanatory filter. A methodology proposed by philosopher and mathematician William Dembski to detect the activity of an intelligent agent. According to the explanatory filter, if an event, system, or object is intentionally produced by an intelligent designer then it will (1) be contingent, (2) be complex, and (3) display an independently specified pattern.

fluid mosaic model. A model that provides the framework for understanding membrane structure and function. This model views the phospholipid bilayer as a two-dimensional fluid that serves as both a cellular barrier and a solvent for integral membrane proteins. It allows the membrane proteins and lipids to freely diffuse laterally throughout the cell membrane.

frameshift mutation. A mutation that results when nucleotides are accidentally inserted or deleted from a gene, leading to a shift in the gene's reading frame.

futile cycle. Paired reactions that cycle back and forth within a cell.

gene. The nucleotide sequence along the DNA strands that codes the amino acid sequence of a particular polypeptide.

gene expression. Refers to the production of the protein encoded by the gene.

gene product. Any functional molecule specified by a gene including proteins, tRNA, and rRNA.

gene regulation. The control of gene expression.

genetic code. A set of rules that relays the information stored in the nucleotide sequences of DNA to the amino acid sequences of proteins.

genome. An organism's total genetic makeup.

genomics. A new life-science discipline that focuses on sequencing and characterizing the structure and function of genomes.

glucose. A six-carbon sugar that releases energy in the process of glycolysis that is used by the cell for energy.

glycerol. A three-carbon compound that forms the backbone of phospholipids.

glycolysis. This biochemical process releases energy from glucose by fracturing it into two molecules of pyruvate. The cell captures a portion of this liberated chemical energy and stores it for later use.

glycolytic pathway. The metabolic process of glycolysis that harvests energy for use by the cell.

Golgi apparatus. Stacks of membranes in eukaryotic cells that function in the processing and sorting of proteins and lipids destined for other parts of the cell and secretion.

guanine. One of four nucleobases found in DNA.

guanosine (G). One of four nucleotides used to build DNA chains. The other three are adenosine, cytidine, and thymidine.

heterotroph. An organism that ingests the organic materials needed for its maintenance and growth.

housekeeping gene. A gene that is expressed, or turned on, nearly all the time because it specifies a protein needed virtually all the time to maintain normal cellular operations.

hydrolytic reaction. A chemical reaction that involves the cleavage of chemical bonds by water.

hydrophilic. "Water-loving"; hydrophilic compounds dissolve readily in water.

hydrophobic. "Water-hating"; hydrophobic compounds are insoluble in water.

indel. A type of genetic mutation that involves the insertion and/or deletion of one or more nucleotides from a DNA sequence.

information. Results when data is processed, manipulated, and organized in a way that adds to the knowledge of the receiver.

intron. A nucleotide sequence in a gene that does not code for anything.

invariable (conserved) position. A position in the amino acid sequence of a polypeptide that doesn't vary in response to mutational pressures. Biochemists regard conserved amino acids as critical to the protein's structure and function.

junk DNA. A region of a genome that does not code for proteins or other functional products. Evolutionary biologists believe that junk DNA results when undirected biochemical processes and random molecular and physical events transform a functional DNA segment into a useless, molecular artifact.

kinesin. A highly efficient and robust molecular motor that moves cellular cargo. Kinesin binds with its cargo and then "walks" in only one direction along microtubules that form part of the cell's cytoskeleton.

knock-out experiment. A protocol that involves either random or systematic mutation of genes to determine those that are indispensable for life.

lipid. A class of chemical compounds that shares the combined properties of solubility in organic solvents and insolubility in water.

lipid bilayer. The tail-to-tail arrangement of phospholipid molecules that forms the matrix of cell membranes.

LUCA (Last Universal Common Ancestor). The hypothetical organism that supposedly gave rise to all life on Earth.

lumen. The single space inside organelles.

macroevolution. Biological evolution at the genus level or higher. Macroevolutionary changes entail major changes in anatomy and physiology.

macromolecule. Any large molecule made up of smaller molecules called subunits.

membrane. A structure that separates the parts of the cell. Internal membrane systems separate organelles within the cell while another membrane forms a boundary for the cell from its exterior surroundings.

metabolism. The sum total of chemical reactions that take place in living systems.

microbe. Any single-cell organism.

microevolution. Evolutionary changes within a species due primarily to altered frequencies of genes within a population.

mitosis. The process of cell division that yields two daughter cells identical to the mother cell.

model. A mathematical or descriptive depiction of a phenomenon in nature. This term is roughly synonymous to a theory or hypothesis.

monolayer. An assembly of molecules that forms a single layer, one molecule in thickness.

monomer. A chemical compound that can be linked with other chemical compounds to form a larger, more complex molecule. Monomers are also referred to as subunits.

monosaccharides. Carbohydrates composed of a single-sugar residue, such as glucose and fructose.

mRNA (messenger RNA). A single-stranded molecule similar in composition to DNA. The cell assembles mRNA using the nucleotide sequence of a gene as a template. At the ribosome, mRNA directs the synthesis of polypeptide chains.

mutation. Any change that occurs in a DNA sequence.

nanotechnology. The scientific discipline that seeks to develop molecular-scale devices and systems.

natural selection. The differential survival of organisms within a population in response to environmental, competitive, and predatory challenges.

nonsense (or stop) codon. This type of codon doesn't specify any amino acids and always occurs at the end of the nucleotide sequence of a gene informing the protein manufacturing machinery where the polypeptide chain ends.

nonuniversal genetic code. A code that employs slightly different codon assignments compared to the universal genetic code; it can be thought of as a deviant of the universal genetic code.

nucleobase. A part of RNA or DNA that extends as a side chain from the backbone of the DNA molecule and serves as an interaction point (like ladder rungs) when the two DNA strands align and twist to form the double helix. Nucleobases include adenine, cytosine, guanine, and thymine.

nucleolus. A dense area within the nucleus of a cell where ribosomes are assembled.

nucleosome. The fundamental organizing structure of chromosomes. A nucleosome consists of DNA wrapped around a histone core and occurs repeatedly along the length of the DNA molecule to form a supramolecular structure that resembles a string of beads.

nucleotide sequence. A sequential string of nucleotides along a DNA strand.

nucleotide. A molecule used by the cell to build polynucleotide chains that form DNA. The four nucleotides used are adenosine (A), cytidine (C), guanosine (G), and thymidine (T).

oligosaccharide. A carbohydrate formed when a handful of sugar molecules are linked together.

operator. One of two key sites within the regulatory region of a gene. The operator binds two types of proteins: the activators and the repressors. The operator functions as a type of on/off switch for gene expression.

operon. A grouping of juxtaposed genes found in bacteria that are involved in the same cellular processes.

organelle. A structure found inside cells, typically surrounded by membranes, that carries out specialized functions.

peptide. A polymer formed by linking together amino acids.

phosphate group. A chemical group consisting of a central phosphorus atom bound to four oxygen atoms. Phosphate groups help form the backbone of DNA and RNA molecules and play an important role in energy usage by the cell.

phosphodiester bond. A bond that forms between a phosphate group and two sugars at the same time to bridge two nucleotides, while retaining a negative charge.

phospholipid. An amphiphilic compound formed from phosphate, glycerol, fatty acids, and amino alcohol. Phospholipids are one of the major components of cell membranes.

photoautotroph. An organism that produces food stuff by using light energy.

plasmid. Small piece of circular DNA found in bacteria. Plasmids exist independent of the bacteria's primary chromosome.

poly(A) tail. A sequence of adenosine nucleotides added to the end of RNA molecules.

polymer. A large chainlike molecule that consists of smaller subunits (called monomers) linked together.

polynucleotide. Chainlike molecules of nucleotides. DNA and RNA are examples.

polypeptide. A synonym for peptide.

polysaccharide. A carbohydrate formed when numerous sugars connect. Starch and cellulose are common examples.

posttranslational modification. The processing of proteins after production at the ribosomes.

primordial soup. The hypothetical mixture of chemical compounds on early Earth that provided the raw materials chemical evolutionary processes supposedly used to generate the first life-forms.

prokaryote. A single-celled organism that lacks subcellular structures, specifically a nucleus. Bacteria and archaea are both prokaryotes.

promoter. One of two key sites within the regulatory region of a gene. The promoter serves as the binding site for RNA polymerase, an enzyme that initiates gene expression by producing an mRNA molecule.

proteasome. A massive protein complex that destroys damaged proteins.

protein coding region. One of two major regions in the gene. It contains information needed by the cell's biochemical machinery to produce the polypeptide or protein chain encoded by that gene.

protein. A biomolecule made by linking amino acids together in a chainlike fashion. Proteins catalyze chemical reactions, harvest chemical energy, serve in the cell's defense systems, store and transport molecules, and more.

pseudogene. Considered to be the dead, useless remains of a once functional gene.

pyruvate. A three-carbon compound produced in the breakdown of a six-carbon compound (glucose) during the process of glycolysis.

reading frame. A contiguous and nonoverlapping set of three-nucleotide codons in DNA. There are three possible reading frames in a single strand of DNA.

regulatory region. One of two major regions in the gene. In effect, the regulatory region consists of "on/off switches" and "volume control knobs" that regulate gene expression, thereby determining the production of the polypeptide chain.

repressor. A protein that binds to DNA. Repressors turn the gene off when they bind, halting gene expression. When a repressor debinds, the gene is activated.

reverse transcription. The process in which mRNA is used as a template to produce the corresponding DNA molecule. This operation, catalyzed by the enzyme reverse transcriptase, reverses transcription.

ribose. A five-carbon sugar that forms part of RNA's molecular structure.

ribosome. A subcellular particle made up of proteins and RNA molecules. This structure plays the central role in protein synthesis.

RNA polymerase. A complex protein that is involved in the production of mRNA.

rRNA (ribosomal RNA). These RNA molecules form the scaffolding of ribosomes. Ribosomal RNA molecules also catalyze the formation of the chemical bonds between amino acids during protein synthesis.

sense strand. The DNA strand in the double helix that harbors a gene. The other strand is referred to as the antisense strand.

sequencing. The process of determining the nucleotide sequence of DNA strands or the amino acid sequence of proteins.

solenoid. A structure formed from coiled nucleosomes. It condenses to form higher-order structures that comprise the chromosome.

stop codons. *See* nonsense codons.

substitution mutation. Replacement of a nucleotide in a DNA sequence with another. This kind of mutation can be catastrophic but more often has a limited effect on protein function.

sucrose. A disaccharide formed from the combination of the sugars glucose and fructose; commonly known as table sugar.

thymidine (T). One of four nucleotides used to build DNA chains. The other three are adenosine, cytidine, and guanosine.

thymine. One of four nucleobases found in DNA.

top-down approach. An approach to account for the origin of life from an evolutionary standpoint. This approach starts with life and seeks to identify pathways that lead backwards to the first life-form.

transcription. The process of copying mRNA from DNA.

transcription factor. A protein that regulates gene expression (transcription) by binding to DNA.

translation. The synthesis of polypeptide chains, directed by mRNA at the ribosome.

tRNA (transfer RNA). An RNA molecule that binds an amino acid, then delivers it to the ribosome. Each of the twenty amino acids used by the cell to form proteins has at least one corresponding tRNA molecule.

Turing machine. A conceptual machine that processes complex computations and operations through a relatively simple process of input, output, and finite control according to a specific set of rules.

universal genetic code. The set of rules, found throughout the living realm, that relate the nucleotide sequences of DNA to the amino acid sequences of proteins. These rules are used during the process of translation.

uracil. A single-ringed nucleobase found in RNA.

vesicle. A small, round membrane-bound sac.

viral capsid. A protein shell that contains the genetic material (DNA or RNA) of viruses.

virus. A subcellular particle composed of a protein capsid that houses genetic material (either DNA or RNA).

INDEX

AAA ring, 81–83
A (accepter) site, 190–91
AcrA/AcrB/TolC complex, 73–74, 76–77
activating enzymes, 195–97
adenine, 158, 160–61, 254–55
alpha helix, 43–44
amino acids, 43, 154
    changes, 128–29
    hydrophilic, 112
    hydrophobic, 112, 115
    sequences, 49–50, 126–28, 130, 142–43, 145–46
    side groups, 112–15
amphiphilic compounds, origin of, 237–38, 242
AQPZ channel, 112–13
aquaglyceroporins, 111–12, 115–17
aquaporins, 112–13, 115–17, 234
arginine-196, 115
artists
    Millais, Sir John Everett, 109–10
    Mondrian, Piet, 126
    Picasso, Pablo, 23–24, 203
    Russell, Charles M., 16
    Vermeer, Jan, 35
artwork
    Artist's Studio, The, 34–35
    calligraphy, 140–42
    Contra-Composition of Dissonances, XVI, 126
    mosaic, 225
    Portrait of Dora Maar, 202
    Riders of the Open Range, 14
    Unknown Masterpiece, The, 22–24, 28, 31–32

asymmetry, 235–36
ATP (adenosine triphosphate), 137–39
ATPase, 78
    F_1-F_0, 71–73, 78, 89
    V-type, 73
autotrophs, 56–57

bacteria, 66
bacterial flagellum, 70–71, 74–75, 271–72
bacteriophage *φX174*, 152–54
base-pairing
    mistakes, 160
    rules, 157–58, 160–61, 218
Behe, Michael, 18–20
beta pleated sheet, 43–44
bilayer, 225–27
    fluidity, 227–28
    lipid, 240
    multilamellar vesicles, 229
    origins, 238–40
    primitive, 242
    sheets, 229–31
    structures, 237
    unilamellar vesicles, 229–31
bilayer-forming molecules, 237–39
bilirubin, 253–54
biliverdin, 253–54
biochemical design, 17–18, 123, 201, 224
biochemical imperfections. *See* suboptimal designs
biochemical information, 142–68, 280
biochemical messages, 233

biochemical redundancy, 260–61, 281
biochemical systems, 20, 26–27
biochemistry, 16–18
biomolecular function, 110–11
biomolecular precision, 110–11
BiP protein, 93–95
Brownian motion, 91–92
Brownian ratchets, 91–95
Buchnera, 60

carbohydrates, 146–48
carbonaceous chondrites. *See* meteorites
carbon dioxide, 264–65
carbon fixation reactions, 65–66, 264–65
carboxysome, 65
Carsonella ruddii, 60
cell
    artificial, 61
    chemical composition, 16
    cycle, 121–22
    quality control, 160, 184–85, 191–97, 280
    reading frame, 154
cell membranes, 36, 38, 45, 242–43, 282
    asymmetry, 235
    domains, 236
    evolution, 240
    fluidity, 227–28
    monolayers, 235–36
    organization, 236, 281
    origin, 237–40, 273–74
    primitive, 241, 273
    stability, 234
    structure, 225–26, 229
    wall, 42
cell theory, 36
cell types. *See* eukaryotes; prokaryotes
chaperones, 106–7
chaperonins, 106–7
charging reaction, 195–96
chicken-and-egg systems, 97–99, 107–8, 271, 279
    proteins and DNA, 98–99, 101
chloroplasts, 41–42
chromosomes, 50–51
class 1 major histocompatibility complex (MHC),
    262–63
coding triplets. *See* codons
codons, 130, 154, 171–74, 187–89
    anticodon, 187–89
    codon changes, 177
    stop codons, 172–73
colicin E, 232

collagenase, 118
collagens, 117
collagen triple helix, 118
cometary ice, 238
Creator, identifying, 28–29, 278
Creator's signature, 29, 33
Crick, Francis, 17
cytoplasm, 36, 38
cytosine, 158, 160–61
cytoskeleton, 39, 64–65

Darwin's Black Box, 18–20
dehydration-hydration cycles, 242
Dembski, William, 25
deoxyribose, 130–34
Design Inference, The, 25
design, appearance of, 205, 270
DNA
    advancing replication fork, 220–21
    analogs, 132–33
    association with histones, 180
    bacterial, 63
    bar codes, 165–66
    computers, 163–65
    daughter molecule, 218
    double helix, 218–21
    encryption, 165
    information storage, 49–50, 52, 143–44
    junk, 255–60
    LINE, 260
    noncoding, 255–60
    packaging motor, 89
    parent molecule, 218
    polymerase, 63–64, 222–23
    repair enzyme, 128
    replication, 84, 99–101, 160, 216–23
        bubble, 220–21
        evolution of, 216
        fork, 221–22
    replication, semiconservative, 218–19
    SINE, 259
    strands, 129–32, 218
        antisense strand, 157–58
        sense strand, 157–58
    strings, 163–64
    structure, 48–49
    sugar-phosphate backbone, 134
    topoisomerases, 64
    transcription, 101
    translocator motor, 78
    viral, 80–81
dynein, 81–83, 265–66

EF-Tu, 196–97
encapsulated self-replicating molecules, 240
endogenous retroviruses, 258–59
endoplasmic reticulum (ER), 40, 93–94, 198
    ER lumen, 198–99
    ER machinery, 199–200
endosymbionts, 59
entropy, 246–48
enzyme, 43, 45
    commission classes, 215
    editing site, 196
    proofreading, 196
error minimization, 158–60
eukaryotes, 36–38, 62–65, 101, 151, 189
evolution, 20
    case for, 246
evolutionary pathways, 204–5, 270–75
evolutionary tree of life, 216–17
exons, 102–3, 152
explanatory filter, 25–27, 277, 288n8
extracellular matrix (ECM), 42, 95

ferredoxins, 178
fibrils, 118
filaments, 39. *See also* microtubules
fluid mosaic model, 48, 225–26, 232–33, 235
fructose, 250, 252
FtsZ protein, 64
FtsZ ring, 65
futile cycle, 250–52, 254

gene
    expression, 136, 259–60
    head-to-head pairing, 151
    organization, 148–49
    overlapping, 152–58
    regulation, 121–22, 135–37, 139, 259
    structure, 135–36, 150
genetic code, 170–74, 176, 181–82, 280
    error minimization, 171, 173, 174–76
    evolution, 175–78, 182
    nonuniversal, 176–77, 247
    origin, 177–78, 182
    universal, 171–72, 174–76, 247, 273
genetic information, 148
genetic letters, 165. *See also* nucleotides
genome, 54–55
    minimum genome size, 56–60
genomics, 55
Gershfeld, Norman, 229–31
giclée, 183–84
glutamate-125, 115

glycine, 115
glycolysis, 137–39, 249–52
God as Creator, 283, 285–86
god of the gaps, 19, 32–33
Golgi apparatus, 40
Gonzalez, Guillermo, 24–25
Gould, Stephen Jay, 205, 246
GroEL-GroES, 107
guanine, 102, 158, 160–61, 254–55

heat production, 251
helicase, 221–22
heme degradation, 253
hemoglobin, 251, 253
hemolysis, 231
Hemophilus influenzae, 55, 215
heterotrophs, 55
high-energy bonds, 138
histidine, 115
histones, 50, 178–79
    association with DNA, 180
    histone-positioning code, 181
    octamer, 178–80
historical contingency, 204–5, 275–76
humanity, 29–30
human origin, biblical account of, 29, 278–79
hydrocarbon chains, 226–28, 234
hydrogen
    bonds, 160–61
    ions, 115–17

image of God, 29–30
immune system, 262–63
indels, 130
information-rich biomolecules, 272–73
information theory, 162
Intelligent Design, 26
intelligent design argument, 19–20, 33, 166–67,
    205, 243, 266, 270, 274, 278, 282–83
introns, 102–3, 152
irreducible complexity, 18–19, 26, 32, 66–67, 96,
    108, 271–72, 279

junk DNA, 255–60

Kai proteins, 88
Kar2p protein. *See* BiP protein
kidney stones, 254–55
kinesin, 93, 265–66

Last Universal Common Ancestor (LUCA), 58,
    216–17
leucine (Leu), 174

life's minimal complexity, 54–62, 66, 281
LINEs (long interspersed nuclear elements),
    258–59
lipids, 45, 227
    aggregates, 233
    annular, 234
    composition, 232
    rafts, 236
liposome, 229–31
lumen, 40
lysosomes, 41

matrix metalloproteinases (MMP), 95
membranes. *See* cell membranes
meteorites, 237–38
    Murchison, 240–41
micelles, 238–39
microtubules, 93, 265–66
minimalism, 53
Min proteins, 64
mitochondria, 41
molecular biology, 50, 52
molecular convergence, 205–6, 223–24, 275–76,
    280
    examples of, 206–15
molecular grammar, 145
molecular messages, 142, 144–45
molecular motors, 70, 87, 89–90, 96, 282. *See also*
    motors
motors
    Brownian ratchets, 91–93
    DNA packaging, 89
    DNA translocator, 78
    F_1-F_0 ATPase, 71–73, 88
    rotary, 71–72, 77
    single-molecule rotary, 90
    synthetic molecular, 90
    viral, 77
mRNA (messenger RNA), 50–52, 102, 119, 134,
    144, 152, 186–87
    degradation, 119–20
    monocistronic, 151
    polycistronic, 151
    production, 193–95
    transcription, 101
multidrug transporter (MT), 77
mutations, 173–74, 247, 256
    DNA, 128–30
    frameshift, 156
    substitution, 156, 173–75
Mycoplasma genitalium, 57–58, 215
myosin, 81–82

NADH (nicotinamide adenine dinucleotide), 137
Nanoarchaeum equitans, 57–58
nanodevices, 87–90
nanotechnology, 87–89
natural selection, 175–78
nonanoic acids, 239–41
noncoding DNA, 255–60
nucleobases, 130–31, 134, 158, 168
nucleosomes, 50, 180
    nucleosome-positioning code, 181
nucleotides, 49, 129–31, 134–35, 154
    sequence, 145–46, 157–58, 160, 180, 193
    See also thymidine; uridine
nucleus, 36, 39

octanoic acids, 239–41
Okazaki fragments, 220–23
oligosaccharides
    $Glc_3Man_9GlcNAc_2$, 199–200
operons, 74–75, 148–49
    lac operon, 149–51
organelles, 36
Origins of Life, 67
oxidation, 129
oxygen, 264–65

P (product) site, 190–91
Paley, William, 85–86
parasites/parasitic microbes, 57–58
parity code, 158–62, 168
pattern recognition, 27–30, 278
Pelagibacter ubique, 55
peptidases, 215
peptides, 154
    antibiotics, 145
    antimicrobial, 145
peristaltic pump, 73–74, 76–77
peroxisomes, 41
phosphates, 130–32
phosphodiester bonds, 131–33
phosphofructokinase, 250, 252
phospholipid, 45, 226–29, 242–43
    asymmetry, 235–36
    composition, 232
    head groups, 226
    with choline (PCs), 228
    with ethanolamine (PEs), 228
    with glycerol (PGs), 228, 232
    with serine (PSs), 228
photorespiration, 264
photosynthesis, 262–64
plasmids, 63

poly (A) tail, 102, 192
polynucleotides, 129
    chains, 48–49, 143–44, 217–18
polypeptides, 43
    chains, 49–50, 126–27, 130
    subunits, 101
posttranslational modification, 198–99
prebiotic Earth, 241–42
Privileged Planet, The, 24
probability arguments, 277
prokaryotes, 36–38, 54, 62–65, 67, 101, 189
proteasome, 121
protein, 120, 126–28, 142–43, 42–43
    asymmetry, 235
    autodestruction, 186
    complexes, 84–85
    degradation, 120–21
        protein-degradation fragments, 262–63
    folding, 105–7, 199–200
    function, 228
    insertion, 232
    membrane, 47–48, 234
    sequences, 129
    structure, 43–45
    synthesis, 101–2, 105, 119, 154, 185–90,
        200–201, 261–62
        error rate, 197–98
protein-coding region, 135–36, 150
proteins
    abnormal, 129
    activators, 136–37, 150
    FtsZ, 64
    globular, 50
    integral, 46–47, 234
    Min, 64–65
    MreB, 65
    peripheral, 46–47
    repressors, 136–37, 150
    TrwB, 73
    viral, 77–78, 262
proton wire, 116
pseudogenes, 256–59
pump-priming reaction, 250

quality control, 160, 184–85, 191–97, 200–201,
    280

radio frequency identification (RFID), 98
reactive oxygen species (ROS), 129, 253–54
reason
    abductive, 276–77
    analogical, 30–31, 86, 278–79
    inductive, 31

red blood cells, 253
regulatory region, 135–36, 150
retroposons, 258–59
retro-translocation, 200
reverse reaction, 251
ribose, 130–34
ribosomes, 39–40, 102, 104–5, 189–90
Richards, Jay, 24–25
RNA, 131–33
    message, 256–58
    polymerase, 84, 101, 136, 193–94
    primer, 222–23
    RNA-world hypothesis, 99
    translation, 101
Ross, Hugh, 67
rRNA (ribosomal RNA), 102, 189–91
RTB creation model, 285–86
rubisco, 262–65

salinity, 232, 241
second law of thermodynamics, 246–48
SINEs (short interspersed nuclear elements),
    258–59
solenoid, 50, 180
spliceosome, 102–3, 151–52
splicing, 151–54, 195
suboptimal designs, 245–49, 266–67, 274–75, 281
sugars, 133, 146–47, 130–32

thioredoxin reductase, 84–85
thymidine, 50, 193. *See also* nucleotides
thymine, 158, 160–61
transcription, 101
transition state complex, 264–65
translation, 101
transposable elements, 258
tRNA (transfer RNA), 105, 187–89, 191
    binding, 195–96
    tRNA-amino acid complex, 190–91, 196
Turing machines, 163, 167–68
type III secretion, 271–72

ubiquitin, 120–21
ubiquitination, 120–21
unfolded protein response (UPR), 200
uracil, 158, 160
uric acid, 254–55
uridine, 50, 193. *See also* nucleotides
UV radiation, 134

viral capsid, 78
viral DNA, 80–81

viral proteins, 77–78, 262   water molecules, 116–17
virus structure, 79   Wright, Frank Lloyd, 204

Watchmaker argument, 85–86, 88, 91, 96, 164   X chromosome inactivation, 259
  criticism of, 86–87

Dr. Fazale Rana is the vice president of research and apologetics at Reasons To Believe. Scientific research in biochemistry provided him with the initial evidence that life must have a Creator. Acting on a personal challenge to read the Bible, he found scriptural evidence that convinced him of the Creator's identity.

After graduating from West Virginia State College (WVSC) with a BS degree in chemistry, Dr. Rana earned a PhD in chemistry with an emphasis in biochemistry at Ohio University (OU). A presidential scholar, Dr. Rana was elected into two honors societies at WVSC and won the Donald Clippinger Research Award two different years at OU. He conducted postdoctoral work at the Universities of Virginia and Georgia. Before joining Reasons To Believe, he worked for seven years on product development for Proctor & Gamble. Dr. Rana also holds an adjunct faculty position at Biola University, teaching in the master's in science and religion program.

Several articles by Dr. Rana have been published in peer-reviewed scientific journals such as *Biochemistry*, *Applied Spectroscopy*, *FEBS Letters*, *Journal of Microbiology Methods*, and *The Journal of Chemical Education*. Recently he published an article on cell membrane origins in *Origins of Life and Evolution of Biospheres*. He has delivered numerous presentations at international scientific meetings. Dr. Rana also has one patent and co-wrote a chapter on antimicrobial peptides for *Biological and Synthetic Membranes*. In addition, he coauthored with Hugh Ross the books *Origins of Life* and *Who Was Adam?*

Dr. Rana travels around the country, speaking on science and faith issues at churches, business firms, and university campuses. He is also a frequent guest on radio and television shows.

Dr. Rana and his wife, Amy, currently live in Southern California, where they homeschool their children.

About Reasons To Believe

A science-faith think tank founded in 1986, Reasons To Believe (RTB) focuses on the relationship between the words of the Bible and the facts of nature. Whether in writing or in talks at universities, research labs, churches, and elsewhere, RTB scholars (of science and theology) present reasons for confidence in the authority of Scripture *and* in the findings of science. They demonstrate how God's verbal revelation proves accurate and wholly consistent with the latest discoveries. A webcast discussing the connections between recent findings and the Christian faith may be heard live every Tuesday from 11 a.m. to 1 p.m. (Pacific Time) via www.reasons.org, where the broadcasts are archived along with each day's "New Reason To Believe" and hundreds of articles. A science-faith hotline operates daily from 5 to 7 p.m. at 626-335-5282. **For an informative brochure and a description of available resources, call 800-482-7836 or visit www.reasons.org.**

REASONS T̲O̲ BELIEVE